Export Prospects for the Republic of Vietnam

Development and Resources Corporation

by

Frederick T. Moore
D. M. I. Thomas
Charles W. Peters
Richard N. Pigossi

The Praeger Special Studies program—utilizing the most modern and efficient book production techniques and a selective worldwide distribution network—makes available to the academic, government, and business communities significant, timely research in U.S. and international economic, social, and political development.

Export Prospects for the Republic of Vietnam

PRAEGER SPECIAL STUDIES IN INTERNATIONAL ECONOMICS AND DEVELOPMENT

Praeger Publishers   New York   Washington   London

PRAEGER PUBLISHERS
111 Fourth Avenue, New York, N.Y. 10003, U.S.A.
5, Cromwell Place, London S.W.7, England

Published in the United States of America in 1971
by Praeger Publishers, Inc.

Library of Congress Catalog Card Number: 74-133364

Printed in the United States of America

TO OUR VIETNAMESE COLLEAGUES

IN THE FORMER JOINT DEVELOPMENT GROUP

This volume is a revised version of a study with the same title that was completed in December, 1969, together with a supplement to that study, completed in February, 1970. The study was prepared by Development and Resources Corporation as a part of its work under a contract with the U.S. Agency for International Development. The latter agency does not necessarily subscribe to the materials or conclusions presented in the report.

Several members of Development and Resources Corporation's professional staff were involved in the substantive work, which was carried out to provide a basis for the study itself, and in writing the study. Four of these are given special mention on the title page for their role in the preparation of the study in its final form. Others contributed to the study in many ways. Particular mention should be made of Thomas A. Mead, who headed the Corporations's resident staff in the country. In the early phases of the work on the study, Abraham Serfaty prepared material on several commodities, and he is responsible for the appendix to the chapter on natural rubber. Pasqual A. Donvito also contributed material on some of the commodity studies. In addition to the Development and Resources Corporation staff members, government officials and businessmen in all the countries covered in Part II generously provided information and data, which have been utilized extensively in the volume. Unfortunately, there are too many of them to list individually.

We believe that the information contained in this report can be helpful in encouraging substantial efforts to increase Vietnam's exports.

CONTENTS

xi

xiv

LIST OF TABLES

xv

Tables   Page

LIST OF FIGURES

xxi

Export Prospects for the Republic of Vietnam

One of the most important problems to be faced by Vietnam in the postwar period is that of expanding foreign exchange earnings from exports to sustain the demand for capital goods and other commodities necessary for the nation's development. In The Postwar Development of the Republic of Vietnam: Policies and Programs,[1] a strategy for development is outlined that forecasts independence from concessionary aid in approximately a decade. If this is to occur, it is essential that great emphasis be given to expanding exports.

Vietnam--the term used for the Republic of Vietnam unless otherwise stated--has always had an unfavorable balance of trade, but under the French and during the present war, the deficit was made up through capital inflows and foreign aid. Exports have been a small and diminishing proportion of the GDP. Unlike some of its neighboring countries, Vietnam's exports have not risen as high as 5 percent of the GDP in the recent past, even when the war was at a low level.

At the present time, Vietnam is a high-cost economy and probably cannot compete successfully in world markets for many of the commodities that it might export. Its success can be achieved, provided the general level of prices and costs can be altered. The present exchange rate is an artificial one and should be readjusted in the future. It is not possible at this point to conclude what level of devaluation may be required but, on present evidence, it will require a devaluation on the order of 100 percent. Obviously, conditions can change in a short period of time, and, for that reason, this tentative conclusion must be viewed cautiously.

Although the market demand forecasts indicate that a small country such as Vietnam can probably obtain a share in the commodity markets, this can be achieved only if the marketing institutions and incentives are effective in the country. There is now no program for stimulating exports; yet, we are convinced that, even now, under conditions of war, exports can be expanded in a short period of time. We are persuaded that it is possible to double or triple exports from the very low level to which they have sunk; over the long run, the prospects for expanding far beyond that are reasonably good.

Market analyses support the conclusion that the prospects for export from Vietnam are probably not demand limited, but they may very well be supply limited. It will take some time to readjust production and to take advantage of market opportunities. Although short-run increases, two or three times higher than present levels, can probably be achieved easily, the absolute amount of such increases will be modest. Over the long run, the growth from this base will require a vigorous program of promotion.

EXPORT PROSPECTS AND PROBLEMS

The export problems of developing countries are receiving a great deal of attention at the present time. The activities of the United Nations Conference on Trade and Development (UNCTAD) keep these problems fresh in the minds of those who are concerned with development. Although conditions affecting exports from the developing countries are not uniform, there are common themes or hypotheses as to where the difficulties lie. It is not the purpose of this study to survey these discussions in any detail, for the problems of a single country are not necessarily reflected in the average problems of all countries. Yet, a few comments are warranted, if only because some of the uncertainties and concern are reflected in Vietnam.

A fear is commonly expressed that the developing countries are capable of exporting only primary products and raw materials and must import manufactured and capital goods. It is felt that this arrangement will, in the long run, be disadvantageous to the developing countries, because the demand for primary products is apt to be weakened through the use of substitutes and because fewer units of input are required per unit of output. It is also said that the price trends and income elasticities for such commodities are generally unfavorable. It is argued that the foreign exchange earnings will be unstable and that the terms of trade may move inexorably against primary producing countries.

The evidence on these points is ambiguous at best. The statistics do not support, to any strong degree, the propositions stated in the previous paragraph. It is true that there is instability in the

TABLE 1

Behavior of Exports From Developing Countries,
1950-53 and 1960-63
(In Millions of Dollars)

Exports	1950-53 Average	1960-63 Average	Percentage Change
Major Exports	$6,778.3	$6,736.1	-0.6
Minor Exports,	3,465.9	5,223.8	50.7
of Which Major Exports Accounting for Less than 5 percent of a Country's Total Exports	640.4	1,112.0	73.6
Total Exports (29 Countries)	$10,224.2	$11,959.9	16.7

Source: Barend A. DeVries, The Export Experience of Developing Countries, World Bank Staff Occasional Papers No. 3 (1967).

export earnings of the developing countries. This seems to result primarily from fluctuations in the volume of exports, rather than fluctuations in price.[2] But the record of fluctuations varies among commodities, with some important ones, such as coffee and sugar, showing long-run unfavorable aspects, whereas for other commodities, particularly those that are used as inputs in manufactured products, there is greater stability and strength in demand.

A recent study of the World Bank indicates that, although traditional products that have constituted a major part of exports of developing countries have tended to stagnate, exports of minor products have shown a great buoyancy. This is briefly shown in Table 1.

The conclusions of the World Bank study are particularly appropriate to Vietnam. The study ends with the following statement:

Most of the developing countries have a relatively small share in the markets of major commodities, and they also have relatively small domestic markets. For these countries, a policy of encouraging exports seems clearly indicated. Outward orientation need not exclude industrialization or an expansion of exports of manufactures. The countries which have had success with industrialization under outward orientation policies, (e.g. Jamaica, Taiwan, and Thailand), have not attempted to produce intermediate goods (e.g. steel) but have relied on imports of industrial raw materials and intermediate products for the output (and export) of finished goods, including labor-intensive capital goods. Where such a strategy of industrialization has been induced by the scarcity of natural resources, an initial obstacle to development has been turned into an economic advantage. For both minor and major exports, the greatest improvement was achieved by countries which had small external market positions and a policy of outward orientation.[3]

It is clear that there is no unique relationship between exports and growth, but it is equally clear that, unless Vietnam can expand its export trade, the only alternatives open to it are to accept a low, and probably unsatisfactory, rate of growth or to become a permanent dependent on concessionary aid from the lending countries of the world. The alternatives to an expansion of exports are not acceptable as a long-run solution.

It has not been demonstrated that the terms of trade necessarily move against primary producing countries. Much depends on the period of time and the countries that are chosen for analysis. It has been shown, for example, that the commodity terms of trade for India have not deteriorated over the long run.[4] On the other hand, it is clear that an expansion of exports is probably a necessary, although not a sufficient, condition for growth. One study concludes that, for a cross section of countries, for each 2.5 percent increase in exports, the real per capita GNP increases about 1 percent.[5]

The average experience of developing countries is not a sufficient guide to the likely experience of Vietnam in the future. Nevertheless, the evidence is at least reassuring and goes some way to allay fears about future prospects. As will be shown in Part I, the market demand for the products that Vietnam may export in the future is, on the whole, reasonably favorable, although this potential cannot be realized unless specific action is taken to stimulate exports.

RECENT HISTORY OF EXPORTS FROM VIETNAM

The history, extent, and direction of Vietnam's external trade is illustrated in Tables 2 to 5, from which we make the following observations:

TABLE 2

Volume and Value of Exports from Vietnam, 1955-68

Year	Quantity (In Metric Tons)	Value	
		Hundreds of Thousands of Vietnamese Dollars	Thousands of U.S. Dollars
1955	430,825	$24,237	$69,000
1956	126,845	15,788	45,100
1957	388,971	28,192	80,500
1958	243,569	19,321	55,200
1959	441,666	26,273	75,100
1960	567,225	29,941	84,500
1961	389,336	24,777	69,800
1962	312,916	19,813	56,600
1963	586,519	26,835	76,700
1964	389,206	16,960	48,400
1965	176,751	12,422	35,400
1966	67,639	14,952	27,600
1967	49,242	13,128	16,400
1968	32,416	9,355	11,700

Sources: Data for quantity and value in terms of U.S. dollars from Directorate General of Customs, Joint Economic Office, USAID/ Vietnam, Annual Statistical Bulletin (1969); data for value in terms of Vietnamese dollars from National Institute of Statistics, Statistical Yearbook, 1967-68 (1969).

TABLE 3

Volume of Exports of Selected Commodities from Vietnam, 1955-68
(In Metric Tons)

Commodity	1955	1956	1957	1958	1959	1960	1961	1962	1963	1964	1965	1966	1967	1968
Rice and Brokens	69,619	24	183,872	112,702	245,689	340,042	154,452	83,915	322,570	48,651	0	0	0	0
Rubber	61,858	63,642	75,972	68,491	78,427	70,121	83,403	74,497	68,926	71,630	58,162	44,897	37,563	29,247
Tea	168	252	456	276	465	1,059	1,655	1,931	1,995	2,148	2,341	1,863	1,047	726
Coffee	56	0	0	0	0	n.a.	0	0	35	660	200	0	576	325
Duck Feathers	1,020	360	1,068	420	405	664	625	570	513	745	625	529	504	340
Duck Eggs	2,740	139	0	0	20	743	1,429	1,870	1,749	1,824	521	0	0	0
Fish Products	418	56	288	413	521	413	633	727	928	913	854	862	572	79
Vegetable Oils	318	573	1,135	702	0	860	3,300	2,411	233	887	2,468	171	0	0
Oil Cake	3,315	2,292	1,346	2,575	3,785	4,981	2,952	4,591	4,051	5,362	8,856	6,355	100	0
Peanuts	252	10	n.a.	22	381	1,143	1,599	807	399	4,745	6,020	310	0	0
Sesame	n.a.*	n.a.	n.a.	n.a.	n.a.	328	199	278	343	452	54	121	3	0
Fresh Fruits	3	465	1	n.a.	8	490	290	363	280	1,568	483	101	5	0
Fresh Vegetables	680	15	284	491	1,221	402	210	140	201	1,153	123	0	0	0
Cinnamon	30	27	527	1,040	1,478	999	819	239	328	553	387	29	38	22
Kapok	55	49	17	5	n.a.	n.a.	409	1,041	708	763	580	346	151	107
Salt	52,968	35,401	70,113	29,590	83,636	51,900	22,050	36,250	20,595	39,050	5,000	0	0	0
White Sand	0	0	32	7	5	47,035	82,555	80,770	136,885	199,165	79,910	5,700	4,177	0
Beer	6,060	3,900	4,032	4,908	978	3,649	4,749	2,908	2,316	0	14	0	0	0
Wood Products	711	1,246	2,217	730	1,447	367	605	282	55	8	62	44	5	0
Iron Scrap	20,508	20,812	22,932	9,933	12,658	15,400	7,360	6,696	9	0	0	2,751	1,277	0

*The symbol n.a. indicates either an insignificant amount or that data is not available.

Sources: Joint Economic Office, USAID/Vietnam; National Institute of Statistics; Directorate General of Customs.

TABLE 4

Value of Exports of Selected Commodities from Vietnam, 1955-68
(In Thousands of Dollars)

Commodity	1955	1956	1957	1958	1959	1960	1961	1962	1963	1964	1965	1966	1967	1968	Total	Distribution (In Percent)
Rice and Brokens	$ 7,981	$ 3	$19,979	$13,493	$23,394	$27,270	$14,598	$ 8,760	$35,736	$ 5,353	-	-	-	-	$156,567	20.8
Rubber	40,085	39,291	48,797	35,560	46,913	47,998	43,832	37,917	33,480	33,299	$26,011	$22,035	$13,268	$9,706	478,192	63.6
Tea	120	240	360	360	501	1,046	1,612	1,893	1,858	1,888	2,135	2,142	955	689	15,799	2.1
Coffee	102	n.a.	n.a.	n.a.	n.a.	n.a.	n.a.	n.a.	17	349	88	n.a.	244	145	945	0.1
Duck Feathers	1,440	480	1,320	480	362	589	689	914	659	1,091	868	770	542	348	10,552	1.4
Duck Eggs	954	36	n.a.	n.a.	62	229	636	875	443	657	181	n.a.	n.a.	n.a.	4,073	0.6
Fish Products	185	42	128	171	228	186	357	495	646	632	852	959	550	142	5,573	0.8
Vegetable Oils	59	195	475	300	n.a.	291	877	557	61	284	826	27	n.a.	n.a.	3,952	0.5
Oil Cake	173	139	79	158	208	298	153	247	287	362	532	449	7	n.a.	3,092	0.4
Peanuts	82	6	n.a.	4	72	205	311	157	66	927	1,237	65	n.a.	n.a.	3,132	0.4
Sesame	n.a.	n.a.	n.a.	n.a.	n.a.	94	35	60	59	74	11	22	n.a.	n.a.	355	n.a.
Fresh Fruits	n.a.	25	1	n.a.	n.a.	24	18	12	n.a.	97	23	5	n.a.	n.a.	205	n.a.
Fresh Vegetables	69	1	41	44	81	27	9	12	18	90	n.a.	n.a.	n.a.	n.a.	392	0.1
Cinnamon	16	14	235	396	785	617	502	185	254	931	778	58	84	83	4,938	0.7
Kapok	37	29	12	2	n.a.	n.a.	56	9	33	1	179	72	40	28	498	0.1
Salt	238	167	450	135	325	330	99	163	91	175	22	n.a.	n.a.	n.a.	2,195	0.3
White Sand	n.a.	n.a.	n.a.	n.a.	n.a.	163	283	280	476	685	289	19	17	n.a.	2,212	0.3
Beer	960	720	840	960	124	636	872	555	449	n.a.	3	n.a.	n.a.	n.a.	6,119	0.8
Wood Products	78	94	132	39	51	79	130	66	2	3	7	73	3	n.a.	757	0.1
Iron Scrap	2,280	240	840	378	495	525	524	1,043	2	n.a.	n.a.	111	89	n.a.	6,527	0.8
Others	14,158	3,385	6,856	2,695	1,462	3,844	4,173	2,427	2,034	1,562	1,448	774	611	553	45,982	6.1
Total	$69,017	$45,107	$80,545	$55,175	$75,063	$84,451	$69,766	$56,627	$76,671	$48,460	$35,490	$27,581	$16,410	$11,694	$752,057	100.0

Note: The symbol n.a. indicates either an insignificant amount or that data is not available. Before August 1, 1966, the conversion was based on VN$35/U.S.$1, after August 1, 1966, the rate used was VN$80/U.S.$1. Values are on a customs clearance basis (f.o.b. Vietnam).

Sources: Joint Economic Office, USAID/Vietnam; National Institute of Statistics; Directorate General of Customs.

TABLE 5

Export and Import Trade of Vietnam with Specified Countries, 1958-67
(In Millions of Dollars)

	1958 Exports	1958 Imports	1959 Exports	1959 Imports	1960 Exports	1960 Imports	1961 Exports	1961 Imports	1962 Exports	1962 Imports	1963 Exports	1963 Imports
France	29.7	58.8	23.8	40.6	30.6	51.1	25.5	38.8	20.4	35.0	18.7	31.4
Germany	0.8	13.1	11.4	13.2	5.8	13.7	7.1	14.7	6.0	10.3	6.6	7.1
England	1.2	6.3	2.3	5.9	4.7	6.6	8.0	7.6	8.8	4.5	5.6	4.3
Japan	0.6	45.0	1.9	47.6	2.4	52.7	1.4	59.9	2.9	44.6	4.3	27.6
Hong Kong	0.9	1.6	5.3	1.4	7.4	0.7	5.7	0.9	3.1	0.9	7.0	1.7
Singapore	6.1	0.8	4.6	0.8	5.2	0.1	1.7	0.2	2.0	0.4	8.0	0.4
Indonesia	3.4	14.5	0.8	15.6	7.0	15.5	4.3	15.2	0	14.2	1.1	18.9
United States	5.1	54.9	6.4	58.5	3.7	61.2	3.6	68.3	1.8	97.2	1.1	107.0
Italy	n.a.*	5.3	1.6	5.2	1.2	8.6	1.1	7.3	1.2	4.9	1.2	6.4
Netherlands	0.1	1.3	1.6	1.7	1.4	1.7	1.2	1.6	0.6	1.0	1.2	1.2
China (Taiwan)	n.a.	5.6	n.a.	6.1	0.9	5.0	2.2	14.3	0.3	25.0	0.2	37.5
Korea (Republic)	n.a.	-	n.a.	0.1	n.a.	0.1	n.a.	0.2	n.a.	0.7	1.2	13.5
India	0.1	4.2	0.1	4.0	n.a.	1.9	n.a.	0.7	n.a.	1.5	1.0	6.7
Thailand	n.a.	0.4	0.1	0.3	n.a.	0.2	n.a.	3.3	0.1	2.7	0.1	2.4
Belgium	n.a.	4.1	2.0	6.5	0.4	4.2	0.5	5.4	0.3	2.7	0.3	0.8
Other	7.2	16.2	13.2	17.1	13.8	17.0	7.5	16.7	9.1	18.9	19.1	19.3
Total	55.2	232.1	75.1	224.6	84.5	240.3	69.8	255.1	56.6	264.5	76.7	286.2

	1964 Exports	1964 Imports	1965 Exports	1965 Imports	1966 Exports	1966 Imports	1967 Exports	1967 Imports	Cumulative 1958-67 Exports	Cumulative 1958-67 Imports	Trade Balance 1958-67 Plus	Trade Balance 1958-67 Minus
France	15.5	18.2	11.9	12.0	10.6	16.0	5.8	17.8	192.5	319.7		127.2
Germany	8.4	8.4	5.6	8.1	3.0	14.4	2.4	15.4	57.1	118.4		61.3
England	5.1	4.9	4.4	6.0	4.5	9.8	2.3	7.1	46.9	63.0		16.1
Japan	4.3	32.1	3.9	32.9	3.6	71.9	2.8	148.7	28.1	563.0		534.9
Hong Kong	2.4	1.7	1.8	2.6	0.3	7.0	0.2	3.6	34.1	22.1	12.0	
Singapore	2.3	3.5	2.4	2.7	0.8	3.4	0.4	18.6	33.5	30.9	2.6	
Indonesia	2.1	13.2	0	2.5	0	1.9	0	0.3	18.7	111.8		93.1
United States	2.0	126.3	1.4	161.9	1.1	200.3	0.4	174.2	26.6	1,109.8		1,083.2
Italy	1.6	8.5	1.7	7.2	1.5	17.5	1.2	23.1	12.3	94.0		81.7
Netherlands	1.0	1.7	0.6	2.0	0.4	2.5	0.3	4.0	8.4	18.7		10.3
China (Taiwan)	0.7	38.3	0.5	47.1	0.6	71.2	0.2	80.5	5.6	330.6		325.0
Korea (Republic)	n.a.	7.0	n.a.	18.2	n.a.	14.2	n.a.	5.3	1.2	59.3		58.1
India	n.a.	6.4	n.a.	8.0	n.a.	7.6	n.a.	7.3	1.2	48.3		47.1
Thailand	0.1	4.0	n.a.	4.1	n.a.	4.6	n.a.	0.6	0.4	22.6		22.2
Belgium	0.3	1.6	0.4	2.3	0.2	3.4	0.1	2.8	4.5	33.8		29.3
Other	2.6	22.0	0.8	39.7	1.0	48.5	0.3	28.7	74.6	244.1		169.5
Total	48.4	297.8	35.4	357.3	27.6	494.2	16.4	538.0	545.7	3,190.1		2,644.4

*The symbol n.a. indicates either an insignificant amount or that data is not available. Before August 1, 1966, conversion was based on VN$35/U.S.$1, after August 1, 1966, the rate used was VN$80/U.S.$1. Values are on customs clearance basis (f.o.b. Vietnam).

Sources: Joint Economic Office, USAID/Vietnam; National Institute of Statistics; Directorate General of Customs.

Between 1955 and 1964, export volumes were erratic, but they did not decline seriously until 1965, when deteriorating security conditions began to affect agricultural production. Volumes achieved their highest levels in 1960 and 1963 (nearly 600,000 tons), but, by 1968, volume had fallen to a mere 32,000 tons. The decline in export values was slightly less sharp, partly because of changes in exchange rates and partly because values reflected differences in the mix of commodities exported. In terms of value, the best year for Vietnamese exports was 1960, when foreign exchange earnings from this source amounted to the equivalent of $84.5 million at then prevailing rates of exchange.

Rubber and rice have always dominated the export trade, but rice has been the more erratic of the two, and there have been no rice exports at all since 1964. Tea, duck feathers, and oil seed cake have been small, but relatively stable, sources of foreign exchange earnings. Certain trade commodities--cinnamon, salt, beer, and scrap iron, for example--achieved encouragingly high export volumes and values in the 1950's, but then either declined or disappeared entirely from the list of significant exports. In a few other cases-- duck eggs, sesame, peanuts, fresh fruits, kapok, and glass sand--a promising export trade began to develop after 1960, but was slowed or halted by the spread of the war in 1964 and 1965. The trade in commodities such as these may reasonably be expected to resume when security returns to the countryside.

Traditionally, Vietnam has had trade dealings with a rather large number of countries, but the bulk of its exports have gone to not more than ten of them. The principal regional markets for Vietnamese produce have always been East Asia and Western Europe. In East Asia, Japan, Hong Kong, Singapore, and Indonesia have been the most important individual outlets for the export trade, and, in Europe, France, West Germany, the United Kingdom, and Italy. Outside these two major regions, only the United States has been a significant customer for Vietnamese trade commodities.

The relative importance of these nine countries to Vietnam's external trade has shifted frequently, depending largely on changes from year to year in the types of commodities that Vietnam has had to offer. Whenever foodstuffs, particularly rice, enter largely into the out-shipments, the East Asian markets absorb more than their normal share of total export volumes; whenever industrial commodities, such as rubber, are predominant, the export trade is mostly with the markets in Western Europe.

The rapid decline in exports has been accompanied by just as rapid an increase in imports, so that, since 1964, what had been a regular imbalance in Vietnam's external trade has become a huge one. In 1958, the ratio of import to export values was about four to one, which was bad enough; by 1967, with a loss over the intervening years of $40 million in exports and an increase in imports by $306 million, the ratio was more than thirty-three to one.

The current situation is largely a result of the war and, to some extent, would be corrected when the war ceases. Import levels are artificially inflated by demands associated with military needs and can be expected to decrease. But the necessary expansion of exports will not occur automatically. Export trade must expand to levels never achieved before, when, however, there was no great incentive to expand. The chapters that follow discuss the commodities and the markets that may be exploited to achieve the export levels that are required for future growth of the country.

NOTES

1. Joint Development group, The Postwar Development of the Republic of Vietnam: Policies and Programs (New York: Frederick A. Praeger, Inc., 1970).
2. Cf. UN, Instability in Export Markets of Underdeveloped Countries (1952).

3. Barend A. DeVries, The Export Experience of Developing Countries, World Bank Staff Occasional Papers No. 3 (1967).

4. D. R. Appleyard, Terms of Trade and Economic Development: A Case Study of India, American Economic Review (May, 1968).

5. R. E. Emery, "The Relations of Exports and Economic Growth," Kyklos, Vol. II (1967).

MARKET DEMAND
FOR SELECTED COMMODITIES

Rice has been one of the two traditional large exports from Vietnam and is a logical candidate for export in the postwar period. Rice and rubber together have typically accounted for over 85 percent of total exports in years past, but rice exports have fluctuated from year to year, even in the early 1960's; at a maximum, they were over 300,000 metric tons. The Postwar Development of the Republic of Vietnam: Policies and Programs,[1] projected a decreased percentage share for these two products but an increasing value and tonnage of exports in the period to 1980 and beyond. Rice exports ceased after 1964, and, since then, Vietnam has been a net importer, with tonnages of imports in the last few years higher than the maximum exports previously achieved. This turnaround in the rice trade in Vietnam was caused by the war; domestic production has fallen and, at present, is insufficient to meet domestic demand. But Vietnam has the production capability to become a rice exporter in the postwar period, so that an analysis of world rice markets and trade possibilities in the future is needed in order to assess the prospects for exports from Vietnam. It is the market demand factors that are of primary concern here; production capabilities and supplies are dealt with summarily. Expansion of production is provided for in the development plans for agriculture.

As incomes rise during the course of development and as populations continue to grow, the demand for goods also rises, and imports (and, sometimes, exports) also tend to increase, often at rates different from the rate of increase of income. For several reasons (to be examined later), the demand for rice may behave differently from the demand for other kinds of goods; the problem is to determine the likely increase in the demand over the next ten years or so by major market areas and to determine, in addition, the extent that a rising market demand for rice will be translated into higher volumes

of trade among the countries, particularly those countries in Asia in
the area from Pakistan to Japan that are both the major consumers
and producers of rice.

Future rice production and trade depend on several different
factors that may partially offset each other or may be reinforcing.
First, on the demand side, rising real income in developing countries
raises the demand for all products; per capita consumption will rise
through the direct income effect, and aggregate demand rises both
for that reason, plus the increase in population. But, as incomes rise,
there is a tendency for consumer preferences for goods to change, so
that substitutions may take place in the composition of consumer expenditures. Spending on fish, meat, and vegetables may be substituted
for spending on rice. The income effect always increases the demand
for a product, but the substitution effect may work either way. The
net change in demand, as a result of these factors, depends on the
relative strength of each of them, and that is dependent on the average
income from which an increase occurs, on the distribution of income,
and on other economic and institutional conditions of the consumer.
These are the elements that must be analyzed in arriving at a judgment
as to future per capita and aggregate demand for rice and the prospects
for trade in the product.

The volume and direction of the trade in rice also depends on
the advances made in production in each country, particularly through
the wider use of the new high-yielding varieties (HYV's) of rice (notably, IR-5 and IR-8). To the extent that a country can rapidly increase its domestic production to meet a growing demand from a
rising population, it will decrease its dependence on imported supplies
of rice. As will be seen below, many of the Asian countries are large
importers of rice, and the deficits in supply have often tended to increase. Self-sufficiency in basic cereal production is frequently a
high-priority objective of development, and the efforts in each country
to supply all demands through domestic production appear to have the
additional effect of decreasing future prospects for trade. It is based
on an assumed great success in the HYV's of rice as part of a determined policy of self-sufficiency that causes some observers to predict a long-run market decline and decreased export possibilities for
rice. There are, however, certain limitations on the expansibility of
production--both economic and technical--and the time period required
to achieve these results is also extremely relevant, since the prospects
for trade may be quite good for five or ten years, but much less certain in the longer run.

The future of rice trade and the volume and sources of exports
depends on all of the factors mentioned previously: the rate of increase of demand for rice as affected by population increases and

rising incomes; the relative success of production increases stemming from the use of HYV's of rice; and the policies of governments
toward agricultural development in each of the countries, with particular reference to trade restrictions and agricultural price supports.
These are the market factors that will affect the prospects for exports
of rice from Vietnam in the next decade.

TRENDS IN PRODUCTION AND TRADE

Over the past ten to fifteen years, and particularly in the last
few years, there have been significant changes in production and in
the pattern or structure of trade. World rice production has increased
by about a third, at an annual rate slightly above 2 percent in this
period, or at about the same rate as population increases in those
countries in Asia that are both the largest producers and the largest
consumers of rice. The UN Food and Agricultural Organization (FAO)
reported that, from 1950 to 1962, production rose "at nearly double
the rate of population growth,"[2] but this refers to world totals and
not to the experience of the countries of Asia. It is the latter that is
the most relevant to the rice trade. In the past two years, production
has continued to increase, and the 1968/69 rice crop (excluding the
Communist countries of Asia) is estimated at 181 million metric tons
of paddy.[3] This is an additional increase of 8 percent over the average production of 1961-64.

The production increases of the past ten years are not necessarily reliable guides to the likely experience of the next ten years.
A simple extrapolation of the trend would suggest that production
increases would just keep pace with population increases. The President's Science Advisory Committee estimated that, if the production
trends of 1960-70 continued up to 1980, total grain production (wheat,
rice, and coarse grains) would grow at a rate of 2.7 percent, or very
slightly better than projected population. The committee also pointed
out that "production has been increasing at a slower rate than dis-
appearance in the developing countries and the growing gap has been
made up by increased imports.[4] It is possible that this conjecture
does not, however, give appropriate weight to the productivity advances possible with the new Mexican wheat and HYV's of rice.

Increases in total production are the result of two separable
factors: (a) an increase in the acreage planted and (b) productivity
increases (that is, yields per acre). Until very recently, the increases
in production were primarily attributable to extensions of acreage
rather than to increases in yields. This is true for virtually all of the
major producing areas, including the Far East and Southeast Asia,
but is the opposite for the United States, where productivity increases

dominate. The figures for 1968/69, compared to average 1960-65, show the following relative importance of the two factors in accounting for production increases (in percent).[5] For example:

	World	Asia
Production	100	100
Acreage	61	56
Productivity	39	44

This means that 61 percent of world production increases were attributable to additional acreage and 39 percent to productivity. More sophisticated statistical analyses for the Philippines have strongly substantiated this conclusion.* In the world, the acreage devoted to rice is now about 238 million acres, with about 90 percent of it in Asia.

It is becoming increasingly difficult to expand rice acreages in most countries, because of the need to move to soils or areas that are far less favorable to rice production, plus the fact that the competition for the land for alternative crops or uses becomes more intense. It seems probable that the extension of acreages will be a much less important source of growth in production in the next decade or so than it has been in the past, perhaps on the order of only half as significant a source. That places major reliance for increased output on raising yields. The new high-yielding rice varieties have already demonstrated that a significant jump in productivity can be achieved. What the total impact on production might be in the next ten years, as well as the possible limits on the rate of increase, are specifically considered in the next section.

About four-fifths of world rice production is produced in Asian countries that are also the major consumers of rice. This matching of demand and supply means that the international trade in rice is a far smaller proportion of total production than is true of a commodity such as wheat, where the matching is not so close. As Table 6 shows, the percentage of production entering trade is about 4 percent of the total. Only about 10 percent as much rice is traded as wheat; but the amount is significant, particularly because it fluctuates in response to changes in production and demand and because, in the future, the volume of trade and the origins and destinations by market may be

---

*Cf. unpublished work of V. Ruttan at International Rice Research Institute, Philippines.

TABLE 6

World Rice Production and Trade, 1950-67
and Projections for 1980
(In Millions of Metric Tons Milled)

(1) Year	(2) Production	(3) Trade	(3/2) Percent
1950*	133	5.6	4.2
1961-64*	168	6.5	3.9
1965	178	7.5	4.2
1966	170	7.0	4.1
1967	171	6.8	4.0
1980	262	6.1	2.3

*Average.

Sources: Figures through 1967 from FAO; 1980 estimate from President's Science Advisory Committee, The World Food Problem (May, 1967), Vol. II, p. 170.

even more responsive than now to changes in market prices. When production is depressed, due to drought or other causes, prices rise and the volume of trade may tend to drop, as smaller supplies are available for trade. In 1967, which was relatively low for production and trade, prices rose rapidly; however, the total value of trade in rice exceeded $1 billion for the first time. The price rises more than offset the decrease in volume traded. Rationing of demand took place through the normal market price changes. Thus, it would be incorrect to assume that rising production in the world will automatically lead to a long-term downward trend in the volume of trade. For technical and economic reasons, volume of trade and the markets for it may very well stabilize or grow somewhat, even in the face of rising yields and the pursuit of policies of self-sufficiency in rice by many countries. (This conclusion is amplified and buttressed in a later section.)

The figures for 1980, shown in Table 6, should not be construed as a prediction that trade as a percent of production will sharply decline. The Committee, in making these estimates, simply assumed that production would grow by 4 percent annually and that U.S. exports would be exactly the amount needed to meet the net import demands in the world market. These assumptions are an oversimplification of the situation.

Major changes have taken place in the international rice trade in the last five years. Intraregional trade in Asia, which accounted for about three-fourths of all trade in the recent past, has declined rather sharply in the last few years. This has occurred for several reasons. There has been a decline in the production and exports of such countries as Burma, Cambodia, Vietnam, and, to some extent, Thailand. Exports from these traditional producers have been offset by a large and rapid increase in exports from the United States, particularly under PL-480 programs of support to India, Vietnam, and Indonesia. The major shift has been a replacement of Southeast Asian countries as the primary source of exports by the United States. In 1960-64, the United States had 16 percent of world exports; by 1967, this had grown to 26 percent and seems likely to go somewhat higher in the immediate future. Unlike most other producer countries, which retain the largest part of their production for domestic consumption, over 70 percent of U.S. production is exported. Although government programs have risen, commercial sales have risen more rapidly, including, until recently, substantial sales to Japan.

Short-term shifts from one year to the next, or even over a few years, do not necessarily signal a permanent change in the structure of the rice trade. Surely, the Vietnam War, plus bad weather over several years and the impact of government policies in certain countries, have caused a shift recently in trade patterns. The question is whether these are likely to persist over the longer run and whether changes in economic market conditions and government policies in other countries might change the outlook for trade that Vietnam would face in the immediate and the more distant future.

PROJECTIONS OF FUTURE DEMAND, SUPPLY, AND TRADE

Projections of future production levels by countries and regions, consumption, and trade balances have been made by a number of agencies, notably the FAO, the U.S. Department of Agriculture (USDA), and the President's Science Advisory Committee, as well as by individuals. The several estimates are frequently hard to compare in any simple way, because they differ as to the time periods for which projections are made and, most importantly, in their basic assumptions

about future population and income growth, consumption patterns,
price behavior, the character of government policies toward agriculture and foreign trade, and other factors that critically affect the
estimates that are finally made.

Tables 7 and 8 show two separate estimates of production, consumption, and trade balances for major regions and countries and for
world totals (for 1975 in both cases and for 1980 in the case of Table
8). The FAO estimates for 1975 (in Table 7) are shown for an assumed
low rate and high rate of increase of the GDP. The differences in the
results are striking. Under the low GDP assumption, import deficits
are large and are concentrated in the Far East, where demand is
projected to exceed production by 1.5 million tons. World production
is projected to increase by 2.5 percent annually, which is based primarily on the recent historical trends. But Pakistan is projected to
be a net exporter, and India is assumed to be about self-sufficient.
Vietnam is projected to have exports of rice of about 100,000 tons,
on the assumption that the war will have ceased.

The major change foreseen under the assumption that incomes
rise more rapidly is a big increase in the production of the developing
countries, particularly those in the Far East. The traditional exporters
in the Far East (Burma, Cambodia, Taiwan, Thailand, and Vietnam)
are estimated to increase their exportable surpluses from 4.6 to 6.2
million tons, and the traditional importers (Ceylon, India, Indonesia,
and Malaysia) are projected to cut their import needs from 6.1 to
1.6 million tons. For the world total, a net exportable surplus of 5.9
million tons is foreseen. The FAO report concludes that, in the long
run: "The trends point to a massive increase in world requirements
of rice in the next twenty years--an additional 100 million tons (milled)
per annum by 1985" and that this demand would be "mostly concentrated in the traditional rice consuming countries of the Far East."[6]
Even if population growth were decreased, it is likely that demand
would be cut by about 10 million tons. This upward trend of demand
would have the effect of raising the volume of the rice trade from the
1967/68 level of about 6 to 7 million tons to 9 to 11 million tons, which
would maintain trade at the same level relative to production as has
obtained in the past.

Table 9 presents some alternative estimates of production, consumption, and trade for 1975 and 1980, but without the distinctions
made by the FAO as to alternative rates of growth of population and
income. They are essentially based on trend projections, but with
adjustments for (an assumed) more rapid growth of production, based
on the new varieties, a gradual falling of prices, as surpluses are
generated, and a return to normal marketing arrangements in Asia.
According to these estimates, Southeast Asia will again become a

TABLE 7

Rice: Production, Total Consumption, and Balances,
1961-63 Averages and Projections for 1975
(In Millions of Tons, Milled Equivalent)

| Regions and Countries | 1961-63 Average | | | 1975 | | | | | |
| | | | | Low GDP Assumption | | | High GDP Assumption | | |
	Production	Consumption	Trade	Production	Demand	Balance	Production	Demand	Balance
Developing Countries:	89.3	88.6[a]	(-)	125.4	127.8	2.4	137.5	132.6	-4.9
Far East Exporters:	19.2	14.4[a]	-4.0	24.6	20.0	-4.6	26.7	20.5	-6.2
Burma	4.9	3.3	-1.6	6.2	4.5	-1.7	6.8	4.6	-2.2
Cambodia	1.7	1.2	-0.3	2.1	1.7	-0.4	2.3	1.8	-0.5
China (Taiwan)	1.8	1.7	-0.1	2.4	2.3	-0.1	2.6	2.2	-0.4
Thailand	6.1	4.2[a]	-1.5	8.2	6.1	-2.1	8.6	6.2	-2.4
Vietnam	3.3	3.2	-0.1	4.2	4.1	-0.1	4.7	4.3	-0.4
Far East Importers:[b]	60.1	63.4[a]	3.3	85.8	91.9	6.1	93.9	95.5	1.6
Ceylon	0.7	1.2[a]	0.5	1.1	1.9	0.8	1.4	2.0	0.6
India	34.6	35.1	0.5	51.0	51.0	-	53.7	52.9	-0.8
Indonesia	7.9	8.9	1.0	9.9	12.1	2.2	11.3	12.6	1.3
Malaysia	0.7	1.3	0.6	0.9	1.9	1.0	1.0	1.9	0.9
Pakistan	10.9	10.9	(-)[c]	16.1	15.7	-0.4	17.4	16.1	-1.3
Philippines	2.6	2.7	0.1	2.9	4.6	1.7	4.4	4.8	0.4
Latin America:	5.7	5.9[a]	0.2	8.5	8.9	0.4	9.5	9.2	-0.3
Brazil	3.9	3.9	(-)[c]	5.9	5.9	(-)[c]	6.3	6.1	-0.2
Africa	2.3	2.8[a]	0.5	3.3	3.9	0.6	3.9	4.2	0.3
Near East:	2.0	2.0[a]	(-)[c]	3.2	3.1	-0.1	3.5	3.2	-0.3
U.A.R.	1.2	0.9[a]	-0.3	2.0	1.4	-0.6	2.0	1.5	-0.5
Developed Countries:	15.0	14.4[a]	-0.7	16.8	16.1	-0.7	16.0	16.1	0.1
North America	2.0	0.8[a]	-1.2	2.7	1.1	-1.6	1.9	1.0	-0.9
Western Europe	1.1	1.4[a]	0.3	1.2	1.7	0.5	1.3	1.8	0.5
Japan	11.9	12.1[a]	0.2	12.7	13.1	0.4	12.5	13.1	0.6
Centrally Planned Countries:	58.2	58.1	-0.1	78.7	78.1	-0.6	80.9	79.8	-1.1
Eastern Europe and U.S.S.R.	0.3	0.8[a]	0.5	0.7	1.0	0.3	0.9	1.0	0.1
China (Mainland)	54.0	53.4	-0.6	72.7	71.9	-0.8	74.4	73.4	-1.0
World Total	162.5	161.1	-0.8	220.9	222.0	1.1	234.4	228.5	-5.9

[a]Including changes in stocks.
[b]Countries (excluding Japan) with net trade deficit in all cereals in 1961-63, though Pakistan and Korea (Republic) export rice.
[c]Less than 100,000 tons.

Source: FAO, Agricultural Commodities--Projections for 1975 and 1985 (1967), Vol. I, p. 106.

TABLE 8

World Rice Trade, By Regions And Countries, 1967/68 and Projections for 1975 and 1980
(In Thousands of Metric Tons Milled)

Country or Region	1967/68	1975	1980
United States	1,826	2,444	2,767
Southeast Asia	918	2,150	2,350
West Asia	-366	-490	-500
South Asia	-625	-800	-950
East Asia and Oceania	-1,574	-1,624	-1,490
Communist Asia	1,100	700	700
Japan	-298	-100	-100
Rest of World	-1,119	-1,636	-2,010
Net Trade	-136	644	767
World Production	186,230	215,729	236,140
World Consumption	183,842	215,085	235,373
Trade	4,624	6,169	6,642
Trade as Percent	2.5	2.9	2.8

Source: USDA unpublished data.

+ exports

- imports

23

TABLE 9

Comparison Of Three Projections Of World Rice
Production And Trade, 1975 and 1980
(In Millions of Metric Tons Milled)

Source	Production	1975 Trade	Percent	Production	1980 Trade	Percent
FAO:						
Low Income Growth	221	9	4.1			
High Income Growth	234	11	4.7			
USDA	216	6	2.9	236	7	2.9
President's Science Advisory Committee				262	6.1	2.3

24

leading source of exports, together with the United States. The major concentrated markets will be in Asia, including Indonesia, India, South Korea, Ceylon, and Japan. Exports from Thailand and Taiwan are projected to drop somewhat from the levels recently achieved. By 1975, Vietnam is expected to become a net exporter of about 125,000 tons and to expand that figure in the succeeding five years.

Three selected projections of production and trade in rice are compared as to their chief features in Table 9. (The details regarding individual country or regional markets are omitted.) Though the differences in the estimates are substantial in some cases and are explicable in terms of differences in underlying assumptions, as well as in methodology, a few features of all the estimates are particularly significant for the prospects for future trade in rice. Regardless of the sometimes rapid estimated rate of growth of production, all three estimates foresee a volume trade in rice that does not decline below the levels now being experienced, and, in the case of the FAO estimates, trade (as measured by export levels) is expected to rise rather dramatically. Trade may become a smaller percentage of production than now (an aspect of policies aimed at self-sufficiency). The absolute level of trade is not expected to fall. There will continue to be an international trade in rice. This is not to say that there will not be imbalances between potential exports and import demand; the FAO estimates, for example, foresee the possibility of excess supplies overhanging the market in the future. However, none of these projections go on to analyze in any detail what this might do to prices and how price declines in export trade might affect the domestic production plans of major importers. That problem requires further exploration.

These aggregate analyses of production, consumption, and trade prospects require elaboration in the form of market analyses of the demand for products in specific markets. (See later chapters.) Moreover, the demand and supply characteristics warrant some further analyses, particularly with respect to the following points: (a) how does population and income growth affect per capita and total demand, if export prices are also changing; and (b) what are the limitations on expansion of production through use of the HYV's of rice. A discussion of these points will improve an understanding and judgment on the credibility of the aggregate projections that are made and will permit an assessment of the probable market for Vietnam rice exports in the future.

FACTORS AFFECTING FUTURE DEMAND

Rice is the basic foodstuff of a very large number of people in the world, but particularly in Asia. The demand for it, on either a

per capita or an aggregate basis, depends on the levels and distribution of income, the rate of increase of income, population growth,
the price of rice, and the prices of other competing (e.g., wheat) or
complementary foods. It has already been noted that, as incomes
rise, the demand for rice (and other goods) increases, but, at some
point or level of incomes, there is a perceptible tendency to substitute
expenditures on other goods for further·expenditures on rice. The
income and substitution effects may offset one another for basic cereals
at lower levels of income than is true, say, of milk or meat. The key
question is at what levels of income that tendency really appears and
how that relates to the incomes and rates of increase of income of the
Asian countries that are major consumers of rice. The income
elasticity of demand measures the percent change in the demand for
a product relative to a percent increase in per capita income.

In a simplified way (that is, abstracting from price and certain
other changes), we can relate the increase in the demand for rice to
population increases and increases in per capita income. The relationship in symbols is:

$$\dot{r} = \dot{p} + e\,\dot{y}$$

where r is the rate of growth of rice demand, $\dot{p}$ and $\dot{y}$ are the rates of
increase of population and per capita income, and e is the income
elasticity of demand for rice. A change in any of the three variables
on the right-hand side of the equation will change the rate of demand
for rice.

The rate of population growth is the more important of the two
factors on the right side in accounting for increases in rice demand.
The FAO projections for a low and a high population growth rate used
1.6 percent and 2 percent, respectively, in general. These are definitely low for Asian countries at the present time, for population
growth rates in this area (except for Japan) are generally between 2
and 3 percent and, sometimes, higher. Of course, the rates used in
the projections are meant to represent conditions as they will be in
1975-85, but this means that, within fifteen years, population growth
rates must decrease 50 to 70 percent to make the forecasted figures
valid. Because of this possible bias, the estimates of rice consumption are also biased, and an underestimate of future demand conditions may exist in these data.

In the detailed country forecasts of production and consumption,
the same apparent bias occurs. For example, Table 10 shows the
population growth rates used in the detailed estimates for Vietnam.
The rate from 1967-75 of 2.1 percent is lower than the 2.6 percent
experienced in the early 1960's, and estimates of current (1969)

TABLE 10

Assumptions Underlying Estimates for Vietnam

Estimates	Percentage Rates of Increase		
	Popu-lation	Income Per Capita	GDP
FAO's Estimates:			
1965-75 (High Income Estimate)	2.1	1.9	4.0
1975-85:			
Low Population; High Income	1.4	3.6	5.0
High Population; High Income	1.7	3.3	5.0
Authors' Estimates:			
Low Population; Low Income	2.0	1.0	3.0
Low Population; High Income	2.0	3.0	5.0
High Population; Low Income	3.0	1.0	4.0
High Population; High Income	3.0	3.0	6.0

experience in the larger urban areas of Vietnam have ranged above 3 percent. Similar experience can be found in most Asian countries. Birth rates do not seem to be coming down very fast, but death rates do, and, as a result, net population growth rates have not declined very much, if at all. This will sustain the demand for rice in the future.

Various estimates have been made of the income elasticity of demand for rice. The FAO estimated the following for selected countries in the Far East: Burma, .1; Ceylon, .6; India, .5; Indonesia, .6; Japan, -.1; Pakistan, .4; and Thailand, .2. These show a wide variation among countries with many similarities in income levels and past levels of per capita consumption of rice, but India and Indonesia, two of the largest aggregate consumers, have quite high income elasticities of demand, meaning that for a 1 percent increase in income, rice demand would increase by .5 or .6 percent.

TABLE 11

Income Elasticities of Demand for Rice in Selected Countries

Country	Elasticity
Vietnam	.59
India:	
Developmental Areas	.38 - .39
Nondevelopmental Areas	.24 - .27
Pakistan	
East Pakistan	.38
West Pakistan	.61
National	.55
Japan	.13 - .28

Sources: Vietnam--based on data in USAID, Rural Income and Expenditure Survey (1965); India--National Council of Applied Economic Research, All India Consumer Expenditure Survey (1967), Vol. II, Table 26; Pakistan--S.A. Abbas, Supply and Demand of Selected Agricultural Products in Pakistan 1961-1975 (1967), p. 196; Japan-- Institute of Agricultural Economic Research, Japanese Import Requirement: Projections of Agricultural Supply and Demand for 1965, 1970, and 1975, For Urban and Rural Areas (1964), pp. 74-76.

Table 11 shows some different estimates of elasticity, based on special studies. Again, the variation is rather wide. All such estimates are uncertain, because the typical data available and the statistical methods do not permit separating out the pure income effects on the demand for rice. There is a mixture of other factors. It must also be pointed out that the elasticity coefficient normally would not be the same at an income level of, say, $100, as it is at $500 or $1,000. It would be higher in the case of the lower income level and usually will decline as income rises to the higher level, though for a range of incomes near the lower end of the scale, this decline in the elasticity will be small. That is, an income level of $100 is very low and is not

capable of supplying even basic needs in more than very modest a-
mounts. An increase in income, at that level, is apt to be spent, in
large part, on additional food, and, in Asian countries, that means
rice, particularly. When an income level of $500 or more is reached
(as in Japan), a further increase in income will not be spent so much
on food as on other goods. The substitution effect becomes dominant.
In the case of Japan, this shows up in a negative elasticity coefficient
in the FAO estimates, meaning that there is a net decline in rice consumption per capita as income rises.

Table 12 shows the per capita and total estimates of demand
prepared by the FAO. For the developing countries of the Far East,
the increases in per capita consumption are in the range of 5 to 10
percent in 1985, a quite modest increase, considering the low current
levels of income in many of these countries. Among the cereals, rice
competes with wheat in certain instances, and it is possible that this
will increase in the future. It is said that the "convenience" features
of wheat (i.e., in the form of bread, biscuits, and so forth) is one reason for the fact that substitution takes place in Japan. In the case of
India, there seems no doubt that PL-480 shipments of wheat have
decreased the import demand for rice in recent years. Without such
concessionary shipments of wheat, the demand for rice would have
been greater.

Rice is not, however, a homogenous product. There are a large
number of varieties, which differ as to quality, and those varieties
that are now causing a "revolution" in production with their high
yields are apparently an inferior grade in terms of taste, and that
affects the current and future demand for these grades. One report
says flatly: "Burmese farmers do not like to eat IR-8 rice, but they
willingly sell it to the government. There is not a black market for
IR-8 rice."[7] The same conclusion has been frequently voiced by
others. Demand is high for the better-quality rices, and producing
countries are responding to it. Rice from Communist China commands a premium because of its quality. Pakistan has been exporting
a quality variety (basmati) and importing cheaper grades for domestic
consumption. The composition of exports from Thailand has shifted
toward parboiled, and the demand for brown rice in Europe has been
growing. In short, the demand for higher-quality varieties will continue to grow, and unless further experimentation can improve the
taste, texture, and aroma of the current so-called high-yielding varieties, such as IR-5 and IR-8, they will sell in export markets at lower
prices and in a weak position, relative to other varieties. This shift
in composition will become accelerated as incomes increase, and the
higher-quality varieties are not necessarily those with the highest
yields. This poses a problem for production planning and export
promotion in the producing countries.

TABLE 12

Rice: Total and Per Capita Consumption,[a] 1961-63 and Demand Projections for 1985

Regions and Countries	1961-63 Average		1985							
			Per Capita Demand				Total Demand			
	Per Capita[b]	Total[c]	Low GDP High Population[b]	High GDP High Population[b]	Low GDP Low Population[b]	High GDP Low Population[b]	Low GDP High Population[c]	High GDP High Population[c]	Low GDP Low Population[c]	High GDP Low Population[c]
Developing Countries:	58	80.9	62	64	62	64	152.4	158.8	148.8	154.1
Far East Exporters:										
Burma	133	3.1	134	133	135	133	5.2	5.2	5.1	5.0
Cambodia	149	0.9	149	149	149	149	1.7	1.7	1.6	1.6
China (Taiwan)	132	1.5	132	122	131	121	2.6	2.4	2.4	2.2
Thailand	123	3.4	128	129	128	129	6.7	6.8	6.5	6.6
Vietnam	168	2.5	173	178	174	177	4.0	4.2	4.0	4.0
Far East Importers:[d]										
Ceylon	110	1.1	116	124	120	124	2.4	2.6	2.3	2.3
India	72	32.5	80	83	80	83	60.4	63.0	59.3	61.5
Indonesia	85	8.4	86	99	87	99	14.8	17.0	14.7	16.6
Malaysia	120	1.2	123	119	123	118	2.5	2.4	2.5	2.4
Pakistan	94	9.8	101	100	101	100	18.5	18.3	18.0	17.8
Philippines	89	2.6	94	99	95	99	6.3	6.6	6.2	6.4
Latin America:	24	5.4	25	27	26	27	10.8	11.3	10.3	10.7
of Which Brazil	48	3.6	51	53	51	53	7.1	7.4	6.8	7.0
Africa	11	2.6	12	13	12	14	4.9	5.6	4.8	5.5
Near East:	19	1.9	21	22	21	22	3.9	4.1	3.8	3.9
of Which U.A.R.	32	0.9	34	35	35	35	1.8	1.9	1.8	1.8
Developed Countries:	19	13.1	17	17	17	17	15.6	15.6	15.2	15.2
North America	3	0.6	3	3	3	3	0.9	1.0	0.9	0.9
Western Europe	3	1.2	4	4	4	4	1.7	1.8	1.7	1.8
Japan	116	11.1	109	108	109	108	12.8	12.6	12.5	12.3
Centrally Planned Countries:	50	53.6	57	58	57	57	92.2	93.3	85.4	85.6
Eastern Europe and U.S.S.R.	2	0.7	3	3	3	3	1.2	1.2	1.1	1.1
China (Mainland)	69	49.4	74	75	75	75	84.3	86.0	78.7	78.8
World Total	47	147.6	52	54	52	53	260.2	267.7	249.4	254.9

[a]As food.
[b]In Kilograms.
[c]In millions of tons.
[d]Countries (excluding Japan) with net trade deficit in all cereals in 1961-63, though Pakistan and Korea export rice.

Source: FAO, Agricultural Commodities--Projections for 1975 and 1985 (1967), Vol. I, p. 111.

A final factor affecting future demand is the likely level of market prices for rice if production grows more rapidly than consumption in the near future. In some producer areas, rice production has been stimulated by the high price levels after 1966, compared to the lower and relative stable prices in the late 1950's and early 1960's. Drought and bad weather led to a low production, rising prices, and a rapid decrease in stocks of rice in 1966-68.

	1956-58 Average	1963-65 Average	1966	1967
Price per Ton	$117	$125	$141	$159
Stocks (In Thousands of Tons)	600*	659**	160	40

If the net effect of the forecasted increases in production and a slower growth in consumption is a growing surplus of rice available for export, prices will decline from the recent high levels, perhaps to the levels of the 1950's. However, prices and increased competition will put heavy market pressure on the high cost, or marginal producers, or areas and may well result in forcing some of them out of production. Countries that are efficient (low-cost) producers and/or with quality varieties for export will be in a strong position in the market. There is evidence that the countries of the Mekong, which include such traditional exporters as Thailand, Cambodia, and Vietnam, are, or can be, among the most efficient producers and, hence, in the long run, should be in a good structural or competitive position in export markets.

An analysis of the possible impacts of declining prices and large exportable supplies concluded that

at the very time the 'green' revolution will be faced with its greatest challenge of moving into more marginal areas of production, one of its greatest incentives--favorable producer prices--may have disappeared and/or come under the support of government subsidies. Few governments in the developing world are structurally or financially capable of supporting producer prices during prolonged periods of deficit spending.[8]

Thus, with higher production and declining prices, the geographical pattern of rice production may alter in the future.

---

*1955-57.
**1962-64.

FACTORS AFFECTING FUTURE PRODUCTION AND SUPPLY

The successes achieved so far with the HYV's developed by The International Rice Research Institute (IR-5 and IR-8) seem to promise a revolution in yields and production throughout the Far East. Acreages planted with these varieties have increased rapidly, and a black market in the seeds exists in some areas. In 1968/69, Burma increased the acreage planted with IR-8 from 2,832 hectares to 223,000 hectares, or to about 4 percent of total paddy area. In India, the acreage planted with these varieties rose 40 percent and, in the Philippines, 11 percent of the rice area was planted with these varieties.[9] Ceylon, Malaysia, and Thailand have been developing their own adaptations to meet local conditions, and preliminary results are favorable. The HYV's seem capable of causing a real revolution in rice production throughout producing areas.

However, there may be some problems, both technical and economic, in sustaining the boom and in spreading these varieties to all acreage. In the previous section on demand, it was noted that the current HYV's have not had wide consumer acceptability, but further experimentation could correct this. That, however, will take some time. Another cycle of experimentation, field testing, seed propagation, and production use will take at least a few years. Meanwhile, the current varieties will sell at a discount, compared to other traditional quality grades. Equally important is the economic effect of falling market prices, if production begins to rise rapidly. This would put heavy financial pressure on governments that try to sustain producer prices through subsidies. In the final analysis, that factor may be the dominating one that determines the structure and location of rice production and trade.

The greatest benefits may occur to those areas that can adopt the new varieties quickly to meet current shortages, before increased competition and falling prices force a readjustment. The capability to expand production with the HYV's depends on the availability of other production inputs, such as water, fertilizers, pesticides, credit, technical training, and on government policies toward agriculture. It has been observed that "the new varieties are generally produced under the best conditions, and, therefore, it would be misleading to compare their yields with average yields of traditional varieties and then assign all the differences to the genetic characteristics."[10] And it was concluded that the yield increases "fall generally in the range of 30 to 100 percent when planted under conditions of adequate irrigation and a high level of fertilization . . ."[11] The underlined qualification is significant because, without irrigation, water availability and control, and high applications of fertilizer, the new varieties apparently give no better yields than traditional varieties. This means that the increased yields will involve increased costs of these other inputs, and the amount of these inputs that is economically profitable to use will depend on the price of the output (rice) and the price of the inputs (fertilizer, water, and so forth). For example, if the price of fertilizer is high relative to the price of rice, the farmer simply cannot afford to use much fertilizer. The benefit cost calculation is unfavorable for high use. The ratio of fertilizer prices to rice prices varies a good deal, as shown in the following list.[12]

Country	Rates
India	4.35
Pakistan	1.56
Japan	1.16
Philippines	2.50
Thailand	4.55
United States	1.72

These ratios represent the kilograms of increased production of rice required to equal the cost of one additional kilogram of fertilizer at the prevailing prices for the commodities. In some instances, both the price of rice and the price of fertilizer are subsidized by the country, so that a special bias is introduced into the ratio and into the calculations of the farmers. It is entirely possible that, in order to achieve the increases in rice production that are projected in country development plans to achieve self-sufficiency, and to save foreign exchange, the countries will have to spend more on imports of fertilizers and pesticides or obtain investment funds to build domestic production facilities. In either case, additional resources must be committed to raising agricultural production.

At present, about 6 million metric tons of fertilizer are used in the developing countries of Asia, Africa, and Latin America. It is estimated that, by 1985, 40 million tons will be required if they are to achieve their production goals. An increase of 34 million tons of fertilizer will require a capital investment of about $17 billion and annual costs to farmers of about $9 billion.[13] This rough estimate applies to all crops and three continents, but the implication is clear that expansion of the capacity for this agricultural input for rice production will involve substantial costs to the producer countries.

Water and irrigation are the other major inputs needed to achieve high yields. One observer comments that "the shortage of irrigation systems with adequate water supplies may turn out to be the most critical physical factor limiting the further spread of the new grain varieties."[14] According to a survey of the Asian Development Bank, the amount of land available for double-cropping of rice with existing irrigation systems is less than 10 percent of the total rice area now under cultivation in South and Southeast Asia.[15] Irrigated areas undoubtedly can, and will be, expanded in the coming years, but the preparatory work takes time, and costs are often high on a per hectare basis, ranging upwards of $1,000. Expansion obviously will not come overnight.

Production of rice will continue to expand in the Asian countries, but probably with some moderation of the rate of increase, as increased technical difficulties and unfavorable economic factors appear. The unqualified conclusion that HYV's will permit all countries to achieve self-sufficiency easily and quickly is a poor guide to the future. There are many uncertainties still to be resolved on both the supply and the demand sides. Forecasts about the future export trade in rice should be conditional and qualified, but some judgments for policy and action are desirable.

PROSPECTS FOR VIETNAM'S RICE EXPORTS

At its peak, in the early 1960's Vietnam exported over 300,000 tons of rice, at a time when exports from Far Eastern countries were about 3.8 million tons. The market share was slightly under 10 percent, and the principal markets were in the region, notably Hong Kong and Singapore. When the war ends, Vietnam should be able to find a market again for available rice exports. This conclusion and the qualifications behind it are based on the following factors, which seem to summarize the foregoing discussion.

Relative Pace of Supply and Demand
in Different Countries

Although rice production in the Far Eastern countries is likely to increase fairly rapidly, at least for a time, the relative pace of supply and demand in different countries will vary, and, in the aggregate, world trade in rice in the next ten years will be on the order of 5 to 6 million tons annually under favorable production outcomes, and at least 6 to 7 million tons, or higher, if production plans are not fully realized. Bad weather and drought, which occur through extensive areas of the region, could push trade demand much higher than this, and in any one or more years, the variation could be great.

Growth of Demand in Far East

Demand in all of the Far Eastern countries will continue to grow, due to high population rates of growth and, secondarily, in a number of countries, through rising per capita consumption, as incomes rise from the levels that predominate in this region. These factors will more than offset the decline in per capita consumption noted in several of the more affluent countries. The increases in demand will be a strong sustaining market force in export trade.

After End of War

Within a few years after the end of the war, Vietnam could re-establish itself in traditional markets (Hong Kong, Singapore), in the sense that the demand would be there. In the longer view, it should look to other markets, particularly to Indonesia and, possibly, to Japan and to India. The case of Japan is special. Its rice production is maintained because of a support price that is about three times the world price. Although officially dedicated to a long-term policy of rice self-sufficiency, Japan has now started a policy aimed at diverting land from rice to other crops. Initially, 300,000 hectares (about 8 percent of total) is affected. As industrialization continues to press on demand for labor, it is possible that Japan will de-emphasize agricultural production and may conceivably become a large potential rice importer.

Long-Run Pressures on Prices

Long-run pressures on prices seem probable, and competition will increase in intensity. Vietnam and other countries in the Mekong Basin seem in a fortunate production position and should be able to keep costs down. Emphasis on quality grades of rice, as demand is upgraded, should provide a guide to production policy.

Demand Consideration

Based on demand consideration primarily, it is estimated that Vietnam could have a market for 150,000 tons within five years of the end of the war and, in ten years or so, could reasonably expect to reestablish its previous market share and export 500,000 tons-- and, provided it is in a competitive price position, raise this to 700,000 tons. Under more favorable conditions or a more intense promotion program, Vietnam might raise these levels and attain a higher market share.

Exchange Earnings

At 1968 unit export values for medium-quality rice exported from Thailand and Burma, the projected level of exports would yield $72 to $100 million annually. These exchange earnings could be achieved within a decade or less.

These appear to be the main elements in an evaluation of rice export prospects for Vietnam in the next ten years.

NOTES

1. Joint Development Group, The Postwar Development of the Republic of Vietnam: Policies and Programs (New York: Frederick A. Praeger, Inc., 1970).

2. FAO, Agricultural Commodities--Projections for 1975 and 1985 (1967), Vol. I, p. 105.

3. USDA, Rice Situation, RS-13 (March, 1969), p. 8.

4. President's Science Advisory Committee, The World Food Problem (May, 1967), Vol. II, p. 172.

5. Derived from USDA, op. cit., Table 25.

6. FAO, op. cit., p. 110.

7. USDA, The Agricultural Situation in the Far East and Oceania, ERS-Foreign 262 (April 29, 1969), p. 7.

8. USDA, The World Rice Situation and Outlook, Preliminary Draft (1969).

9. Ibid.

10. J. W. Willet, The Impact of the New Varieties of Grain in Asia, USDA Working Draft (June, 1969).

11. Ibid.

12. Cited in President's Science Advisory Committee, op. cit., p. 156; data are for 1964.

13. Ibid

14. Willet, op. cit.

15. Cited in Willet, op. cit.

In the past, the major portion of Vietnam's foreign earnings has been derived from rubber exports. It is possible for natural rubber again to attain its position of importance in export earnings, although there are some uncertainties in the market. The uncertainty stems from the changing position that natural rubber occupies in the world market for elastomers, as well as the ability of Vietnam's production to acquire some portion of that market. It appears that Vietnamese rubber enjoys a favorable production environment and, also, a ready market in at least a few areas. Both conditions of demand and supply lead to optimism about future exports from Vietnam.

The total market for rubber has been expanding considerably. Synthetic rubber has been growing more rapidly than natural rubber and has been acquiring a larger and larger share of the total market. Table 13 shows, for recent years, the consumption and production of rubber and the amounts that are represented by natural and synthetic rubber.

As calculated from the data in Table 13, world consumption of natural rubber has been increasing at about 3.5 percent per annum. Increases in the consumption of synthetic rubber, however, have been much more substantial, averaging about 10 percent per annum. The percentage of the total market that is represented by synthetic rubber has almost doubled in a period of a little over a decade.

Trends in the consumption of natural rubber for different countries are quite varied. Some nations are increasing their consumption markedly; among them are many of the underdeveloped countries. Consumption quantities in other nations remain relatively unchanged, while still others are experiencing net decreases in the consumption

TABLE 13

World Rubber Production and Consumption, 1953-65
(In Thousands of Tons)

Market	1953-55	1962	1963	1964	1965
Production:					
Natural Rubber	1,849	2,164	2,101	2,268	2,332
Synthetic Rubber	1,083	2,889	3,243	3,753	4,048
Consumption:					
Natural Rubber	1,802	2,227	2,266	2,256	2,367
Synthetic Rubber	1,062	2,819	3,156	3,654	3,913

of natural rubber. The United States and France, for example, are experiencing absolute declines in the use of natural rubber. There does not appear to be any systematic pattern in these consumption changes. Consumption of natural rubber in low-income Brazil is decreasing, while consumption in high-income Canada is increasing. The natural rubber market share, however, appears to be decreasing in all areas. Table 14 shows, for a number of countries, past trends and projections of the market share of natural rubber.

In spite of the displacement of natural rubber by synthetic rubber in the total market for elastomers, there are indications that the consumption of natural rubber in quantitative terms will increase in the future. The market for natural rubber has grown in the past and, recently, has been growing at an accelerating rate. Indications are that consumption will continue to grow in the future. This market can provide a place for increased Vietnamese production, provided that marketing channels are maintained and that prices are comparable to competing suppliers.

A number of projections have been made of the future consumption of natural rubber. Although there are differences of degree, all of the studies examined in the course of this analysis were in agreement that consumption would continue to grow. The growth rate envisaged is moderate. In addition to examining studies conducted elsewhere, an independent estimate for 1980 was prepared. The method and its results appear in the appendix to this chapter. As in the other studies, the mathematical estimate projects forward from 1966 data, using past growth rates and rates of substitution between natural and synthetic rubber for extrapolation to 1980. Like the other studies, a moderate growth rate has been calculated for the future.

TABLE 14

Natural Rubber: Share in Total Rubber Consumption, by
Major Consuming Countries, 1954-66 and
Projections for 1975
(In Percent)

Country	1954	1958	1962	1966	1975
United States	48	36	27	25	22
Canada	58	44	32	31	24
Belgium-Luxembourg	87	67	48	41	31
Germany (Federal Republic)	88	70	53	42	32
France	90	71	54	43	28
Italy	84	67	52	42	29
Netherlands	94	80	60	47	33
United Kingdom	96	74	56	49	31
Other Western Europe	93	80	60	50	32
Eastern Europe (Excluding U.S.S.R.)	48	50	52	40	26
Japan	98	90	65	50	30
Australia	99	68	57	49	38
Brazil	99	96	58	38	28
India	100	91	83	75	50

Source: FAO, Agricultural Commodities--Projections for 1975 and 1985 (1967), Vol. I.

Among the other studies examined was a projection made by the International Rubber Study Group. [1] They estimated that consumption of natural rubber would increase to 3 million long tons in 1975. This projection was made primarily on the basis of surveys and information obtained from rubber-using industrial firms. This estimate is almost certainly too low.

The FAO also prepared projections of the consumption of rubber. (See Table 15.) The projections of demand were made for each country or group of countries, primarily on the basis of assumed population and income growth. Income elasticities of demand, derived from time series and covering the years 1954-65, were developed and used in the analysis. World elastomer demand (including demand in centrally planned economies) in 1975 was projected by the FAO to be 39 to 67 percent greater than in 1966. The share of the world elastomer market going to natural rubber is projected to decline to 34 percent. World demand for natural rubber is projected to rise by 7 to 30 percent over that of 1966, reaching 2.7 to 3.3 million tons, depending on high or low GDP assumptions in the consuming countries.

Another projection for the consumption of natural rubber was developed by A. Maizels. [2] Maizels developed consumption ranges for a high-income growth assumption and for a low-income growth assumption. For the low-income growth assumption, demand is projected for 1975 at between 2.7 to 3.3 million tons. For the high-income growth assumption, demand for 1975 is placed at between 3 to 3.6 million tons.

These projections are all fairly consistent with one another. They all fall within Maizels' low of 2.7 million tons and high of 3.6 million tons for 1975. Our independent projection for 1980, at 3.4 million tons, is also essentially in agreement with the others.

However, in the light of the latest consumption statistics, these projections all appear to have been too modest. In 1968, world consumption of natural rubber reached 2.8 million tons, which puts consumption already above the lower end of the ranges projected for 1975. Monthly statistics available for early 1969 [3] indicate that consumption may have reached 2.9 million tons in 1969. These latest figures would point toward a consumption of at least 3.6 million tons in 1975, which exceeds most other projections and occupies the highest point in Maizels' upper range. Thus, on present evidence, the future market consumption of natural rubber appears favorable.

NATURAL RUBBER PRODUCTION

An evaluation of Vietnam's future role in world markets for natural rubber must consider the relationship of the future world

TABLE 15

Rubber Consumption: Demand Projections for 1975
(In Thousands of Tons)

Country	1966 Natural	1966 Synthetic	1966 Total	1975--Low Natural	1975--Low Synthetic	1975--Low Total	1975--High Natural	1975--High Synthetic	1975--High Total
Developed Countries:	1,653	3,009	4,662	1,642	4,298	5,940	1,920	4,955	6,875
North America:	606	1,808	2,414	627	2,203	2,830	695	2,445	3,140
United States	559	1,699	2,258	580	2,055	2,635	641	2,274	2,915
Canada	47	109	156	47	148	195	54	171	225
Western Europe:	769	914	1,683	756	1,524	2,280	902	1,798	2,700
European Economic Community:	411	558	969	376	874	1,250	432	1,008	1,440
Belgium-Luxembourg	18	26	44	16	34	50	19	41	60
Germany, Federal Republic	158	212	370	141	299	440	166	354	520
France	124	167	291	109	281	390	122	313	435
Italy	91	129	220	90	220	310	104	256	360
Netherlands	20	24	44	20	40	60	21	44	65
Northern European Countries:	270	275	545	215	445	660	255	525	780
United Kingdom	184	193	377	124	276	400	146	324	470
Southern European Countries	88	81	169	165	205	370	215	265	480
Japan	216	222	438	200	460	660	255	585	840
Oceania:	41	41	82	41	69	110	47	78	125
Australia	34	37	71	36	59	95	40	65	105
New Zealand	7	4	11	5	10	15	7	13	20
South Africa	21	24	45	18	42	60	21	49	70
Centrally Planned Countries:	579	865	1,444	745	1,725	2,470	885	2,135	3,020
U.S.S.R. and Eastern Europe:	411	820	1,231	535	1,635	2,170	665	2,015	2,680
U.S.S.R.	273	610	883	355	1,125	1,480	425	1,335	1,760
Eastern Europe	138	210	348	180	510	690	240	680	920
Centrally Planned Countries in Asia	168	45	213	210	90	300	220	120	340
Developing Countries:	285	223	508	310	440	750	459	616	1,075
Latin America:	112	141	253	122	253	375	175	340	515
Argentina	24	22	46	17	38	55	25	55	80
Brazil	30	51	81	35	95	130	50	120	170
Mexico	18	32	50	20	60	80	30	85	115
Africa	6	4	10	16	14	30	21	19	40
Near East:	13	6	19	27	18	45	43	27	70
U.A.R.	5	3	8	12	8	20	18	12	30
Far East:	154	72	226	145	155	300	220	230	450
India	67	22	89	70	70	140	105	105	210
World Total	2,517	4,097	6,614	2,697	6,463	9,160	3,264	7,706	10,970

Source: FAO, Agricultural Commodities--Projections for 1975 and 1985 (1967), Vol. I.

43

demand to future world supplies, including likely production cost levels in competing areas. The supply of natural rubber is relatively in- elastic. Short-term fluctuations in demand result in little change in production. Seven years from planting are required before rubber trees can produce, and a tree produces at full capacity roughly from ten to twenty years after being planted.

Vietnam's production of natural rubber is only a small portion of the total world production, representing in Vietnam's most pro- ductive years only about 4 percent of the world total. Malaysia is the world's largest rubber producing country, followed by Indonesia, Thailand, and Ceylon, in that order. These four countries account for approximately 85 percent of the world output and about the same percentage of world exports.

A number of estimates of future production also have been made. These estimates were developed as part of the studies referred to in the discussion above on future consumption. Estimates of production from the different sources are essentially in agreement. The ranges of estimates overlap, and all show moderate growth. All, except one, are basically in agreement that production will exceed demand. The exception was a group from the United Kingdom, which forecast that supplies of natural rubber will not be sufficient in the future. This group maintained that "more and more rubber is being produced, but not enough to satisfy growing demand."[4]

The estimates prepared by FAO show a range of production for 1975, from 3.3 million tons (low GDP) to 3.8 million tons (high GDP).[5] When compared with the FAO demand projections (Table 15), the pro- jections of production suggest that some 18 percent of the natural rubber produced in 1975 would be in excess of requirements on the low GDP assumption and that 16 percent would be in surplus on the high GDP assumption. A surplus of this magnitude would indicate a definite tendency to oversupply, which would be reflected in the ac- cumulation of heavy stocks and in severe pressure on natural rubber prices.

Table 16 shows past trends in the production of natural rubber and FAO projections for 1975. Notice that the Vietnamese production is projected to fall from about 4 percent of the world total to less than 3 percent of the world total in 1975, but, in absolute terms, output is projected to increase 33 percent over the 1961-63 average.

The range of production estimates developed by Maizels[6] over- laps the FAO estimates. Maizels' estimates range from 3.15 to 3.50 million tons for 1975. Projections prepared by the International Rubber Study Group (see page 42) are very close to the projections

TABLE 16

Natural Rubber: Production in 1953-55, 1961-63, and 1966,
and Projections for 1975
(In Thousands of Tons)

Region or Country	1953-55 Average	1961-63 Average	1966	1975 Low	1975 High
Latin America:	31	29	31	40	55
Brazil	24	22	24	30	40
Africa:	88	150	174	300	400
Nigeria	25	60	74	115	150
Liberia	38	43	53	75	100
Congo (Kinshasa)	22	38	25	60	90
Far East:	1,747	1,951	2,231	2,960	3,325
Malaysia:	656	839	1,004	1,445	1,610
Malaya- Singapore	609	771	943	1,350	1,500
Sarawak	29	46	37	45	50
Sabah	18	22	24	50	60
Indonesia	737	648	711	770	830
Thailand	116	190	207	275	340
Ceylon	97	102	131	185	210
Vietnam	58	75	49	100	110
Cambodia	25	41	51	70	85
India	22	32	53	85	95
Burma	12	10	9	10	15
World Total	1,886	2,130	2,436	3,300	3,780

Source: FAO, Agricultural Commodities--Projections for 1975 and 1985
(1967), Vol. I.

45

developed by Maizels.   The study group developed estimates for 1975, ranging between 3. 125 and 3. 375 million tons.

Later data indicate that world production for 1968 amounted to 2. 6 million tons. [7] These projections, therefore, appear reasonable in the light of recent data.   The trend indicates a production of 3. 3 million tons in 1975, which is about the midpoint of a composite of all the ranges discussed.   This projected level of production does not indicate a serious future oversupply of natural rubber, when matched against the projected level of demand.

PRICES

An unfavorable aspect of the world rubber trade in recent years is the falling price of natural rubber.   Since the recent high point of 1960, the price of natural rubber has dropped almost in half, primarily as a result of competition from synthetics.   Table 17 shows the average annual prices of natural rubber from 1960 to 1968.

These price changes have resulted in a decrease in the foreign exchange earnings of natural rubber.   In spite of increased volume, earnings from rubber exports have diminished significantly.   Over the eight-year period covered in Table 17, consumption increased about 25 percent and prices decreased by 50 percent, leaving the value of exports reduced significantly.

Decreases in the price of natural rubber have brought its price very close to the price of synthetic rubber.   Eliminating price differences may serve to strengthen the future of natural rubber.   The International Rubber Study Group concluded that there was a significant zone of price competition between natural and synthetic rubber.   Within this zone, substitution could take place without major technical difficulty.   It was estimated that a change of $0. 035 per pound could switch 5 to 10 percent of the market from one to the other.   Thus, as natural rubber prices drop toward the price of synthetic rubber, substitution may work in favor of the former or, at least, dampen the incentive to increase the use of synthetic.   Obviously, the relationship of the two prices is an important determinant of the relative demand for each.   Although export earnings are diminishing with dropping prices, the production of rubber can remain remunerative, since there are active programs in most countries to raise productivity.   Replanting of pedigree clones is doing much to increase productivity.   New pedigree clones have raised productivity, in some cases, to 2, 000 pounds per acre, from an output of 400 pounds per acre from unselected stock.   One estimate puts the costs of natural rubber, with a 1, 500 pounds per acre yield, at $0. 12 to $0. 13 New York c. i. f. price. [8]

TABLE 17

Average Price of Ribbed Smoke Sheet No. 1, 1960-68

(c.i.f.--New York)		Export Price (f.o.b.--Saigon)	
Year	Cents	Piasters per Kilogram	Cents per Pound
1960	38.16	27.32	35.41
1961	29.50	20.96	27.17
1962	28.56	19.66	25.48
1963	26.26	18.26	23.66
1964	25.24	16.96	21.98
1965	25.69	17.47	22.55
1966	23.62	26.21	20.92
1967	19.90	30.77	17.44
1968	19.84	n.a.	n.a.

Source: Rubber Statistical Bulletin (London), various issues.

At those cost levels, production of natural rubber is profitable, even with present low prices.

Whether Vietnam can again regain export markets for its rubber will depend on conditions of production and cost in other countries and how these compare to conditions in Vietnam. A recent survey of the rubber plantations in Vietnam that covered actual physical inspections of a large part of the planted area concludes that conditions for future expansion are quite favorable and that present conditions do not pose any insuperable problems of rehabilitation. [9] This study notes a number of factors that are favorable to production over the long-run:

1. Rubber in Vietnam is grown on some of the best (most productive) soils, altitudes, and other physical conditions. This contrasts to the experience and practice in many other countries.

2. There is a virtual absence of any serious diseases that attack rubber trees.

3. The clones being used are among those that have proved to give good yields in Vietnam, and there is great familiarity with their use.

4. There is an absence of high winds, which cause serious damage in other countries. The rubber expert "hazard(s) a guess that if all the areas destroyed by bombing and shell fire alone were added up, the total would not equal the destruction that I have seen caused by a few heavy winds."[10]

5. There is an organization that is active in research and production problems of the Vietnamese rubber industry.

All of these factors (and others of lesser importance) strongly indicate that, in the postwar period, the rubber plantations will be able to produce at competitive costs and will have the basis for expansion of production. These are factors on the supply side. In the next section, it is shown that there are other favorable demand conditions.

VIETNAM'S RUBBER TRADE AND FUTURE PROSPECTS

Rubber has traditionally been of considerable importance in Vietnam's export trade. In the mid-1960's, when production was at relatively high levels, rubber represented almost three-fourths of Vietnam's total export earnings. The proportion of rubber to total exports has been relatively constant, even though rubber exports from Vietnam have dropped off considerably. The export of other products has dropped off as much or more.

Trade ties with France have been very strong, since a number of large plantations are French-owned. Other than France, the substantial importers of Vietnam's rubber are the United States, the United Kingdom, and West Germany. Table 18 presents data on exports according to the recipient country.

Although present conditions in Vietnam are depressing, there are favorable prospects for future market demand. World production of natural rubber has not, in the past several years, kept pace with expanding world consumption. Natural rubber stocks have been drawn down, and sales have been made from U.S. stockpiles, which have had the effect of filling the gap between production and consumption. This gap between consumption and production reached about 200,000 metric tons in 1968. The demand situation, as compared with production, both at present and in the future, indicates sufficient room for increased exports. Vietnam has a tradition of exporting natural rubber, and trading channels have been established, even though currently disrupted.

The figures on the destination of exports indicates the close

TABLE 18

Vietnam's Rubber Exports, by Recipient Country, 1958-67
(In Thousands of Dollars)

Country of Destination	1958	1959	1960	1961	1962	1963	1964	1965	1966	1967
Total	$35,560	$46,913	$47,998	$43,832	$37,917	$33,480	$33,299	$26,012	$22,034	$13,211
France	28,515	21,058	29,751	25,164	19,459	18,072	14,954	11,441	10,090	5,458
Germany	740	10,996	5,171	6,257	4,919	5,936	7,660	5,047	2,716	2,165
United Kingdom	1,171	1,921	3,670	6,610	7,256	3,858	3,500	2,528	2,402	1,304
Japan	83	578	725	126	1,706	2,267	2,767	3,095	3,095	2,273
Italy	8	1,576	1,145	954	1,100	1,215	1,595	1,694	1,535	1,218
Netherlands	88	1,375	1,132	601	427	573	662	553	408	218
United States	4,500	5,285	2,831	2,917	1,333	377	448	101	320	41
Belgium	17	2,018	425	508	265	255	288	387	165	61
Singapore	191	1,880	2,824	180	206	61	176	122	292	107
Other	247	226	324	515	1,246	866	1,249	1,044	1,071	366

Source: USAID--Vietnam, Annual Statistical Bulletin (1968).

TABLE 19

Vietnam's Rubber Exports, by Type, 1958-67
(In Metric Tons)

Type	1958	1959	1960	1961	1962	1963	1964	1965	1966	1967
Total	35,560	46,913	47,998	43,832	37,917	33,480	33,299	26,012	22,034	13,211
Latex	383	2,178	1,703	982	1,704	534	1,727	n.a.	n.a.	n.a.
Smoked Sheets	26,617	32,993	34,135	32,650	26,949	24,542	23,643	n.a.	n.a.	n.a.
Crepe Sole and Ordinary Sole	7,617	9,448	10,451	7,846	7,097	7,004	6,652	n.a.	n.a.	n.a.
Other	943	2,294	1,709	2,354	2,167	1,400	1,277	n.a.	n.a.	n.a.

Source: USAID--Vietnam, Annual Statistical Bulletin (1968).

ties that have existed with France; these ties continue to exist through French ownership of plantations and in other ways. The Société de Caoutchoucs d' Extrême-Orient and the Société de Plantations des Terres Rouge maintain their interests in the long-run future of rubber production in Vietnam, and they have pointed out that there is a ready market in France for virtually all the forseeable production expansion in the near future.

The potential of the existing estates, only 50 percent of which are now being exploited, is between 70,000 and 80,000 metric tons. This level of production could be achieved readily without new investment in replanting. Admittedly, yields on existing plantations will decrease in the medium term, as a result of the failure to replant over the past five or six years, but there should be no drastic falloff in the short term. Cutting out old trees and rejuvenation by new planting continued in the large estates up to 1964/65. There are, therefore, immediate prospects of export earnings up to $35 to $40 million, once access is obtained to the estates that are now too insecure to be worked. Indeed, if production in 1961--the last relatively peaceful year--were to be taken as an indication of potential yields, plus the additional hectarage planted from then to 1965, the theoretical production level is as high as 120,000 metric tons, but, since then, some abandoned estates have been absorbed by the forest, and, of course, some physical damage has been inflicted by the war. (See Table 19 for list of Vietnam's rubber exports by type.)

There is no doubt in the minds of the main rubber producers of their ability to dispose of this quantity of rubber--and considerably more. They point to the relative superiority of the product, as a result of favorable soil and climatic conditions, its freedom from serious disease, and the skill and productivity of the Vietnamese labor force, derived from over sixty years' experience of rubber cultivation. The problem is not one of demand but of supply. At prevailing world market prices, Terre Rouge, Michelin, and the other large estates could absorb up to 150,000 metric tons (less than 5 percent of total world production) themselves. That is, there could be a tied market for the commodity in France--apart from the prospects of selling additional quantities to brokers in Singapore or to Japan.

With this in mind, the estates have proposed to the government of Vietnam a scheme for expansion, involving the creation of 10,000 hectares of new plantations each year for a five-year period, to be implemented as soon as security conditions permit. They consider this degree of expansion an objective capable of effective realization. Suitable land is available in Phuoc Long Province and near Tay Ninh and Ban Me Thuot. Since 80 percent of existing capacity is foreign-owned, the large estates, realistically, consider that the greater portion of new plantations should be under the operation and control of small holders, although they themselves would be prepared to provide the investment necessary for some of the new planting, if the government would allocate further concessions to them. Their most important role, however, and one that they are eager to fill, would be in providing technical, processing, and marketing services for the small holders.

The new estates, planted with high-yielding clones, could have a potential production of up to 2 metric tons a hectare, as opposed to present average yields of 1 ton. As production on the older estates initially declines from 70, 000 to around 50, 000 tons, there would be a progressive increase in production from the new plantations, which would secure an overall annual output of 150, 000 tons by the end of ten years. At current prices, this would represent export earnings of almost $70 million. This would be a significant part of total export earnings for the country.

The International Rubber Study Group estimated in 1966 that natural rubber production in Vietnam would reach 100 to 110 thousand metric tons in the 1970's. This might be regarded as the lower end of the reasonable range, with 150,000 tons as the upper end. After allowing for a growth in domestic consumption to as much as 10,000 tons per year, and at 1968 unit export values for Malaysia of about $0. 20 per pound, the forseeable export earnings from rubber would be in the range of $44 to $62 million. This appears to be the outlook for rubber exports in the postwar period.

NOTES

1. International Rubber Study, Working Party on the Prospects for Natural Rubber (UNCTAD, June, 1966).

2. A. Maizels, Exports and Economic Growth of Developing Countries (Cambridge University Press, 1968).

3. Unpublished USDA statistics.

4. Plantation Crops (London: Commonwealth Secretariat, 1967), p. 156.

5. FAO, Agricultural Commodities--Projections for 1975 and 1985 (1967), Vol. I.

6. Maizels, op. cit.

7. Rubber Statistical Bulletin (London) (August, 1968).

8. M. J. Hooft Welvaars, The International Organization of Commodity--Trade: Case Study of Rubber (UNCTAD, 1966).

9. See K. G. McIndoe, A Preliminary Survey of Rubber Plantations in South Vietnam, Development and Resources Corporation Vietnam Working Paper No. 3 (September, 1969).

10. Ibid.

APPENDIX TO CHAPTER 3

PROJECTION OF DEMAND FOR NATURAL RUBBER IN 1980

For the purposes of projecting the demand for natural rubber in 1980, the elasticity of substitution of synthetic rubber for natural rubber is defined as:

$$E_s = \frac{\text{Percentage change in the ratio of } \frac{\text{natural rubber}}{\text{total rubber}}}{\text{Percentage change in consumption of total rubber}}$$

Mathematically, where $\frac{N}{T}$ is the ratio of natural to total rubber:

$$E_s = \frac{\Delta\left(\frac{N}{T}\right)}{N/T} \bigg/ \frac{\Delta T}{T} \quad \text{or} \quad \frac{\Delta\left(\frac{N}{T}\right)}{N/T} \cdot \frac{T}{\Delta T}$$

On the assumption that the denominator is positive, i.e., consumption of total rubber increases over time, then the elasticity can be interpreted as follows:

$$E_s > 0 \longrightarrow \text{gain}$$

$$E_s = 0 \longrightarrow \text{no substitution}$$

$$E_s < 0 \longrightarrow \text{displacement}$$

The values we obtained (see Table 20) are all negative, implying displacement over time by synthetic substitutes. The magnitudes, however, differ substantially, varying from -.06 in the Eastern European countries to -.98 in the United Kingdom, with the fastest relative growth of synthetic rubber, due undoubtedly to the remarkable development of the petrochemical industries in the 1960's.

TABLE 20

Consumption of Natural Rubber, Projections for 1980[a]

Markets	(1) Total Consumption of Rubber--Projected Increase, 1966-80 (In Percent)	(2) Trend E_s	(3) Percent Change in N/T	(4) N/T at Base Period 1966	(5) Projected N/T in 1980	(6) Projections of Rubber Consumption [from (1)]	(7) Projections of Natural Rubber Consumption in 1980	Total of (7) as percent of Total (6)
United States	(2,258)[b] 71	-.65	-.53	.25	.15	3,950	580	
Canada	(156) 124	-.44	-.54	.30	.15	346	50	
European Economic Community	(969) 85	-.44	-.51	.42	.27	1,900	500	
United Kingdom	(377) 57	-.98	-.56	.49	.28	600	170	
Japan	(438) 190	-.13	-.65	.49	.20	1,300	260	
Australia	(71) 68	-.89	-.60	.48	.20	130	25	
U.S.S.R.	(883) 130	-.04	-.20	.31	.25	2,100	525	
Eastern Europe	(348) 230	-.06	-.13	.40	.35	1,150	400	
Latin America	(253) 170	-.38	-.65	.45	.20	680	135	
Asia	(89) 200	-.08	-.30	.68	.45	270	120	
Other	(635) 370	-.16	-.60	.61	.25	2,300	600	
Total						14,726	3,365	23

[a]Explanation of symbols used in table in text.
[b]Figures in parentheses represent total consumption of rubber in thousands of tons at base period 1966.

The steps followed in Table 20 for arriving at a forecast of natural rubber consumption are as follows:

1. Computation of the trend elasticity of substitution from historical data.

2. Finding the percentage cumulative increase in total consumption of rubber to 1980, as projected from weighted trends.

3. From the two magnitudes obtained in step 1 and step 2, the percentage change in the ratio of natural to total rubber is computed, and given the ratio in the base year 1966, the projected ratio in 1980 can easily be obtained.

4. From step 2, we can compute the actual projected consumption of total rubber in 1980, and given the projected ratio in 1980 obtained from step 3, we can arrive at an estimate of the consumption of natural rubber for that year.

Wood and wood products constitute a heterogeneity of items, with marked differences among them in terms of their prospects in the development of an export trade for Vietnam. In general, wood and wood products can be considered in four categories: (a) logs or round wood, which consist of cut but unprocessed materials; (b) sawn wood, which involves the primary processing of timber into lumber or dimensions; (c) wood panel products, which consist of plywood, fiberboard, particle board, and, at times, insulation board; and (d) pulp wood, wood pulp, and paper products. A distinction needs to be made between the hardwoods and the conifers. The market for the hardwoods and the conifers, although overlapping at times, is significantly different. Likewise, a distinction needs to be made as to the availability of supplies of these two basic types of wood.

Although some attention will be given to supply conditions, the primary consideration here, as for the other commodities in this study, will be with demand or market conditions.

World consumption and international trade in wood and wood products is growing. This growth presents Vietnam with a good opportunity to market its wood resources abroad. Vietnam possesses considerable forest resources, which, at present, are largely unexploited. Due to existing war conditions, this timber is, in most cases, as yet inaccessible to lumbering operations.

PRODUCTION AND CONSUMPTION TRENDS

World production figures over the past years illustrate the expanding use of timber and timber products. Table 21 presents data on world production since 1950.

57

TABLE 21

Timber and Timber Products:
Value of World Production, 1950-68
(In Millions of Dollars)

Commodity	1950	1960	1965	1968	Percentage Average Annual Increase
Processed Wood	$10.3	$13.5	$15.1	$15.9	2.5
Panel Products	1.0	2.7	4.4	5.4	10.0
Pulp Products	8.7	12.2	16.2	19.0	4.5
All Other	3.9	5.5	5.3	5.2	1.6
Total	$23.9	$33.9	$41.0	$45.5	3.5

Source: FAO, Yearbook of Forest Products (1969), p. xiv.

As can be seen from the figures in Table 21, wood and wood product markets have been expanding substantially. The 3.5 percent increase per annum since 1950 is substantial; however, it tends to obscure the remarkable 10 percent average per annum increase that was experienced in the production and use of such products as wood panels. Also, the world production data shown in Table 21 do not reveal development in particular regions or individual countries. The consumption of wood and wood products in Asia (discussed below), although at relatively low levels at present, is expanding at a far greater rate than world consumption.

Various timber trend studies have been made in the recent past, and virtually all conclude that the consumption of industrial wood for most purposes and in most regions is likely to increase substantially in the future. Further developments will depend on a number of factors, including the rate of economic development, population growth, availability of supplies, competition from substitute materials, and relative prices.

There are substantial differences in market trends between the developed countries of North America and Europe and the countries of Asia. Consumption of wood in the developed countries is high, both per capita and in total. However, substitute materials, technological developments, and increasing efficiency in the use of wood limit prospects for overall future expansion. For certain items, there has been a net decrease in usage. The Asian countries, however, reflect the opposite. Consumption levels, when compared with the developed countries, are quite low (both per capita and in total), but the rate of increase in wood usage is generally quite high. An export strategy for wood and wood products must weigh the alternatives of whether to stress penetrating the large but competitive markets of the developed countries or whether to concentrate on the smaller but rapidly growing markets in Asia.

Substitution of materials is a key market consideration, particularly in the developed countries. Wood products are becoming more highly finished. For example, plywood is being substituted for sawn wood in construction uses, which sometimes results in a net decrease of wood consumed. Even more significantly, materials, such as metal and plastics, are being substituted for wood products. For example, flexible floor materials are being substituted for wood floors. Substitution has been taking place because of quality differences and because of price. In many instances, the prices of substitute materials have been falling, relative to the price of wood. If the relative prices of substitutes continue to fall, future demand for wood products will be adversely affected. This substitution away from woods that characterize the markets of the developed countries does not appear, at the present time, to be very much in evidence in the developing countries. This substitution process affects different items to different degrees, of course. Sawn wood seems particularly adversely affected, while paper products remain, to a large extent, without substitutes. Beyond a certain point, of course, it becomes increasingly difficult to substitute, so that, in the developed countries, demand for wood may grow in absolute terms, but at a much lower rate than other materials.

Technological developments, substitution of materials, and future relative prices all contribute to uncertainty in gauging future prospects in international markets. And these uncertainties increase as the time horizon is extended. Nevertheless, the current and near-term prospects for Vietnam's participation in a foreign trade in wood and wood products appear very favorable, particularly in the Asian countries.

Prospects for exports are not limited to the Asian area, however. Asian countries have, in certain items of wood products, demonstrated a good capability to export to developed countries. Production and exports from South Korea, Taiwan, Japan, and the Philippines have played an important role in the development of a market for wood panel products in the United States, particularly plywood and veneers of hardwood.

WORLD TRADE IN WOOD AND WOOD PRODUCTS

World trade in wood and wood products has been expanding more rapidly than world production. The rate of expansion in world trade has been almost three times that of world production, which, as shown in Table 21, has averaged 3.5 percent per annum in value since 1950. Table 22 presents import data covering the years 1958-67. The total for the Asian countries is shown, together with world totals for various wood products. Table 23 shows average annual percentage increases for similar wood products, worldwide and for Asia.

The participation in trade of the developing countries has been growing more rapidly than has total world trade. This is accounted for both by an increase in exports directly to the developed countries of the world and an increase in interregional trade, particularly among countries in Southeast Asia (but including Japan and South Korea). The latter element of trade has been primarily an export of lumber and sawn wood (i.e., raw and semifinished products) from a group of primary producers, such as Malaysia, Indonesia, and the Philippines, to a few other countries (Japan, South Korea, and Taiwan) that process the materials into plywood, veneer sheets, and similar products, for export to the developed countries. The domestic consumption of both raw and manufactured wood products by Japan has also been growing rapidly in the last ten years and will continue at a high rate in the next ten.

Over the past ten years, world trade in wood products has increased at about 10 percent per year, but the developing countries trade has grown more rapidly. Exports of logs and sawn wood from Asian countries still account for over 90 percent of exports, but exports of wood panels has also been growing. Total exports have been increasing, on the average, about 15 percent per year, but, in the last two years (1967-69), they have been growing at over 20 percent per year. For at least the next few years, the high rate of growth is almost certain to continue.

LOGS AND SAWN WOOD

In markets for logs and logs and sawn wood, a clear distinction must be made among geographic areas. Worldwide figures--those most heavily influenced by the heavy consumption in developed countries--shown very modest increases in the past, with an actual

TABLE 22

Imports of Wood and Wood Products: Asia and World, 1958-67

Year	Pulpwood[a]	Logs[a] Conifer	Logs[a] Broadleaved	Sawn Wood[a] Conifer	Sawn Wood[a] Broadleaved	Veneer Sheets[a]	Plywood[a]	Wood Pulp[a]	Newsprint	Pulp Products[b] Printing and Writing Paper	Other Paper and Paperboard	Fiberboard
Asia[c]												
1958	144	635	4,097	901	171	1	62	158	227	107	293	39
1959	159	1,034	5,263	1,209	208	2	94	257	268	120	318	32
1960	213	1,274	5,832	1,052	186	3	65	359	268	144	349	37
1961	429	2,827	6,977	1,378	177	5	68	470	324	150	378	35
1962	533	3,488	8,207	1,524	228	3	80	610	267	159	394	34
1963	525	4,922	9,830	1,686	259	2	96	833	296	174	434	43
1964	668	6,009	10,878	1,835	566	4	124	895	383	175	517	83
1965	635	7,689	12,471	1,727	557	42	122	820	345	156	521	80
1966	996	9,285	16,131	2,078	528	34	155	1,049	407	189	603	87
1967	1,025	14,180	18,293	2,834	577	39	164	1,194	493	250	738	81
World Total												
1958	8,858	2,948	8,950	28,873	3,740	309	1,144	7,596	6,830	625	2,874	613
1959	8,988	3,726	10,803	31,951	4,015	422	1,526	8,453	7,084	650	3,132	713
1960	11,284	4,690	12,774	35,054	4,340	407	1,517	9,619	7,577	796	3,610	766
1961	13,620	6,501	13,796	36,060	4,143	439	1,561	9,882	7,900	1,000	3,949	772
1962	12,903	7,494	14,676	37,912	4,051	494	1,784	10,212	7,754	968	4,159	857
1963	11,681	9,019	16,851	40,501	4,386	552	1,963	11,403	7,770	1,072	4,623	974
1964	12,511	10,039	18,946	43,471	5,184	646	2,401	12,378	8,547	1,285	5,295	1,138
1965	13,497	12,116	20,205	43,083	5,416	772	2,571	12,428	8,931	1,712	5,442	1,115
1966	12,778	13,754	23,952	41,384	5,524	798	2,821	13,318	9,757	1,660	6,354	1,060
1967	13,331	18,833	26,142	42,696	5,469	811	3,106	13,254	9,352	1,830	6,678	1,162

[a] In thousands of cubic meters.

[b] In thousands of metric tons.

[c] Asian countries include the following: Brunei, Burma, Cambodia, Ceylon, China (Mainland), China (Taiwan), Hong Kong, India, Indonesia, Iran, Iraq, Israel, Japan, Jordon, Korea (Republic), Kuwait, Laos, Lebanon, Malaysia (West Malaysia, Sabah, Sarawak), Pakistan, Philippines, Ryuku Islands, Singapore, Syria, Thailand, Turkey, Vietnam.

Source: FAO, 1968 Yearbook of Forest Products (Rome: 1968).

TABLE 23

Average Annual Percentage Increases in Wood and Wood Products in
International Trade, 1958-67

Region	Pulpwood	Logs Conifer	Logs Broadleaved	Sawn Wood Conifer	Sawn Wood Broadleaved	Veneer Sheets	Plywood	Wood Pulp	Newsprint	Printing and Writing Paper	Other Paper and Paperboard	Fiber-board
Asia	61.2	213.3	34.6	21.4	23.7	380.0	16.4	65.6	11.7	13.4	15.2	10.8
World	5.0	53.8	19.2	4.8	4.6	16.2	17.2	7.4	3.7	19.3	13.2	9.0

Source: FAO, Yearbook of Forest Products (1968), passim.

downturn in recent years. This development is due primarily to the
substitution of newer (and, often, less costly) materials for wood and
to more efficient uses being made of wood.

In Asia, the situation is quite different. There is a vigorous and
expanding market in Asia for logs and sawn wood. This growing market has resulted in a substantial increase in the Asian trade of logs
and, to a somewhat lesser extent, sawn wood.

Tables 24 and 25 show the total exports and imports of logs and
sawn wood of selected Asian countries. The largest exporters of logs
and sawn wood are Indonesia, Malaysia, and the Philippines. The dominant position of this form of exports is quite clear, and the largest
importers are Japan, South Korea, and Taiwan, which manufacture
wood-based panels and paper for export. In the future, the trade volume of logs and sawn wood will be dictated by two separate elements:
(a) the demand for plywood, paper, and similar manufactured products
in the developed countries (the United States, Japan, and Western Europe), and (b) the domestic demand for sawn wood for construction
purposes in the Asian countries themselves. Their demand for manufactured products, particularly paper products, will very likely rise
at the most rapid rate of all products, but the per capita consumption
of these products is now very small. The future growth in this demand
holds promise for active markets in the future.

Log exports from Southeast Asian countries approximately doubled between 1956 and 1962.[1] This growth in the export of logs results in large measure from increases in the production of plywood
and veneers. Between 1965 and 1975, the consumption of plywood is
expected to double in North America and Asia and to total approximately 25 million cubic meters.[2] If Southeast Asian exports doubled
as a result, log exports would increase approximately 11 million cubic
meters. How much of the total market or the increase could be acquired by Vietnam depends primarily upon the supply situation relative to prevailing prices. Because Vietnam now has high-cost logging operations (due, in large part, to an overvalued currency) and
because trade channels have not been established, it does not appear
likely that Vietnam would capture any significant part of the current
market. Vietnam can, however, acquire some portion of the projected
increase, estimated at 10 to 20 percent of the total increase. This
portion of the projected expansion of the market would mean from 1
to 2 million cubic meters per year for Vietnam by 1975. Exports of
hardwood logs from Sarawak and Sabah (1968 prices) indicate an export value of about $20 per cubic meter. Vietnam's potential trade,
even assuming a modest proportion of 10 to 20 percent of the projected
increase, can be placed conservatively at $20 million per year and,
optimistically, at $40 million. This would represent a modest 1 to 2
percent of the world market.

TABLE 24

1968 Exports of Logs and Sawn Wood
from Asian Countries
(In Millions of Dollars)

Country	Total	Raw and Semi-finished Form	Manufactured Form
Burma	$ 32,567	$ 32,546	$ 21
China (Taiwan)	88,241	20,139	68,102
Indonesia	60,586	60,535	51
Japan	273,747	21,774	251,973
Korea (Republic)	66,357	46	66,311
Malaysia	244,961	230,921	14,040
Philippines	234,500	196,700	37,800
Thailand	12,630	11,785	845
Vietnam	—	—	—

Source: FAO, Yearbook of Forest Products (1969), p. 123.

TABLE 25

1968 Imports of Logs and Sawn Wood into Asian Countries
(In Millions of Dollars)

Country	Total	Raw and Semi-finished Form	Manufactured Form
Burma	$ 6,035	$ –	$ 6,035
China (Taiwan)	45,037	41,882	3,155
Indonesia	9,922	347	9,575
Japan	1,374,769	1,284,456	90,313
Korea (Republic)	125,914	117,185	8,729
Malaysia	30,113	2,570	27,543
Philippines	32,255	4,785	27,460
Thailand	28,764	2,114	26,650
Vietnam	8,266	1,143	7,123

Source: FAO, Yearbook of Forest Products (1969), p. 129.

Sawn woods also show some promise, but export markets are smaller and, also, more uncertain. On the basis of the performance of Vietnam's neighboring countries, an export quantity ranging from a conservative estimate of 100,000 cubic meters to an optimistic estimate of 400,000 cubic meters can be made for Vietnam. This means from $4 to $16 million per annum, using 1968 export values from Sarawak for pricing.

WOOD PANELS

As mentioned above, the increased demand for hardwood logs is the result of a marked increase in demand for plywood veneers and other panel products. Percentage increases are fairly uniform regionally, but the developed countries are the big markets--especially the United States. World consumption of wood-based panels has been growing faster than consumption of any other forest product.

Wood panels have competed successfully with sawn wood, particularly in the developed countries. This was due partly to falling panels prices during a period when sawn wood prices rose or remained unchanged and partly to the adaptability of panels to mechanized processes, permitting standardization. In addition, new applications have been found for panel products. The factors influencing usage of wood panels are the following: (a) the prior level of use of sawn wood; (b) prices and trends in prices of panel products relative to sawn wood, as well as other substitutes; and (c) forest resources and supplies (which are necessarily related to prices).

The expansion in the use of panel products should give Vietnam a good opportunity to enter export markets. In the decade 1955-65, world per capita consumption of plywood almost doubled, increasing from 3.8 m^3 per 1,000 population in 1955 to 7.1 m^3 in 1965. Although from a smaller base, even greater percentage increases have occurred for particleboard. World per capita consumption of particleboard increased from 0.2 m^3 per 1,000 population in 1955 to 1.6 m^3 in 1965. World consumption of fiberboard increased from 1.1 m^3 per 1,000 in 1955 to 1.8 m^3 in 1965.

These increases in the market for panel products have been quite uniform in all regions. Although percentage increases are about the same, there are wide differences in the absolute levels of consumption. The large markets are in North America, where, for example, U.S. consumption per 1,000 population in 1965 was 68 m^3. By contrast, for the Asia-Pacific region, the average consumption of plywood in 1965 was 0.7 m^3 per 1,000. World consumption rose to 33.8 million m^3, which represents an annual increase of 9.6 percent.

Three-fourths of the growth in the consumption of wood-based panels took place in developed countries, which absorb 82 percent of the world total.

The continued heavy concentration of consumption and production of forest products in the high-income countries has coincided with the pattern of international trade in wood and wood products. In 1959-61, the flows among high-income countries accounted for more than 80 percent of total trade in forest products. Since the early 1960's, however, the shifts in the pattern of demand for wood products and pressures on the indigenous resources of the developed countries have stimulated flows from new sources of supply. The developing countries, particularly those of Asia, have recently provided a major portion of the growth of supplies. Most of Southeast Asian exports were destined for the U.S. market, either through direct exports of plywood and veneers or through the more indirect method of exporting logs to Japan, Taiwan, or South Korea, which, after processing into plywood, have been reexported to the United States.

Several Asian countries have been very successful in acquiring market shares in the United States in recent years. In 1960, Japan supplied almost a half of U.S. imports of plywood; Taiwan and South Korea together supplied 1 percent. By 1969, Japan supplied only 18 percent of the total, and the other two countries supplied almost 60 percent. Since total imports were rising, the relative rate of growth of Taiwan and South Korea was approximately 40 percent annually during this period.

The decline in the Japanese share of the U.S. market cannot be ascribed entirely to displacement by other Asian suppliers, inasmuch as the domestic demand for plywood in Japan also has increased very rapidly in recent years. Since plywood is a product with high-income elasticity, a continuation of the present upward trend in domestic consumption for Japan is reasonable. In the foreseeable future, then, Vietnam's main competitors for the U.S. market in plywood should be Taiwan, South Korea, and the Philippines.

U.S. imports of plywood in 1969 amount to about $240 million annually. Over 90 percent in volume comes from Asia. Assuming that imports of plywood from Asia rise at the same rate as U.S. consumption, imports of plywood into the United States will reach $400 million per annum by 1980. This is the largest market and offers opportunities for new entrants, such as Vietnam. By 1980, it is estimated that Vietnam could have an annual export capacity of 100,000 to 200,000 metric tons (about 150,000 to 300,000 cubic meters). At 1968 unit export values for Asia, this would amount to about $20 to $40 million. Some of the capacity would operate on imported logs, at

TABLE 26

Production of Wood Pulp and Pulp Products: Asia and World, 1958–67
(In Thousands of Metric Tons)

		Wood Pulp		Pulp Products[b]				
	Year	Mechanical	Chemical	Newsprint	Printing and Writing Paper	Other Paper and Paperboard	Fiberboard	
Asia	1958	935	1,781	890	936	3,402	107	
	1959	1,088	2,391	1,035	1,134	4,496	142	
	1960	1,206	3,026	1,111	1,279	5,279	223	
	1961	1,271	3,680	1,205	1,473	6,121	274	
	1962	1,304	3,813	1,354	1,469	6,560	315	
	1963	1,322	4,247	1,517	1,745	7,218	391	
	1964	1,375	4,661	1,693	1,909	8,080	464	
	1965	1,434	4,836	1,692	1,800	8,183	476	
	1966	1,504	5,377	1,723	2,095	8,982	516	
	1967	1,535	5,899	1,871	2,225	9,589	538	
World Total	1958	16,074	33,835	12,124	11,444	39,116	3,660	
	1959	17,301	37,604	13,061	12,538	43,310	4,111	
	1960	18,270	40,908	13,976	13,493	46,050	4,345	
	1961	18,654	43,986	14,370	14,308	48,827	4,636	
	1962	19,166	45,933	14,566	14,842	51,357	4,957	
	1963	19,790	49,948	14,998	15,999	54,644	5,436	
	1964	20,827	54,431	16,307	17,213	58,681	5,954	
	1965	21,661	57,540	16,986	18,098	62,196	6,265	
	1966	22,913	61,790	18,274	20,117	66,348	6,291	
	1967	22,393	62,747	18,362	20,438	67,220	6,183	

Source: FAO, Yearbook of Forest Products (1968).

least in the first few years. Even if the U.S. market were the sole
target, the implied market share for Vietnam would be under 10 percent, or less than half that achieved by South Korea in 1968. Alter-
natively, some of the output could be sold in Asian markets.

Japan, which is a leading exporter of plywood to the United States,
only exports about 10 percent of its production to the United States.
Most of the balance is for the Japanese market. Between 1965 and
1969, production in Asia increased a remarkable 128 percent. The
major Asian importing countries show imports of over 160,000 cubic
meters in 1967.[3] At an estimated value of $130 per cubic meter (1969
unit value), the value of this trade amounts to $20 million. This Asian
market promises to double in the next decade. Conservative to optimistic estimates for Vietnam would range from $2 to $4 million per
annum for the developing future Asian market. These would offer
additional opportunities.

WOOD PULP PRODUCTS

Virtually all wood pulp is used for the making of paper and paperboard products. World production of pulp and pulp products has been
expanding considerably in recent years. As can be seen in Table 26,
production of most items has approximately doubled in the decade
1958-67.

As with other processed wood products, consumption of paper
and paper products is heavily concentrated in the developed nations.
North America accounts for approximately a half of the world's consumption and Europe for approximately a third. Underdeveloped
Africa, Asia, and South America together only consume about a tenth
of the world total. Table 27, which shows the observed relationship
between income and consumption of paper and paperboard, shows a
marked positive relationship between income and consumption. At
low levels of income, the income elasticity is high, at 2.5 to 3.0. The
elasticity falls, however, with rising levels of per capita income. Future developments in the consumption of paper and paper products are
expected to be determined, as in the past, mainly by the rate of growth
and level of income per capita. Estimates of future consumption have
been made and appear in Table 28. The Asian estimates are based
on a GDP growth rate per capita of 2.5 percent per annum.

The markets projected for pulp, paper, and paper products, therefore, are substantial. In percentage increases, the Asian market is
among the highest of the geographic regions. This growth could present
Vietnam with potential markets for exports.

TABLE 27

Estimated Total Consumption of Wood Products, per 1,000 Capita, by Income Class, 1967
(In Dollars per Person)

Income Class	Region	Paper and Paperboard
More than $2,000	United States	190.9
$1,500-$2,000	Northern Europe	104.1
	Canada	125.2
	Pacific	78.5
$1,000-$1,500	European Economic Community	63.2
	United Kingdom and Ireland	97.8
	Central Europe	36.0
$500-$1,000	Eastern Europe	26.8
	U. S. S. R.	15.9
	Southern Africa	21.5
	Japan	53.1
$300-$500	Southern Europe	9.8
	Mexico	15.4
	Caribbean	11.1
	Northern South America	13.0
	Southeast South America	22.7
	Mediterranean Basin	11.2
$150-$300	Central America	6.4
	Brazil	9.4
	Southwest South America	8.6
	Northern Africa	5.7
	Southwest Asia	1.8
	Arabian Peninsula	0.8
	East Asia (less Japan)	7.8
Less than $150	Western Africa	0.8
	Eastern Africa	1.3
	Continental Southeast Asia	1.9
	Insular Southeast Asia	1.8
	South Asia	1.2
	China (Mainland)	3.7

Source: FAO, Wood: World Trends and Prospects (1967).

TABLE 28

Estimated Consumption of Paper and Paperboard, by Category, 1975

Region	Newsprint		Other Printing and Writing Paper		Industrial Paper and Paperboard	
	Millions of Metric Tons	1961 = 100	Millions of Metric Tons	1961 = 100	Millions of Metric Tons	1961 = 100
Europe	8.10	196	10.40	215	32.10	231
U. S. S. R.	1.40	327	3.20	441	10.40	449
North America	9.90	139	9.50	149	37.00	155
Latin America	1.80	248	1.20	259	3.80	263
Africa	0.50	286	0.60	240	1.50	303
Asia–Pacific	4.60	242	5.70	353	20.20	303
World Total	26.30	182	30.50	215	105.10	215

Source: FAO, Wood: World Trends and Prospects (1967).

Vietnam is now a relatively high-cost producer of pulp. Production of hardwood bleached sulphate pulp was reported at twice the cost in the United States and approximately 60 percent higher than Scandinavia.[4] This situation could, however, change in the future if efficient scales of plant are built. Production of chemical pulp from conifers appears feasible for Vietnam, together with the production of newsprint. A development plan for Vietnam recommended the production of 100,000 tons of chemical pulp a year as a first-priority investment and an allocation of 60,000 tons per year for export, which would yield $8 to $10 million annually.[5]

Inasmuch as most other countries in the region are not endowed with similar timber resources, they will require imports to satisfy their growing needs for newsprint. Consumption of newsprint should double in the nearby Asian area by 1980. The future market increase for all paper by 1975 is projected at about 300,000 tons per year. Of that market, 30 percent, or about 100,000 tons, is expected to be for newsprint. Vietnam could satisfy one-third to one-half of the increase; this would amount to 30,000 to 50,000 tons in exports, or $6 to $10 million (at 1968 unit values) per year.

Imports of printing and writing paper constitute about 30 percent of the total paper imports into Southeast Asian countries. Vietnam possibly could supply 20 to 30 percent of the total projected increase of printing and writing paper; this would provide an additional $7 to 10 million. The balance, which is 40 percent of the total, is made up of various types of specialized paper and packaging materials. Vietnam's possibilities for exporting specialized products is so uncertain that they have been omitted from consideration.

Vietnamese resources of fibrous raw materials are abundant and varied. Conifers are found in the high plateau, mainly in the Dalat region. It is estimated that there are approximately 120,000[6] hectares of pine stands in Dalat. It is further estimated that at least 2 m^3 and possibly as high as 8 m^3 a year can be produced from a volume of 80 m^3 per hectare.

Potential production of pulp in Vietnam is substantial. An estimate of 85,000 tons per year of pulp production has been made by the FAO.[7] As mentioned earlier, the Joint Development Group recommended that a facility producing 100,000 tons per year be constructed. Production potential is greater than foreseeable domestic demand. However, with world supplies more than adequate, price is the problem. As with the hardwoods (mentioned earlier), price of pulp in Vietnam is high now. New facilities, however, could make the difference. The Joint Development Group maintains that, if the pulp and paper industry is properly planned and integrated, Vietnam

TABLE 29

Vietnam's Potential Export Earnings
from Wood and Wood Products, 1980
(In Millions of Dollars)

Product	Conservative Estimate	Optimistic Estimate
Logs	$20	$40
Sawn Wood	4	16
Plywood	20	40
Pulp	8	10
Newsprint	6	10
Paper	7	10
Total	$65	$126

could well become one of the low-cost pulp and paper producers in
Asia.[8]

SUMMARY

The prospects for logs, sawn wood, plywood, pulp, and paper
have been considered as to their earning potential in export. Ranges
of earnings were estimated for each category. In summary, the
earnings possibilities within ten years are projected, as shown in
Table 29.

NOTES

1. FAO, Wood: World Trends and Prospects (1967).

2. FAO, Yearbook of Forest Products (1968).

3. Ibid. (1969).

4. FAO, Pulp and Paper Prospects in Asia and the Far East, Vol. I, (1968), p. 67.

5. Joint Development Group, The Postwar Development of the Republic of Vietnam: Policies and Programs (New York: 1970).

6. FAO, Pulp and Paper Prospects in Asia and the Far East, Vol. II, p. 125.

7. Ibid., p.132.

8. John W. Delaplaine, The Vietnamese Industrial Sector, Working Paper No. 2 (August, 1967), p. 10.

5

Any examination of future Vietnamese export possibilities should give serious consideration to fishery products, one of the fastest-growing branches of world trade. This growth has been reflected in past Vietnamese fishery exports, which rose steadily from $171,000 in 1958 to $959,000 in 1966, a compound rate of increase of 24 percent per annum.[1] Total fishery export earnings during that period were $9.6 million, representing over 6 percent of total Vietnamese exports after rice and rubber.

Although the war has had an adverse effect on exports, particularly after 1966, Vietnam's fish landings have held up amazingly well. In 1969, the catch was 464,000 metric tons, or about 7 percent of the total catch in East and Southeast Asia. Vietnam ranked about twenty-fifth among all countries of the world in the size of catch; it ranked above Malaysia, but fell far short of Thailand.[2] If Vietnam can hold up this well under extremely adverse conditions, which affect the area fished and the improvement of the fleet, there is every reason to expect that, after the war, it can expand the size of the catch rapidly.

A glance at the structure of past Vietnamese fishery exports in Table 30 provides some indication of future export opportunities. Of particular significance is the rapid increase of crustacean and mollusc exports, primarily to Japan. The increasing relative importance of these higher-value products to a position of clear dominance of all fish trade at the end of the 1960-66 period certainly contributed (as did inflation) to a rise in the average unit value of Vietnamese fishery exports, from about $450 per ton in 1960 to over $1,100 per ton in 1966. As we shall see below, these products again should provide the greatest opportunities for exports in the postwar period.

TABLE 30

Vietnam's Exports of Fishery Products, by Country of Destination, 1960-66
(In Metric Tons)

Product	1960	1961	1962	1963	1964	1965	1966
Fresh Fish:							
Total:	245	390	231	367	362	169	156
Singapore	238	365	229	367	361	166	156
Hong Kong	7	25	2	-	-	3	-
Others	-	-	-	-	1	-	-
Fresh and Dried Crustaceans and Molluscs:							
Total:	163	240	493	561	551	685	702
Japan	-	-	30	349	76	278	398
Hong Kong	31	133	395	130	245	197	100
France	3	8	6	36	108	40	142
United States	75	55	42	36	31	152	62
Others	54	44	20	10	91	18	-

Source: Vietnam Statistical Yearbook (1966-67).

The purpose of the following analysis is to assess the potential world market for Vietnamese fishery products coming primarily from the nearby waters of the South China Sea. It is not anticipated that during the period through 1980, which is the scope of this study, Vietnam could become a major force in world fishery trade--as it probably will become in rice. Thus, the feasibility of expanding Vietnamese exports in the postwar decade will depend primarily on the following: (a) the expansion of world markets at a rate that exceeds the growth of supplies, and (b) the ability of Vietnam to meet the pricing structure and marketing conditions that will be imposed on it from the outside. If these two conditions can be satisfied, then it is likely that the growth of export earnings from fisheries will be constrained not by export markets but by Vietnam's supplies.

PRODUCT DESCRIPTION

The following paragraphs contain a discussion of the following: (a) fishery products in general, including fresh, frozen, cured, and canned fish and shellfish, fish meal, and fish oils; and (b) crustaceans and molluscs, a subcategory, which includes shrimp, crabs, lobsters, oysters, clams, mussels, snails, squid, octopuses, and so forth. The category of crustaceans and molluscs is usually divided in statistical references into fresh, frozen, dried, and salted products, on the one hand, and processed products and preparations, on the other. In the following analysis, the two groups are combined and sometimes referred to as shellfish and shellfish products--not an exact definition, but appropriate for present purposes.

Highest world consumption levels are found in the Far East and many African countries, where a half or greater of total animal protein consumption is of fishery origin.

WORLD CONSUMPTION PATTERNS

Fisheries contribute about 1 percent of the total world food supply. The dietary role of fish, however, varies greatly from country to country; in some, very little is consumed, but, in others, particularly in developing countries of the Far East and Africa and developed countries with major fishery industries and traditional food preferences for fish, only cereals, starches, and fruits are consumed in larger quantities than fish. [3] This is illustrated by the following FAO statistics for 1960-62, which shows the percentage of total animal protein consumption provided by fish:

Developed Countries		Developing Countries	
United States	3.9	Argentina	2.1
Australia	4.4	Pakistan	8.1
West Germany	7.1	India	8.3
France	7.2	China (Mainland)	20.9
United Kingdom	7.9	Indonesia	40.0
Denmark	14.3	Vietnam	·49.5
Norway	19.9	Philippines	54.2
Spain	26.1	China (Taiwan)	58.8
Portugal	47.4	Thailand	59.3
Japan	55.0	Korea	64.8

TRENDS IN PRODUCTION AND TRADE

All Fishery Categories

World production of fish and fish products has increased steadily during the past decade, doubling from 30 million metric tons in 1957 to almost 60 million tons in 1967. [4] The cumulative annual rate of increase between 1957 and 1963 was 8.4 percent, dropping to 4.9 percent in the 1963-67 period.

Similarly, world trade in fish and fish products rose from 3 million tons in 1957 to over 6 million tons in 1967, at a cumulative annual rate of 11 percent between 1957 and 1963 and 3.7 percent during the 1963-67 period.

Thus, trade grew faster than production between 1957 and 1963 (11 percent versus 8.4 percent) but the trend reversed during 1963-67, with production growing faster than trade (4.9 percent versus 3.7 percent). This reversal probably was due to two major factors: (a) an increase in the domestic consumption of exporting countries, leaving a smaller proportion of production for export, and (b) greater efforts towards self-sufficiency in many importing countries. A third factor to be considered is the exceptional fourfold expansion of world fish meal exports that occurred between 1957 and 1963, from 500,000 tons to almost 2 million tons over the six-year period. During the subsequent four-year period through 1967, an additional export gain of 50 percent was achieved--representing a much slower rate of increase. [5]

In 1965, twelve countries accounted for nearly three-fourths of world fisheries production: developing countries--Peru and India; socialist countries--Mainland China and the U.S.S.R.; and developed countries--Japan, the United States, Norway, South Africa, South West Africa, Spain, Canada, Iceland, and the United Kingdom. Nearly all of the developing countries of Asia in recent years have shown a rising catch trend, chiefly for domestic food requirements and intra-regional trade, plus growing volumes of crustaceans and tuna, for export to Japan, North America, and Europe.

Over two-fifths of the total world catch is by Asian fisherman. [6] The Japanese catch increased from 5 million tons (1955-57 average) to almost 8 million tons in 1967. [7] Despite these production increases, Japanese domestic consumption has grown even faster, causing imports to increase rapidly over the past decade (about 42 percent per annum). [8]

Over 70 percent, by value, of world exports of fish and fish products is destined for markets in six amjor developed countries: the United States, the United Kingdom, West Germany, France, Italy, and Japan. In 1965, these countries absorbed about three-fourths of total fishery exports from the developing world [9]

The United States is the largest importer, its primary purchases being fish meal (from Peru), shrimps (from Mexico--the world's leading fish exporter--Latin America, and Asia), and tuna (from Japan).

In Asia, Japan is the dominant importing (and exporting) nation, its major imports being fresh and frozen shrimps, seaweed, and fish meal. Its chief sources for all but fish meal are the developing countries of the Far East and Mainland China.

To provide some indication of the general market situation that might face Vietnam in the postwar period, Table 31 summarizes past trends in the major world import markets, looking particularly at the countries that could be the primary trading partners for Vietnam. If past results are any indication of the future--and, in this case, it probably is safe to assume that they are--Asia clearly has the fastest-growing major import markets (Japan, in particular) and, thus, should provide the best opportunities for Vietnam to gain a foothold. This tentative conclusion will be examined below, but first, we shall look more closely at the high-value shellfish products, which are in strong demand in the major import markets.

Crustaceans and Molluscs

Between 1958 and 1967, world production of crustaceans and molluscs and their products and preparations increased almost three-fold, from 446,000 metric tons to 1.075 million metric tons, [10] or about one and a half times as fast as the growth of total fish production.

During the same period, world trade (exports) in these products increased from 220,000 to 388,000 metric tons, an increase of 75 percent. Thus, trade increased at only one-fourth the rate of production growth, indicating a significant increase in domestic consumption of producing nations.

Worldwide, average export unit values for crustaceans and molluscs increased 105 percent between 1955 and 1966, compared with 38 percent for total fishery products (Figure 1). The comparative increase for the processed products and preparations of shellfish during that period was 44 percent, the total volume of trade in this category by value being less than a third of the total for unprocessed products. [11] The strongest demand and lowest price elasticity, therefore, applies to the category of crustaceans and molluscs consisting mostly of fresh and frozen products.

The most important shellfish product, by value, is frozen shrimp. It is caught all over the world, and production has increased rapidly in recent years, in response to increasing demand in high-income countries, especially the United States, which is both the world's largest importer and producer of crustacean products and accounts for about a fifth of world crustacean production. [12]

In 1964, developing countries exported $122 million worth of crustaceans and molluscs to the United States, equal to 80 percent of their total exports of these products. [13] The total value of the U.S. crustacean and mollusc market in 1967 was $254 million, followed by that of Japan ($99 million) and of France ($43 million). [14]

As can be seen in Figure 2, Far Eastern exports of shellfish and shellfish preparations and products increased 62 percent more than total world exports during the 1955-67 period (an absolute increase of 136 percent for the former, compared with 84 percent for the latter). Thus, Vietnam finds itself located in one of the most dynamic trading areas for these products in the world. This is particularly true when we see that Japanese imports of these products increased at a compound annual rate of 78 percent between 1962 and 1967 (some, of course, for reexport). [15]

The dominant position of Japan in Asia as both an importer and

TABLE 31

Import Demand for Fishery Products, by Major Market Region, 1958-67
(In Thousands of Metric Tons)

Region	1958	1962	1963	1964	1965	1966	1967	Compound Annual Rate of Increase 1962-67
United States	594	827	911	981	856	1,112	1,232	8.3
Europe:	2,128	3,315	3,526	3,854	4,123	3,919	4,387	5.7
United Kingdom	471	673	650	768	777	700	905	6.0
West Germany	418	721	704	796	827	753	860	3.5
France	166	294	296	321	338	325	335	2.7
Italy	152	227	249	260	292	272	285	4.7
Asia:*	388	401	488	571	612	689	653	10.3
Japan	8	60	125	190	233	266	264	34.6
Hong Kong	58	49	53	69	67	73	73	8.3
Philippines	65	39	50	50	52	50	n.a.	6.4
Malaysia (West)	24	35	42	43	41	49	41	3.2
Singapore	64	77	79	79	87	91	n.a.	4.2
Thailand	5	8	7	8	12	10	n.a.	5.7
Oceania:	33	48	39	63	70	80	80	10.8
Australia	27	39	28	47	53	60	56	7.6

*Excluding China (Mainland).

Source: Compiled from FAO, Yearbook of Fishery Statistics (1967).

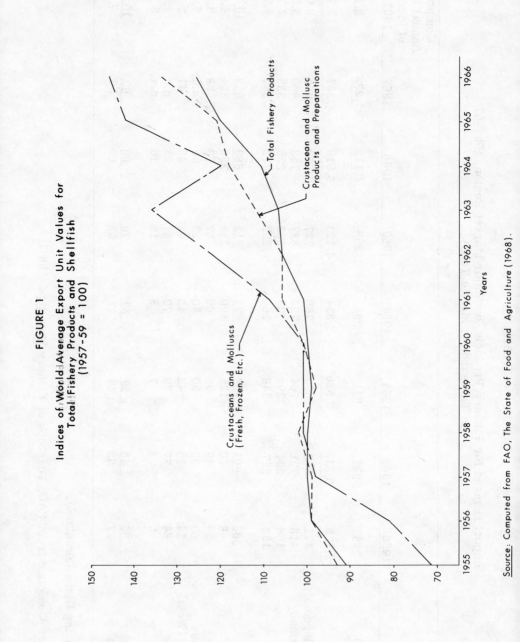

FIGURE 1

Indices of World Average Export Unit Values for
Total Fishery Products and Shellfish
(1957–59 = 100)

Total Fishery Products

Crustacean and Mollusc
Products and Preparations

Crustaceans and Molluscs
(Fresh, Frozen, Etc.)

Years

Source: Computed from FAO, The State of Food and Agriculture (1968).

82

exporter of shellfish and shellfish products can be seen in Table 32,
which is derived from FAO statistics for 1966. Here we see that
Asian imports exceeded exports by 39,000 tons, due, in large part, to
net Japanese imports of 61,400 tons. Other Far Eastern net importing
nations in 1966 were Hong Kong, Singapore, and Thailand, providing
some indication of specific Vietnamese export markets in the postwar
period. Likewise, these recent figures indicate that export competition
in Asia probably can be expected primarily from South Korea, India
(depending largely on its own internal consumption growth), Malaysia,
and Pakistan.

Australia and the rest of Oceania are a separate matter. While
Australia was a net exporter of shellfish in 1966, its major export
product was the rock lobster, a product that is not competitive with
present and potential exports of Vietnam. Because, in addition, Australia's past imports have been quite small and the potential for demand
growth in this rather limited high-income population (with a very low
per capita demand for fish products) is similarly limited, the future
Asian and Far Eastern trade balance, as seen by Vietnam, is unlikely
to be altered significantly by Australian trade (or that of the whole of
Oceania). Therefore, we shall not include this region in the projections
of future trade balances described below.

PROJECTIONS OF FUTURE DEMAND,
SUPPLY, AND TRADE

Projections for Total Fishery Products

For purposes of this analysis, the projections offered by the
FAO will suffice to indicate the future world consumption and trade
patterns that might be expected during the period through 1980. [16]

During the 1962 base period used by FAO, wide ranges of income
elasticities of demand for fish and fish products were found. In North
America, for example, a 10 percent increase in income indicated a
2 percent increase in fish consumption. At the opposite extreme,
the same 10 percent increase in income in India and Pakistan indicated
a 15 percent increase in fish consumption.

The FAO projects that such elasticities will change over time,
the general trends through 1985 being--

1. An increase, but at the declining rate of per capita consumption in most developed countries and a few Latin American countries, with per capita consumption never reaching the saturation
level.

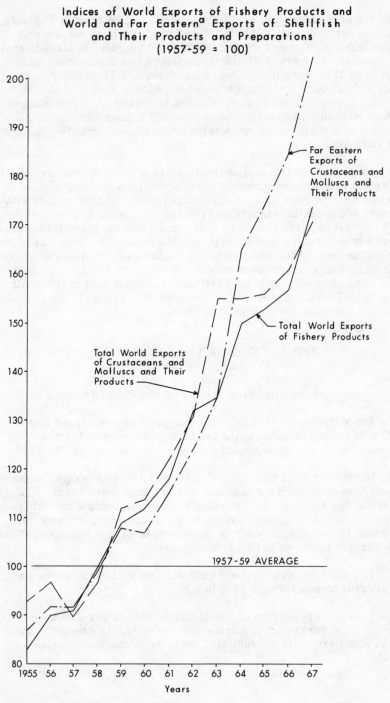

FIGURE 2

Indices of World Exports of Fishery Products and World and Far Eastern[a] Exports of Shellfish and Their Products and Preparations
(1957-59 = 100)

Far Eastern Exports of Crustaceans and Molluscs and Their Products

Total World Exports of Fishery Products

Total World Exports of Crustaceans and Molluscs and Their Products

1957-59 AVERAGE

Years

[a]Excluding Mainland China.

Sources: Compiled from FAO, The State of Food and Agriculture (1968), and FAO, Yearbook of Fishery Statistics (1967).

TABLE 32

1966 Trade Balance and Value of Major Import Markets
for Shellfish and Shellfish Products
(In Thousands of Metric Tons)

Region	Gross Exports	Gross Imports	Net Exports	Net Imports	Value of Gross Imports (In Millions of Dollars)
Asia Total:	109.0	148.0		39.0	$106.2
Japan	31.2	92.6		61.4	75.6
Hong Kong	8.2	18.1		9.9	14.9
Singapore	4.3	14.4		10.1	4.6
Thailand	7.1	8.1		1.0	1.9
China (Taiwan)	1.0	1.7		0.7	1.0
South Korea	15.3		15.3		
India	11.3		11.3		
Malaysia (West)	14.0	6.2	7.8		3.2
Pakistan	6.2		6.2		
Macao	5.2	0.6	4.6		0.2
Other Asia*	5.2	6.3		1.1	4.6
Oceania Total:	9.3	3.5	5.8		4.9
Australia	8.9	2.5	6.4		3.9
Other Oceania	0.4	1.0		0.6	1.0
Grand Totals	118.3	151.5	51.6	84.8	$111.1

*Excluding China (Mainland).

Source: Compiled from FAO, Yearbook of Fishery Statistics (1967).

2.   A tendency towards saturation of per capita demand in Portugal, Spain, Japan, and South Korea.

3.   Increasing per capita consumption at fairly constant elasticities for the large majority of developing countries, indicating consumption per capita far below the saturation level.

The FAO projections of fish requirement in 1975 (in millions of metric tons) are as follows:

<u>World Total</u>	**47**
Developed Countries	19
Socialist Countries	15
Developing Countries	13

World requirements are further projected to rise by an additional 30 to 60 percent between 1975 and 1985. To meet the nutritional targets set by the FAO for 1975, fish protein supplies will have to increase 2.33 times over 1960 levels.

In the developed countries, future demand is expected to be strongest (highest income elasticity) for a few high unit-value fishery products (such as shrimp) and much lower elasticities are expected for staple-type products (in some cases, even negative elasticities).

In the developing countries, the urgent need will be for increased fish protein supplies. Unfortunately, these countries lack the financial resources and skills necessary for large-scale production and distribution of fish and fish products; in addition, they lack the foreign exchange needed to import even the cheapest varieties in large enough quantities. Thus, the transfer of technological skills to the developing world, and probably concessionary aid, will be primary conditions for the FAO goals to be achieved.

Summing up the FAO projections, we have interpolated between their figures for 1975 and 1985, to provide, in Table 33, estimates of world and regional demand for fish (for food) in 1980. Of particular significance to Vietnam are the developed countries and countries of Asia and the Far East. The former group shows the lowest expected growth over 1965 demand (between 28 and 36 percent), but still this represents annual increases of well over 1 million tons per annum. In Asia and the Far East, an increase of 63 to 95 percent above 1965 demand levels is forecasted, or an average increase of up to 400,000 tons per annum (not including Mainland China).

TABLE 33

Projection of Food Demand for Fish, by Region, 1980
(In Millions of Metric Tons)

Region	1965 Food Fish Supplies	1980 Demand [a]	
		Low GDP Growth Rate	High GDP Growth Rate
World Total:	36.1	53.4	60.7
Developed Countries	16.0	20.5	21.8
Socialist Countries [b]	10.6	17.2	20.4
Developing Countries:	9.5	15.7	18.5
Asia and Far East [c]	6.3	10.3	12.3
Latin America	1.5	2.5	2.8
Africa	1.4	2.3	2.7
Near East	0.3	0.6	0.7

[a]Projected from 1965 base.
[b]Including China (Mainland).
[c]Excluding China (Mainland).

Source: Computed from interpolation of FAO estimates for 1975 and 1985 in Argicultural Commodities--
Projections for 1975 and 1985 (1967).

In order to achieve the nutritional targets set by FAO's Third World Food Survey, fish protein as a percentage of total protein in the Far East must rise from 3.9 percent in 1960 to 7.0 percent by the end of this century. [17] Translated into quantities, this means almost a sixfold increase in Far Eastern food fish catches in forty years, from 14 million tons in 1960 to 82 million in 2000 (figures including Mainland China). Clearly, these tremendous requirements are attractive to a fish-exporting nation like Vietnam.

But alone, these figures do not justify an expansion of Vietnamese fish-exporting industries, for nutritional requirements cannot be translated directly into potential trade for surplus producers. The essential fact is that the developing countries of Asia (and the world, generally) with the greatest needs for increased consumption of fish protein will not have the financial resources necessary to import their requirements and will be forced, instead, to increase domestic production or forgo consumption.

The most attractive export markets for Vietnam, therefore, are not likely to be in those countries requiring large volumes of low-value fishery products but, instead, are probably those countries with an increasing demand for high unit-value products, such as crustaceans and molluscs. These markets clearly are in North America, Europe, and parts of the Far East.

Projections for Crustaceans and Molluscs

Looking first at the Far East, Japan is today, and undoubtedly will continue to be, the largest Asian importer of these products. In Table 34, we have computed a range of probable Japanese imports, taking into consideration past trends and expected future patterns of production, consumption, and exports.

Exports have been extrapolated directly along the 1958-67 trend line to an annual level in 1980 of 100,000 tons. Japanese production, however, is not likely to rise above 500,000 tons in 1980, due to pressures of rising labor costs and diminishing opportunities for exploitation of new fishing grounds. This estimate is some 200,000 tons below that which might be expected from extrapolation of 1958-67 production trends.

Because Japanese consumption of crustaceans and molluscs has increased so rapidly in recent years, it is hard to judge how high per capita consumption will rise before leveling off, as it has begun to do in other high-income countries. For this reason, we have attempted to provide a range of possible future consumption levels.

TABLE 34

Japanese Consumption of Shellfish and Shellfish
Products, 1958-67 and Projections for 1980
(In Thousands of Metric Tons)

Item	1958	1962	1963	1964	1965	1966	1967	1980 Projections Low Per Capita Consumption	1980 Projections High Per Capita Consumption
1. Production (+)	153	267	288	169	250	265	380	500[a]	500[a]
2. Imports (+)	3	6	15	34	63	93	108	400[b]	600[b]
3. Exports (-)	23	24	27	30	31	31	38	100[b]	100[b]
4. Consumption = (1+2-3)	133	249	276	173	282	327	450	800	1,000
5. Population[c]		95	96	97	98	99	100	112	112
6. Consumption Per Capita[d]		2.6	2.9	1.8	2.9	3.3	4.5	7.1[e]	9.0[f]

[a]Assumes growth of production below 1958-67 trend. (See text.)
[b]Assumes growth of production and exports along 1958-67 trends.
[c]In millions.
[d]Kilograms per capita.
[e]Assumes growth of per capita demand for shellfish along trend projected by FAO for all fish products.
[f]Assumes linear extrapolation of 1962-67 per capita demand trend.

Source: Historical data compiled from FAO, Yearbook of Fishery Statistics (1967); population projection interpolated from FAO, Agricultural Commodities--Projections for 1975 and 1985 (1967).

As a low estimate, it is assumed that per capita consumption of these products through 1980 will rise in direct proportion to the increase projected by the FAO for all Japanese fishery products. The high estimate assumes per capita consumption growth along a linear extrapolation of the 1962-67 demand trend. It is quite unlikely that demand will fall below the lower estimate, for this would mean a radical reversal of the growth patterns observed in recent years. Furthermore, the upper limit could well be exceeded if growth occurs exponentially for the next few years, as it has in the past two or three years. It is likely, therefore, that, if anything, both estimates could be on the conservative side.

Multiplying the high and low per capita consumption projections by a projected Japanese population of 112 million in 1980 gives an approximate range of consumption levels of 800,000 tons to 1 million tons. Adding projected exports to consumption to give total requirements and then subtracting the projected production level yields a rough estimate of probable Japanese import requirements in 1980: 400,000 to 600,000 tons. Net imports of crustaceans and molluscs in that year, therefore, would be 300,000 to 500,000 tons (recognizing, of course, that "net" figures conceal the considerable physical differences between imports and exports; exports, in many cases, are likely to be processed versions of imports).

For the balance of Asia, we have projected a likely export surplus, ranging from 70,000 to 120,000 tons in 1980. This range is based on figures roughly 20 percent above and below a linear extrapolation to 1980 of the 1962-67 trade balance trend for Asia without Japan. The projected trade deficit for Japan, however, is so large that Asia as a whole is likely to have a net import demand of 230,000 to 380,000 tons in 1980. The breakdown of these projections is shown in Table 35, together with similar trade deficit projections for North America and Europe, the other two regions most likely to be customers for Vietnamese crustaceans and molluscs. Together, Asia, North America, and Europe will probably have a net import demand for these products ranging from 380,000 to 620,000 tons in 1980, as indicated in Table 35.

Note that the past trade balances for North America that have been used in computing the above projections already include the large volume of shrimp exports from Mexico, the world's largest shrimp exporter and the main foreign supplier to the huge U.S. market. The projections assume that these Mexican exports will continue along the 1962-67 trend line and, thus, do not consider the possibility of any extraordinary growth in Mexican exports that could upset the present balance of trade in North America. This, in fact, is unlikely, for total Mexican exports actually decreased by almost 10 percent between 1962 and 1967. [18]

TABLE 35

Crustaceans and Molluscs: Projections of Net Import Demand, by Major Market Region,[a] 1980
(In Thousands of Metric Tons)

Region	Actual Net Imports						1980 Projections[b]	
	1962	1963	1964	1965	1966	1967	Low	High
Asia:	-15[c]	-17	-1	20	39	46	230	380
Japan	-18	-12	4	32	62	70	300	500
Asia less Japan	3	-5	-5	-12	-23	-24	-70	-120
North America	37	42	40	46	50	52	70	110
Europe	20	26	33	47	38	44	80	130
Total	42	51	72	113	127	142	380	620

[a]Excluding China (Mainland).
[b]See text.
[c]Minus (-) indicates net exports.

Source: Actual net imports compiled from FAO, Yearbook of Fishery Statistics (1967).

Similarly, the projections of European and Asian trade balances in 1980 do not account for the possibility of extraordinary deviations up or down from 1962-67 export trends within those regions.

In summary, Vietnam, in 1980, is certain to face very attractive levels of net import demand in the three regions discussed above. Even in the worst of circumstances, it is unlikely to find in these three regions net import markets totaling less than 300,000 tons per annum, and, possibly, this will range well beyond 600,000 tons. Within Asia, North America, and Europe, we have already accounted for local competition through the use of net instead of gross import figures. In Asia, of course, it is quite possible that countries such as Malaysia or Thailand might undertake large-scale development of export-oriented shellfish industries that would cut into Vietnam's potential share of regional import markets or that other importing nations (probably not Japan) might make significant strides in increasing production for domestic use. Nevertheless, on the whole, the projected deficit is not likely to be reduced significantly from the range indicated above, and Asia presents Vietnam with some excellent market possibilities in the future--Japan, Hong Kong, and Singapore, in particular, all with growing populations and personal incomes.

In the North American market, competition is likely to be felt from growing South American exports (up 54 percent between 1962 and 1967),[19] and, in Europe, even stronger competition is likely from African exporting nations, many of which have preferential trade arrangements with the European Economic Community (EEC). In West Africa, for example, considerable investment is being made in cold storage and freezing facilities, to provide for increased exports of fishery products.[20]

On the whole, while increasing competition is probable in the Asian, North American, and European shellfish trade, Vietnam can probably anticipate markets far in excess of its feasible levels of export production in 1980, provided, of course, it can match world patterns of product quality and price. The implications of this optimistic picture on Vietnamese earnings are considered in final section, below.

CONCLUSIONS FOR VIETNAM'S
EXPORT EARNINGS

A recent preliminary estimate of future Vietnamese agricultural production levels [21] indicates a potential exportable surplus of 15,000 tons of fishery products (all types) in 1980.

This estimate, however, did not take adequate account of offshore fishing, which should provide the majority of exports. By 1980, it is estimated conservatively that Vietnam could expand its landed catch to 700,000 tons and export 8 to 10 percent of the total. This allows a generous margin for increased domestic consumption. The estimated export levels of 55,000 to 70,000 tons and the landed catch are less than Korea actually achieved in 1968. Considering the actual catch of 464,000 tons in 1969, these estimates are not overly generous. The major emphasis should be on high-value crustaceans and molluscs, possibly produced in fish-farming operations along the Vietnamese coast and inland river beds. About a half of the exports are estimated to be of these products.

While considerable investment in increased production facilities for exports would appear to be justified now, the actual upper goal to be sought should be revised during the next two to three years, when--

1.   The actual long-term trend in Japanese per capita consumption of shellfish products should become clearer (if it continues to grow at the 1962-67 rate, then, the previously forecasted upper limit of net Asian imports is almost certain to be exceeded).

2.   The probable long-term growth rate of Japanese production will be more easily identified.

3.   The changes in past trends of export and import substitution production in the other parts of Asia should begin to take form.

4.   A better assessment of the role to be played by Mainland China can be made (today, it exports shrimps to Japan--in the future, it could well become a major export market for Vietnam or, possibly, even a competitor).

At the present time, the estimated export levels are taken as 55,000 to 70,000, with the possibility that these could be revised upwards. About a half of the total should be high-value items, such as shrimps and crabs; the remainder, fish. Based on 1968 unit export values for South Korea and the estimated product mix, the value of exports would vary between $66 and $84 million. This would be an extremely high level of exports, compared to levels previously achieved, but in view of current achievements and the rapidly growing demand for these products in Japan and high-income countries, the estimate should be achievable in a decade.

NOTES

1. USAID Mission to Vietnam, Annual Statistical Bulletin No. 11 (1969).

2. FAO, Yearbook of Fishery Statistics (1969), Tables AO-2 and AO-3.

3. FAO, Fisheries in the Food Economy, Basic Study (1968).

4. FAO, Commodity Review (1968).

5. FAO, Yearbook of Fishery Statistics (1967).

6. FAO, Fisheries in the Food Economy, Basic Study.

7. FAO, Yearbook of Fishery Statistics (1967).

8. FAO, Agricultural Commodities--Projections for 1975 and 1985 (1967).

9. FAO, Fisheries in the Food Economy, Basic Study.

10. FAO, Yearbook of Fishery Statistics (1969).

11. Ibid.

12. Ibid.

13. FAO, Fisheries in the Food Economy, Basic Study.

14. FAO, Yearbook of Fishery Statistics (1967).

15. Ibid.

16. FAO, Agricultural Commodities--Projections for 1975 and 1985, and FAO, Fisheries in the Food Economy, Basic Study.

17. FAO, Fisheries in the Food Economy, Basic Study.

18. FAO, Yearbook of Fishery Statistics (1967).

19. Ibid.

20. FAO, Fisheries in the Food Economy, Basic Study.

21. Development and Resources Corporation, Projected Need for Agricultural Production in the Delta, 1970-1990 (October, 1969).

Before World War II, Indochina was the largest producer and exporter of corn in the Far East, but this production was an early casualty of the war, and it did not recover thereafter. Except for minor and sporadic instances, Vietnam has not raised feed grains (i.e., corn, sorghum, and so forth) for export since that time, and total production in the country is minor, in comparison to rice. The reason for including feed grains in this study is due to the rapid expansion of the market for feed grains to support a growing livestock industry in many countries and because physical and soil conditions in Vietnam are favorable to an increase in production. The success of Thailand in raising corn for export to Japan is one that could be matched by Vietnam in the future.

Export opportunities in feed grains are heavily influenced by world supply conditions, and these, in turn, are dominated by the concentration of production in a relatively few countries, particularly the United States. The United States is by far the world's largest producer of coarse grains, and it is the most efficient producer. Eastern Asia, on the other hand, is characterized by low yields and low production of feed grains. The Far East countries, on the average, have the lowest yield per hectare in the world. At the two extremes, therefore, are the United States, with production at almost 5,000 kilograms per hectare and Far East Asia, with 1,100 kilograms per hectare.[1] The large production of the United States, its highly efficient production, and the sizable surpluses available for export are bound to influence the prospects of any country entering the world trade of feed grains.

The ability of a Southeast Asian country to develop an export market for feed grains has been demonstrated in recent years by Thailand. In the past decade, Thailand began with virtually no grain exports. In 1961-63, it produced about 0.7 million tons for export and, according to FAO projections, should triple that figure by 1975. Yet, the amount produced is only a small part of projected import demand in the markets of the region. That is an encouraging factor in the development of a market for Vietnam exports.

WORLD PRODUCTION AND CONSUMPTION
OF FEED GRAINS

The amount of feed grains being produced and consumed worldwide has been growing at an annual rate of about 3 percent. Barley and corn have been showing strong growth, while millet, rye, and oats have been lagging. Corn is, by far, the most important feed grain, with a production that almost equals the combined output of all other coarse grains. Productivity increases in corn have been higher than in other feed grains. In the decade up to the mid-1960's, acreage in corn increased by 15 percent, while production increased 38 percent. Yields grew very significantly, especially in the United States, where yields increased 75 percent in the decade.

Table 36 presents the quantities produced for the crop years 1963/64 and 1966/67, including the percent increases.

Although production and consumption of feed grains have been, in the aggregate, increasing steadily, production, when matched with consumption in individual countries, has been very uneven. The tendency has been for the developed countries to produce in excess of their needs and for the developing countries to lag behind their demand. In the developing importing countries, including those of Southeast Asia, increases in the production of grains have not been very high, averaging only about 1.9 percent per annum, which is less than increases in population. The average world rate of increase in production of grain crops has been 2.9 percent per annum. An increase in grain production of 950 million tons by 1975 has been projected by the FAO.[2]

Most of this increase projected for all grains will be in the coarse or feed grains, inasmuch as per capita consumption of grain as food is expected to stabilize. Total feed demand is determined by the size and composition of the livestock population, the relative importance of concentrates in the feed ration, and the share of grains in total concentrates. These factors differ among countries and change over time. Countries with rapidly expanding livestock and poultry industries are clearly the best markets for feed grains. The FAO has made projections of animal feed on the basis of projections of meat and egg production, taking into account past trends and patterns

TABLE 36

World Production of Feed Grains, * 1963/64 and 1966/67
(In Millions of Metric Tons)

Grain	1963/64	1966/67	Percent Increase
Barley	85.5	98.3	15.0
Oats	45.8	46.1	1.0
Corn	194.6	215.2	10.6
Millet and Sorghum	55.7	60.7	9.0
Mixed Grains	6.3	5.9	-7.4
Rye	30.4	31.0	2.0
Total	418.3	457.2	9.3

*Excludes China (Mainland), North Korea, and North Vietnam.

Source: International Wheat Council, Review of the World Wheat Situation (1968).

of grain feeding as shown by time series data on grain utilization. The projections have been made on two alternative assumptions in regard to the growth of domestic output in the countries. These projections show annual increases in the future to be on the order of 3 percent per annum with a low GDP estimate and 3.3 percent per annum assuming a higher GDP. These projections are on the same order as increases of the past. Production and consumption of feed grains are projected to attain levels in 1975 ranging from a low of 640 million tons to the high of 665 million tons.

The agriculture policies of governments will determine, to a considerable extent, the levels of world production and trade. Such measures, in the past, have affected wheat more than feed grains. Farm subsidies, price supports, and acreage allotments all influence

TABLE 37

Coarse Grains: Production, Total Consumption, and Balances,
1961-63 Average and Projections for 1975
(In Millions of Tons)

| | 1961-63 Average | | | 1975 Projections | | | | | |
| | | | | Low GDP Assumption | | | High GDP Assumption | | |
Regions and Countries	Produc- tion	Consump- tion	Trade[a]	Produc- tion	Demand	Balance	Produc- tion	Demand	Balance
Developing countries:	97.6	94.3	-3.4	136.0	136.3	0.3	150.3	141.7	-8.6
Importers:[b]	88.4	88.9	0.6	119.8	128.3	8.5	134.1	133.5	-0.6
Latin America[c]	21.2	21.8	0.6	34.0	34.0	0.0	35.8	34.5	-1.3
Africa	27.7	27.5	-0.2	37.4	41.2	3.8	42.9	42.5	-0.4
Near East	8.3	8.1	-0.1	10.4	10.4	-0.0	11.3	12.2	0.9
Far East:[d]	31.2	31.5	0.3	38.0	42.7	4.7	44.1	44.3	0.2
India	23.7	23.7	0.0	29.1	32.2	3.1	33.0	33.2	0.2
Pakistan	1.3	1.3	0.0	1.5	1.8	0.3	1.9	1.9	0.0
Major Exporters:	9.2	5.4	-4.0	16.2	8.0	-8.2	16.2	8.2	-8.0
Argentina	8.5	5.4	-3.3	13.8	7.9	-5.9	13.8	8.1	-5.7
Thailand	0.7	0.0	-0.7	2.4	0.1	-2.3	2.4	0.1	-2.3
Developed Countries:	224.2	230.1	2.2	308.2	313.0	4.8	310.1	322.2	12.1
Importers[b]	69.5	90.3	20.3	94.8	125.8	31.0	96.7	131.7	35.0
Japan	1.8	4.6	2.6	1.3	10.5	9.2	1.3	11.3	10.0
Major exporters:	154.7	139.8	-18.2	213.4	187.2	-26.2	213.4	190.5	-22.9
United States	133.9	122.8	-14.9	184.5	163.8	-20.7	184.5	166.6	-17.9
Centrally Planned Countries	147.5	147.3	-0.2	196.3	195.6	-0.7	203.9	204.2	0.3
World Total	469.3	471.7	1.3	640.5	644.9	4.4	644.3	668.1	3.8

[a]The trade figures shown are not equal to the difference between production and consumption because of stock changes.
[b]Includes other than major exporters.
[c]Excludes Argentina.
[d]Excludes Thailand.

Source: FAO, Agricultural Commodities--Projections for 1975 and 1985 (1967), p. 90.

98

the amount that will be produced, marketed, and consumed. Government policies have been steadily extended in scope and effectiveness over the past several decades. They have, at the same time, encouraged production and discouraged growth in foreign trade by isolating domestic markets from foreign competition with special incentives and the like. Yet, the financial burden of such policies and subsidies may very well prove greater than the countries can maintain in the long run.

Table 37 presents the FAO projections for coarse grains in 1975 and compares them to the average experience in 1961-1963. Unlike the projections for cereal grains (wheat, rice), which are not widely used in feeding operations, the projections for these feed grains show an aggregate world demand that exceeds expected production, regardless of the level of domestic product (or income) increases. Among the Far East regional markets, the projections for Japan are startling. Imports are projected to grow from 2.6 million tons in 1961-63 to between 9 and 10 million tons in 1975, or about a 300 percent increase during this period. An extension of the period to include later years would show the trend continuing to rise. Only Thailand among the Far East countries is a net exporter, with the major exporters to Japan being the United States, Canada, and Australia. Thus, the prospects for Vietnam will depend on the behavior of the United States in particular. The United States can act in a way to make it easy for Vietnam to get a share in the market, if it chooses to do so.

Although world consumption has increased but moderately, international trade in feed grains has been expanding considerably. Over the past decade, the amount of coarse grains entering foreign trade has more than doubled. Table 38 shows the quantities of coarse grains imported and exported in the past years.

The pattern of world trade is predominantly a movement from the extensive agriculture of the United States, Argentina, and South Africa (and, more recently, Thailand and Mexico) toward the densely populated areas of Europe and Japan, where the growing demand for livestock products results in a derived demand for feed imports.

As can be seen from Table 38, corn is the major feed grain in foreign trade. Over a half of the corn exports are supplied by the United States, though substantial shipments have been made in some years by a number of other countries, including South Africa, Argentina, Rumania, and Thailand. Trade in the other grains has not been growing to the extent of corn, primarily because of increasing self-sufficiency in barley and the declining usage of rye and oats.

World trade in feed grains, on balance, promises rapid growth in the future. All grains will not benefit equally. Corn and sorghum,

TABLE 38

Coarse Grains: World Imports and Exports; by Type,
1951/52-1955/56, 1960/61, 1963/64, and 1967/68[a]
(In Thousands of Tons)

Market	1951/52-1955/56[b]	1960/61	1963/64	1967/68[c]
Imports:				
Rye	1,120	880	560	430
Barley	5,420	5,750	6,610	6,240
Oats	1,510	1,240	1,170	1,280
Corn	4,970	12,360	21,050	27,070
Sorghum and Millets	1,620	2,640	3,450	6,140
Total	14,640	22,870	32,840	41,160
Exports:				
Rye	1,110	1,020	580	430
Barley	5,550	5,820	6,850	6,320
Oats	1,560	1,200	1,190	1,190
Corn	5,060	12,130	21,040	27,350
Sorghum and Millets	1,660	2,830	3,570	6,120
Total	14,940	23,000	33,230	41,410

[a]Totals do not include trade between the centrally planned countries.
[b]Average.
[c]Preliminary.

Source: FAO, World Grain Trade Statistics, 1967/68 (1968).

because of their cost advantage, can be expected to take up increasing shares of the total market. This favorable outlook for corn and sorghum in international markets, together with the Southeast Asian potentials for corn production, can serve as the basis for South Vietnam's entry into the feed grain market.

Feed grain prices have been relatively stable since the mid-1950's, mostly ranging between $50 to $60 per metric ton. National

and international policies have had the objective of reducing extreme
price fluctuations. These policies apparently have had an effect, since
prices of the various grains have not been fluctuating as much as before
World War II.

Transportation costs represent significant portions of the total
market price of corn in Southeast Asia and will continue to affect trade
patterns and competition in the future. Using Saigon as an example of
a point of destination, U.S. exports of corn involve a freight cost of
$25.60 per ton. Exports from Thailand to Saigon involve a freight cost
of $6.90 per ton.[3] Landed costs in Saigon are as follows:

imported U.S. corn, $76.90 per ton; and
imported Thailand corn, $67.80 per ton.

There are also quality differences that affect price. A reddish-colored
corn is grown in Southeast Asia, and Japanese feeders have a color
preference for this corn, with the result that colored corn commands
a premium on world markets. This advantage may not be long lasting,
however, since there is little difference in nutrition between the yellow
and reddish varieties.

PRODUCTION AND MARKETING IN VIETNAM

The area that now includes Vietnam has historically been an
important producer and exporter of corn. Some production of sorghum
also has taken place. Corn production in this region by Far East
standards was substantial. The peak production year was 1937, when
621,000 tons were produced. A key producing area was the Mekong
Delta. In that peak year, exports reached 550,000 tons. Importers
of corn produced in Indochina were Japan, Africa, and, particularly,
France.

The list appearing below shows the annual corn production figures
for Indochina for the years prior to, and including, World War II.[4]
No differentiation is made in these quantities between the glutinous
varieties grown for human consumption and the varieties grown as
animal feed.

In the years since World War II, production has varied somewhat
at relatively low levels. From an exporting region, Vietnam now must
import quantities of corn. For one three-year period, 1960-62, some
exporting of corn was getting underway. However, exports fell off
completely in 1963 and have remained so since that time. From 1955
to the present time, the cultivated area in corn varied only slightly,
and production has ranged from about 30,000 to 45,000 tons.

Year	Tons
1936	504,000
1937	621,000
1938	568,000
1939	534,000
1940	365,000
1941	301,000
1942	262,000
1943	207,000
1944	196,000

Table 39 shows the regional distribution of the areas under cultivation and their production quantities for the year 1965.

VIETNAM'S PROSPECTS FOR EXPORTING FEED GRAINS

The export market for feed grains, as discussed earlier, is expanding at a rapid rate. World production, and, more importantly, world capacity to produce, is likewise expanding. Historically, Vietnam has demonstrated a capacity to participate in the world market. The feed grains most promising for future exporting are corn and sorghum; both are well suited to cultivation in Vietnam.

Markets dispersed worldwide are not promising for Vietnam. In the more distant markets, Vietnam must compete with the large producers--the United States, Canada, Argentina, France, and Australia. However, freight costs become a substantial part of the final prices, which make the Asian markets more attractive for Vietnam. Japan, in particular, serves as a promising market. Because of rising incomes in Japan, accompanied by increases in the production and consumption of meat, the demand for feed grains has been rapidly expanding. This increased demand for feed grains is largely being met through imports, especially corn, sorghum, and millet.

TABLE 39

Cultivated Areas and Production of Corn in
Vietnam in 1965

Region	Area (in Hectares)	Production (In Metric tons)
Mekong Delta:	15,170	17,530
Chau-Doc	2,400	1,090
An-Giang	1,320	1,470
Kien-Phong	2,220	2,890
Long-Khanh	2,200	2,200
Phuc-Tuy	1,300	1,300
Central Coastal Lowlands:	16,390	18,780
Quang-Ngai	4,760	4,850
Quang-Nam	3,200	6,870
Binh-Dinh	1,700	2,000
Phu-Yen	1,500	1,500
Ninh-Thuan	1,900	760
Khanh-Hoa	1,000	1,000
Central Highlands:	4,620	7,510
Darlac	1,700	4,700
Phu-Bon	1,040	1,200
Total	36,180	43,820

Source: Ministry of Land Reform and Agriculture, Agricultural
Statistics Yearbook (Saigon: 1966).

Table 40 presents the Japanese import figures for corn, sorghum,
and millet. As can be seen from the table, there has been a fivefold
increase in corn imports and, from the very low base of 12,000 tons,
there has been a twenty-five-fold increase in the importation of sorghum
and millet.

None of the other Asian countries show similar import activity
in feed grains. One possible exception is Taiwan, which, in the more
recent years, has begun importing feed grains in significant quantities.
In the 1967/68 crop year, 292,000 tons of feed grains were imported
into Taiwan.

TABLE 40

Imports of Corn, Sorghum, and Millet
into Japan, 1958/59-1967/68
(In Thousands of Tons)

Year	Corn	Sorghum and Millet
1958/59	855	12
1959/60	1,018	199
1960/61	1,708	114
1962/63	2,396	541
1963/64	3,076	984
1964/65	3,222	1,317
1965/66	2,887	1,704
1966/67	3,837	3,259
1967/68	4,592	2,712

Source: FAO, Production Yearbook (1969).

Because of the expanding international market for corn and
because Vietnam has a tradition in its growing and exporting, corn
is the most promising feed grain in Vietnam's export future. As was
mentioned earlier, a temporary reestablishment of the corn export
trade did occur in the years 1960-62. The Joint Development Group,
on the basis of its survey of corn planting, recommended the development of corn planting until a production level of 1 to 1.5 million tons
was reached. [5] Production costs developed by the Joint Development
Group indicated that corn can be produced in Vietnam at costs below
world market corn prices. These estimated production levels are not
realistic, even over a decade. They may involve replacement of rice
with corn, particularly in the Mekong Delta, and that substitution is
economically undesirable. The natural production region for corn
in Vietnam is the central highlands and, to some extent, the coastal
lowlands. In the former area, corn plantings depend on a greater
clearing of the land and, hence, might follow (and, in some cases,
accompany) timbering operations. This will be a slow process, and
it is unlikely to have dramatic effects in the short run. It should be
possible to raise productivity to about 2.5 tons per hectare without
too much trouble. We estimate, at a maximum, that 200,000 to
250,000 hectares could be in corn in ten years. After allowing for
some domestic use (livestock is not expected to increase rapidly),
the exportable surplus would be 400,000 to 550,000 tons. At 1968
export prices for corn, this amounts to $20 to $28 million in export

earnings. To achieve such a target is almost certainly more difficult than virtually all of the other commodity targets discussed in this study, but the market prospects are so bright that every effort should be made to develop production capability in corn.

Japan is the world's largest importer of sorghum. This market recently reached the level of 3 million tons annually. The increasing need for grains as animal food in Japan holds promise for future expansion. The United States supplies the world with most of the millet and sorghum imports. In 1968, the United States exported 4.5 million tons out of a total of 6 million tons. Thailand also participates in this trade. Thailand exported a total of 266,000 tons in the past three years.

By 1980, Vietnam should be able to find markets for approximately 100,000 tons per year (ranging up to perhaps 150,000 tons). Thailand only built up its trade in sorghum and millet since 1964. This development also should represent a demonstration of the possibilities that exist for entering the export trade. The growth in Asian sorghum and millet imports (which include shipment into India) shows a tenfold increase between 1958 and 1968. This represents an increase from about 500,000 tons to 5 million tons. An annual export of 100,000 tons of sorghum and millet is a reasonable target and would result in export earnings to Vietnam of about $5 million.

Although world production of barley has increased considerably, foreign trade in barley has diminished. Nevertheless, there is a sizable barley trade in the Far East. In the crop year 1967/68, Japan imported 637,000 tons of barley--mostly from Australia, Canada, and the United States. Although barley can be grown in semitropical regions, South Vietnam's production of barley has not been significant. It would appear extremely difficult, in the small grains, to compete in the near future with the large growers and exporters, such as Argentina, Australia, Canada, the United States, France, and the United Kingdom.

In summary, Vietnam's prospects for grain exports are centered essentially on corn and sorghum. The range of estimates reflects the uncertainty involved. The list below summarizes the estimates of Vietnam's potential export earnings from feed grains (in millions of dollars):

	Low of Range	High of Range
Corn	$20	$28
Sorghum	5	5
Total	$25	$33

It is important to note that these are estimates derived from a market demand analysis. It seems likely that supply and production limitations will be the governing factors for some time in the expansion of Vietnam's trade in feed grains.

NOTES

1. FAO, Production Yearbook (1969), Table 19.

2. FAO, Agricultural Commodities--Projections for 1975 and 1985 (1967).

3. Joint Development Group, Development of Corn Planting in Vietnam, Working Paper No. 49 (Saigon: 1968).

4. Union Nationale des Coopératives Agricoles de Cereales, Le Mais (Paris: 1950).

5. Joint Development Group, op. cit.

Vegetable oils and their by-products, oil cake and meal, have never ranked as major exports of Vietnam, but, still, they have provided a significant source of foreign exchange in the past that might be increased in the future. Between 1958 and 1965, Vietnam exported a total of $3.2 million worth of vegetable oils and $2.2 million of oil cake. Together, these products comprised almost one-tenth of Vietnam's minor exports during that period (total dollar exports after rice and rubber). Past vegetable oil earnings have fluctuated widely, reaching annual highs of over $800,000 in 1961 and 1965. Oil cake earnings rose steadily between 1958 and 1965, reaching an annual level of over $500,000 in 1965. In more recent years, exports of oil and cake have turned downward, due to the effects of the war.

The two major oils exported from Vietnam are coconut and peanut oil; in both cases, Vietnam has only a very small fraction of world trade. Thus, the market conditions under which it must operate are largely dictated to it from the outside.

World markets for oils and oil cake and meal are highly complex and defy anything but the most speculative forecasting of future market conditions. We shall concentrate here on identifying, in a general manner, the main countries and regions that have promise as export markets for expanded Vietnamese production in the postwar period.

PRODUCT DESCRIPTION

Oils and fats provide essential constituents of human diets throughout the world. In the developing world, particularly, they serve as a primary means of increasing nutritional levels. Per capita consumption of oils rises rapidly with incomes, making substantial

107

contributions to caloric intake. Nevertheless, oils contain no proteins or minerals and, sometimes, no vitamins. Above certain income levels, increases in per capita consumption of oils tend to taper off, reaching a saturation level of about 1,000 calories per day in the highest income countries, such as the United States, Sweden, and the United Kingdom. [1]

Thus, the proportion of domestic production in developing countries entering world trade has been decreasing, and the reverse has been seen in the high-income countries. African exports of peanuts during the past decade, for example, have risen only 1 percent, while production has risen 3 percent. On the contrary, during this same period, soybean exports from the United States have risen 8 percent, while production has gone up only 4.5 percent.

The secondary products of oilseed crushing, oilseed meal and cake, display a very different demand structure. In recent years, world demand for these products, primarily in the developed world, has been rising rapidly--more so than for fats and oils--as their use for high-protein livestock and poultry feed has increased. The result has been expanded production of oil as a by-product of meal and cake, reversing the traditional relationship and contributing to an oversupply of some vegetable oils on world markets. Thus, markets for both oil and cake or meal are tightly interconnected. The situation is further complicated as modern crushing and refining techniques make different types of oil increasingly interchangeable and competitive with one another. Therefore, an assessment of Vietnam's export potential for oils and their meals should not be based on a look at its two major oils, coconut and peanut, but on the broader market for all types of vegetable oils and meals.

TRENDS IN PRODUCTION
AND TRADE

General Fats and Oils

In 1968, world exports of oilseeds, oils, and fats were 11 million metric tons (fat and oil equivalent) out of total world production of 37 million tons. [2] A breakdown of world production and exports, according to the most recent UN figures, is shown in Table 41. The differences between the developed and developing nations are marked. From the mid-1950's through the average of 1964-66, production in the developing nations rose at a compound annual rate of only 2.2 percent, or less than population growth. Developed and centrally planned country exports, however, rose 3.1 and 3.4 percent per annum, respectively, during this period. The differences in export volumes

TABLE 41

World Production and Exports of Oils and Fats, [a] 1955-66

Production and Exports	Rates of Change (In Percent)			Total (In Millions of Metric Tons)	
	Average 1955-57 to 1964-1966	1964 to 1965	1965 to 1966	1965	1966
Production:					
Developed Market Economies	+3.1	- 3.1	+2.6	15.4	15.8
Developing Countries	+2.2	+ 5.5	-0.9	11.5	11.4
Socialist Countries	+3.4	+12.0	+1.1	8.8	8.9
Total	+2.9	+ 3.2	+1.1	36.0	36.4
Volume of Gross Exports:					
Developed Market Economies	+5.1	- 5.1	- 1.6	5.3	5.2
Developing Countries	+1.5	- 0.1	+ 2.0	4.1	4.2
Socialist Countries	+5.3	+24.3	+35.9	0.7	1.0
Total	+3.5	- 1.4	+ 2.6	10.1	10.4
Value of Gross Exports:					
Developed Market Economies	+5.3	+ 6.3	+ 3.0	$2.2 [c]	$2.3 [c]
Developing Countries	+2.1	0	- 4.3	1.3 [c]	1.3 [c]
Socialist Countries	+3.2	0	+20.1	0.3 [c]	0.4 [c]
Total	+3.9	+ 3.5	+ 2.0	$3.8 [c]	$4.0 [c]

[a] In terms of oil, including animal and marine fats (butter, lard, tallow, whale oil, fish oil).

[b] Percent per annum.

[c] Total value of gross exports for 1965 and 1966 in millions of dollars.

Source: FAO, Commodity Review (1967).

and values can be seen to be even greater. Exports of developing countries rose one-third slower than production, due largely to increased domestic demand. On the other hand, the tendency toward demand saturation in the developed economies and expanding import markets (including developing countries) caused their exports to grow an average two-thirds faster than production. Similar performance was attained by the socialist countries, with their maximum export gains in the most recent years.

Overall, the developing world's share of expanding world export markets has fallen from 55 percent in the early 1950's to about 45 percent today. It has imported, on balance, about as much as it has exported during the past decade, although this disguises national differences, some of which are considerable. Imports would surely have outstripped exports in the developing world in the past if not for the constraints of foreign exchange shortages and low purchasing power, which have held down per capita consumption levels in many developing nations.

Vegetable Oils, Oilseeds, Oil Cake and Meal

Looking specifically at oilseed products, which make up about two-thirds of world fats and oils production, we can see, in Table 42, the large differences in both production and export growth that have existed between the developed and developing worlds. On average, principal exports of the former nations have increased at rates that are over twelve times faster than those of the latter, and production has increased at rates that are three times faster. (Note, however, that the products of these two groups are totally different, and the domestic consumption has increased much faster in the developing nations.) The greatest single influence on this pattern has been the rapid increase in soybean oil trade, principally exports from the United States to Japan and Western Europe. Today, that one product accounts for about a fifth of world trade in fats and oils. [3]

Total world exports of the two major product categories, vegetable oils and oilseeds (oil equivalent) and oil cake and meal, are shown in Figure 3. While exports of the former category have increased fairly steadily since the mid-1950's, with Western Europe as the main importer, exports of oil cake and meal have grown much more rapidly. The demand for soybean meal as a high-protein source of feed for livestock and poultry (again, primarily in Western Europe) has been the primary force behind this trend. The combination of high U.S. soybean production levels, encouraged by price support programs, and rapid growth in livestock production in Europe have led to great increases in European demand for cake and meal and

TABLE 42

Trends in World Production and Exports of Principal Edible Vegetable Oils and Oilseeds, 1956-58 to 1964-66

Exports	Rates of Change, 1956-58 to 1964-66 (In Percent per Annum)		Average 1964-66 (In Thousands of Tons)	
	Production	Exports	Production	Exports
Exported Almost Entirely by Developing Countries:				
Coconut	0.3	0.5	2,182	1,337
Peanuts	3.2	1.9	3,256	999
Palm	0.5	0.2	711	565
Palm Kernel	-0.7	-1.3	405	370
Sesame	2.1	5.9	584	70
Total	1.6	0.7	7,138	3,341
Exported Almost Entirely by Developed Countries:				
Soya	5.4	7.0	4,182	1,621
Sunflower	5.7	17.7	2,395	407
Rapeseed	3.2	12.9	1,363	230
Total	5.1	8.9	7,940	2,258

Source: FAO, Commodity Review (1967).

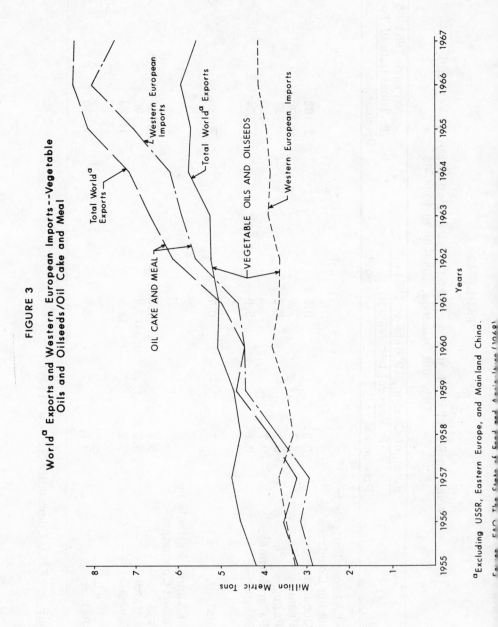

FIGURE 3

World[a] Exports and Western European Imports--Vegetable
Oils and Oilseeds/Oil Cake and Meal

[a]Excluding USSR, Eastern Europe, and Mainland China.

112

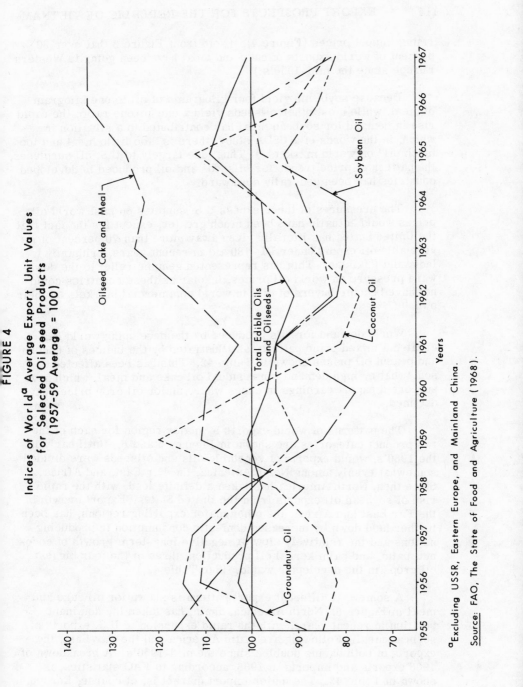

FIGURE 4

Indices of World[a] Average Export Unit Values
for Selected Oilseed Products
(1957-59 Average = 100)

Oilseed Cake and Meal

Soybean Oil

Coconut Oil

Total Edible Oils
and Oilseeds

Groundnut Oil

Years

[a]Excluding USSR, Eastern Europe, and Mainland China.

Source: FAO, The State of Food and Agriculture (1968).

rising import prices (Figure 4). (Note from Figure 3 that over 80 percent of world exports of cake and meal have been going to Western Europe since the mid-1950's.)

Because soybeans yield four kilograms of oil to one kilogram of meal, while most other oilseeds yield a one-to-one ratio, the rapid rise in demand for soybean meal has contributed to a situation in which, in the words of a USDA study, there is "too little meal and too much oil" on world markets. [4] Thus, due largely to U.S. oil surpluses, the pattern of price trends for oilseeds and oil produced in developed countries has been generally downward.

The pressures of these excess U.S. supplies on past world oil prices would actually have been much greater, except for the fact that the United States has literally given away more than 70 percent of its vegetable oil export under PL-480 aid in recent years, primarily to India and Pakistan. This has represented genuine relief to the downward pressure on world oil prices, insofar as these countries could not have become buyers of oils in world commercial markets on their own. [5]

World demand for oils produced by the developing world has created a mixed price pattern, as illustrated by the indices of coconut and peanut oil prices shown in Table 42. This has been affected somewhat by high demand for residual oil cake and meal, which have supported export earnings in cases where major oil crop prices have declined.

The patterns of world exports by major region for each of the two product categories are shown in Figures 5 and 6. Until early in the 1960's, world exports of vegetable oils and oilseeds were divided somewhat evenly among North America, the Far East, and Africa. Since then, North America has taken a definite lead, with the rapid rise of soybean oil exports from the United States. Export growth in the Far East and Africa, the other major exporting regions, has been further held down by increased domestic consumption in producing nations and the relatively slow or negative long-term growth of coconut, palm, and palm kernel oil production, three of the four biggest oil crops in the developing world. (See Table 42.)

A somewhat different export pattern is shown for oil cake and meal in Figure 6. North America, again, has taken the dominant position in recent years, with the rapid expansion of U.S. exports of soybean meal. Following are Latin America and the Far East, the exports of both having doubled since the mid-1950's. A breakdown of 1966 exports and imports in 1966, according to FAO statistics, is shown in Table 43. The major import market is, of course, Europe,

FIGURE 5

World Exports by Major Region:
Vegetable Oils and Oilseeds

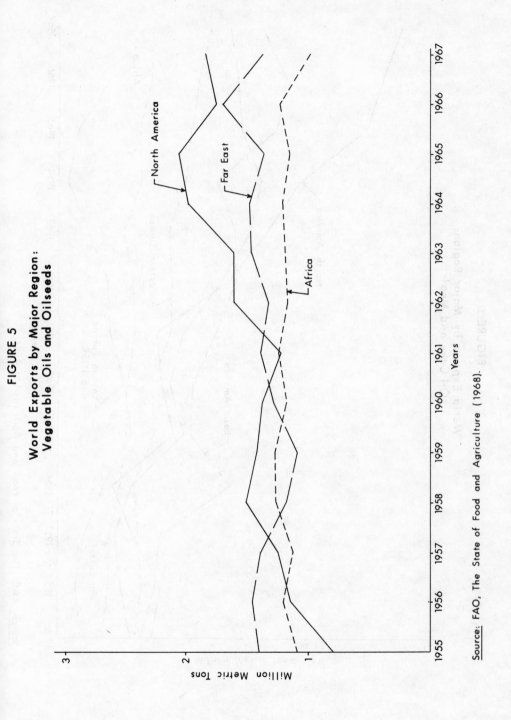

Source: FAO, The State of Food and Agriculture (1968).

115

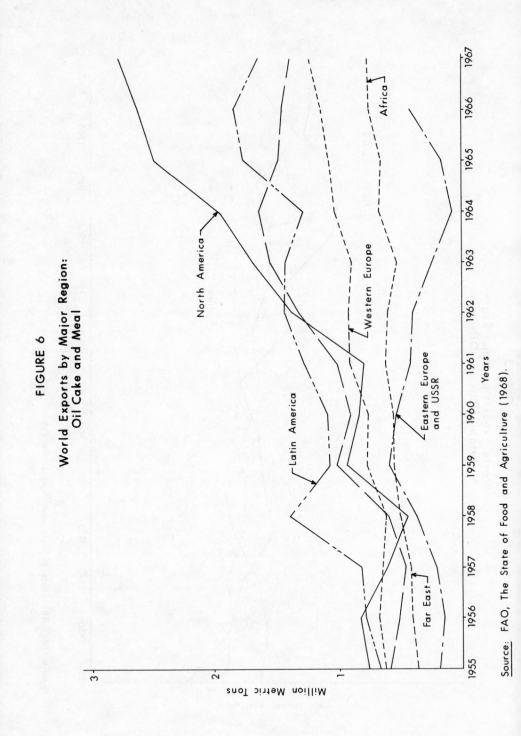

FIGURE 6

World Exports by Major Region:
Oil Cake and Meal

Source: FAO, The State of Food and Agriculture (1968).

116

TABLE 43

Oilseed Cake and Meal:
Regional Breakdown of 1966 Exports and Imports

	Regions and Countries	Percentage of World Market	Volume (In Millions of Metric Tons)
World Total:		100	8.79
Exports	Europe	14	1.22
	U.S.S.R.[a]	4	.39
	North and Central America:	33	2.86
	United States	(86)[c]	2.46
	South America:	16	1.37
	Brazil and Argentina	(88)	1.20
	Asia:	24	2.13
	India[b]	(40)	.84
	Philippines	(11)	.23
	Africa	9	.80
World Total:		100	9.29
Imports	Europe:	93	8.64
	France	(13)	1.09
	Germany	(28)	2.40
	United Kingdom	(12)	1.06
	Asia:	3	.26
	Japan	(60)	.15
	Other	4	.39

[a]Exports in 1966 from the U.S.S.R. were the largest since the early 1960's.

[b]India had 52 percent of Asian exports in 1965, a more typical year.

[c]Numbers in parentheses indicate percentage of regional category immediately above.

Source: Computed from FAO, Trade Yearbook (1967).

TABLE 44

Oilseed Cake and Meal:
Range of Total Values of Major Import
Markets, 1961-66
(Annual Market Value in Millions of Dollars)

Regions and Countries	Minimum	Maximum
Europe:	$ 363	$ 827
France	33	110
Germany	69	226
United Kingdom	93	117
Asia:	13	23
Japan	2	13

Source: Computed from FAO, Trade Yearbook (1967).

led by West Germany, France, and England. The Japanese market, although much smaller, is the major one in Asia and has been growing rapidly. As shown below, it presents, perhaps, the best single opportunity for Vietnamese exports of cake and meal in the postwar period.

Table 44 shows the approximate maximum and minimum sizes of these major import markets during the period 1961-66. The European markets can be seen to be so large that a relatively small producer like Vietnam might not be too optimistic to believe that it could squeeze in for a small but significant fraction of the total. Thus, together with Japan, the future European market for cake and meal will be given closest consideration in the projections that follow.

PROJECTIONS OF FUTURE DEMAND, SUPPLY, AND TRADE

Fats and Oils

As noted previously, reliable projections of future markets and trade in the products under consideration are difficult to achieve. For purposes of this analysis, we shall use variations of recent FAO projections for 1975 and 1985 as the basis for forecasting the general world outlook for fats and oils. (See Table 45.)

TABLE 45

World Production of Fats and Oils, 1961-63 Average and Projections for 1975 (In Millions of Metric Tons)

	Region	Average 1961-63	Projected 1975
Total Fats and Oils	World Total:	33.1	45.7
	Developed Countries	14.4	19.5
	Socialist Countries	8.1	11.7
	Developing Countries	10.1	14.5
Vegetable Oils	World Total:	15.8	23.3
	Developed Countries	5.7	8.5
	Socialist Countries	3.9	6.0
	Developing Countries	6.2	8.8

Source: FAO, Agricultural Commodities--Projections for 1975 and 1985 (1967).

Of particular importance here is the projected increase in production of soybean oil (from the United States) contributing to the large gain in production in the developed countries. Smaller but substantial increases are projected for peanut oil (in the developing countries) and sunflowerseed oil (especially in the U.S.S.R.). The figures also assume successful implementation of planned expansion of palm oil production in the developing countries.

The FAO projections of per capita consumption increases assume a continuation of past consumption trends. Per capita demand growth in the developed countries is expected to slow down and approach saturation, even in Southern Europe. The exception is Japan, for which 1985 per capita consumption of fats and oils is projected to more than double over 1965 levels. These projections are shown in Table 46, together with forecasts of per capita consumption increases in the developing world and socialist countries. Of particular interest to Vietnam are the high expected increases for South Asia (57 percent over the twenty-year period) and East and Southeast Asia (76 percent). Perhaps even more striking is the projected increase per capita of 119 percent for Mainland China, certainly an important export market for Vietnam in a long-term political and economic framework.

Projected world consumption ranges for 1975 and 1985 are shown in Table 47. Again, the differences between the developed and developing worlds in terms of both total and per capita consumption growth can be seen.

The most important results of the FAO series of projections are summarized in Table 48. Here can be seen the range of probable trade balances for the major exporting and importing countries in 1975. Worldwide, there is projected a trade equilibrium in that year. The structural changes from past years within this balance have significant implications for Vietnam's trade outlook.

Net import demand of the developed countries is projected to decline by more than 1 million metric tons over average 1961-63 levels, reflecting increased availabilities of 2 million tons (mostly U.S. soybean oil) and increased gross import demand of 1 million (more than half to Japan). At the same time, projected increases in exportable supplies from the developing countries are twice as large as projected increases in gross import demand of the developed countries. Developing country exports now go mostly to developed countries, which, in 1961-63, accounted for about 80 percent of world gross imports. With these markets expected to decrease in the future, the developing world must look elsewhere. Perhaps, the socialist countries will prove to be attractive (potential net import increases

TABLE 46

Percentage Increase In Per Capita GDP and Per Capita Consumption of Fats and Oils, by Region, 1965-85*

Regions and Countries	Per Capita GDP in 1962	Percentage Increase 1965-85	
		Per Capita GDP	Fats and Oils Consumption
Developed Countries:	$ 1,368	105	9
North America	2,603	71	-1
European Economic Community	1,123	133	10
Northern Europe	1,302	106	3
Southern Europe	304	165	22
Japan	521	294	109
Oceania	1,237	81	0
South Africa	480	69	31
Socialist Countries:	314	126	65
U.S.S.R.	820	176	60
Eastern Europe	696	149	17
China (Mainland)	105	78	119
Developing Countries:	126	67	52
Central America	407	77	24
Western South America	273	74	41
Eastern South America	223	52	21
Northwest Africa	190	52	44
West Africa	92	58	51
Central Africa	80	52	37
East Africa	76	58	51
Near East	159	81	49
South Asia	97	17	57
East and Southeast Asia	78	64	76

*Average figures from ranges of FAO projections.

Source: FAO, Agricultural Commodities--Projections for 1975 and 1985 (1967).

121

TABLE 47

Fats and Oils:
World Consumption, 1961-63 Average and 1975 and 1985 Projections

Region	Total Consumption (In Millions of Metric Tons)						Per Capita Consumption (In Kilograms per Capita)		
	Average	1975		1985			Average 1961-63	1975*	1985*
		Low	High	Low	High				
Total World:	32.8	45.5	48.8	57.2	68.5		8.1	9.0	10.1
Developed Countries	16.6	20.4	20.8	22.9	24.5		17.7	18.9	19.6
Socialist Countries	8.3	12.9	14.3	17.4	21.5		6.0	8.0	9.8
Developing Countries	7.8	12.2	13.7	16.9	22.1		4.7	5.7	6.8

*High/low average.

Source: FAO, Agricultural Commodities--Projections for 1975 and 1985 (1967).

of more than 1 million tons per annum by 1975), but this is uncertain, as the U.S.S.R. might become a large vegetable oil exporter in the future, as it has been in the past three years. That leaves trade among the developing countries themselves for potential new markets. More than a half of gross import needs for these countries are projected for India and Pakistan, but they rely today on PL-480 soybean oil to a large measure. It is questionable whether they will be able to enter commercial markets on their own for many years. In addition, many other developing countries are constrained by balance of trade problems and cannot increase imports significantly without concessionary aid. Thus, the overall outlook for fats and oils exports from the developing world does not look very favorable.

Among the developing countries, the main potential competitors of Vietnam in Southeast Asia are the Philippines, Malaysia, and Indonesia. As far as tapping the Western European market, Vietnam's most formidable competitors are the West African nations, the main exports of which have preferential trade arrangements with the EEC and the British Commonwealth.

Looking specifically at Vietnam's most attractive markets and areas of greatest competition, trade balances to 1980 have been projected as linear extrapolations of FAO's 1975 projections. The results are shown in Table 49.

The overall balance between the main exporting and importing countries in 1980, compared to 1963, shows a change from a deficit to a surplus, due to the relatively high increases projected for the United States and West Africa, while the European deficit is not expected to increase significantly.

The projected balances for the Asia region look less pessimistic, as seen in the following list, which shows the estimated trade balances in 1980 for the Asian region (in thousands of metric tons):[6]

Importers of Fats and Oils		Exporters of Fats and Oils	
Japan	1,340	Australia	500
Burma	80	Ceylon	160
India	900	Indonesia	160
Pakistan	450	Malaysia	340
China (Taiwan)	130	Philippines	1,120
Total	2,900	Total	2,280

TABLE 48

Fats and Oils: World Net Trade, by Regions and Selected
Major Importing and Exporting Countries, 1961-63 Average and Projections for 1975
(In Millions of Metric Tons)

Regions and Countries	Net Imports Average 1961-63	Net Imports 1975 Low	Net Imports 1975 High	Net Exports Average 1961-63	Net Exports 1975 Low	Net Exports 1975 High
Developed Countries:	4.8	5.6	6.0	2.6	4.7	4.8
North America	-	-	-	2.0	4.0	4.1
Western Europe:	4.4	4.5	4.7	-	-	-
European Economic Community	2.4	2.4	2.4	-	-	-
United Kingdom	1.4	1.4	1.4	-	-	-
Oceania	-	-	-	4.8	6.5	6.8
Japan	0.4	1.1	1.3	-	-	-
Centrally Planned Countries:	0.4	1.3	1.6	0.1	-	-
U.S.S.R.	-	0.1	0.2	0.1	-	-
China (Mainland)	-	0.6	1.0	0.1	-	-
Eastern Europe	0.4	0.6	0.5	-	-	-
Developing Countries:	0.8	2.2	2.6	3.2	4.5	5.4
Latin America	0.3	0.6	0.6	0.6	0.8	0.9
Near East	0.2	0.5	0.5	0.1	0.2	0.2
Asia:	0.3	1.2	1.5	1.2	1.4	1.7
Burma	0.02	0.05	0.07	-	-	-
India	0.01	0.7	0.8	-	-	-
Pakistan	0.1	0.3	0.4	-	-	-
China (Taiwan)	0.1	0.1	0.1	-	-	-
Ceylon	-	-	-	0.1	0.1	0.1
Indonesia	-	-	-	0.3	0.1	0.1
Malaysia	-	-	-	0.1	0.2	0.3
Philippines	-	-	-	0.8	0.9	1.1
Africa:	-	-	-	1.3	2.1	2.6
Nigeria	-	-	-	0.6	1.0	1.3
Senegal	-	-	-	0.2	0.4	0.4
Congo (Kinshasa)	-	-	-	0.2	0.2	0.3
Antarctic	-	-	-	0.3	0.03	0.04
Grand Total*	6.0	9.1	10.2	5.9	9.2	10.3

*Totals represent only a part of world import and export trade, as the figures are on a net basis. Actual world trade in 1961-63 was 8.8 million tons.

Source: FAO, Agricultural Commodities--Projections for 1975 and 1985 (1967).

124

TABLE 49

Fats and Oils: Projected Trade Balances to 1980
(In Millions of Metric Tons)

Region	Production	Consumption	Trade Balance	1963 Balance
North America	13.4	8.5	+4.9	+2.0
Western Europe	6.6	11.3	-4.7	-4.4
Japan	0.3	1.6	-1.3	-0.4
West Africa	3.4	1.1	+2.3	+1.1
Philippines	1.5	0.4	+1.1	+0.7
			+2.3	+1.0

+Net exports
-Net imports

Source: Computed from FAO, Agricultural Commodities--Projections for 1975 and 1985 (1967).

In an Asian market of about 3 million tons, Vietnam's potential share, given present estimates of its exportable surplus, would be a small fraction of the total. For this reason, it is quite possible that Vietnam could find an Asian export market for whatever surpluses it might generate during the next decade.

Vegetable Oils

The most attractive overall market for all oilseed products from Vietnam would appear to be Japan. We have noted previously the expected doubling of Japanese fats and oils consumption between 1965 and 1975. Similar increases are expected for vegetable oils alone (79 percent of total Japanese fats and oils).[7] The USDA has estimated the Japanese demand for vegetable oils in 1971 will be 832,000 metric tons, up 13 percent from 1967 levels.[8] Much of this increase will come from U.S. soybean oil imports, which undoubtedly will remain the most formidable competitor for the growing Japanese oil market. As was shown in list showing estimated trade balance in

1980 for the Asian region, the primary Asian competitor for Vietnam for coconut oil sales in the Japanese market will probably be the Philippines. Vietnam's ability to meet Philippine prices will be decisive. A similar conclusion would apply in other vegetable oil markets that Vietnam might seek.

Oil Cake and Meal

Worldwide, the demand for cake and meal is expected to grow much faster than that of oil,[9] and this probably presents an export opportunity for Vietnam that is better than for foreseeable oil exports. The two major markets will be Japan and Western Europe. In both cases, Vietnam will have to compete with U.S. soybean protein meal, which is low in cost and has a desirable amino acid balance for livestock and poultry feed. Demand growth for cake and meal could slow down with expanding use of high-lysine corn and urea. Nevertheless, Vietnam's potential exports, again, will only be a small fraction of world trade, and it should not have great difficulty in gaining a small fraction of the market growth that is certain to occur under any circumstances.

CONCLUSIONS FOR VIETNAM'S EXPORT EARNINGS

It is the basic conclusion of this analysis that Vietnam should be able, by 1980, to export a substantial (for Vietnam) volume of oilseed products during the first decade following the war. The outlook for vegetable oil exports, while not outstanding, is still somewhat bright. The best opportunities will lie within Asia, where a net supply deficit is expected in 1980. Within this regional market, Japan will provide the best opportunities. The outlook for oil cake and meal is certainly brighter. In addition to Asian markets (again particularly Japan), Vietnam can look toward Western Europe.

Using estimates of potential agricultural export surpluses in 1980,* it appears possible that Vietnam could export in that year 3,000 to 4,000 tons of peanut oil, 15,000 to 20,000 tons of coconut oil, and 20,000 to 30,000 tons of oil cake and meal. These are only rough estimates, but are sufficient to indicate the magnitude of potential earnings. Using 1968 unit export prices (e.g., export price in Ceylon for coconut oil), the foreign exchange earnings that might be expected from these products is shown in Table 50.

---

*Authors' estimates.

TABLE 50

Vietnam's Potential Earnings in Peanut Oil, Coconut Oil, and Oilseed Cake and Meal

Commodity	Price (In Dollars per Metric Ton)	Earnings (In Thousands of Dollars)	
		Low	High
Peanut Oil	$300	$ 900	$1,200
Coconut Oil	250	3,750	5,000
Cake and Meal	80	1,600	2,400
Total Earnings		$6,250	$8,600

Thus, under the reasonable expectation that Vietnam will be able to find a market for these comparatively small export surpluses, it can expect, by 1980, annual export earnings of perhaps $6 to $9 million. This would be tenfold increase over the average annual earnings from vegatable oils and cake during the 1958-65 period.

NOTES

1. FAO, Agricultural Commodities--Projections for 1975 and 1985 (1967).

2. USDA, Foreign Agriculture Circular, FFO 13-68 (October, 1968).

3. FAO, op. cit.

4. USDA, op. cit.

5. U.N. Commodity Survey (1967).

6. FAO, op. cit.

7. Ibid.

8. USDA, op. cit.

9. Ibid.

8

Aside from rice and rubber, tea has been Vietnam's largest source of export earnings over the past decade. Between 1958 and 1967, tea exports totaled $14.4 million, or almost a fifth of all exports after the two major items. Until 1966, when the growth of this industry was attenuated by the escalation of fighting, the volume of tea exports grew at a compound rate of over 35 percent per annum (Table 51). Earnings, however, grew more slowly than the volume of trade during this period, due largely to a downward trend in world prices.

The largest single market for Vietnamese tea is the United Kingdom, which has accounted, in recent years, for over 90 percent of exports. The only other markets of significance to Vietnam, at present, are France, Singapore, Germany, and Hong Kong.

In the opinion of British tea importers, Vietnamese tea is a "plain" or "common" variety, not commanding premium prices, as do some of the choice varieties of North India, Ceylon, and Kenya, which are used for blending.[1] This is not to say that better varieties could not be produced in Vietnam, but merely that the exacting environmental requirements of elevation, climate, and soils for producing more than average teas are not met at the sites of present Vietnamese plantations.

For present planning purposes, it is prudent to assume that future Vietnamese tea production will not be of the premium variety and, thus, will be more subject to general world price and market trends than would pertain if special characteristics were to allow Vietnamese tea to carve out a differentiated market of its own.

TABLE 51

Exports of Tea from Vietnam, 1958-67

Export Volume and Value	1958	1959	1960	1961	1962	1963	1964	1965	1966	1967
Total Export Volume	276	465	1,059	1,655	1,931	1,995	2,148	2,341	1,863	1,047
Total Export Value[a]	$ 360	$ 501	$1,046	$1,612	$1,893	$1,858	$1,888	$2,135	$2,142	$ 955
Export Unit Value[b]	$1,304	$1,077	$ 986	$ 974	$ 980	$ 931	$ 878	$ 912	$1,149	$ 912

[a]In thousands of dollars.
[b]In dollars per metric ton.

Source: USAID Mission to Vietnam, Annual Statistical Bulletin No. 11 (1968).

TRENDS IN PRODUCTION AND TRADE

Production

With the main exceptions of the U.S.S.R. and Japan, tea is produced almost entirely in developing countries. World production grew from an annual average of 846,000 tons during the 1955-57 period to a 1965-67 average of 1.2 million tons, an annual rate of increase of about 3.3 percent (Table 52). Over this period, however, there were significant differences among the growth rates of the main producing regions. Production in Ceylon and India, together the source of half the world's tea, grew by 2.5 and 1.9 percent per annum, respectively, while African production, amounting to almost 7 percent of the world total, grew by over 9 percent annually. Latin America showed the fastest production growth, 21 percent per annum, but today only accounts for 2 percent of world production. Annual growth rates in Mainland China and the U.S.S.R., together accounting for 18 percent of world production, were 3.5 and 7 percent, respectively.

Exports

During this same period, world exports of tea grew at a rate of 1.8 percent per annum, or only slightly more than half the growth rate of production (Table 53). This can be attributed to increasing domestic consumption in producing nations and a sluggish growth of import demand in the major market areas of Europe and North America.

Again, there were considerable differences among the main producers. Indian exports actually decreased slightly between the 1955-57 and 1965-67 averages, due largely to a rapid rise in domestic consumption and to the comparatively slow expansion of production during this period.[2] In Ceylon, where internal demand is much smaller, exports increased at roughly the same rate as production. This, also, was the case in Africa, where rapid production increases far exceed the growth of domestic demand.

Imports

The major importers of tea are the developed countries, but their total demand increased by less than 1 percent per annum during the 1955-57--1965-67 period. The largest consuming country, and therefore the largest importer, is the United Kingdom, accounting for well over a third of world net imports and over 60 percent of those of the developed world (Table 53). The import market of the United

TABLE 52

World Tea Production,
by Major Region, 1955-67
(In Thousands of Metric Tons)

Regions and Countries	1955-57 Average	1962-64 Average	1965	1966	1967	Percent Change, 1955-67 Average to 1965-67 Average
Developed Countries:						
Japan	74	90	90	105	111	+38
	72	81	77	83	88	+15
Developing Countries:						
Asia:	630	786	835	865	864	+36
	595	713	751	757	763	+27
Ceylon	175	217	228	222	221	+28
India	309	355	368	375	379	+21
Pakistan	23	26	27	29	30	+25
Africa	32	60	67	87	79	+143
Latin America	3	13	18	21	22	+578
Centrally Planned Countries:						
China (Mainland)*	142	206	209	219	219	+52
	113	159	159	160	160	+41
U.S.S.R.	26	44	45	55	54	+97
World Total	846	1,082	1,134	1,189	1,194	+39

*Estimated.

Source: FAO, Commodity Review (1968).

Kingdom is not growing much at all and, in fact, actually declined slightly between the annual averages of 1955-57 and 1965-67.

The second largest importer is the United States, with about 15 percent of net world imports. The U.S. market grew by 35 percent during the 1955-57--1965-67 period, but the major portion of this growth was concentrated in the first seven years (3.5 percent per annum). Unpublished USDA figures indicate an estimated annual average of 67,000 metric tons imported into the United States during the 1967-69 period, or an annual increase of 2.6 percent over 1962-64 levels.

Thus, it appears that per capita demand is at or near the saturation point in the two major import markets and, in fact, may even be turning downward. In the United Kingdom, studies have shown that demand for tea is highly inelastic with respect to price or income and is dictated more by habit and tradition.[3] With a very slow rate of population growth, and strong evidence that Britions are drinking more coffee (imports up 39 percent between 1961 and 1966),[4] it is not surprising that tea imports from the United Kingdom have decreased over the past decade.

In the United States, tea appeared to be gaining at the expense of coffee early in the past decade, but there, too, increases in per capita demand for tea appear to have slackened. Of the other developed countries, only the EEC has shown any buoyancy of demand; the market there, however, is still quite small.

As shown in Table 53, net imports of developing countries of Asia, Africa, and Latin America have been growing at a rate exceeding the world average, but they still total only one-third of the import demand of the developed world. Import growth in Asia, the most likely outlet for Vietnamese exports of the three regions, has been the slowest. The 1965-67 average net import demand in Asia, in fact, decreased from the average of the previous three years.

Prices and Earnings

While world tea production has increased by over a third during the past decade, net import demand has grown by less than half that amount. Because excess supplies have not been taken up by domestic consumption--particularly in Ceylon with its limited population--and because the income elasticity of demand in major developed country markets has proven to be extremely low, supplies have outstripped demand and prices have fallen steadily (Figure 7). Tea cannot be stores for extended periods of time, as can many other commodities, and increasing supplies can only be absorbed by falling prices and increased

TABLE 53

World Trade in Tea,
by Major Region, 1955-67
(In Thousands of Metric Tons)

	Regions and Countries	1955-57 Average	1962-64 Average	1965	1966	1967	Percent Change 1955-57 Average to 1965-67 Average
Exports from Producing Countries	Developed Countries	12	6	7	4	4	-58
	Developing Countries:	449	533	556	531	573	+23
	Asia:	420	471	484	440	491	+12
	Ceylon	163	206	224	200	217	+31
	India	202	215	199	179	211	- 3
	Pakistan	7	2	3	2	-	-64
	Africa	28	53	58	75	68	+139
	Latin America	-	9	15	16	14	+67[a]
	Centrally Planned Countries[b]	39	31	32	36	36	-11
	World Total	499	569	596	570	613	+19
Net Imports	Developed Countries:	377	408	417	396	432	+10
	Western Europe	266	275	280	257	284	+ 3
	United Kingdom	229	233	236	214	231	- 1
	European Economic Community	17	21	23	23	33	+55
	Rest of Western Europe	20	21	22	20	20	+ 3
	United States	46	59	59	60	67	+35
	Canada	20	20	20	20	19	-2
	Oceania	32	37	38	35	35	+13
	Others	13	18	21	24	28	+87
	Developing Countries:	106	136	130	147	134	+29
	Latin America	6	8	9	11	12	+78
	Asia and Oceania	46	60	55	67	50	+25
	Africa	53	68	66	70	72	+31
	Centrally Planned Countries:	15	24	37	21	24	+82
	Eastern Europe	5	9	12	11	12	+133
	U.S.S.R.	10	16	25	9	12	+53
	World Total	498	568	584	564	590	+16

[a]Increase over 1962-64 average.
[b]Estimates for China (Mainland) and North Vietnam.

Source: FAO, Commodity Review (1968).

134

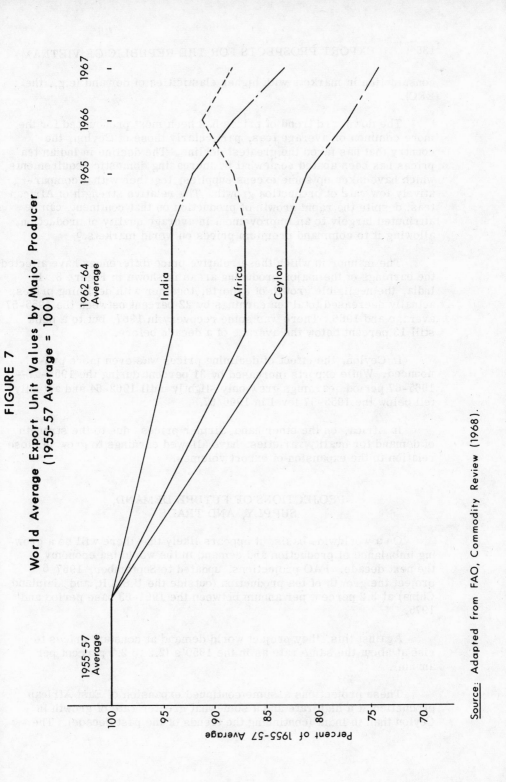

FIGURE 7

World Average Export Unit Values by Major Producer
(1955-57 Average = 100)

India

Africa

Ceylon

1955-57
Average

1962-64
Average

1965   1966   1967

Percent of 1955-57 Average

Source: Adapted from FAO, Commodity Review (1968).

consumption in markets with higher elasticities of demand (e.g., the EEC).

The downward trend of prices has been most pronounced for the more common or average teas, particularly those of Ceylon, the country that has faced the greatest decline. The decline in Indian tea prices has been abated somewhat by increasing domestic requirements, which have taken up some excess supplies, together with a comparatively low rate of production growth. The relative strength of African teas, despite the rapid growth of production on that continent, can be attributed largely to an improvement in average quality of production, allowing it to command premium prices on world markets.[5]

The manner in which these relative price differences have affected the earnings of the major producing areas is shown in Figure 8. In India, the negligible growth of exports, together with declining prices, actually decreased total tea earnings by 22 percent between the 1955-57 average and 1966. There was some recovery in 1967, but to a point still 13 percent below the average of a decade before.

In Ceylon, the effect of declining prices was even more pronounced. While exports increased by 31 percent during the 1955-57-- 1965-67 period, earnings grew only slightly until 1962-64 and actually fell below the 1955-57 level in 1966/67.

In Africa, on the other hand, firmer prices, due to the strength of demand for quality varieties, have allowed earnings to grow in close relation to the expansion of export volumes.

PROJECTIONS OF FUTURE DEMAND, SUPPLY, AND TRADE

On a worldwide basis, it appears likely that there will be a growing imbalance of production and demand in the world tea economy of the next decade. FAO projections, updated to September, 1967,[6] project the growth of tea production (outside the U.S.S.R. and Mainland China) at 3.2 percent per annum between the 1961-63 base period and 1975.

Against this, they project world demand at constant prices to rise at about the same rate as in the 1950's (2.2 to 2.7 percent per annum).

These projections assume continued expansion of East African production at a high rate and a somewhat greater rate of growth in Ceylon than in India (continuing the trends of the past decade). The

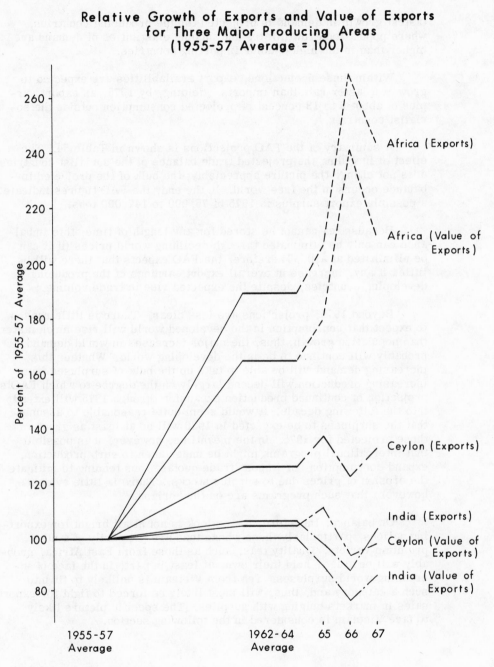

FIGURE 8

Relative Growth of Exports and Value of Exports
for Three Major Producing Areas
(1955-57 Average = 100)

Source: Adapted from FAO, Commodity Review (1968).

137

fastest growth in demand is projected for the producing countries, where population growth rates and income elasticities of demand are higher than in the high-income importing countries.

Within these projections, export availabilities are expected to grow at a faster rate than imports, yielding, by 1975, an export surplus of about 6 to 13 percent of projected consumption outside the socialist countries. [7]

A summary of the FAO projections is shown in Table 54. The effect of including the projected trade balance of the socialist countries does not change the picture appreciably; the bulk of the projected imbalance occurs in the free world. In the end, the FAO figures indicate a possible export surplus in 1975 of 75, 000 to 147, 000 tons.

Because tea cannot be stored for any length of time, this imbalance can only be eliminated through declining world prices (if it can be eliminated at all). Therefore, the FAO expects that there will be little, if any, increase in overall export earnings of the producing developing countries, despite the expected rise in trade volume.

Beyond 1975, projections are less clear. There is little reason to expect that consumption in the developed world will rise much faster than population growth; thus, the major increases in world demand probably will continue to be in the developing world. Whether this increasing demand will be able to take up the bulk of surpluses from increasing production will depend largely on the degree to which FAO's projection of continued production expansion through 1975 will extend into the following decade. It would seem quite reasonable to assume that the surpluses to be expected in 1980 will be at least as great as those projected for 1975. In the meantime, however, it is possible that international programs might be undertaken to curb production, expand consumption, or impose trade quotas, thus tending to mitigate the erosion of prices due to surplus stocks. There is little evidence, however, that such programs are on the horizon.

On balance, therefore, the outlook is not at all bright for exporting nations, particularly those whose teas are primarily of a nonpremium variety. Quality teas, such as those from East Africa, probably will be able to hold their own, at least in part, in the face of increasing world surpluses. Tea from Vietnam is unlikely to fit into such a category and, thus, will most likely be forced to fight for export sales in markets bulging with supplies. The specific picture likely to face Vietnam is considered in the following section.

TABLE 54

Tea: Production, Consumption, and Trade Balance, 1961-63 Average and Projections for 1975
(In Thousands of Metric Tons)

Region	1961-63 Average			Projections for 1975				
					Demand		Trade Balance	
	Production	Consumption	Exports– Imports+	Production	Low	High	Low	High
Developed Countries	84	480	+402	123	566	582	+443	+459
Developing Countries	766	381	-388	1,162	575	625	-587	-537
Total Developing and Developed Countries	850	861	+14	1,285	1,141	1,207	-144	-78
Centrally Planned Countries[b]			-15				- 3	+ 3
World Trade Balance			-1				-147	-75

a Allowing for stock changes.
b Projected balances are net imports of U.S.S.R. and Eastern Europe, plus average net exports during 1961-63 from China (Mainland).

Source: FAO, Agricultural Commodities--Projections for 1975 and 1985 (1967).

OUTLOOK FOR VIETNAMESE TEA EXPORTS

As has been discussed, the outlook for Vietnamese tea exports on the basis of expected world trends is somewhat gloomy. This does not provide, of course, the full picture on which future decisions for the postwar period can be made. It is necessary to look more closely at the specific markets that are likely to be outlets for Vietnam's production before reaching any final conclusions.

To this end, we have the benefit of additional information: Discussions that were held in July, 1969, with a senior partner of George White, Sanderson (Tea Brookers) Ltd. of London, the major importer of Vietnamese tea in the United Kingdom,[8] and several on-site Asian market studies (undertaken as part of this study, which appear in later chapters). The specific markets will be examined individually.

United Kingdom

The markets position of Vietnamese tea in the United Kingdom can be evaluated roughly by glancing at some recent prices on the London market. During the first six months of 1969, the prices offered for Vietnamese tea averaged $726 per metric ton equivalent, better than Argentina ($616), Mozambique ($660), and Malawi ($704), but not as good as South India ($792), Uganda ($924), or Malaysia ($814). The average prices of higher-quality teas were Kenya ($1,100), Ceylon ($1,012), North India ($990), and Tanzania ($1,012).

Within the trade, it is considered that any teas sold in London at less than about $800 per metric ton are probably being grown at a loss (production costs are estimated to be at least $775 per ton). Our London contract expressed doubt whether growers could make a reasonable profit when London prices for their teas were less than $1,050. Only the better medium and choice teas are presently achieving this. (Vietnamese tea receives the benefit of a not insubstantial export subsidy.)

The conclusion of the London discussions was that the best that Vietnam is likely to do in the London market by 1980 would be slightly above the good year of 1965, say 2,300 tons. Assuming continued downward pressure on prices (as expected by the London trade), the price probably would not exceed $800 per ton, meaning total earnings of no more than $1.8 million.

This estimate is probably not far out of line from feasible levels of sales. Technological problems probably will preclude any large

Vietnamese production increases by 1980, and 2,300 tons is not very much in terms of total world trade. Even if world supplies do tend to run ahead of consumption, Vietnam probably can dispose of such an amount on the London market. Its product is a pretty good "common" tea, which sells, generally, at better prices than the products of some other producing countries. On the whole, it has been the poorer of teas that have remained unsold in recent auctions.

However, sales of this order and at these prices would not be profitable to the producers, unless the Vietnamese government subsides continued--or unless, at some future time, a devaluation of the piaster altered significantly the relationship between production costs and export prices.

Hong Kong

Over two-thirds of Hong Kong's tea imports are from Mainland China. Of several other major suppliers, North Vietnam, surprisingly, is one of the most significant, shipping 477 tons to Hong Kong in 1968, an amount equal to 18 percent of non-China tea imports in that year. Because North Vietnam produces black and green teas of similar taste and quality to those grown in South Vietnam, there is no reason why the South should not be able to acquire a large fraction of this market by 1980.

Similarly, Indonesian teas in 1968 accounted for 30 percent of Hong Kong's non-China tea imports. There is a chance that Vietnam might be able to intrude competitively upon this market, also. The other main Hong Kong supplier, Ceylon, probably cannot be challenged by Vietnam, due to differences in product quality and taste.

On balance, it is not beyond reasonable expectation to project 1980 Vietnamese exports to Hong Kong of as much as 450 tons per year. This would represent earnings of about $350,000.

Japan

The Japanese tea import market is small and relatively static ($8 million in 1968). Major suppliers of black tea are India, Ceylon, and United Kingdom re-exports. Green tea imports (only 7 percent of the total) come almost entirely from Taiwan.

It is possible that Vietnam might compete with Taiwan for a share of the green tea market, but it is doubtful that this established supplier much closer to Japan can be displaced to any significant extent. It might also be possible for small quantities of Vietnamese black tea to compete with Argentinian and East African varieties, but again this is not probable.

Singapore

In the past, Singapore has been only a minor importer of South Vietnamese tea. The exception was 1965, when imports reached 222 tons, but this diminished in subsequent years, due to supply problems. North Vietnam and Indonesia, also, have been minor suppliers. It is possible, as with Hong Kong, that South Vietnam might intrude upon the small markets of these two countries. By 1980, it would be reasonable to expect the South Vietnamese exports of black and green tea to Singapore might reach about 120 tons per year, selling for about $100,000.

Others

The EEC countries (primarily France and Germany) have accounted for over 100 tons of Vietnamese exports in past years. These markets might be expected to increase somewhat by 1980. Adding other minor world markets to potential European demand might mean a total of about 200 tons per year, or $160,000.

SUMMARY OF POSSIBLE TEA EXPORTS

None of the above projections has considered the possibility of major price drops due to excess world tea supplies of the magnitude projected by FAO. All of them, therefore, might prove to be optimistic. If a probable range of Vietnamese tea exports in 1980 under optimistic and pessimistic market conditions is assumed, the likely size of the overall Vietnamese export market would be from $1.7 to $2.4 million per annum. This is broken down (in thousands of dollars and in early 1969 export prices) as follows:

Market	Probable Annual Earnings	
	Pessimistic	Optimistic
United Kingdom	$1,300	$1,800
Hong Kong	200	350

(continued)

| Market | Probable Annual Earnings | |
	Pessimistic	Optimistic
Singapore	50	100
Others	100	160
Total	$1,650	$2,410

All things considered, it is likely, therefore, that Vietnamese tea export earnings in the postwar period will not rise much higher than the best that has been achieved in the past ($2.1 million in 1966). They could, in fact, decrease. Thus, tea would not appear to be a product for major emphasis in the postwar reconstruction period.

NOTES

1. T. A. Mead, Internal Memorandum, Development and Resources Corporation (July 9, 1969).

2. UN, Commodity Survey (1967).

3. FAO, Agricultural Commodities--Projections for 1975 and 1985 (1967).

4. FAO, Trade Yearbook (1967).

5. UN, Commodity Survey.

6. FAO, Agricultural Commodities--Projections for 1975 and 1985.

7. UN, op. cit.

8. Mead, op. cit.

9

In addition to the commodities covered in the previous chapters, there are many others that have been exported in the past, plus new commodities that might be added in the future. For any one such commodity, the market demand or the potentially available supplies are relatively small in comparison to rice, rubber, wood products, and those products previously described. They may not add large amounts to export earnings individually, but collectively, they amount to a significant total value. A brief summary of this varied list of commodities is presented in this chapter. It should not be inferred that these are the only minor commodities, since we have not tried to be exhaustive. Nor has there been an attempt to list every new product that might be available in the future; in fact, on new products, only a few, for which it appears to be relatively easy to generate a supply and for which the market demand is strong and growing, have been selected.

CINNAMON

Vietnam produces commercially the product known as Saigon (or Indian) cassia from at least four species of Cinnamomum, found in a wild state in the Indochina Peninsula, all of which yield aromatic barks. True cinnamon derives from a tree of Ceylon, the Seychelles, and Madagascar, whereas cassia comes from trees of the same genus in South China, Indonesia, Malaysia, and Indochina.

Cinnamon and cassia are similar in flavor, although derived from the bark of different trees. End uses are similar, but the FAO considers cassia a cheaper substitute for cinnamon.[1] Nevertheless, the U.S. market considers Vietnamese cassia to be the richest-flavored of all cinnamon products and, thus, places premium prices on it, even though the trade generally considers it to be an inferior product.

145

TABLE 55

Vietnam's Exports of Cassia, 1957-67

Year	Volume (In Metric Tons)	Value (In Thousands of Dollars)	Average Price (In Dollars per Kilogram)
1957	527	$237	$0.45
1958	1,040	396	0.38
1959	1,478	785	0.53
1960	999	617	0.62
1961	819	502	0.61
1962	239	185	0.77
1963	328	254	0.77
1964	553	931	1.68
1965	387	788	2.01
1966	29	58	2.00
1967	38	84	2.21

Source: USAID, Annual Statistical Bulletin, Nos. 10 and 11 (1967 -68).

Disruptions of supplies of Saigon cassia in recent years, due to the war, have resulted in a changing structure of world cinnamon supplies that could have profound effects on the ability of Vietnam to regain or expand its former position in this market. Time is of the essence, for the largest market for Vietnamese cassia, (the United States) is moving rapidly towards synthetics and fortified cheaper cinnamon varieties.

Exports of cassia from Vietnam have fluctuated considerably for more than a decade, as shown in Table 55. Over the period shown, most production was exported to the United States. Since 1965, government export licensing restrictions, designed to deny trade to areas controlled by the Viet Cong, have virtually halted legal exports. Previously, annual production fluctuated widely following the 1959 peak, but, on the average, it declined. No doubt, this was due, in large part, to increasing hostilities in the nothern producing provinces.

The effect of the war is made somewhat clearer, as is one's insight into the past strength of demand for Vietnamese cassia, when one looks at past variations in the average price paid for exports. Between 1957-61, the price varied between $0.38 and $0.62 per kilogram, with higher production generally reflected in lower prices. Production decreased significantly in 1962 and 1963, and prices rose

to $0.77. In 1964, production rose by 69 percent, but prices more
than doubled to $1.68. In the following year, prices rose again to
over $2, while production dropped to a little above 1963 levels (when
the price was $0.77). It appears that the high prices paid during the
1964/65 period reflected an abnormal supply and demand situation
and included a significant increment above the price norm, which was
paid by buyers who, no doubt, feared the eventual disruption of supplies
due to the war. Of course, part of this price rise may have been due
to inflation and higher production costs, but certainly not all of it.
Vietnamese cinnamon demonstrated during this period its ability to
command high prices in periods of market stress.

There is some question whether or not this commanding position
will be retained when production is resumed in the postwar period.
As of the end of 1968, when conversations were held with knowledgeable
U.S. cinnamon importers,[2] the U.S. market still had strong hopes of
resuming purchases of Vietnamese cassia. The United States, however,
had switched largely to supplies from Indonesia (less desired by the
North America palate, but available) and synthetics. At the time, it
was felt these substitutes were gaining consumer acceptance. Nevertheless, there was little question that the Vietnamese product at
reasonable prices would still face a ready market in the United States
if supplies could be resumed in the immediate future. The U.S. market,
in fact, paid $3.30 per kilogram f.o.b. Saigon for some limited supplies
that were made available in 1968. U.S. cinnamon import prices were
generally high in 1968, with over two-thirds of U.S. imports ranging,
on the average, from $1.38 to $2.75 per kilogram.[3]

The conclusion of the 1968 market study* was that Vietnam
would have little trouble selling 3,000 tons of cinnamon in the U.S.
market in the immediate postwar period (if such an amount could be
produced), provided that the price were kept to about $1.65 per kilogram
f.o.b. Saigon. It was estimated that this could easily rise to 6,000
tons by 1980, if supplies were reliable.

A more recent investigation seems to indicate some deterioration
in this outlook. The U.S. baking industry, which is the biggest U.S.
consumer of cinnamon, has been hurt many times since World War II
by disruptions in cinnamon supplies from Mainland China, Ceylon,
Indonesia, and Vietnam, and they are anxious to obtain more reliable
sources. Many have been using fortified cinnamon, which is a mixture
of synthetic cinnamon and which is very cheap, and low-quality cinnamon from the Seychelles (average price in 1968, $0.31 per kilogram).
Others are considering the use of pure synthetics, in order to take
advantage of still lower prices.[4] For the first time, bakers can now

---

*Authors' study.

purchase synthetic cinnamon flavoring, which has advantages of consistency in organic content, as well as assured availability of supply. Taste, apparently, can also be controlled fairly easily.

The key to the matter of synthetic cinnamon is that there still appears to be some consumer reluctance to make the complete switch to synthetics. At least initially, while synthetics are being introduced, the consumer lacks confidence in the new product and tends to consider it an inferior substitute. Nevertheless, confidence grows with usage, and the best time to compete with a synthetic is before the customer has had a chance to develop a taste for it. A similar situation existed in the battle between butter and margarine twenty years ago.

Thus, while there appears to have been some deterioration in the competitive position of Vietnamese cassia in the U.S. market over the past year, it is concluded that Vietnam still can sell $2 to $3 million worth per year if immediate steps are taken to relax the present restrictions on exports. Assuming normal market development over the next decade under more relaxed conditions this might be expected to increase to $6 million by 1980. Further delays in releasing exports might lose the lucrative U.S. market entirely to synthetics and fortified cinnamons from other countries. The United States is not, of course, the only market for Vietnam to consider. Japan, Singapore, and South Korea might be counted upon for future sales, as indicated later in this book. Europe, which accounts for one-fifth of world imports of cinnamon, is less attractive, for the special qualities of Vietnamese cassia are not regarded as highly there as in the United States. Market uncertainties are too abundant to belabor the issue of demand in non-North American markets, particularly when the problem of synthetics is introduced, but it would seem appropriate to estimate that these markets together might comprise an additional demand for Vietnam of about $1 million per annum over the next decade. The main competition for cinnamon (cassia) of the type produced in Vietnam is likely to come from Mainland China, which exports a similar product. It should be pointed out that existing U.S. restrictions on trade with Mainland China provide an enormous prop for Vietnamese exports to the United States. When these restrictions are relaxed, as no doubt they will be sometime in the foreseeable future, Vietnam may indeed find itself fighting to keep the quasimonopolistic position it has held in the past for cassia of the type it produces. Mainland China produces it also.

In summary, Vietnam probably can look forward to a potential world market for cinnamon exports of about $3 to $7 million per annum by 1980 if and only if the following conditions are met:

1. Exports are resumed to traditional markets (mainly the U.S.) at a very early date.

2. Prices f.o.b. Saigon are kept to between $1.50 and $2 per kilogram.

3. Supplies are made continuous and reliable.

4. U.S. restrictions against trade with Mainland China are continued long enough to allow Vietnam to regain a foothold in the U.S. market before facing competition from similar product varieties from Mainland China.

The overriding requirement is the quick resumption of exports, for, as the months go by, Vietnam is losing its traditional market leverage to more reliable (and probably cheaper) substitutes. It cannot count much longer on consumer loyalty in the U.S. market, the only market where it has any real leverage to begin with. If it loses the United States, it will become just another cinnamon producer in a world market that does not hold its product in high regard and has no trouble finding its supplies elsewhere.

FRUITS AND VEGETABLES

The consumption of fruits and vegetables, particularly in the Asian areas, is increasing considerably. This expansion in foreign markets, together with Vietnam's capacity to produce fruits and vegetables, offers a promising opportunity for Vietnam's entry into the trade. Markets in countries within Vietnam's area are growing for both fresh and processed items. However, whereas exporting fresh produce is a more immediate possibility, a food processing industry in Vietnam, capable of supporting an export trade, is a development for the more distant future.

Table 56 presents data on import trends for a number of countries that would be potential importers of Vietnam's produce. For the selection of countries shown in Table 56, the value of imports of fresh fruits and vegetables ranged from $235 million in 1964 to $340 million in 1965. This represents a substantial percentage increase as well-- from 11 to 16 percent (average) per annum.

Import developments for Japan are especially significant. The import level is at $200 million per annum and is increasing on the average at 15 percent per annum. In spite of increased domestic production of fruits and vegetables in Japan, import trends of the recent years point to a substantial market for the future, which could readily be served by nearby Vietnam.

Contrary to the Japanese plans for self-sufficiency (which may not be realized), their imports of fresh vegetables have also been

TABLE 56

Fresh Fruit and Vegetable Imports, Asia and Australia,
1964-67
(In Millions of Dollars)

Country	1964	1965	1966	1967	Average Annual Percentage Increase
Japan	$125	$148	$161	$194	15
Hong Kong	50	66	67	72	14
Philippines	6	8	10	8	11
Singapore	50	55	61	66	11
Australia	15	18	19	20	16

Source: Developed from data presented in UN, Yearbook of
Trade Statistics (1967).

increasing rapidly--at about 15 percent per annum. Specifically,
fresh vegetable imports increased from $69 million in 1964 to $104
million in 1967. Included in these figures are nuts, which, although
they represent only a small fraction of the import total, are increasing
at about the same rate as the total, i.e., 15 percent per annum.

In Vietnam, production of vegetables in general has increased
by 50 percent since 1963; the production level in 1967 reached 192,000
metric tons and has since exceeded 200,000 tons,[5] although all regions
of Vietnam have experienced considerable expansion in vegetable
production.

Approximately one-third of the 1967 production was in Tuyen
Duc Province. Included in this province of the Central Highlands is
the Dalat Plateau, which is particularly well-suited to vegetable production and, in fact, the yield per hectare in this region averages
twice that of the balance of the country. There is the very likely
prospect of increased production in the Dalat Plateau, because large
areas suitable for growing vegetables are now lying fallow, due to the
unsettled conditions. Most of the Dalat-produced vegetables can be
exported, because their quality meets international standards.[6]

Projections of the consumption of fruits and vegetables have been made by the FAO.[7] These projections have been developed as ranges, with the high point based on higher income and population growth assumptions and the low point based on lower income and population growth. For South Asia, the consumption of vegetables between 1965 and 1975 is projected to increase by 36 percent at the lower point and up to 47 percent at the higher point in the range. Projections for increases in the consumption of fruits are somewhat higher: by 1975, assuming higher levels of income and population, up to 37 percent. Vegetable consumption in South Asia is estimated to grow slightly more, at about 4 to 5 percent per annum, and fruit consumption, 4 to 6 percent per annum. FAO projections of the growth in vegetable consumption in Japan are lower--2 to 4 percent per annum, but fruit consumption growth projections are the same as for South Asia.

Except for vegetables in Japan, the increase estimated in the future consumption of fruits and vegetables in Asia is substantial. Although growth of 4 to 6 percent per annum, as shown in FAO data, is substantial, it falls far below the increases in imports now being seen in Asian countries. Table 56 shows annual increases in the recent past, averaging from 11 to 16 percent. This means that trade in fruits and vegetables is growing at a rate that is almost three times that of consumption. Assuming the relationship between consumption and trade to remain constant, by 1975, imports in the countries shown in Table 56 will reach approximately $900 million, an increase of $540 million over 1967. Increases in markets amounting to $540 million would permit sufficient opportunity for Vietnam to enter the trade. The remaining questions concern quality and cost. This estimated increase in imports only applies to the countries that are reasonably close to Vietnam for trading purposes and, further, only applies to fresh fruits and vegetables. Some quantities of processed and canned items could possibly be exported, perhaps even to the United States.

Some estimates have been prepared of export availabilities for certain products produced in the Mekong Delta. These include manioc, mungo beans, certain vegetables, and bananas. As mentioned previously, the prospects for expansion are best in Tuyen Duc and neighboring provinces in the highlands. The physical conditions are extremely favorable; in order to serve a rapidly growing market by the U.S. and other military forces, production of quality vegetables has risen rapidly. Production can be expanded at least two to three times the present levels without great difficulty. In addition to standard products, such as green beans, onions, carrots, tomatoes, cabbage, and other leafy vegetables, the area can concentrate production especially on the high-value products that are in greatest demand in export trade. These products include asparagus, artichokes, peppers, strawberries, and melons. Since most of these products can be grown and marketed at off-season times for markets such as Japan, premium prices can be commanded. It is estimated that the total of fruits and vegetables (primarily fresh but some in dried, frozen, or processed form) could easily reach $15 to $20 million annually. The major markets would be Japan, Hong Kong, and Singapore, where rising incomes, land shortages, and luxury market demand all combine to offer attractive possibilities.

JUTE AND KENAF

Trends in the use of jute and hemp since World War II have varied widely from region to region, country to country, and at different periods of time. For a number of years in the early postwar period, world consumption expanded at a relatively high rate (5 percent per annum); but, by the mid-1960's, the increases moderated considerably. This tapering off in consumption increases is primarily the result of the inroads being made by substitute materials. For example, there has been considerable substitution of jute sacks by multiwall paper sacks. New uses for jute, however, have also been found. Consumption has increased considerably for a variety of more specialized packaging uses and, particularly, for backing material for tufted carpeting.

In addition to substitutes, differences in consumption among countries depend upon the extent to which bulk handling of commodities is practiced. The extensive bulk handling of commodities in the United States, as well as in the developed countries of northern Europe, has, to a considerable extent, been responsible for decreases in the use of bagging for commodity packaging. The demand for jute goods has been rising more rapidly in the developing countries than in the developed countries. For the Asian countries, internal consumption rose by about 50 percent between the mid-1950's and the mid-1960's. This increasing consumption of jute, however, largely reflects developments in India, where consumption in this period increased approximately 250 percent. Thailand and Burma, both of which have newly established jute textile industries, also have shown large increases in the consumption of jute. The greater increases in jute consumption are appearing in the developing countries that also manufacture jute products. According to projections made by the FAO, world consumption is estimated to increase 5 to 30 percent by 1975. The FAO projections were made on the basis of the 1961-63 price levels, but the price has risen since the early 1960's. However, the quantitative projection should not be significantly affected, considering the general upward movement of prices over that time. The FAO projections indicate that world consumption will increase until 1975, with demand more likely to continue rising in the developing countries. Of the total, the share of the low-income countries is projected to increase from 50 percent in the 1961-63 period to 60 to 63 percent by 1975. The FAO projections for jute are shown in Table 57.

TABLE 57

Jute: Estimated World Consumption and Demand,
1961-63 Average, 1966 Preliminary, and Projections for 1975

(a)

(In Thousands of Tons)

Regions and Countries	1961-63	1966	1975
Developed Countries	1,325	1,390	1,080-1,450
U.S.S.R. and Eastern Europe	190	310	300-400
Developing Countries of Asia	623	744	990-1,200
Asian Centrally Planned Countries	368	545	700-800
Other Developing Countries	509	546	640-770
World:	3,015	3,535	3,710-4,620
of which Developing:	1,132	1,290	1,630-1,970
of which Asia	991	1,289	1,690-2,000

(b)

In Percentages

Regions and Countries	1961-63	1966	1975
Developed Countries	44.0	39.0	29-31
U.S.S.R. and Eastern Europe	6.0	9.0	8-9
Developing Countries of Asia	21.0	21.0	27-26
Asian Centrally Planned Countries	12.0	15.5	19-17
Other Developing Countries	17.0	15.5	17
World:	100.0	100.0	100
of which Developing:	37.5	36.5	44-43
of which Asia	33.0	36.5	46-43

Source: FAO, Agricultural Commodities--Projections for
1975 and 1985 (1967).

As can be seen from the wide range in the projections for 1975, uncertainty marks the future of jute in the developed countries. It is in the developed countries that substitutes are making their greatest impact. Paper and plastic sacks are being used increasingly as substitutes for jute ones. Also, polypropylene backing may take larger shares of the market for floor coverings. Further, in the developed countries, to a larger and larger extent, handling of materials is being done in bulk form.

It is difficult to estimate the extent to which increased consumption in the developing countries will result in an increased trade in jute, kenaf, and other such fibres. Many developing countries are encouraging the cultivation of jute, kenaf, and similar fibers. This encouragement has as its objectives: (a) to diversify agricultural production by introducing an additional cash crop with a ready market, (b) to provide a basis for developing a processing industry, and (c) to save import expenditures on packaging materials.

Estimates of production also have been developed by the FAO and appear in Table 58. These projections were made on the basis of development plans and past trends in production. Plans of the Southeast Asian countries for their own production of fibers do not offer much promise for Vietnam as an exporter of jute and kenaf. Some countries, for example, Thailand, already have substantial production and some exportable surplus. By 1975, the combined production of Burma and Taiwan could reach 100,000 tons.

Jute and kenaf are currently being produced in Vietnam, but in limited quantities. The peak production year was in 1962, when about 5,000 tons were raised. Table 59 presents past production figures.

There never has been a significant export trade in these fibers from Vietnam. The domestic market could no doubt take most, if not all, of future increases in production. Placing more emphasis on future expansion possibly could make some quantities available for export. The range of possibilities would be quite limited, however. Recent prices have been relatively stable, primarily as a result of agreements among suppliers. For Vietnam, the upper limit for export possibilities in the 1970's is considered to be 5,000 tons, ranging down to 2,000 tons. At $300 per ton (approximation for Export Firsts, c.i.f. Dundee), the range of export earnings would be from $600,000 to $1.5 million.

SCRAP METALS

Accumulations of ferrous and nonferrous scrap in Vietnam can provide an additional source of future export earnings. As a result of

TABLE 58

Jute, Kenaf, and Allied Fiber Production, 1961-63 Average,
1966 Preliminary, and Projections for 1975
(In Thousands of Tons)

Regions and Countries	1961-63	1966	1975
India	1,387	1,150	1,450-1,980
Pakistan	1,197	1,150	1,200-1,450
Thailand	237	600	600-850
Other Asia	73	102	120-150
Total Asia	2,894	3,002	3,370-4,430
Brazil	59	80	100-130
Other Latin America	11	20	25-40
Africa	17	22	30-40
Near East	7	6	15-25
Total Other Developed Countries	94	128	170-235
U.S.S.R.	60	60	70-85
Asian Centrally Planned Countries	328	475	540-600
Total Centrally Planned Countries	388	535	610-685
World Total	3,376	3,665	4,150-5,350

Source: FAO, Agricultural Commodities, Projections for 1975
and 1985 (1967).

TABLE 59

Jute and Kenaf Production in Vietnam, 1957-66
(In Metric Tons)

Commodity	1957	1958	1959	1960	1961	1962	1963	1964	1965	1966
Jute	655	1,330	1,903	2,441	1,460	2,035	1,338	890	865	790
Kenaf	-	-	1,594	2,724	7,800	3,245	3,600	740		615

Source: Vietnam Statiscal Yearbook (1966-67), Vol. XIII.

the war, there have been huge accumulations of scrap metals, though no one has an accurate measure of what may be available. A Japanese scrap metal export who sought contracts for the delivery of scrap metal visited Vietnam in late 1969 and reported: "Mountains of scrap do exist in South Vietnam, but not any regular scrap business. Eventually that country will try to ship all its scrap and earn money for importing essential products. But my recent visits were premature."[8]

There is a substantial and growing international demand for scrap iron and steel to be used in the production of finished steel. Japan is a heavy importer of scrap and has been expanding the quantities being imported. The United States, a major exporter of scrap iron and steel, is currently Japan's chief supplier, as is shown in these figures on shipments of U.S. scrap iron and steel to Japan (in millions of short tons):[9]

Year	Quantity
1966	3.1
1967	5.3
1968	7.5

These increases in scrap imports are the result of increases in Japanese steel production. Japan is the major steel producer in Asia and is expanding its production rapidly, based primarily on Australian ore. The availability of iron and steel scrap in Japan itself falls far short of meeting the requirements of the steel industry.

Steel production for the years 1962-66 is shown in Table 60 for various Asian steel-producing countries. The average annual increase in steel production from these countries over the 1962-66 time period has been 12.7 percent, whereas increases in steel production worldwide have been considerably less, averaging about 7 percent per annum over the same period of time. Japan, alone, increased its production 73 percent in the four years shown and has continued to expand rapidly since.

Steel consumption in the Asian countries is increasing at approximately the same rate as production, but the absolute volume is lower than production, with the difference being made up with substantial steel shipments from Japan. Table 61 presents data on steel consumption for a number of Asian countries. Consumption has been increasing about 13 percent per annum.

TABLE 60

Crude Steel Production in Asian Countries, 1962-66
(In Thousands of Metric Tons)

Country	1962	1963	1964	1965	1966
China (Taiwan)	182	215	236	260	326
India	5,149	5,970	6,032	6,316	6,606
Japan	27,546	31,501	39,799	41,161	47,784
Korea, Republic	149	160	129	192	216
Thailand	7	3	4	6	6
Total	33,033	37,849	46,200	48,935	54,938
Percent included from Prior Year	-	14.6	22.1	5.9	12.3

Source: UN, Statistical Yearbook (1967).

Increases in both production and consumption of steel in Asia, therefore, indicate that conditions are favorable for exports of scrap from Vietnam in the area. There are certain technical and price developments, however, that cast some doubt on the long-run prospects for scrap. These developments are as follows: (a) increases in efficiency in steel-making and the increased use of basic oxygen furnaces are decreasing the specific consumption of scrap in steel-making; (b) methods for improving the quality of scrap are increasingly being employed; such methods often require heavy investments in processing and handling equipment, which would be difficult to justify for Vietnam; and (c) the price of scrap has been dropping over the past decade.

Prospects for iron and steel scrap exports from Vietnam should be viewed primarily in he short or intermediate run, while the supplies generated by the war can be exploited. The United States is the largest generator of iron and steel scrap, and world prices and trade conditions depend, to a large extent, upon the scrap situation in the United States. With existing accumulations stemming from the war, Vietnam should be able to supply from 50,000 to 100,000 tons of scrap annually. This

TABLE 61

Steel Consumption in Asian Countries, 1962-66
(In Thousands of Metric Tons)

Country	1962	1963	1964	1965	1966
Ceylon	194	95	77	81	90
China (Taiwan)	330	397	483	626	798
Indonesia	246	232	196	320	123
Japan	22,945	24,726	31,417	28,841	36,449
Malaysia	273	249	334	367	334
Thailand	307	365	397	452	806
Total	24,295	26,064	32,904	30,697	38,600

Source: UN, Statistical Yearbook, 1967 (1967).

would represent from $1.5 to $3 million in export earnings annually.
Such an amount of scrap could easily be taken up by Japan, which,
in 1967, imported about $300 million in scrap. After a period of time,
when war sources are exhausted, the supply of scrap will decrease
rapidly.

OTHER COMMODITIES

In addition to the products discussed in previous sections, there
are a number of other minor commodities that should be able to
supplement Vietnam's foreign exchange earnings in the postwar period.
While their total potential is a relatively small portion of total expected
earnings, they might, in time, develop greater potential. Projections
for these commodities in 1980 are contained in Table 62.

These estimates are based on an evaluation of known levels of
production, past capacity to expand production, and the judgments of
producers and other persons who are familiar with markets for these
products. For some of these products, such as duck feathers and
white silica sand, we had the opinions of people who had been engaged

TABLE 62

Minor Export Commodities: Estimated Export Earnings in 1980

Commodity	Previous Peak Exports (In Metric Tons)	Potential Export Supplies in 1980 (In Metric Tons)	Potential Earnings in 1980 (In Millions of Dollars)
Duck Feathers	1,070	4,500	$ 6.6
Beer	4,750	9,500	1.8
Duck Eggs	1,870	4,000	1.8
White Silica Sand	199,000	500,000	2.0
Peanuts	6,020	15,000	2.0
Coffee	660	5,000	2.5
Salt	83,640	165,000	1.0
Pepper	40	500	4.0
Live Buffalo	1,400	5,000	0.5
Cut Flowers and Plants	-	-	0.5
Kapok	750	2,500	0.3
Dry Bones	3,400	7,500	0.2
Sesame	450	2,000	0.2
Roots	1,700	5,000	0.1
Dry Beans	340	2,000	0.1
Medicinal Plants	400	1,000	0.3
Total			$23.9

in the trade or we had evidence of past plans for expansion. The silica sand, for example, is very high quality and is used in optical glass. Plans for expanded exports to Japan were cut off because of the construction of a military base that made access to the deposit very difficult. In some cases, particularly at the lower end of the table, it is difficult, and, perhaps, not very useful, to make any detailed appraisal of export prospects. Here the estimates for 1980 are based on judgment and the peak export volume that has been achieved in the past. For each of the commodities in the table, the maximum previous export price has been used to place values on potential export volumes, although for commodities such as peanuts, coffee, and pepper, unit export values were available. The dollar estimates probably tend to indicate the maximum earnings that might be expected.

For purposes of forecasting potential export earnings in 1980, a range of $20 to $25 million for these minor exports would seem to be appropriate.

NOTES

1. FAO, Spice Trends in World Markets (1962).

2. R. N. Pigossi, Internal Memorandum, Development and Resources Corporation (October 4, 1968).

3. USDA, Foreign Agricultural Circular, FTEAI-69 (April, 1969).

4. The New York Times, August 9, 1969.

5. Government of Vietnam, Agricultural Statistics Yearbook (1967).

6. Future prospects for increasing production in this area of Vietnam are discussed in the Joint Development Group, Vegetable Production Problems in the Dalat, Tuyen Duc Areas of South Vietnam, Working Paper No. 27 (September, 1967).

7. FAO, Agricultural Commodities--Projections for 1975 and 1985 (1967), Vol. II.

8. Reported in American Metal Market (April 14, 1969), p. 7.

9. Institute of Scrap Iron and Steel, Yearbook 1968 (1968).

10

PRESENT PROSPECTS
AND
SOME FUTURE POSSIBILITIES

In this chapter, the export prospects for the commodities that have been previously discussed will be summarized, and some possibilities for the future, which, at present, are too speculative to allow for reasonable judgments to be made about their contribution to export earnings, will be introduced. These possibilities cannot be overlooked, however, since several of them could easily dwarf the contributions of existing commodities. Chief among these is the possibility of the discovery of petroleum deposits in the Gulf of Siam, but one invisible trade item is, also, of importance.

The picture that emerges from the preceding pages is that the world demand outlook for potential Vietnamese exports in the 1970's is rather favorable. Expectations vary, of course, from commodity to commodity, but, on the whole, there is considerable room for optimism. In Table 63, the outlook is summarized by commodity, in terms of the general prospects that are foreseen for expanding past exports, the range of export volumes that might be achieved by Vietnam in 1980, and the approximate levels of foreign exchange that would be earned at such levels of demand.

As stated above, however, these are figures that reflect potential levels of demand; they do not necessarily translate directly into forecasts of actual exports to be expected in 1980. Actual export performance will be determined in large part by the following: (a) the degree to which supplies can be made available in sufficient quantities and at adequate levels of price and quality to meet projected levels of demand, and (b) successful development of institutions and national programs for export promotion and support.

The export promotion problem is addressed in detail in later

TABLE 63

Summary of Vietnam's
Export Prospects in 1980

Product	Prospects for Export Expansion	Potential Market Demand (In Thousands of Metric Tons)	Estimated Range of Potential Export Earnings (In Millions of Dollars)
Rice	Good	500-700	$ 72-$100
Natural Rubber	Excellent	100-150	44- 62
Wood and Wood Products	Excellent	(Variable by product Type)a	65- 126
Fish	Excellent	55-70	66- 84
Feed Grains	Good	400-550 b / 100-150 c	25- 33
Vegetable Oils and Oil Cake	Fair	18-24 d / 20-30 e	6- 9
Tea	Poor	2-3	2
Cinnamon	Good	2-5	3- 7
Fruits and Vegetables	Good	-	15- 20
Jute and Kenaf	Poor	2-5	1- 2
Scrap Iron and Steel	Good f	50-100	2- 3
Other Commodities	Variablea		20- 25
Total			$321-$473

aSee text.
bCorn.
cSorghum.
dOils.
eCake.
fFigures shown are probably more applicable to the 1970-75 period, for prospects will diminish as wartime stocks of scrap are depleted.

164

chapters. The question of supplies has several facets. The feasible
level of rice exports, for example, will depend in large measure on
the implementation of irrigation and land development schemes in the
Mekong Delta and the degree to which they prove successful in raising
rice yields and expanding production above domestic requirements.
Earnings from exports of wood and wood products will depend on levels
of investment in pulp production and plywood manufacturing facilities.
The enormous potential for fishery exports will only be achieved after
high levels of investment in fishing fleets, shellfish farming operations,
and cold storage facilities. Cinnamon prospects will depend on the
early resumption of supplies from presently insecure producing areas
to traditional North American markets, which rapidly are changing to
other suppliers and synthetics.

These are but a few examples, and many will prove difficult.
The levels of investment that can be obtained for export industries
will be determined largely by the following: (a) the success of national
development plans and policies in attracting private investment and
other sources of capital, and (b) the degree to which national priorities
for reconstruction and development can be structured so as to channel
sufficient amounts into the sectors of Vietnam's economy that are
best able to support economic self-sufficiency over the long run. A
reasonable exchange rate policy, combined with realistic tariffs that
encourage efficient domestic production of inputs to the export sectors
will be necessary if Vietnam is to compete with other exporting countries and match them in price and quality.

Thus, the path to success in the field of exports will be arduous,
but the rewards to be gained promise to be considerable. In the book
The Postwar Development of the Republic of Vietnam: Policies and
Programs, * it was estimated that a prerequisite for achieving economic
self-sufficiency in the first decade following the war would be export
earnings of about $400 to $500 million. As Table 63 indicates, the
potential earnings that could be achieved in 1980 range from $321 to
$473 million. The upper figure falls within the target range that was
set by the earlier study; so there is, indeed, a very real opportunity
for the target to be met. The markets do exist, and the challenge to
Vietnam's policy-makers in the decade ahead lies in the selection of
priorities and programs that will allow Vietnam to serve them to the
maximum possible extent.

---

*(New York: Frederick A. Praeger, Inc., 1970)

FUTURE POSSIBILITIES

The foregoing analysis has dealt with trade in commodities that have been exported before or that represent processed forms of previous raw material exports. The problems in these commodities is mainly one of reestablishing markets, stimulating an effective supply, and expanding from a low base level. While these are difficult problems, they are familiar ones, and Vietnam can profit from the experience of other successes, notably Korea. There are other possibilities of export earnings in activities or commodities whose future is more speculative. Four of these will be considered briefly: petroleum, other raw materials, manufactured products, and tourism.

There has recently been considerable interest in the possibilities for discovery of petroleum deposits in the Gulf of Siam. The area of interest extends in an arc from Vietnam, along the coasts of Cambodia and Malaysia. One would have to have current information on the geophysical and other analyses that have been made in order to give a rough probability of discovery, and, even so, the majority of the uncertainties would remain. But the physical structure of the area appears promising, and, of perhaps greater significance, some discussions and preliminary negotiations have been started concerning areas for concessions. A statute covering the petroleum industry has recently been enacted to encourage private investment. Additional ones may be needed on specifics of concessions and exploration. If experience in other countries is any guide, it is not unreasonable to expect that, within the next few years, exploration and preliminary drilling in the offshore waters of the Gulf will occur. Obviously, such a program will take time, but even a modest commercial discovery could dramatically change the export picture in Vietnam. The value of such a discovery is measurable, at the very least, in the tens of millions of dollars. Anything less would be commercially uninteresting. It is fruitless to speculate further since so little is now known, but this study would be incomplete without noting this possibility.

In the future, Vietnam may have export opportunities in other raw materials, principally metallic and nonmetallic minerals. The geological information on the country is fragmentary and anecdotal. What information is available has not been correlated nor has it been analyzed in order to draw inferences about possible areas for further work. The general geological structure and age appears favorable for the existence of a range of minerals. Kaolins and clays represent one product family that may exist in deposits; nonferrous metals are another possibility. Until systematic geological exploration, mapping, and analysis are undertaken, particularly in the highlands, the potential mineral resources of the country cannot be assessed.

Prospects for the export of any range of manufactured products are unfavorable. The textile industry, as presently constituted, is incapable of supplying the domestic market efficiently. Most metals and machinery industries are rudimentary. The best prospects may be in pharmaceuticals, which have grown rapidly during recent years. If the piaster is suitably adjusted to other currencies and price levels and if efficiency-wage costs can be kept low-relative to other neighboring countries, Vietnam may be able to emulate the experience of South Korea and engage in subcontracting, which is the practice of importing a raw or semifinished product, processing it one stage further, and reexporting for final fabrication. Japanese industry has entered such arrangements because of rising wage costs in Japan. Overall, however, in the next ten years, Vietnam will do well to build up light industry that can efficiently replace imports. It can meet its need for export earnings in other ways than the export of manufactured goods.

Finally, there are very real possibilities in tourism. In spite of the war, there has been a small trickle of tourists--the curious and the adventuresome. Vietnam has a number of physical attractions that, in any other country, would provide a base for tourism. These include a number of beach areas, big game hunting, and cool highland areas, all within a relatively short distance from Saigon. On a very realistic basis, counting on the appetite of normal tourists, the attractions to businessmen, and those who may come for special reasons, the earnings from tourism could easily reach $20 million annually within a few years and might greatly exceed that. As in all other calculations, this assumes that Vietnam is open to the outside.

PART

II

**MARKETS
IN EAST ASIA**

GENERAL INFORMATION

The Crown Colony of Hong Kong was acquired by the United
Kingdom from China under three separate treaties: the island of
Victoria, Kowloon Peninsula, and Stone-Cutters Island, altogether
35.75 square miles, were ceded by treaties in 1842 and 1860; the New
Territories, that is the mainland area adjoining Kowloon and 235
adjacent islands, covering a land area of 365 square miles, were
obtained by lease in 1898 for a ninety-nine-year term. Consequently,
91 percent of the land area of Hong Kong is due to revert to Mainland
China in 1997, while the island of Victoria and the Kowloon Peninsula
are, theoretically, British in perpetuity.

These circumstances are relevant to any long-term projections
of trade with Hong Kong. More than half the Colony's population is
living in, and most of its industries are located in, areas due to be
returned to Mainland China in less than thirty years. The urban areas
of Hong Kong are dependent on the New Territories for water and
for a great part of their food supplies, and it is unlikely that Hong
Kong can maintain an independent existence once its hinterland reverts.
It is impossible to predict whether the lease will be permitted to run
its course and whether the Peking Government would honor treaties
entered into by discredited mandarin governments more than 100
years ago. There are no indications that an extension of the lease
could be negotiated.

The long-term implications for the Colony's economy are clear.
In the meantime, Hong Kong enjoys unprecedented prosperity. Exports
were up by 25 percent in 1968, and foreign capital investment continues
at a high level. The banking sector is establishing new records, with
deposits higher than ever before and loans and advances in excess

171

of pre-1967 levels. But as the lease of the New Territories draws nearer its close, foreign investment will inevitably diminish, land values will fall, and emigration will increase, particularly among the wealthier and better-educated members of the community. Unemployment will grow, industrial capacity will diminish, and the Colony's eagerness to import materials to supply its industries will diminish too.

In the shorter term, until 1980, and possibly until 1985, assuming no overt and hostile action by Peking, the economy should continue to grow, though almost certainly not at the phenomenal rates of recent years. This prediction may be falsified by events: if, for example, Mainland China's dependence on Hong Kong trade channels for foreign exchange earnings should decrease--possibly as a result of population redistribution and higher domestic wheat yields--there will be greater chances of earlier interference in Hong Kong's status. But, on balance, it appears that Hong Kong will present opportunities for trade for at least eleven and probably as much as sixteen years.

CHARACTERISTICS OF THE ECONOMY

Hong Kong is an industrial territory with an export-oriented economy. From the 1840's until 1950, it served mainly as a staging post and transshipment center between China and the rest of the world. This dominantly entrepôt role ended with the Korean War and the embargo on the supply of strategic goods to Mainland China; with an influx of people, capital, and industrial skills from Mainland China after 1949, Hong Kong turned to manufacturing for a living. Its government has steadily pursued a policy of free competition, generally refusing demands for protection and for retaliation against the restrictive practices of other countries. In accordance with traditions established in the days of the entrepôt trade, Hong Kong has no tariffs and few restrictions of other kinds on the entry of goods from any part of the world. Only five groups of imported commodities are subject to customs duty--alcoholic liquors, tobacco, hydrocarbon oils, table waters, and methyl alcohol, and excise duties are levied on the same products manufactured locally. Rates of duty are low: on liquor from $0.27 per gallon for domestic beer to $12.05 a gallon for spirits originating outside the Commonwealth. (A Commonwealth preference for beer and liquor is exercised by the imposition of duties ranging from 66 to 89 percent for non-Commonwealth produce.) Duty on tobacco is from $0.42 per pound for Chinese-prepared tobacco to $1.80 a pound on non-Commonwealth cigars. Preferential rates of duty are granted to unmanufactured tobacco of Malawi origin and to tobacco manufactures of Commonwealth origin. Duties on hydrocarbon oils vary from $0.30 a gallon to less than $0.17 a gallon.

The rate of duty on table waters and methyl alcohol are $0.08 and
$1.25, respectively.

Restrictions of other kinds concern the following: (a) rice,
which is imported under quota; (b) coffee, which, because of the United
Kingdom's participation in the International Coffee Agreement, is also
imported under quota, presently 1.6 million pounds a year, much of
it for reexport; (c) wheat, again because of an international agreement,
though, in practice, no quotas are imposed, since all wheat imports
are from subscribing countries; and (d) some licensing of strategic
imports and for exchange control purposes.

Hong Kong is, however, heavily dependent on Mainland China
for many imports, especially for foodstuffs other than rice (which is
on quota), and it is probably true that any country that produces for
export those commodities that form a substantial part of the trade
with Mainland China will not be able to secure a foothold in Hong Kong
against Chinese competition. Subsidization, price manipulation, and
control of the wholesale outlets for certain commodities by the Communist Chinese government are factors with which other trading
partners of Hong Kong will have to contend.

National income statistics are not compiled by the Hong Kong
Government. In 1965, unofficial sources estimated per capita income
at $305 per annum, and it must be appreciably higher now. Industrial
production statistics, except for certain textiles, are not available in
any detail.

The estimated population of the Colony at the end of 1968 was
3.971 million. Projections are complicated, first by the existence of
a war gap in the age structure (50 percent of the population are under
the age of twenty-one, making it inappropriate to use crude birth
rates for the projection of future fertility trends) and second, by
irregular migration. For present purposes, it will be sufficient to
assume that, by 1980, Hong Kong's population will be slightly over 5
million.

EXTERNAL TRADE

In 1968, Hong Kong's external trade increased in value by 20
percent over 1967, reaching a record figure of approximately $3,840
million. Imports were valued at $2,080 million, with foodstuffs,
valued at $412 million, constituting 20 percent of the total. Principal
food items imported were rice, other cereals, fruit and vegetables,
live animals, fish, meat, dairy products, and eggs. Imports of raw
and semimanufactured materials included textile yarn and fabrics,

raw cotton, and base metals. Mineral fuels were imported in large quantities; capital goods imported were mainly machinery and transport equipment.

Proximity, prices, speed of delivery, and traditional trade relationships determine the sources of imports. The last of these factors is of particular interest to Vietnam, with its large Cantonese and Fukien communities, who would be quick to reestablish family ties with Hong Kong traders. Until 1968, Mainland China was Hong Kong's principal supplier, but, in that year, Japan took the lead.

In 1968, five principal suppliers accounted for 67 percent of all imports into Hong Kong. In order of importance they were the following:

Japan, which accounted for 22 percent of all imports. Textile yarn and fabrics constituted over one-third of the supplies from Japanese sources, the rest consisting of a miscellany of manufactured articles, including electrical and other machinery, scientific equipment, photographic equipment, watches, plastic materials, paper and paperboard, and iron and steel.

Mainland China, which had 19 percent of the trade, including 49 percent of all the foodstuffs imported by Hong Kong and also supplied textile yarn and fabrics, made-up articles of clothing, live animals, fruit and vegetables, cereals, meat, fish, and dairy products, and, also, some paper, chinaware, and base metals.

The United States, which accounted for 14 percent of imports, consisting mostly of electrical and other machinery, textile fibers, nonmetallic mineral manufactures, tobacco, pharmaceutical products, and cereals.

The United Kingdom, which accounted for 9 percent of the import trade, supplied electrical and nonelectrical machinery, textile yarn and fabrics, nonmetallic mineral manufactures, and transportation equipment.

The Federal German Republic, which supplied nonelectrical machinery, dyes and other chemicals, textile yarn and fabrics, electrical machinery, and transportation equipment.

In Southeast Asia, Taiwan was Hong Kong's most important supplier, providing about the same value of imports as West Germany, and eight other Asian and Pacific countries supplied 11.6 percent of the import trade, to a combined value of over $250 million; in declining order of importance, these were Pakistan ($60 million), Australia ($52 million), Thailand ($45 million), Singapore ($44.5 million),

Indonesia ($16 million), South Korea ($14.25 million), India ($12 million), and Macau ($8 million).

The pattern of Hong Kong's import trade in the most recent year of record was as follows:[1]

1. Manufactured goods, classified chiefly by material, 32 percent
2. Food and live animals,   20 percent
3. Machinery and transport equipment,   13 percent
4. Miscellaneous manufactured articles,   11 percent
5. Inedible crude materials, except fuels,   10 percent
6. Chemicals,   8 percent
7. Others,   6 percent.

Vietnam's immediate interest is chiefly in the second and fifth categories, which can be broken down into these details (in millions of dollars): [2]

Food and Live Animals	$412
Cereals and cereal preparations	100.5
Fruits and vegetables	84.5
Live animals	59.0
Meat and meat preparations	42.0
Fish and fish preparations	42.0
Dairy products and eggs	37.0
Coffee, tea, cocoa and spices	16.3
Sugar and honey	15.0
Miscellaneous food preparations	12.6

Inedible Crude Materials, Except Fuels	$210
Textile fibers	140.0
Crude animal and vegetable materials	35.0
Wood, lumber, and cork	11.0
Oil seeds	7.0
Metalliferous ores and metal scrap	6.5
Crude rubber, including synthetic and re-claimed	4.5

Hong Kong's exports are dominated by products of the textile and garment manufacturing industries, which account for 48 percent of all exports by value, and by miscellaneous manufactured articles, which provide a further 22 percent. Other light industrial products make up most of the balance. Although these manufactures reach almost every country in the world, the direction of the export trade is influenced importantly by such factors as the preferences granted in the United

Kingdom and other Commonwealth markets and by the commercial policies and economic conditions affecting foreign markets. The United States was easily Hong Kong's best customer in 1968, taking 41 percent of all its exports; other good customers, listed in order of their importance, were the United Kingdom (16 percent), West Germany (6 percent), Canada, Australia, Japan, and Singapore each (3 percent), Sweden, and the Netherlands. Reexports still play a significant role, being valued in 1968 at $358 million. Japan is the most important reexport market, followed by Indonesia, Singapore, the United States, Taiwan, and the Philippines. Reexports consisted mostly of textile fabrics, diamonds, medicinal and pharmaceutical products, and crude and vegetable materials.

TRADE WITH VIETNAM

In the past, Vietnam has had a fluctuating but not insubstantial trade with Hong Kong. The balance of trade in the period 1958-67 has been in Vietnam's favor by some $12 million. These figures do not, of course, take into account offshore purchases by the U.S. Government in Hong Kong nor Hong Kong's lucrative earnings from services to Vietnam--based American personnel on leave in the colony. The details of Vietnamese exports to Hong Kong in the last two years of this period (when the balance of trade went against Vietnam) and the first half of 1968 are shown in Table 64.

In earlier years, however, Vietnam's principal export to Hong Kong was rice; in 1959 and 1960, for example, 46,416 and 52,435 metric tons, respectively, were exported. The trade in rice fell to 16,000 and 13,797 metric tons in 1961 and 1962 but rose to 50,265 again in 1963; since then, Vietnam has been unable to meet its own rice requirements. Other traditional exports to Hong Kong have included beer and duck eggs.

A comparison of these figures, derived from Vietnamese sources, with the comprehensive trade statistics compiled by Hong Kong reveals considerable discrepancies. Hong Kong employs a system of classification based on the Standard International Trade Classification, Revised (SITC), whereas Vietnam uses the Brussels Customs Tariff nomenclature. Hong Kong records show that, in 1967, Vietnam exported goods to the value of $350,000 to Hong Kong and received from it exports to the value of $9.71 million and reexports to the value of $11.74 million. In 1968, Vietnamese exports to Hong Kong fell to $290,000 while Vietnam's purchases from Hong Kong remained at about the previous levels ($10.47 million and $10.99 million, respectively).

A meticulously detailed list of imports from Vietnam is maintained, including customs declarations of items of a value of less than

TABLE 64

Vietnam's Trade with Hong Kong, 1966-68
(In Millions of Vietnam Dollars)

Commodity	1966	1967	1968[a]
Total	$13.6	$18.4	$5.3 [b]
Fish (Fresh, Chilled, or Frozen)	-	-	8.9 [b]
Crustaceans and Molluscs	7.8	5.4	-
Duck Feathers	0.4	3.5	3.9
Dried Beans	1.5	0.4	-
Edible Fruit	0.1	-	-
Tea	0.8	1.2	-
Cinnamon	-	3.2	1.0
Peanuts	0.4	-	-
Other Oilseeds	0.8	-	-
Pharmaceutical Plants	0.5	0.3	0.04
Preserved Fruit	0.3	-	0.2
Metal Scrap	0.4	-	-

[a]First half of 1968.
[b]There is an obvious error in these figures. They are repeated exactly as recorded in the Statistical Yearbook.

Source: Vietnam Statistical Yearbook (1967/68).

$83.30. Significant import items to Hong Kong from Vietnam in 1967 and 1968 were the following:

	1967	1968
Dairy products and eggs	$32,640	$ --
Fish and fish preparations	62,306	12,730
Fruit and vegetables	28,302	2,335
Coffee, tea, spices	47,138	13,750
Metalliferous ores and metal scrap	83,116	125,880
Crude animal and vegetable materials	40,551	80,361

In greater detail, these general classifications comprise the following commodities:

1. Preserved eggs in shell

2. Squid, beche de mer, marine fish, prawns, shrimps,

crustaceans and molluscs, either salted, dried, smoked, or otherwise prepared

3. Largely preserved or prepared fruit and vegetables (little or no fresh fruit and vegetables are exported, at least to this particular market.)

4. Mainly coffee and cinnamon

5. Iron and steel scrap only

6. Animal bones, tortoise shell, and duck feathers.

Other commodities listed, though the trade in them is presently insignificant, are silk, pigments, and tea.

EXPORT OPPORTUNITIES
FOR VIETNAM BY COMMODITY

Rice

Domestic production of rice amounts to less than 5 percent of consumption, so Hong Kong is almost entirely dependent on imports for its supply. Under the pressure of urbanization, the alienation of arable land to industrial use, and the diversification of cropping, particularly to higher-value crops, such as vegetables and cut flowers, both the acreage in rice and production have fallen substantially in the last ten years, and these trends seem certain to continue.

Hong Kong has established a Rice Control Scheme,[3] to ensure that adequate supplies of rice are available to the consumer at a cost commensurate with world selling prices. Under the scheme, the importing of rice is limited to thirty-eight registered quota holders, to whom 110 quota units, each averaging 800 metric tons, are issued in each quarter of the year. This basic quota may be adjusted every three months, upwards or downwards, by up to 20 percent, in response to market conditions at the time. Some 88,000 metric tons are imported quarterly and are disposed of by some forty wholesalers and between 2,400 and 3,000 retailers, who are not controlled in any way.

The aggregate minimum reserve stock that registered importers are required to keep is 44,000 tons, plus a working balance of 25,000 to 30,000 tons, to provide for rice in transit, minor interruptions in supply, and so on. Thus, at any one time, stocks will amount to 70,000 to 75,000 tons, about two and one-half month's supply at an average daily consumption of 1,000 tons.

Importers have their own established sources of supply. It is only the volume of rice imports that is controlled, and there is no discrimination as to source, with the single exception of Mainland China. A quota of not more than 30 percent of total imports is imposed upon imports from Mainland China, in order to reduce Hong Kong's dependence on a source of supply liable to interruption because of internal deficits and other causes.

Importers usually buy from their suppliers c.i.f. and terms of payment are mostly by letter of credit.

Under the provisions of the scheme, quota holders are not permitted to extend credit to wholesalers for more than thirty days. Wholesalers, on the other hand, often extend forty to fifty day's credit to their retail outlets, which, in turn, give credit to the consumer. It is estimated that some $8 million of rice business is being financed on credit at any one time. Regularity of supply is regarded by importers as more important than the terms of credit, because of their obligation to fulfill their quotas.

In the past, Hong Kong has obtained its rice supplies from other Southeast Asian countries, principally Thailand and Mainland China, but because of regional shortages, the United States has also become a substantial supplier. (See Table 65.)

A significant trend is toward the consumption of better-quality rice, that is, reasonably long-grained whole rice (maximum broken contents 15 percent). The average quality marketed is represented by Thai 100 percent third-grade whole (very similar in quality to American blue-bonnet). Rice from Mainland China is deemed to be the best quality and sells at a premium.

Per capita consumption has declined steadily between 1961 and 1966 but now appears to be leveling off, and there are indications that a new consumption platform of about 155 catties* a year (ninety-three to ninety-four kilograms) has been reached.

Relatively greater affluence permits a higher protein content in average diets, but other factors are the popularity of electric rice-cookers, which eliminate waste, and the convenience of substitutes, such as bread or processed noodles.

Rice is purchased in a multitude of types and varieties, but the

_____

*Measurements--100 catties equal 1 picul; 16.53 piculs equal 1 metric ton.

TABLE 65

Hong Kong: Rice Imports, by Source, 1959-67

Year	Thailand Thousands of Metric Tons	Thailand Percent	China (Mainland) Thousands of Metric Tons	China (Mainland) Percent	Vietnam Thousands of Metric Tons	Vietnam Percent	Cambodia Thousands of Metric Tons	Cambodia Percent	United States Thousands of Metric Tons	United States Percent	Others Thousands of Metric Tons	Others Percent
1959	161.2	48	57.1	17	45	13	39	12	-	-	34	10
1960	172	48	71	20	54	15	52	15	-	-	7	2
1961	185	53	83	24	19	5	43	12	-	-	18	6
1962	215	60	82	23	10	3	21	6	-	-	18	8
1963	185	49	93	25	50.8	14	29	8	-	-	10	4
1964	195	56	84	24	7	2	49	14	-	-	14	4
1965	199	58	88	26	-	-	53	15	-	-	4.5	1
1966	209	62	99	30	-	-	15	4.5	-	-	13	3.5
1967	219	53	82	21	-	-	36	9	45	11	14	6

Source: Hong Kong Trade Statistics (1968).

TABLE 66

Hong Kong: Rice Prices, 1963-68
(In Dollars per Metric Ton)

| Year | Prices c.i.f. Hong Kong | |
	Average Grade	Low Grade
1963	$150.88	$110.39
1964	141.67	98.67
1965	137.91	98.67
1966	162.66	126.04
1967	217.28	162.61
1968	231.05	181.17

Source: Daily Commodity Quotations (Hong Kong), derived from various issues.

prices of two grades--Thai 100 percent whole third-grade and Thai 100 percent broken A-1 supergrade--can be used as indicators for prices movements of average- and low-grade rice. (See Table 66.)

On several occasions within the last decade, Vietnam has been the third most important supplier of rice to Hong Kong, after Thailand and Mainland China, and, in one particular year, it contributed 15 percent of a market of 356,000 metric tons. Provided that quality, regularity of supply, and competitive prices can be assured, there would appear to be no reason why Vietnam should not recapture a comparable share of the future market.

On the assumption that per capita consumption will stay at about 155 catties per annum and that Hong Kong will have 5 million people by 1980, its consumption of rice will increase by that year from a present 310,000 metric tons (valued at $64.6 million at current prices) to 470,000 metric tons, worth $108 million at current prices for the better rice qualities, or at least $97 million, taking grade variations into account.

Imports from Mainland China will probably continue to provide 30 percent of supplies, as they do now; it seems unlikely that political pressure will be applied to increase the quota, for there are rice deficit areas in Mainland China, and a low value crop rice is not given as much export priority as other commodities designed to earn foreign exchange.

At 15 percent of the projected market (what, in fact, it has previously achieved), Vietnam could look forward to a trade of the order of 75,000 metric tons by 1980, worth $13.1 million at current prices. It might not be unduly optimistic to look forward to a 30 percent share, which would be worth $26 million. Bangkok is marginally further from Hong Kong than Saigon, and, other things being equal, Thai rice would incur higher freight charges.

Quality is important. An extract from the daily commodity quotations for June 9, 1969, gives the following spot ex go-down prices per picul for 100 percent whole white rice. (See Table 67). It is clear that Chinese rice is preferred and that this particular type is price inelastic. Cambodian rice, in spite of considerably lower prices, commands only a limited market. Thailand will be Vietnam's most serious competitor in the open rice markets of Hong Kong, and promotion policies must take this into account.

Wood and Wood Products

Hong Kong's imports of wood in 1968 and the sources from which these came are recorded under the appropriate categories of the SITC classification system.

In all, imports of timber, both logs and lumber, amount in value to $10.8 million. There is a good demand for the luxury timbers, teak and rosewood (traditionally used for Chinese furniture), largely supplied

TABLE 67

Hong Kong: Spot Prices for Rice Ex Go-Down,
June 9, 1969
(In Hong Kong Dollars per Picul)

Grade	Thailand	United States	Cambodia	Canton
Special	$87.50	-	$87.30	$96
First Grade	85.50	88	77.50	95
Second Grade	84.00	-	76.50	92.50
Third Grade	82.50	-	66.00	90

Source: Daily Commodity Quotations (Hong Kong), June 9, 1969.

by Sabah and Sarawak, although Indonesia, Burma, and Thailand share
to varying degrees a not insignificant part of the market. Utility hardwoods for construction are mainly red and white Seraya, also imported
from Sabah and Sarawak. In 1968, the market for hardwoods was worth
$9 million.

The much smaller market for soft woods is supplied principally
by Mainland China. China fir is durable, highly priced, and easily
worked, and is in demand, particularly for junk masts.

The principal uses for timber are for building construction,
furniture, and boat building. Consumption fell off in 1966/67, but is
now increasing. A feature of the trade is the deliberate importation
of relatively poor-quality logs, in order to give users a price advantage
on the finished product. Lack of quality is made up by the very high
degree of utilization that Hong Kong's sawmills achieve in converting
logs to lumber; there is practically no wastage.

Long-term demand trends for logs and lumber are unclear.
However, building construction activity should remain at a fairly high
level for the next fifteen years, and exports of finished timber products,
such as furniture, will certainly continue to grow. On the other hand,
the formerly significant demand for timber for pleasure boat construct-
tion is dwindling, as manufacturers turn to fiberglass. The needs of
the fishing fleet will continue to be substantial (there are now 6,687
vessels) but the fleet is slowly shrinking, as it becomes more specialized and efficient and modern, and the use of ferroconcrete for hull
construction will probably be introduced.

There is a surprisingly valuable market in charcoal, just over
$1 million, now dominated by Malaysia, but this presents no long-term
opportunities. There will always be a small demand for charcoal for
specialized industrial and cooking uses, but charcoal is rapidly being
replaced by superior fuels--electricity and butane gas, particularly--
for general domestic purposes.

Imports of wood pulp are negligible, a mere $600 worth in 1967
and 1968, and imports of veneers (about 200,000 square feet, worth
$12,000) are small, but there is a big demand for plywoods, and, in
1968, 92.7 million square feet, worth almost $6 million, were imported.

The principal suppliers are Taiwan, with more than half the
entire market, supplying four times as much by value as its nearest
competitor, Mainland China, followed by Singapore, the Philippines,
and Sabah. Grades and values vary considerably; and there are, in
all, a score of suppliers of small, specialized quantities, though 99
percent of all supplies come from neighboring Asian countries.

The conclusions are that there will continue to be a fairly constant demand for logs and lumber, particularly for luxury woods and hardwoods, and that there will be an expanding demand for plywoods and, also, for veneers. Mainland China has only a small share of the total market, mainly softwoods and 12 percent of plywood requirements, and it has no position of special advantage in this particular sector. Quality is not a prime consideration in the hardwood log and baulk market, and sources of plywoods and veneers, and of logs as well, are determined largely by considerations of price. Vietnam is unlikely to be able to supply the luxury woods (teak, rosewood, and sandalwood), but should find a ready market in Hong Kong for other hardwoods and for plywoods, if these can be supplied at c.i.f. prices, competitive with those obtaining for the products of Taiwan, Singapore, and Sabah. On the assumption that the demand for logs will remain fairly static but that there will be an annual growth of 5 percent in demand for plywoods, then, by 1980 and at current prices, the total market should be worth $21.6 million. If Vietnam can acquire 15 percent of this trade, its earnings from the export of wood and woodproducts to Hong Kong will, by then, amount to $3.25 million, possibly made up by 50,000 cubic meters of logs and baulks and 1.4 million square meters of plywood and veneers. It may be able to do rather better than this.

Rubber

There is no local production of rubber, but not inconsiderable quantities of both natural rubber and synthetic substitutes are imported for industrial uses, mostly for the manufacture of a miscellany of light articles, including shoes, sandals, sports equipment, and flashlight cases, and for tire retreading. In 1968, rubber imports consisted of 9,200 tons of natural rubber, worth $3.6 million, and 2,650 tons of synthetic rubber, worth a little over $1 million. Natural rubber is imported in four forms: smoked sheet (47 percent of total natural rubber imports in value), latex crepe (31 percent), rubber sole crepe (14 percent), and rubber latex (8 percent). The main sources of synthetics are the United States and Japan; and the main suppliers of natural rubber are Western Malaysia, Singapore, and Sabah, which account for 61 percent of this market. Small quantities of natural rubber are also purchased from Thailand, Ceylon, Sarawak, and the Philippines.

The figures of imports for a single year do not give a true picture of the distribution of consumption between synthetic and natural rubber. In fact, this is almost two-to-one in favor of synthetics, roughly what it is in the world as a whole. Although Hong Kong does not produce in any quantity the specialized high-quality and high-performance products (such as aircraft tires) for which natural rubber is preferred to synthetics, it is becoming an increasingly large producer and exporter of furniture and carpets, which require latex for upholstery and backing. However, this potential growth in demand for natural rubber is offset, to some extent, by the facility with which synthetics can be substituted for natural rubber or used together with it in many cheaper products, such as shoes. The rate of substitution appears to depend almost entirely on relative prices.

On balance, the rate of growth in demand for rubber will probably be small but steady. Provided Vietnam meets the high standards of preparation and quality control applied by its competitors and provided it can produce and sell at world prices, there is no reason why it should not edge its way into this market and share a little of the growth. A cautious estimate is indicated: possibly 10 to 15 percent of a 1980 market for 15,000 tons, or possibly about 1,500 to 2,000 tons, could be captured, which, at current prices, would be worth approximately $600,000 to $800,000.

Tea

In 1968, Hong Kong imported 11.066 million pounds of China tea, valued at slightly over $4 million and exported or reexported 3.369 million pounds. There is unlikely to be any place for Vietnam in this particular market. There should be better opportunities in the trade in other types of tea, of which Hong Kong imported 5.873 million pounds, valued at $1.815 million, reexporting very little of this. The other teas are used almost entirely for consumption in Hong Kong, some of them being blended with China teas. The principal suppliers are Ceylon (1.994 million pounds), Indonesia (1.742 million pounds), North Vietnam (1.049 million pounds), and Singapore (889,576 pounds).

The significant position held in this trade by North Vietnam, which produces black and green teas of similar taste and quality to those grown in South Vietnam, is noteworthy.

Domestic consumption of tea in Hong Kong is high, but the public preference is for China tea. It is unlikely that local demand will increase to any great extent, but the prospects of a small but reasonably lucrative market in Hong Kong are reasonably good. Vietnam is unlikely to make much impact on the market enjoyed by Ceylon, but it should certainly be able to acquire some of the trade now held by North Vietnam, and could probably do so almost immediately; the qualities and prices of Indonesian teas, which seem to gain a small but ready acceptance in Hong Kong, warrant investigation, in case Vietnam could intrude competitively upon this segment of the market, as well. Vietnam disposes of 1 million pounds of tea a year, worth

about $350,000 to Singapore, and might well achieve the same level
of exports to Hong Kong.

Livestock

Pigs

The Chinese like fresh meat, and those who live in Hong Kong
are no exception. Between 5,000 and 6,000 pigs are slaughtered daily
for local consumption, 85 percent supplied by Mainland China and 15
percent produced locally. Very little pork imported chilled or frozen
is consumed.

In 1968, 48 million pounds of pork, with a value of approximately
$11 million, were imported into Hong Kong. Of this quantity, Mainland
China provided 44.5 million pounds, the only other significant importer
being Denmark, with 3.5 million pounds, worth $752,800, the Danish
pork being consigned almost entirely to the luxury hotel and restaurant
trade.

In accordance with what appears to be deliberate economic policy,
Mainland China has recently increased its pork prices to a level at
which supplies from such countries as Taiwan and Indonesia might
well be attracted to compete, especially since Hong Kong has no livestock health restrictions. But without a guaranteed market (which
would be incompatible either with Hong Kong's trading principles or
its relations with Mainland China), it is unlikely that any competitor
with Mainland China would take the risk of competing with a country
that can readily manipulate prices to its advantage--and has not hesi-
tated to do so.

Without some unexpected changes in Mainland China's economic
policy, there will be no market for Vietnamese pork in Hong Kong.
There may, however, be a very small opportunity for pigbristle,
which Mainland China cannot supply in quantity, because it has so improved the quality of its pigs that they are now permanently clean-
shaven. This particular little market is now dominated by South Korea,
which sends some 15,000 pounds of bristle, worth $11,000, into Hong
Kong a year. The total value of such imports in 1968 was only $37,500,
but the demand for bristle may grow.

Cattle

Hong Kong slaughterhouses import nearly 200,000 head of live
cattle a year, worth $13 million. The Colony's own cattle population
in 1967/68, including buffalo, was only 17,000, either serving the

small dairy industry or being used as draft animals. There are no present plans to expand production. Mainland China supplies 60 percent of import requirements, or 110,000 head of cattle, mostly with animals of poor quality. Indonesia provides 40,000, also of inferior quality, and Thailand and Cambodia between them have what is left of the market--only 40,000 head, but worth about $6 million, almost half the value of total cattle imports.

Average prices per head are $116 and $114, respectively, for animals of Cambodian and Thai origin, as against $69 for Indonesian cattle and $39 for Chinese ones.*

As standards of living improve in Hong Kong, there is a steady trend towards a higher protein diet, and, of course, there is also a growing demand for good-quality beef from the hotel and restaurant trade. Unless Mainland China improves the quality of its beef, more and more of this increasing demand will be for Thai and Cambodian cattle. At a minimal compound growth rate of 5 percent, Hong Kong will require at least 268,000 head by 1975 and 340,000 by 1980. Much of this increasing demand, which will normally be directed at Thai and Cambodian sources of supply, could be diverted to Vietnam, if Vietnam can emulate the quality production achieved by its neighbors. Indeed, in these circumstances, Vietnam could obtain a share of the existing market. There are good opportunities for Vietnam to export at least 75,000 to 100,000 head of cattle a year to Hong Kong by 1980, if it can raise them. At current prices for Thai cattle, such a trade would be worth $8 to $11 million.

Poultry

Local production of chickens has increased considerably in recent years, the estimated chicken population rising from 2.121 million in 1964/65 to 3.257 million in 1967/68. Between 25 to 30 percent of consumption is now met by locally raised fowls.

Imports of live chickens in 1968 amounted to 19.500 million pounds, of which China supplied 19.468 million. The value of this trade was $4.322 million. For reasons already stated in this chapter, Mainland China's domination of this market is unlikely to be disturbed.

_____

*There could be a little distortion here, because trade figures do not differentiate between cows, oxen, and buffalo; buffalo are not imported in significant numbers, however, and the inferences as to quality are generally correct.

On the other hand, there has been a distinct trend toward consumption of frozen chicken, and the demand for this commodity now exceeds that for live poultry--28.2 million pounds of frozen chicken, worth $6.3 million, were imported in 1968. A little over 25 percent came from Mainland China, 50 percent from the United States, and the balance from several Western European countries. It is unlikely that Vietnam can compete for many years against such low-cost, efficient, large-scale production.

There is a large market for ducks; 27.5 million pounds of which, worth $5 million, were imported in 1968. Mainland China completely monopolizes the trade in live ducks, and it virtually monopolizes the demand for preserved or smoked ducks, as well.

The dominance of Mainland China is not quite as complete in the importation of fresh and preserved eggs, but it is still considerable: 390,000 gross of chicken and duck eggs are produced locally, but this represents only 8 percent of consumption. While Hong Kong has the capacity to increase local production, and is doing so, local production is unlikely to do much more than keep pace with population growth, and the percentage of its requirements met from domestic sources will probably remain the same. About 92 percent of its fresh eggs and 93 percent of its preserved eggs are imported from Mainland China. The only possibilities for trade here would appear to be in preserved duck eggs, of which, in 1968, North Vietnam sent 9,345 gross to Hong Kong, worth $35,000, but this is a very small and specialized trade, with a very limited potential for development.

Fish and Fish Products

Of all the marine fish consumed, 80 percent are produced locally; the balance, imported from Mainland China, largely represents landings by the Hong Kong fishing fleet in that country. There are no prospects for the export to Hong Kong of fresh, chilled, or frozen fish; but one demand not satisfied by domestic fisheries is for crustaceans and molluscs, since the inshore grounds have been taken out of production by Chinese restrictions on Hong Kong vessels. Shrimps are in particularly strong demand, 11 million pounds, worth $5 million, being imported in 1968. Of this, 55 percent came from Mainland China and the rest from a number of different sources, including Cambodia, Taiwan, Indonesia, and Thailand; 750,000 pounds of other crustaceans and molluscs, valued at $1.3 million, were imported from as far afield as Australia and South Africa. There is, also, a steady demand for salted, dried, or smoked marine products, as Table 68 demonstrates.

TABLE 68

Hong Kong: Imports of Salted, Dried, and Smoked Marine Products, 1968

Product	Quantity (In Hundredweight)	Value
Marine Fish	85,438	$ 1,945,340
Shrimps	33,400	1,588,800
Oysters	6,180	483,100
Abalone	1,964	1,153,700
Crustaceans and Molluscs	5,197	883,800
Sharksfin	36,998	3,611,100
Beche de Mer	23	482,000
Squid	52,862	2,010,000
	222,062	$12,157,840

Source: Hong Kong Trade Statistics (1968).

Mainland China supplies 63 percent of the volume of this market, mainly in dried and salted fish. The high-value abalone, oysters, and crustaceans are imported from other neighboring countries--particularly Japan in the case of abalone; North Vietnam appears in the trade statistics for salted and dried marine fish, for abalone, and for squid, although its share of the trade is very small. South Vietnam also appears as a supplier of preserved crustaceans and molluscs (in 1968, seventy-four hundredweight, worth $13,000).

Supplies of sharksfin, the most important import item in value, come from forty-seven different countries. Hong Kong will buy all the sharksfin Vietnam can possibly produce that is surplus to its own needs.

It is hazardous to forecast a possible Vietnamese share of this market without better statistics of local production. It is clear, however, that it is a seller's market and that the share Vietnam will get of it depends primarily on its capacity to produce surpluses of these commodities.

Live pond fish represent an even more lucrative market than preserved marine fish. Local production is small and limited by land shortage. In 1968, Hong Kong imported 598,000 hundredweight, valued at $15.55 million, 97 percent of which came from Mainland China. Cambodia, however, claimed a small but profitable share in this trade, valued at $275,000, by sending Hong Kong luxury fresh-water fish of species that Mainland China cannot supply. Demand for these is as yet unsatisfied.

A small sideline: Hong Kong happens to be one of the world's largest exporters of aquarium fish, some $2 million worth of which were sent by Hong Kong all over the world in 1968. The fry, imported mainly from Thailand and Singapore, were worth $100,000 in that year. This is a rapidly growing industry, in which the Chinese are particularly adept, and it presents another small opportunity for Vietnam.

Fruit and Vegetables

Vegetables

Hong Kong produces 40 to 50 percent of the vegetables it consumes from one-third of the available hectarage of irrigated land. The balance of its requirements comes from Mainland China, but if this source were to be denied or if prices of Chinese imports rose to the point at which local production would be advantageous, Hong Kong could readily double its own production. A wide variety of vegetables are produced and imported from Mainland China, and the only prospects for Vietnam would appear to lie in the market for a few luxury items, especially for the growing hotel and tourist industry. Hong Kong now has 8,000 double first-class hotel bedrooms, with more under construction. It has a regular hotel occupation rate well in excess of 10,000. There is also a substantial canning industry for export.

Vegetables in this category include artichokes, asparagus (although Taiwan is reported as overproducing this commodity), lettuce (which is imported by air from the United States and Japan at over $1 a head for this special market), and mushrooms (Taiwan is a seasonal producer). In the luxury trade, there is consumer resistance to many locally produced vegetables, since, in most places, they are grown on nightsoil. The selected statistics in Table 69 display the range of other possibilities.

Vegetable Oils

In order of importance, the vegetable oils that Hong Kong imports and Vietnam is probably capable of producing are soybean, cotton-seed, peanut, rapeseed, copra, tung, and sesamum. Mainland China

TABLE 69

Hong Kong: Selected Vegetable Imports, 1968

Commodity	Origin	Value
Dried Beans	China (Mainland)	$1,217,000
	Thailand	848,000
	Others	135,000
	Total	$2,200,000
Fresh Tomatoes	China (Taiwan)	$ 297,000
	Japan	11,000
	China (Mainland)	90,000
	Total	$ 398,000
Fresh Ginger	China (Taiwan)	192,000
	Philippines	310,000
	China (Mainland)	53,000
	Singapore	37,000
	Others	22,000
	Total	$ 614,000
Temporarily Preserved Ginger	China (Taiwan)	$ 328,000
	Others (Philippines, Thailand, Singapore)	22,000
	Total	$ 350,000

Source: Derived from official Hong Kong trade statistics.

almost monopolizes the cottonseed, rapeseed, and tung oil markets, but the other vegetable oils present opportunities. Imports of peanut oil in 1968 were valued at $5.5 million, more than a half from Mainland China but, also, from South Africa, Japan, Indonesia, Singapore, and several other countries. Imports of soybean oil were valued at $1.7 million, almost entirely from the United States and Japan. In addition, Hong Kong bought $147,000 worth of coconut oil from Singapore and Sarawak and $282,000 worth of sesamum from Japan and Mainland China.

There is a market worth $14,400,000 in plants for perfumes and pharmaceuticals. Mainland China supplies 80 percent of this market, but profitable shares in it go also to Cambodia ($240,000),

Taiwan ($217,000), South Korea ($570,000), and Singapore ($600,000), and smaller shares to Burma, Laos, and Malaysia. Vietnam already has a minute part of this trade, worth $5,500 in 1968.

Fruit

Imports from Mainland China satisfy virtually all of Hong Kong's demand for lychees, stonefruit, pears, and fresh tropical fruits other than mangoes, pineapples, papaya, and oranges. The Philippines is easily Hong Kong's largest supplier of mangoes, and Taiwan supplies most of its pineapples. The largest demand is for oranges, of which $13.8 million worth were imported in 1968. Well over a half of the trade in oranges was taken by the United States, but Mainland China, South Africa, Australia, and Taiwan were also substantial suppliers, Taiwan's share amounting to $880,000.

The possibility of South Vietnam acquiring part of the Philippines' business in mangoes or Taiwan's business in pineapples, oranges, and papaya depends entirely on questions of quality and price and is worth exploring further. So is the trade in dried citrus fruit (of which North Vietnam has a present monopoly, worth $900,000), avocados, and fresh grapes. The latter market is worth, at present, $350,000 and is supplied entirely by the United States.

Silk

There is a small market for silk, which suggests that the encouragement of this traditional Vietnamese industry may be justified. The total value of imports in 1968 was $1.23 million, Mainland China supplying $913,000 worth and Japan, Thailand, South Korea, Cambodia, and Vietnam all sharing in the trade. In 1968, Vietnam sent to Hong Kong 10,000 pounds of unreelable cocoons and 2,420 pounds of raw silk, together to the value of $5,000. The current price for A-grade silk is $7.25 a pound.

The markets for jute, hemp, ramie, sisal, coir, and other vegetable textile fibers are negligible. The market in cinnamon is small, and Vietnam has better prospects for trade in this commodity elsewhere.

SUMMARY OF CONCLUSIONS

These are set out in Table 70. The principal opportunities for exports to Hong Kong are in rice and timber. Of the former commodity, it is possible that, by 1980, up to 150,000 metric tons might

TABLE 70

Export Possibilities, Vietnam to Hong Kong, 1980

Commodity	Volume	Estimated Value[a] (In Millions of Dollars)
Rice[b]	75,000 - 150,000	$13.1 - $26.2
Hardwood Logs[c]	50,000	2.25
Plywood and Veneers[d]	1,400,000	1.0
Rubber[b]	1,500 - 2,000	0.6 - 0.8
Tea[e]	1,000,000	0.35
Beef Cattle[f]	75,000 - 100,000	8.0 - 11.0
Molluscs and Crustaceans	-[g]	-[g]
Sharksfin	-[g]	-[g]
Live Freshwater Fish	-[g]	-[g]
Dried, Smoked, and Salted Fish	-[g]	-[g]
Preserved Duck Eggs	-[g]	-[g]
Vegetables (Artichokes, Asparagus, etc.)	-[g]	-[g]
Pharmaceutical Plants	-[g]	-[g]
Raw Silk	-[g]	-[g]
Fresh Fruits	-[g]	-[g]
Total		$25.3 - $41.6

[a]1968 prices, in $U.S. Millions.
[b]In millions of tons.
[c]In tons.
[d]In square meters.
[e]In pounds.
[f]By head.
[g]Not estimated: either small or dependent entirely on production capacity.

193

be sold, worth, at current prices, some $26 million; timber sales by
the same year may reach 50,000 cubic meters of logs and baulks and
1.4 million square meters of plywood and veneer, together worth $3.5
million. There should also be a small but steady growth in the consumption of natural rubber in Hong Kong, and, within the next decade,
there is no reason why Vietnam should not be able to sell between
1,500 and 2,000 tons a year--at current prices, approximately $600,000
to $800,000. The Hong Kong tea market should also by then be able
to take up to 1 million pounds of tea, worth $350,000. There is little
prospect of Vietnam being able to sell pigs to Hong Kong, but there is
a growing demand for beef cattle. If Vietnam succeeds in increasing
and improving its production so as to compete effectively with Thailand
and Cambodia, it may be able to claim a share in the growing market
for beef cattle. A share amounting to 75,000 to 100,000 head would be
worth $8 to $11 million at current prices. The poultry market is
dominated by Mainland China, but there may be a small specialized
market for preserved duck eggs. Although Hong Kong is almost self-
sufficient in its production of fresh marine fish, there is a steady unsatisfied demand for fresh crustaceans and molluscs, particularly
prawns and shrimps, and a fairly large market for dried, smoked, or
salted marine products. Provided Vietnam can produce a surplus of
these commodities, it should find a ready sale for them in Hong Kong.

There are few opportunities for exporting fresh vegetables to
Hong Kong, although a small, specialized, and profitable trade is possible in such vegetables as artichokes, asparagus, ginger, and, possibly,
mushrooms. There is some demand for vegetable oils and for plants
used in perfumes and pharmaceuticals. Taiwan and the Philippines
dominate the markets for mangoes and oranges, but there are chances
of expanding trade in other fresh fruits, such as pineapples and papaya,
and Vietnam could also expand its trade in raw silk with Hong Kong.

The balance of trade is presently strongly in Hong Kong's favor;
until and unless Vietnamese manufacturing industry can compete with
imports of manufactured goods, this favorable balance of trade for
Hong Kong will probably continue. In an open economy like Hong Kong's
there is no prospect of official negotiation of arrangements to control
the direction of trade. At this point, one can say simply that profitable
trade possibilities exist; whether Vietnam will fully exploit these
possibilities depends substantially on its ability to produce and its
competence to compete with other Southeast Asian countries in price,
quality, and regularity of supply.

NOTES

1. Hong Kong Trade Statistics (1968).

2. Ibid.

3. Report on the Operation of the Rice Control Scheme in 1967 (Hong Kong: Government Printer, 1968).

CHAPTER 12

GENERAL INFORMATION

With a population of 102 million compressed into an area of 370,000 square kilometers, only 16 percent of it cultivable, increasingly unable to supply its own requirements for most agricultural products, with rising per capita incomes, and, in recent years, considerable and growing foreign exchange reserves, Japan is unquestionably one of the most valuable markets in the world for the agricultural export commodities. Its buoyant economy grew by over 16 percent in 1968 and achieved a GNP exceeded only by that of the United States and the U.S.S.R. Its balance of payments is strongly favorable. There is no doubt that in the future, Japan will require, greater volumes of imported agricultural commodities than it does already.

Japan's total exports in 1968 expanded much more rapidly than total imports, a trend that continued into 1969. There are now visible favorable trade balances with numerous countries, and, under pressure to reduce these imbalances, Japan is pursuing a trade policy designed to diversify sources of supply of farm products and, thereby, to broaden the export markets for its manufactures. Associated with this policy is a desire to assist the economic growth of those developing countries that are potential sources of supply of the foods and fibers which Japan requires for the sustenance of its population and for the raw materials that it requires for its industries.

This is the origin of a major dilemma for Japan and its expansionary economic policies. In 1968, of total imports valued at $13 billion, more than a half came from the developed countries: the United States, Canada, Western Europe, Australia, New Zealand, and South Africa. The United States was Japan's biggest supplier, with food and raw materials worth $3.5 billion, or 26 percent of all imports

197

by value. The proportion of supplies taken from the developed countries is actually increasing and may be expected to continue to increase. The reason is clear: Japan necessarily buys in the most competitive markets, and it buys in great bulk. It buys what it needs, homogeneous commodities in large quantities, shipped with regular precision. Grain, for example, is now shipped to Japan from the United States and Canada by the tanker load; it is the cheapest way to do it. Unless, therefore, the developing countries can produce in sufficient and standardized quantities the materials Japan requires, offering Japan the economies resulting from efficient marketing and large-scale transportation (which few are able to do), they will not be able to compete with the large developed producers: when, in fact, they can do this, they cease to be developing countries.

The trend away from the smaller, less-sophisticated countries is reinforced by the fact that the high labor costs of Japanese manufacturing now threaten to price it out of many of its markets, emphasizing the need for low-cost raw materials. The British electronics industry, for example, finds it only marginally profitable nowadays to purchase Japanese components rather than domestic ones; when carriage, insurance, freight, and forward dollar cover are added to the price, it is really only the preshipment financing provided to the exporter at soft rates by the Japanese Export-Import Bank that keeps the product competitive.

Japan has one other major dilemma of particular concern to Vietnam, its price support policies for rice. This is discussed in the section of this chapter devoted to that commodity.

Japan takes a national census every five years and has comprehensive and accurate population data. The last census was in 1965, when total population was 98.282 million, and the most recent estimate was 101.362 million in 1967. Since World War II, there has been a significant shift to a "developed country" pattern of population growth, with, as a corollary, a marked tendency for households to decrease in numbers. Japan has the lowest annual average population growth rate of any country in the Far East and Southeast Asia, a little over 1.1 percent.

Over the period 1965-85, the population is estimated to increase by 18 million, to a total of 116.558 million; in this time, it is expected that the numbers of Japanese in the fifteen to twenty-nine age bracket will decrease by 430,000, those in the thirty to fifty-nine age bracket will increase by 11.280 million, and those over sixty will increase by 7.200 million (who will then constitute more than 14 percent of total population). This conspicious increase in the numbers of elderly and mostly economically inactive people may create difficult social and economic problems for Japan. This twenty-year period is also expected to display continuing and growing trends towards urbanization: by 1965, 68.1 percent of the Japanese people were already living in the cities and their suburbs; by 1975, 73.4 percent are expected to be doing so; and, by 1985, 78.2 percent.

CHARACTERISTICS OF THE ECONOMY

The economy is now remarkably buoyant. Foreign capital inflows are strong and rising, there is a very healthy balance in the external trade account, and continuing expansion is expected, though the long-term prospects obviously depend upon the conditions prevailing in the major markets to which Japan exports. High investment and aggressive modernization and rationalization in industry has resulted in increases in productivity that more than compensate for rising wages. Wages rose sharply in 1968, by about 12 percent, but productivity increased in the same year by 14 percent. Export earnings are more than enough to cover rising expenditures on imports, while the low prices of Japanese securities in relation to earnings have attracted record inflows of foreign capital.

In June, 1969, a record surplus of $280 million was realized on the total balance of payments account, owing to large foreign investment and a trade surplus of $350 million. In that month, gold and foreign exchange reserves stood at $2.748 million, an increase of $1.018 million in a year. In the early postwar years, balance of payment difficulties were a primary factor in restricting Japanese economic growth, and, in the early 1960's, the target growth rate for the economy was set at a comparatively low 7.2 percent per year to avoid excessive imports; in the 1970's, it begins to look as if this anxiety had been laid to rest, permitting Japan to aim at higher growth rates, to increase public investment, and, also, to increase economic aid to developing territories.

The Japanese Economic Research Center predicts an average growth rate of 11.5 percent per year between 1970 and 1975, leading by that year to a GNP of $418 billion, a per capita income of $3,776, and to exports valued at $41.1 billion. If such a growth rate is achieved, the GNP will then be greater than that of the entire EEC today, income per capita will be as high as it now is in Sweden, and exports, by value, will exceed current U.S. export values by a substantial margin.

These are formidable targets, and the predictions are possibly somewhat overoptimistic. Whether Japan can reconcile rapid economic growth with high public investment in the infrastructure and in social welfare, where it is most needed, remains to be seen. Some weaknesses are already apparent. Consumer prices rose 6 percent in 1968 and have risen even more rapidly in 1969; even wholesale prices, which have hitherto been a remarkably stable feature of the economy, are being affected. There is a growing shortage of skilled workers, resulting in regular, substantial wage increases: 12 percent in 1968, followed by further increases of 15 percent in 1969. There are signs of increasing industrial unrest, for Japanese workers are no longer satisfied that nonfinancial benefits and other inducements are acceptable substitutes for more pay. If labor costs continue to rise and if heavier government subsidies are nor forthcoming, the Japanese manufacturing industry could lose some of its ability to compete. The impact of the more liberal trading practices to which Japan is committed, both by its General Agreement on Tariffs and Trade (GATT) obligations and because it is under pressure from its trading partners, has yet to be assessed--and so has that of the reduction of the agricultural base by the diversion of arable land to industrial use and the effects on food imports in the next ten years of the country's diminishing farm population. The main problems for Japan in the 1970's are more likely to lie in shortages of labor than in the balance of payments.

The situation of Japanese agriculture calls for some special observations in this context.

A main feature of the last decade has been the exodus of young workers from the countryside to the cities as a result of industrial growth. The drop in the farm population has been rapid. In 1950, 45 percent of the nation's work force was in agriculture; this declined to 40 percent in 1955, to 31 percent in 1960, and was estimated to be only 20 percent in 1968. By 1985, it is believed that only 10 percent of the working population will be working on farms. Even today, farmers earn just about as much from off-farm activities as they do from farming; the production of wheat, barley, and soybean is falling off, as more and more farmers, seeking to enhance their incomes by temporary factory employment in the cities, neglect the planting of the fall crops.

To stem this movement out of the countryside, the government applies high rice support prices, in an effort to equalize farm and factory incomes. Other measures, not yet successfully implemented, aim at enlarging the scale of individual farm enterprises, by relaxing restrictions on the sale, purchase, and lease of farms.

At the same time, every year, 20,000 hectares of arable land are being taken out of cultivation, to provide for the growth of industry, the industrial infrastructure, and housing. It is, therefore, not surprising that Japan now supplies from its own resources only 75 percent of its requirements in food and that this proportion is falling by about

1 percent each year. Japanese food prices are among the highest in the world. The place of agriculture in the Japanese economy is well illustrated by Table 71.

The drop in the farm labor force and the continuing contraction of the area in cultivation have prompted a drive toward increased efficiency by the creation of larger farm units, more mechanization, and higher yields. In some areas, farming technology has made truly remarkable advances.

Recent projections by the Ministry of Agriculture and Forestry of domestic production demands and import requirements are shown in Table 72.

A few observations are also appropriate on Japanese attitudes toward trade and aid.

Economic aid given by Japan in 1968 amounted to $1,000 million, 0.98 percent of national income. This is an impressive total. However, Japanese aid is not more unreservedly altruistic than that of some other developed countries. More than a half of the aid given was in the form of deferred payments on Japanese exports, and most of the assistance went to Asian countries, which provide Japan's second most important export market, taking 30 percent of its total exports last year. Unless the economies of these countries grow stronger, Japan cannot expect to export more to them. Moreover, Japan follows a policy of diversifying its sources of food and fiber, and much of its interest in the developing Asian countries is to establish for itself, wherever possible, larger and lower cost supplies for import into Japan.

This "develop and export" formula, together with Japan's declining ability to meet its own needs in farm produce and its improved ability to purchase, has caused both governmental and private interests to accelerate their efforts to develop agriculture in the Asian countries. In 1968, twenty-four private companies participated in the Overseas Agricultural Development Company, which provides Japan's neighbors with technical assistance and farm supplies. Projects are being implemented in Indonesia, Thailand, Cambodia, and Malaysia. There is also an Overseas Technical Co-operation Agency, specializing in the technical assistance aspects of the foreign aid program, which is growing in staff and experience, has helped to develop corn and sorghum production in Indonesia, Thailand, and Cambodia, and is now proposing to help in the improvement of soybean, sesame, kenaf, and cassava production in these countries, as well. Japan's External Trade Organization (JETRO) had a 1969 budget of 1.6 billion yen for similar purposes throughout Asia, and it cooperated closely with the Ministry

TABLE 71

Japan: Status of Agriculture, 1960, 1966, and 1967
(In Billions of Dollars)

	1960	1966	1967
Private Consumption Expenditure	$24.3	$55.0	$63.0
Food Consumption Expenditure, as a Percentage of Private Consumption Expenditure	43.4	37.6	36.9
NDP	36.3	81.4	96.4
Net Agricultural Product, as a Percentage of NDP	10.0	7.7	8.0
Total Exports	4.0	9.7	10.4
Agricultural Exports, as a Percentage of Total Exports	4.1	1.6	1.6
Total Imports	4.5	9.5	11.2
Agricultural Imports, as a Percentage of Total Imports	19.7	23.8	20.2

Source: The State of Japan's Agriculture (Tokyo: Ministry of Agriculture and Forestry, 1968).

of International Trade and Industry in this endeavor. The Ministry of Agriculture and Forestry is also involved in the foreign aid effort and has entered into agreements to provide technicians to Cambodia, to assist that country in production of corn, a project in which five Japanese trading companies are also involved.

A principal ingredient in these policies is the development of joint ventures between Japanese and local interests. Several joint ventures have recently been established in Indonesia. A good example is that of a new company, capitalized at $1.5 million, to grow corn on an area of 12,000 hectares for export to Japan. In the same way, other corporations are participating with the Thai government and private Thai interests in building corn storage and shipping facilities

TABLE 72

Japan: Estimates of 1977 Demands for Selected Agricultural Commodities
(In Thousands of Metric Tons)

Commodity	Domestic Production	Demand	Import
Rice	12,442	12,171-12,442	0
Wheat	795	5,790- 5,848	4,955-5,053
Barley	902	1,995- 2,058	1,093-1,156
Soybeans	121	4,149- -	4,028-
Peanuts	187	284- 295	97- 108
Vegetables	17,447	17,175-17,528	272- 81
Fruit	9,725	10,786-11,693	1,061-1,968
Meat (Beef, Pork, Poultry)	2,300	2,439- 2,771	139- 471
Eggs	1,907	1,887- 1,987	20- 80
Animal Feed	15,875	28,783- -	12,908- -

Source: Long-Range Outlook for Demand, Supply and Production of Agricultural Commodities in Japan (Tokyo: Ministry of Agriculture and Forestry, 1968).

in Bangkok. The big paper producing industries have set up a number of joint ventures in Cambodia, producing wood pulp, timber for plywood, and kenaf. They have also invested in harbor facilities near Kompong Som to facilitate shipments to Japan.

Although Japan has bilateral trade agreements with some forty-five countries, most of these either provide for importation by Japan of agricultural commodities or raw materials, or are with Communist bloc countries, or concern bulk supplies of essential commodities by international tender. The possibility of negotiating long-term bilateral agreements for the rectification of presently adverse trade balances is remote. Japan enjoys too favorable a balance of trade with too many nations to make it favor such arrangements. The economic relationships it is developing with Asian countries for the exploitation of industrial raw materials and the diversification of low-cost sources of supply are more profitable to it.

There is little doubt that, once political conditions permit, Vietnam, too, may benefit from Japanese investment in pursuance of these policies in fields such as fishing and animal feed production, where economies of scale are possible. It may benefit, in fact, from investment in any agricultural activity that involves a high labor content, as long as labor costs seem likely to permit a profitable return to the investors. Japan's interest in low-cost labor will continue, for it needs to expand production and labor shortages, and rising living costs make domestic production less competitive. However, investment will not be confined to agricultural production; as in South Korea, Hong Kong, Taiwan, and many other Asian countries, Japanese capital investment can be expected in Vietnam in any high-labor content industries, such as electronics, where low-cost manipulative and mechanical skills are important.

EXTERNAL TRADE

In Japan, the trade in many of the commodities of potential interest to Vietnamese exporters is either carried on by the government or regulated by it. Essential commodities, such as wheat, barley, rice, tobacco, and salt, are imported only by agencies of the government, while imports of many foodstuffs are under quota or are otherwise restricted. Japan however, has been under heavy pressure to liberalize its commerce in items on which it still retains import restrictions contrary to GATT.

Progressive liberalization of Japan's trade policies seems fairly certain, for Japan wishes to avoid retaliation against its own exports. The probability is that, in the long term, apart from rice, to which special considerations apply, few, if any, of Vietnam's potential agricultural surpluses will attract restrictions of a quantitative nature. This is significant, for, where quotas apply, import permits are granted to trading companies on the basis of past performance, and the companies subdivide the quotas among their traditional suppliers. It is possible for new suppliers to invade a restricted market only by offering concessionary (and, often, initially subeconomic) prices.

Other restrictions on imports that will continue in force are the food additive regulations, based on World Health Organization (WHO) specifications (which are enforced rigidly), and plant and animal quarantine rules, which are similar to those applied by the United States.

There are several categories of customs duties, but, in general, rates are moderate, and the system is relatively uncomplicated. In comparison with those of other major importing nations, tariffs range from medium to low on major unprocessed agricultural commodities. As might be expected, they are high on processed imports.

In 1968, Japan's exports were valued at $13,717 million, an increase of 27.3 percent over the $10,774 million registered in 1967. Imports totaled $13,290 million, a 10.2 percent increase over those of the previous year.

By major destinations, 51.6 percent of all exports went to advanced countries, 43.8 percent to developing countries, and 4.6 percent to Communist bloc countries. Of all imports, 52.4 percent were derived from advanced countries, 41 percent from developing countries, and the balance from Communist ones. Imports from Southeast Asia totaled $2,043 million, or 15.4 percent--an increase of 12.1 percent over 1967.

The direction of trade is clearly illustrated in Table 73.

Of exports, 68.3 percent were classified as heavy industrial and chemical products and 27 percent as light industrial products; only 3.1 percent were foodstuffs, both natural and processed. Of imports, 19.3 percent were classified as consumer goods, 70.4 percent as industrial raw materials, and 9.7 percent as capital goods.

TRADE WITH VIETNAM

Figures taken from the Vietnam Statistical Yearbook show that, from 1959 to 1968, the balance of visible trade with Japan was in Japan's favor, to an annual average of $25 million.* (See Table 74.)

In recent years, imports from Japan have covered a wide range of commodities. On a customs clearance basis, f.o.b. (which will account only partly for the discrepancy between Vietnamese and Japanese trade figures), Japanese statistics indicate that, in 1967, Vietnam imported goods to the total value of $174.6 million from Japan, ranging from transistor radios, motorcycles, and electrical

---

*Other sources show the balance to be even more heavily adverse.

TABLE 73

Japan: Exports and Imports by Destination
and Origin, 1968
(In Millions of Dollars)

Area	Exports	Percent	Imports	Percent
United States	$4,311	31.4	$3,532	26.6
Canada	330	2.8	655	4.9
Western Europe	1,710	12.5	1,320	9.9
South Africa	188	1.4	336	2.5
Australia	425	3.1	1,003	7.5
New Zealand	70	0.5	127	1.0
Southeast Asia	3,865	28.2	2,043	15.4
Near and Middle East	588	4.3	1,855	14.0
Latin America	788	5.7	1,005	7.6
Africa	706	5.0	471	3.5
Communist Bloc	622	4.3	861	6.5
Other Countries	114	0.8	72	0.6
Total	$13,717	100	$13,290	100

Source: Japan Tariff Association, Japan--Exports and Imports (1968).

machinery to synthetic fabrics and heavy chemical and industrial products.

Exports to Japan, on the other hand, are recorded as reaching $4.57 million, of which $813,000 worth were foodstuffs (including fish to the value of $747,000), $3.60 million were industrial raw materials (including rubber to the value of $3.02 million,) and 159,000 consisted of other categories of goods.

In greater detail, and on Vietnamese records, exports to Japan during 1966-68 have been as shown in Table 75.

Unimpressive as this record is, it represents 14 percent of Vietnam's total exports in 1966, 16 percent in 1967, and 21 percent for the first six months of 1968, a sizable proportion of the trade and one that is increasing. Rubber, of course, accounts for the major share--81 percent by value in 1967. After France, which took 40 percent of the volume of Vietnam's rubber exports in 1967, Japan was the most important customer, taking 18 percent.

TABLE 74

Vietnam: Imports from, and Exports to, Japan, 1959-68
(In Thousands of Dollars)

Trade	1959	1960	1961	1962	1963	1964	1965	1966	1967	1968*	Total
Imports	$14,139	$15,637	$17,760	$13,244	$8,183	$9,526	$9,752	$36,614	$100,811	$32,720	$258,386
Exports	576	702	422	867	1,283	1,276	1,168	1,777	1,035	708	9,814

*First six months.

Source: Vietnam, Statistical Yearbook (1969).

TABLE 75

Vietnam: Exports to Japan, 1966-68
(In Thousands of Dollars)

Commodity	1966	1967	1968*
Live Animals	$ 0.2	$ 325.0	-
Crustaceans and Molluscs	201.0	264.0	74.0
Bones and Other Animal Wastes	27.3	52.5	-
Fruit	1.4	-	-
Glass Sand	12.8	11.3	-
Rubber	1,480.0	1,541.0	632.0
Raw Silk	19.6	-	-
Duck Feathers	4.7	4	-

*First six months.

Source: Vietnam, Statistical Yearbook (1969).

In addition to the items listed above, there has, in the past, been a minor commerce with Japan in such items as sesame (exports were worth VN$183,464 in 1963), peanuts (VN$808,500 in 1965) and bananas (VN$1.486 million in 1964).

EXPORT OPPORTUNITIES FOR VIETNAM BY COMMODITY

Rice

Rice has always been Japan's dominant domestic crop. It is the staple food; 40 percent of all cultivated land is devoted to its production, 80 percent of all farms allocate some portion of their production

to it, and it accounts for 45 percent of all farm incomes. In pursuit
of the policy of equalizing farm and city incomes, it is the crop that
the Japanese government selects for high support prices, now equal
to $13.88 per hundredweight for rough rice, treble the support level
in the United States. The support price has been increased steadily
in recent years, and, although in 1969 it was ostensibly pegged to 1968
levels, more generous subsidies on fertilizers had the effect of
improving the support price by about 2 percent.

The direct result of the support price policy, together with
favorable weather, improved production techniques, and higher yields
was a 1968 rice crop of 14.5 million metric tons (husked, unpolished)
and a stockpile of embarrassing proportions (2.7 million tons in
October, 1968, and 5.7 million tons today), creating acute disposal
and storage problems and increasing the already considerable financial
burden being carried by the Japanese government.

Meanwhile, demand has been falling, and is now about 1 million
tons less than the peak of 13.51 million tons (husked rice equivalent)
reached in 1963/64. In all income groups alike, the income elasticity
of demand for rice is now negative, and, even taking into account
population growth, it is difficult to believe that total demand will ever
exceed the present 12.5 million tons a year. This is the direct and
natural effect of changes in diet patterns inspired by increases in per
capita income. A similar tendency for per capita rice consumption
to fall has been observed in Hong Kong, but there are indications that
at least a temporary platform has been reached. No such leveling
off can be discerned in Japan, where people continue to improve and
diversify their diets.

A basic problem for Japanese agricultural policy today is to
bring rice production more into line with demand, and herein lies the
second major dilemma mentioned earlier in this study. Even though
the stockpile continues to grow excessively, it is extremely difficult,
both because of its incomes parity policy and for political reasons,
for Japan to reduce the rice support price or to transfer the subsidy
to other crops. There is actually a black market in fresh rice, as
consumers begin to reject the dated releases from the stockpile.

In 1969, for the first time, the government is providing for payments to farmers, at the rate of 200,000 yen a hectare, to switch
from rice to other crops. The initial target is 300,000 hectares but
the efficacy of the scheme has yet to be proved. The political difficulties are formidable; the target will only be realized if the basic
agricultural land law is changed, and politicians are not eager to
sponsor the necessary amending legislation. Meanwhile, the rice
support price continues to produce excessively abundant crops.

Remarkably, even in this predicament, Japan imported 270,000 tons of rice in 1968, to the value of over $50 million! More than a third came from Mainland China, but Thailand and Taiwan were also large suppliers, and small quantities came from Burma, the United States, South Africa, and Kenya. There are two main explanations. The first is that much of this rice was glutinous, a variety not grown extensively in Japan but in great demand as an accompaniment to sushi (the Japanese raw fish delicacy). The second is that much of the remainder stemmed from a bilateral trading arrangement with Communist China, which could not be varied at short notice. In fact, in the first eight months of 1969, imports were reduced drastically. Only 43,355 metric tons were imported, 98 percent of this being glutinous rice from Thailand. Curiously, the records also show a nine tons, valued at $1,236 being imported from Vietnam.

Excessively high purchase prices, of course, also operate against Japan's disposing of its surpluses by export and sale to other countries. In 1968, Japan managed to dispose of only 367 metric tons by sale, although a further 300,000 tons were supplied to South Korea on soft loan terms.

The important question for Vietnam is whether Japan will continue to pursue a policy of self-sufficiency in rice into the 1970's. Ministry of Agriculture and Forestry projections show that domestic supply and demand will be in balance by 1977 at 12.4 million tons and that there will be no import requirements. On purely economic grounds, such a policy is extremely difficult to justify: it implies that, in a time of labor shortages and with a declining area of arable land, men and resources are being devoted to producing a low-value crop--and to producing it at increasing cost in the effort to enhance yields by adding to the inputs. Japan could more sensibly purchase its rice requirements from neighboring countries, including Vietnam, where costs will probably be lower, and diversify its own production into higher value crops, such as fruit, vegetables, and dairy products, for which demand is increasing and imports of which are a drain on foreign currency resources.

Three reasons are advanced by Japanese to explain why their country is unlikely to be able to do this. The first is the traditional nature of the crop and the conservative instincts of the small farmer; the second is psychological in nature--the basic food shortages suffered by Japan in World War II created a deep dislike of independence on any other nation for a staple foodstuff; and the third appears to be purely political, in that whereas urban voting patterns are becoming more flexible, the rural prefectures, whose representatives are dominant in the Diet, demand from the latter a rigid adherence to traditional patterns and the status quo. It is further argued that the cost-benefit

ratios of crop diversification should not ignore 1,000 years of investment in water control and irrigation works specifically designed to
serve a rice monoculture.

It appears, therefore, that Japan may very well cling to a policy
of self-sufficiency in rice, regardless of cost, and that it will be imprudent to assume a large market in that country for surpluses that
Vietnam may produce in the next ten years. It would be attractive
to suppose that conservatism and political and psychological factors
are bound eventually to yield to the realities imposed by economic
forces; that greater emphasis will be placed on diversification out of
rice in the early 1970's; that there will be a gradual fall in rice production to below 12 million tons after, say, 1974; and that, from then
on, Japan might become an increasingly valuable customer for other
countries' rice. But there can be no promise that this will happen:
and even without any price support, domestic rice production will
probably always be substantial in Japan, possibly 6 to 8 million tons,
so there is never any likelihood that Japan will ever turn to foreign
suppliers for more than a half of its needs. Increasing industrial
demands on labor and limited land area may, however, force a major
change in the next ten years.

Timber

In 1967, imports of logs and baulks were 28 million cubic feet,
worth $934 million, an increase of 38 percent over 1966. In 1968,
imports increased still further, to $1,165 million, 24 percent over
1967. In the first eight months of 1969, $824 million worth have been
imported, and, although the rate of growth is slowing, a further increase of some 7 percent was expected by the end of the year. Dependence on external sources of supply for timber is, of course, the
result of shortages of supplies from Japan's native forests, even
though these cover three-fifths of its total land area. Timber imports
in 1967 amounted to 33 percent of total requirements, and the proportion will continue to increase. Timber was, in fact, Japan's second
largest import commodity in 1967 (after crude oil), accounting for
almost 9 percent of all imports. In addition to timber, there are also
substantial imports of wood pulp and waste paper, $119 million worth
in 1968. Most of the timber imported in 1968 consisted of logs or
roughly squared wood ($1,035.8 million, including $17.4 million of
pulp woods--in addition to the pulp and paper imports), and there
were also considerable imports of shaped or simply worked woods
($125.0 million).

There are three separate possibilities of Vietnam's capturing a
share of this extremely important market for wood and wood products.

First, and the one that lends itself most readily to exploitation in the early future, is the market for hardwood sawlogs and veneer logs. The 1968 imports into Japan amounted to $360 million (excluding specialized species, such as mahogany, ebony, lignum vitae, teak, and sandalwood), and no less than thirty-nine separate countries shared in the trade. About three-quarters of this market, however, went to the Southeast Asian countries, especially Sabah, Sarawak, and Indonesia, though Thailand, Cambodia, Burma, West Malaysia, India, and the Philippines also claimed portions of it.

More research is needed into the range, variety, and technical qualities of Vietnamese hardwoods before categorical statements can be made concerning the export prospects. (Japanese saw and veneer mills will not, of course, be interested in logs that have suffered damage in the course of military operations.) It is clear, however, that there is a large and growing demand in Japan for Asian hardwoods, which can only be satisfied from widely diverse sources of supply. If, as seems highly probable, there are species of Vietnamese hardwoods that are acceptable to the trade, there are immediate prospects for export of veneer logs; if it is in a competitive position vis-a-vis other suppliers with respect to quality and price, this could amount to $10 million in the early future and would thereafter grow to an extent limited only by the supply. A trade to the value of from $30 to $50 million may be entirely possible by 1975-80.

Secondly, Japan is the third-largest paper-producing country in the world, ranking after only the United States and Canada. An idea of the scale of the Japanese pulp and paper industry can be gathered from the fact that ten Japanese shipping companies employ a fleet of twenty specially constructed carriers solely for the shipment of wood chips from North America. Demand for pulp and paper is growing by 10 percent a year.

Pulp wood exports from America are increasingly restricted, and Japanese pulp and paper manufacturers have been turning to Southeast Asia for their raw materials, frequently by establishing jointly owned mills in association with local companies. One manufacturer made a survey of the coniferous forests of Vietnam as early as 1957, and a proposal has already been received from another company for a pulp and paper mill at Dalat, with a capacity of 20,000 tons a year. It seems reasonably probable that, once conditions permit, substantial Japanese investment in the pulp and paper industry may be expected in Vietnam. Doubts have been cast recently on the capacity of the Tuyen Duc pine forests to support an economic scale of operation, but technological improvements have made some of the hardwoods, kenaf, and other materials acceptable for pulp manufacture; eventually, of course, there should be reforestation in pine and eucalyptus to supply the materials for large-scale production.

A 20,000-ton capacity pulp mill, as proposed, would not be a large earner of foreign exchange for Vietnam. Even if its entire production were surplus to domestic requirements (which is improbable, for it would barely satisfy the internal market), it would bring in only $2.8 million in foreign exchange. The proposals put forward in the Joint Development Group's report* were more ambitious: these contemplated a mill with a capacity of 100,000 tons of pulp a year, of which 40,000 tons would be used for paper manufacture in Vietnam and 60,000 tons would be available for export. At this level of operation, earnings from wood pulp would be roughly $8 to $9 million. Whether this scale of operation will be feasible in the next ten years will depend on the results of studies presently in progress into the availability of natural resources.

Thirdly, the demand for veneer sheets and plywoods for building, furniture, and other industrial uses is increasing, to the extent that Japan's own large plywood manufacturing capacity is finding it difficult to supply the market. In 1968, $3.1 million worth of these supplies were imported from widely scattered sources. The proportion of this market captured by Asian countries, 65 percent, is growing. If plans for the construction of plywood and veneer mills in Vietnam materialize, then Japan will offer a ready and expanding market for their products, though probably not, at the start, a very large one.

Rubber

Japan's consumption of both natural and synthetic rubber is increasing steadily; it rose from 516,000 metric tons in 1967 to 602,000 metric tons in 1968, and the Japanese Rubber Industry Association estimated that it would reach 665,000 metric tons in 1969. Synthetic rubber presently supplies 57.3 percent of Japanese needs and natural rubber 42.7 percent; the value of the natural rubber imported in 1968 was $95 million. The principal sources of supply were Malaysia (with 77,563 tons of rubber and 27,033 tons of natural latex), Thailand (77,262 tons), and Indonesia (49,538 tons); smaller quantities were purchased from Singapore, Sarawak, Sabah, Cambodia, Ceylon, Nigeria, and Vietnam, the last of which supplied 6,400 metric tons, worth $2.1 million.

---

*Joint Development Group, The Postwar Development of the Republic of Vietnam: Policies and Programs (New York: Frederick A. Praeger, Inc., 1970).

Vietnamese rubber is highly acceptable, even though it is not presently being exported in great volume. It is thought that production of rubber in Vietnam might be increased to 150,000 tons over the next ten years, and, if Japan takes 20 percent of this (roughly the proportion it now does, and not an unduly large share of a market that is increasing by 30,000 tons a year), this would be worth $11 million at current prices. In this market, as in several others, the problems are ones of supply, not of demand.

Tea

The area under tea in Japan, 49,000 hectares, has remained fairly constant in recent years and supplies the greater part of the nation's needs. Although a traditional beverage, tea consumption per capita is declining slightly; even taking population growth into account, it is unlikely that demand will increase. There is a small market, however, for imported tea, worth $8 million in 1968, especially for black tea, which, in that year, made up 93 percent of all imports. The principal suppliers of black tea are Ceylon (2,510 tons, valued at $4.1 million) and the United Kingdom (905 tons, valued at $2.2 million), followed by India, Kenya, Taiwan, Malaysia, and a few others. Imports of green tea come almost exclusively from Taiwan, which supplied over 1,000 tons, valued at $658,000 in 1968.

It is, of course, possible that Vietnam may be able to compete with Taiwan for a share of the limited market for green tea, but it is unlikely that against so well-established a supplier, having the advantage of lower freight charges, Vietnam will succeed in capturing more than a minute portion of it. It is also possible that small quantities of Vietnamese black tea might gain acceptance over Argentinian and the cheaper East African black varieties, but again, the market for these is tiny (less than $7,000 in 1968) and is relatively static. Any share of Japanese tea imports that Vietnam can hope to win by 1980 will be too small to be worth counting.

Livestock and Meat

The Ministry of Agriculture and Forestry estimates that by 1977, Japan will be producing 2.3 million metric tons of meat, including 308,000 of beef, 1.364 million of pork, 617,000 of poultry, and 11,000 of other meats. Consumption is expected to range from 2.44 to 2.77 million metric tons, resulting in an import requirement of between 139,000 and 471,000.

Demand for meat is growing fast as incomes rise. Nevertheless, per capita consumption of animal protein is still low, only one-seventh of what it is in the United States. The contrast is modified by Japanese consumption of fish protein, five times greater per capita than it is in the United States, but American consumption of proteins, as a whole, is still more than twice that of the Japanese.

Japan places great emphasis on expansion of the livestock industry. Poultry meat production in 1968, for instance, was about 335,000 metric tons, 15.5 percent higher than in 1967. By the end of 1969, it was expected to have increased by another 19 percent, up to about 400,000 tons. Even so, Japan still had to import 15,500 tons of poultry in 1968, 39 percent of this coming from the United States. Competition for this market is severe, and barter-type arrangements with Eastern European suppliers have been cutting into the large U.S. share of the market in recent years. Although imports of frozen poultry meat are expected to continue at present levels ($11 million), little opportunity is seen for Vietnam in a market that will surely continue to be dominated by these large-scale producers.

Domestic pork production has been fluctuating. In 1968, 575,000 metric tons were produced, 7 percent less than in 1967; in 1968, imports of 10,500 tons were permitted, in order to stabilize prices, about 90 percent of this coming from the United States and much of the balance from Mainland China. In 1969, production was expected to increase sharply to the detriment of imports, and the indications are that Japan will remain largely self-sufficient in pork.

Beef and veal production in 1968 was 152,000 metric tons, 9 percent higher than in 1967, and 1969 production was expected to increase by 10 percent over 1968. Beef imports in 1968 were 13,500 metric tons, valued at $13.1 millions; they were obtained almost entirely from Australia and New Zealand. The demand for beef should continue to grow, but, insofar as low-cost beef is concerned, the market will probably be retained by the present suppliers, with the United States meeting a larger share of the demand for high-quality meat. Imports of live cattle are relatively small, 4,465 head, worth $4.7 million in 1968, almost all from the United States, Canada, and the European countries, and intended entirely for breeding purposes. There is little or no opportunity for Vietnam in this particular field. There are better prospects for supplying an ancillary commodity-- animal feedstuffs.

Feedstuffs

Even though domestic mixed feed production was more than 11 million metric tons in 1968, it is increasing substantially and is expected to reach 15,875,000 tons in 1977. It is estimated that, in that year, Japan will still have to import 12.9 million tons of feedstuffs, principally concentrates.

Actual 1968 imports and the sources of supply are shown in Table 76.

A further 1.102 million metric tons of unmilled corn was imported for other than feeding purposes, primarily for the manufacture of corn starch.

Although the big bulk suppliers, the United States and South Africa, dominate this trade, Table 76 illustrates the extent to which Japan is seeking to diversify its sources of supply. Supplies from Thailand are beginning to approach those of South Africa in volume; the rapid increase in production of corn for export in Thailand arises in no small part from direct Japanese investment in this source of supply. There is, obviously, a large and growing market in corn for Vietnam, too, if surpluses can be produced and marketed in sufficient bulk and at prices that will meet Japanese requirements. A similar market exists in sorghum, which was responsible for $136 million of the value of the 1968 imports of feedstuffs. Of the market in sorghum, 81 percent was supplied by the United States and 11 percent by South Africa.

It is difficult, without further information than is now available on production possibilities and costs, to attach a figure to potential exports of corn and sorghum from Vietnam to Japan, but it is clear that, at least to some extent, Vietnam is capable of doing what Thailand has done. Its share of the market in these two commodities might amount to anything from $6 to $24 million in ten years time; there are other, though less important, possibilities in other commodities used for animal feeds.

Because of its own surplus production of rice, Japanese demand for imported rice bran is very small, amounting in 1968 to only 1,749 metric tons, valued at $85,000, but cake and meal from vegetable oil residues were imported in larger quantities, offering a market valued at $12 million in 1968 and capable of rapid growth. The largest share of this market, some 73 percent, was claimed by U.S. suppliers, but imports included soybean cake and meal from Brazil, as well as the United States; coconut cake and meal from South Korea, Mainland China, and Indonesia; linseed products from South Korea; cottonseed cake and meal from Mainland China, the United States, and Brazil; and peanut cake and meal from India, Brazil, the United States, Mainland China, and Burma. However, imported cake and meal reflect only a small proportion of Japanese import demand for these products, since crushing for oil and meal is done mostly in Japan. Japanese domestic soybean production, for example, satisfies only 7 percent of the country's requirements, 2.241 million metric tons being imported in 1968, 83 percent from the United States and the balance

TABLE 76

Japan: Imported Feedstuffs, 1968

Source	Quantity (In Metric Tons)	Value (In Millions of Dollars)
Korea (Republic)	1,670	$ 0.1
North Korea	4,903	0.3
China (Mainland)	48,584	2.89
China (Taiwan)	703	0.04
Thailand	623,246	36.2
Indonesia	8,762	5.1
Cambodia	9,614	0.64
United States	2,397,424	144.6
Mexico	182,910	10.7
Mozambique, Canada, and Lesotho	-	0.5
South Africa	750,241	44.8
Malawi	1,004	0.5
Total	4,042,154	$241.7

Source: Derived from Japan Exports and Imports (1968).

from Mainland China. Soybean is, by far, the most important import in this category, peanuts, copra, and other oilseeds or nuts being imported in much smaller quantities. Some details of oilseed imports are given in the next section of this chapter.

In the face of competition from the bulk suppliers and, in the case of Mainland China, of bilateral trade agreements, Vietnam will not find it easy to enter the soybean market, but the demand is there and so is the desire to diversify sources of supply. The difficulty will be to supply in sufficient volumes to attract the interest of Japanese importers. On the other hand, some coconut cake and peanut cake can be sold to Japan, since these commodities are dealt with in comparatively small lots and since Vietnam will have an advantage of lower freight costs over India and Brazil, two present suppliers. Initially, the value of this market to Vietnam will probably be small, perhaps $250,000, but it is a trade that is likely to grow and could be worth several million.

Oilseeds and Kernels

The previous section stated Japan's present import requirements for soybean and Vietnam's probably limited opportunities in this trade. There should be better opportunities for trade in other oilseeds and kernels, peanuts, copra, castor, sesame, and kapok, which are imported from many different sources and less commonly in bulk shipments.

In 1968, for example, Japan purchased from other countries 49,500 metric tons of peanuts, valued at $11.3 million, 36 percent from Mainland China, 42 percent from Nigeria and the Sudan, and small quantities from Thailand, Indonesia, India, South Africa, and North Vietnam (338 tons). Import requirements in 1977 are expected to amount to between 97,000 and 108,000 metric tons, twice what they are now. Japan also imported 126,000 metric tons of copra, worth $27.2 million--mostly from the Philippines, Indonesia, and Oceania; 43,400 metric tons of castor beans, worth $7.5 million--54 percent from Thailand, and the balance from Mainland China, Indonesia, Pakistan, and several African countries; 39,200 metric tons of sesame, valued at $9 million--57 percent from the Sudan and Ethiopia, but significant amounts, also, from Thailand, Indonesia, Cambodia, Pakistan, and South America; and 36,500 metric tons of kapok seeds, worth $2.4 million--one-third of it from Thailand, nearly a half from Indonesia, and most of the rest from Cambodia.

The market in these five commodities, all of which appear to have production potential for Vietnam, now amounts to $47.5 million and is one in which steady growth is discernible. The official Japanese estimate of 1977 consumption of vegetable oilseeds puts it at 60 percent above present demands. A conservative target for Vietnam to aim at is 5 percent of this market, and this, by the mid-1970's, will probably be worth $3 to $4 million.

Coffee

Import restrictions have been relaxed. Demand is likely to be stable at about the 1968 level of 45,000 metric tons, although there is a slight increase in consumption of coffee, with the decline in consumption of tea. Taking population growth into account, coffee imports may climb to somewhat more than 50,000 tons in the next ten years. The present market is worth $27.6 million at current prices. Sources of supply are extremely varied, 63 percent of Japan's coffee by value coming from eleven South American countries and 32 percent from seven African countries. The share obtained by Asian countries is very small and is worth only $550,000--661 tons in 1968 from Indonesia, 117 tons from West Malaysia, 8 tons from Sabah, and 1 ton from North Vietnam.

The prospects of Vietnam's obtaining even a small part of this
trade would appear remote against low-cost and high-quality South
American and African production. There is, however, an advantage
of location, which cannot be completely discounted. If an acceptable
coffee is developed, small quantities may possibly be disposed of to
Japan, but, on the whole, coffee is unlikely to be a significant earner
of foreign exchange for Vietnam in this particular market.

Silk

Japanese exports of manufactured silk are now only one-tenth
of what they were ten years ago, when silk ranked as a major Japanese
export commodity, but there is still a substantial domestic market
for silk, based on the faithful attachment of Japanese women to the
kimono. While 1968 exports were only 9,436 bales of 60 kilograms,
domestic deliveries were about 342,000 bales. Three-quarters of
Japan's requirements for silk are met from domestic production, but
this still leaves a valuable import market. In 1968, Japan purchased
380 tons of wild raw silk, valued at over $3.0 million, mostly from
Mainland China, with small quantities from North Korea and Taiwan;
30 tons of double cocoon silk, mostly from South Korea, but, also,
from Italy, North Vietnam, and Mainland China, valued at $416,000;
and 1,690 tons of raw silk other than wild silk, worth $23.6 million,
from ten different countries, including Mainland China and South
Korea (the two principal suppliers), North Korea, Bulgaria, Italy, the
U.S.S.R., Brazil, North Vietnam, Yugoslavia, and Taiwan.

There is little prospect of much growth in this market, but
Vietnam should certainly be attracted by an import requirement,
worth over $25 million, which is now being met in part by countries
as far away and as diverse as Eastern Europe, the countries of the
EEC, and South America. It is unlikely that the Chinese and South
and North Korean shares of the market (80 to 85 percent) can be
captured to any great extent, but the balance, worth from $4 to $5
million, should operate in favor of the revival of Vietnam's traditional
raw silk industry. When this happens, it will not be overoptimistic
to expect exports to Japan worth anything from $150,000 to $750,000.

Fruits and Vegetables

Production of both fruits and vegetables is increasing in Japan.
The expectation is that, by 1977, Japan will either be producing
vegetables in excess of its needs (apart from a few specialized crops,
for which a limited import market will still exist) or that its import
requirements will be reduced to, at most, 80,000 tons. The only
present export possibilities are in fresh green beans, imported to

the value of $5.6 million in 1968, almost all from Burma and Thailand; french beans, for which there is a current demand worth $4.4 millions, nearly a half of it met from Burma and the rest from the United States, Mexico, Malagasy, and South Africa; and fresh onions, of which $3.6 million worth were imported last year, more than a third from the United States, but substantial quantities from Thailand ($191,000), Burma ($114,000), Africa ($105,000), and South America. Small quantities of these particular vegetables can probably be sold to Japan and so can small quantities of such items as asparagus, artichokes, and mushrooms, but the market is not likely to amount to much and has no real long-term significance.

An interesting and potentially profitable activity is the cultivation of lotus. In Japan, the root, deep fried, is a highly prized delicacy, said by some to possess potent medicinal qualities, but its harvesting is a dirty, unpopular, labor-intensive job, for which current daily wage rates in Japan are about the equivalent of $10.00. Like many other labor-intensive agricultural products, lotus could probably be harvested competitively in Vietnam, and the wage differential, together with the value of the crop, might justify the use of air freight to exploit this specialized market.

Imported citrus fruit (other than mandarin orange, in which Japan is self-sufficient) is in substantial demand and so are fresh pineapples, papaya, and bananas. The United States supplies almost the entire market in all these fruits, except that for bananas, for which demand is quite exceptional. The 1968 import statistics are worth quoting in full. (See Table 77.)

This amounts to a $100 million market, virtually shared between Taiwan and Ecuador, which shows indications of increasing by as much as 20 percent per annum, though it is impossible to say how long this rate of growth can continue. However, in the first eight months of 1968, imports have been at the rate of $123 million a year, and the official forecast is that, by 1977, imported fruit requirements will be at least 1.061 million metric tons--and may be as high as 1.968 metric tons--largely explained by this Japanese addiction to bananas.*

---

*A footnote of some social interest: "In the good old days, Japanese housewives used to cook their husbands a decent breakfast. Now, they just throw them a couple of bananas." Anonymous Japanese businessman, interviewed in Saigon, October 13, 1969.

TABLE 77

Japan: Imports of Bananas, 1968

Origin	Quantity (In Millions of Tons)	Value (In Thousands of Dollars)
China (Mainland)	1,204	$ 126
China (Taiwan)	355,338	55,966
Philippines	320	44
Mexico	6,075	1,006
Guatemala	217	45
Honduras	28,577	5,935
Ecuador	246,063	37,936
Total	637,794	$101,058

Source: Japan Tariff Association, Japan Exports and Imports, 1968 and August, 1969.

Serious consideration should obviously be given to the possibilities of Vietnam's entering this extremely lucrative market. The problems are not purely ones of agronomy. Consumer preference is for the Taiwan variety, to which the Ecuador banana is similar; so, clearly, Vietnam must first produce an acceptable fruit; but exploitation of the market will also require very large investments in production, transportation, and marketing arrangements. Refrigerated vessels are necessary, and bulk supplies of a standardized, homogeneous product have to be available at the right time and in the right place. It will take some time to build the infant Vietnamese banana industry up to the point at which it can meet these requirements. The experience of Taiwan will be a valuable guide.

Tobacco

Nearly 60 percent of Japan's 1968 leaf imports came from the United States, and most of the balance came from Turkey, Greece, and India. Small quantities were, however, purchased from Asian countries other than India, for instance, 1,780 tons from Thailand, 421 tons from the Philippines, 26 tons from Indonesia, 25 tons from Korea, and 10 tons from Taiwan. Thailand's share of this market was quite a substantial one, worth $2.412 million.

Japanese domestic leaf production is declining slowly, from 209,000 metric tons, or 8 percent of consumption, in 1967 to 194,000 metric tons in 1968, while consumption continues to increase modestly, by 1.3 percent in 1968.

The Asian share of the market is only 13 percent of the whole, but it is worth nearly $7 million. Vietnam may be able to capture a little of this trade, especially from Thailand and India; however, after meeting its own requirements--now met almost entirely by imports-- it is unlikely to capture enough of it to make a significant difference to export earnings.

Spices

Although Japan has relaxed its controls on the importation of these commodities, import volumes have not fluctuated greatly in recent years, and demand appears fairly stable. However, the import trade is not inconsiderable. It amounted to about $4.0 million in 1968, pepper, pepper seed, and pimento being the principal items, valued at $1.7 million. Of particular interest to Vietnam were imports of cinnamon, worth $980,000; other spices represented in the trade were mace and cardamon, anise, fennel and coriander, and ginger.

The trade in pepper is dominated by Sarawak, although most Asian countries, Indonesia and Pakistan in particular, also contribute small quantities. There is an opportunity for South Vietnam to take a small share of this, possibly worth $100,000. South Vietnam exported to Japan 37.5 metric tons of cinnamon, worth $30,000, in 1968, and North Vietnam exported 68 tons, worth $58,000. In fact, Mainland China supplies 86 percent of Japan's requirements for cinnamon, and the special qualities of Vietnamese cinnamon do not appear to be as highly esteemed in Japan as they are in the United States. Nevertheless, Vietnam should certainly be able to expand its dealings with Japan in this commodity to about $100,000.

Japanese statistics for 1968 also show Vietnam as having supplied five metric tons of spices in the category anise, fennel, coriander, cumin, caraway, and juniper, worth $2,500, but no details are available. North Vietnam is shown as having exported twelve and a quarter tons of the same group worth $4,800. This market is largely supplied by Mainland China, Iran, Morocco, and Rumania; the market for ginger is met substantially by China. Overall prospects for the export of spices and pepper are not encouraging.

Marine and Freshwater Products

The difficulties of the Japanese fishing industry originate in labor shortages and rising living costs, which have together so inflated the operating costs of deep-sea, distant water fishing that almost exceptional catch rates of selected commercial fish varieties (such as mackerel, tuna, salmon, swordfish, marlin, squid, deep sea smelt, and red snapper) are required for it to be profitable. At the same time, the operational range of Japanese fishing fleets is becoming more restricted, partly by international agreements and controls on fisheries and partly because of the assertion by many maritime nations of sovereign rights outside the traditional three-mile limit.

Heavy capital investment in equipment and intensified activity have kept total deep-sea fishing production at a fairly constant level, but there is a fall in the catch rates of quality fish. Meanwhile, domestic demand continues to increase, especially for those high-value fish listed above, while the demand for shrimps, lobsters, and other crustaceans appears to be quite insatiable. Imports are regularly increasing, by as much as 15 percent annually. The principal foreign suppliers of fish to Japan are South Korea (17 percent), Mexico (11 percent), Mainland China (10 percent), and the United States (8 percent); over 160,000 metric tons of fresh, chilled, or frozen high-quality fish were imported in 1968, to a total value of $118 million. The most significant items were shrimps, prawns, and lobsters, 35,204 tons, worth $78 million; other crustaceans and molluscs, 44,348 tons, worth $10.9 million; and bonito and tuna, 28,965 tons, valued at $10.7 million.

A modern fishing industry in Vietnam would find a ready market for the dozen or so species that Japan regularly imports; however, at this stage of development, the most obvious opportunity is the export of shrimps and lobsters.

In 1968, Japan obtained its shrimps and lobsters from no less than forty-eight different countries. It scours the world for these delicacies, the demand for which is rapidly expanding, going as far afield as Mexico and Cuba. Wholesale market prices for shrimps and lobsters rose 70 percent between 1960 and 1967 and have gone considerably higher in 1968 and 1969, so that, at current prices, frozen shrimps could be shipped to Japan by air and still sold profitably. For Vietnam, the problems are solely those of supply and processing.

Other possibilities for the Vietnamese export trade reside in the Japanese market for dried, smoked, or salted marine products.

This is not large: its value was approximately $1 million in 1969, and it was supplied by Mainland China, South Korea, and the United States; however, small quantities could be sold, including such high-value items as dried sharksfin, since Chinese cuisine is gaining some popularity in Japan. Fish meal for cattle feed could be yet a more profitable item of Vietnam's fish exports to Japan. In 1968, 150,000 metric tons were imported, worth $20 million, besides 65,000 tons of flours and meals from meat, crustaceans, and molluscs, worth $6.7 million.

Once Vietnam can succeed in producing surpluses of the right species for export, it is not overoptimistic to expect a market worth $5 million, capable of very considerable growth over the next ten years. The trade will be limited by not much more than the capacity of the fishing industry to produce.

Miscellaneous Nonagricultural Items

Natural Quartz Sand

Japanese imports in 1968 amounted to 104,000 metric tons, valued at a little over $1 million. Australia supplied 84 percent, but Vietnam was the second largest supplier, with 11,600 metric tons, valued at $113,000.

Demand for sheet glass increased significantly in 1968, and the glass industry predicts additional growth of 11 percent in domestic demand and 7 percent in exports in 1969. Vietnam's glass sands are of high quality and huge volume, and there should be no difficulty in expanding exports to $250,000 and, quite probably, more.

Salt

Salt production and importation are a government monopoly, but production costs are high, and Japan is looking for low-cost sources of supply. Imports are presently restricted to supplies from Chile (15,000 metric tons, worth $930,000, in 1968). Another minor opportunity for Vietnamese industry is likely to be presented by this commodity.

SUMMARY OF CONCLUSIONS

While Japan provides, without any doubt, one of the most valuable and most rapidly expanding markets for agricultural exports in the world, the opportunities for Vietnam in Japan may not be quite as certain or extensive as many people think for the following reasons:

1. There is a distinct trend toward reliance on bulk producers in the developed countries for certain foodstuffs and for many industrial raw materials.

2. Although there is a well-defined policy of diversifying the sources of supply of raw materials for the use of Japanese industry, Japanese investment is much more readily available for the production of raw materials than it is for the processing or semiprocessing of raw materials for shipment with added values.

3. There is a distinct reluctance to enter into bilateral negotiations for the correction of trade imbalances.

4. Most disappointing of all, there is a rigid determination to keep Japan self-sufficient in rice.

Although Japan may eventually be persuaded by its own interests to modify the last of these policies, there is no sign whatever that it will do so in the short or medium term. In the longer run, the prospects for rice exports are much more favorable.

What Vietnam can reasonably be expected to sell to Japan is set out in Table 78. The four most promising commodities are timber, rubber, fish, and animal feedstuffs.

Japanese demand for tropical hardwoods is growing, and immediate prospects are seen for exports of veneer logs, possibly up to a value of $10 million, if Vietnam succeeds in producing at competitive prices and qualities. By 1980, this trade might become a very considerable one. The potential for plywood and veneer exports is less important, but cannot be ignored, because Japanese consumption exceeds the capacity of its industries, and there is an existing market, capable of growth, and already worth about $3 million, 65 percent of which is supplied by Asian countries. Pulp, pulp wood, and wood chip for the paper industry are greatly needed, but it cannot yet be said with certainty that Vietnam will be able to complete with the big producers, though there are fairly good chances that it can do so and excellent chances that it can do so in time.

A modern deep-sea Vietnamese fishing fleet would have no difficulty at all in disposing of its surpluses of high-quality fish to Japan, and the fishing industry has, therefore, obvious potential for early investment. The most profitable immediate prospect lies in the production and export of frozen shrimps. Vietnam is excellently placed--especially in relation to such distant suppliers as Cuba,

TABLE 78

Export Possibilities, Vietnam to Japan, 1980

Commodity	Volume	Estimated Value[a] (In Millions of Dollars)
Wood and Wood Products:		
Hardwood Logs[b]	650,000-2,000,000	$30.0 -$ 50.0
Plywood and Veneers[c]	350,000	0.25
Wood Pulp[b] [d]	20,000-60,000	2.8 - 8.0
Rubber[e]	30,000	11.2
Feedstuffs:		
Feed Grains[b]	80,000-320,000	6.0 - 24.0
Cake and Meal[b]	30,000-240,000	0.25- 2.0
Tea	[f]	[f]
Oilseeds[b]	15,000-20,000	3-4
Silk[b]	15-75	0.15- 0.75
Fruit and Vegatables (Except Bananas)	[f]	[f]
Bananas[d]	-	-
Tobacco	[f]	[f]
Pepper, Cinnamon, and Other Spices[b]	400	0.2
Fish:		
Crustaceans and Mulluscs[b]	3,000-5,000	5.0 - 8.0
Dried, Smoked, or Salted	-	-
Fishmeal	-	-
Glass Sands[b]	250,000	1.00
Salt	-	-
Total		$59.85-$109.40

[a]1968 prices.
[b]In tons.
[c]In square meters.
[d]Indicates new production; feasibility presently uncertain.
[e]In millions of tons.
[f] Not estimated or insignificant.

Mexico, and the European countries--to capture a good share of this expanding and valuable trade. It may be selling as much as $5 million worth of fish and shrimps to Japan by 1975, and increasing this substantially by 1980.

Japan's imports of animal feeds, mainly corn and sorghum, are thought likely to increase to about 12.9 million tons by 1977. Bulk suppliers, like the United States and South Africa, now dominate the trade, but Japan seeks additional suppliers, and Vietnam might well be able to follow the example of Thailand, which now sells to Japan $36 million worth of these commodities. Sales of up to $10 million by 1975 would not be an unreasonable expectation. There is less, but still some, potential in feed cake and meal, but probably not in soybeans, which are virtually monopolized by large-scale low-cost producers.

Japan is a traditional purchaser of Vietnamese rubber, and its consumption of both the natural and the synthetic product is growing fast. On assumptions that Vietnam's production can be increased within ten years after the end of the war (which implies, certainly, some extensive replanting in the very early future) to 150,000 metric tons and that Japan will continue to purchase 18 to 20 percent of the output, by 1980 this trade would be worth $10 million at current prices.

It is unlikely that Vietnam will find easy entry into the rather small and slowly declining market for tea, unless it can compete with Taiwan in meeting demand for the green variety. Nor is Vietnam likely to be able to sell Japan any poultry and pork, nor, at least, for the foreseeable future, any beef. If a fairly large-scale cattle industry were to establish itself in Vietnam, a small share of Australia's and New Zealand's trade might be obtained, but this is not going to be a quick or easy process.

There is a $47.5-million market, showing steady growth, for oilseeds and kernels. The best opportunities for Vietnam appear to be in peanuts, copra, castor, and sesame, and a 5 percent share of the trade in these commodities would yield $3 to $4 million by the mid-1970's.

Coffee does not look like being a good export crop. Raw silk, on the other hand, offers profitable prospects, though small ones. The current import requirement is for 1,750 metric tons, worth $25 million. Mainland China and South Korea supply most of this market, but there are several other sources, and it should be possible for Vietnam to sell Japan unprocessed silk worth up to $750,000.

There is likely to be a growing market in vegetables, mainly in specialized items, such as asparagus, artichokes, and mushrooms, although lotus root is suggested as a high-value crop for which there is a good demand.

The potential banana market is a very large one, and merits serious investigation. A steady Japanese demand for peppers and others spices is met by exports from neighboring Asian countries, and, while prospects for growth are not encouraging, some small portion of the market, possibly worth as much as $250,000, can probably be won. Similarly, the Asian share of Japan's market for tobacco, although only 13 percent of the total, is worth $7 million, and some opportunities, not very considerable ones, exist for the displacement of neighboring competitors. The value of such a trade to Vietnam is hardly likely to exceed $500,000.

Finally, two minor industrial possibilities have been indentified in glass sands and salt.

An unavoidable inference is that Vietnam's export opportunities in Japan, although they are varied and not without value as foreign exchange earners, are not extensive, in relation to the size of the Japanese import trade as a whole. The wealthiest nation in Asia, with a projected economic growth rate of 11.5 percent per year, generates demands for agricultural imports and other raw materials that are almost without parallel. But it is the bulk suppliers, against whom developing Asian nations will find it most difficult to compete, who monopolize the main requirements. What is left is a miscellany of comparatively minor items, which, in total, may still make Japan Vietnam's most important customer, but for which less-exacting markets also exist in such places as Hong Kong and Singapore. In the early future, these smaller markets may, in fact, be more natural trading partners for Vietnam, more adapted to the marketing techniques and supply characteristics of the Vietnamese economy, readier to give consideration to matters of mutual benefit, and more easily capable of development than the huge, industrialized economy of Japan. In the longer run, hopefully, as Vietnamese production becomes more efficient, this need not be the case.

GENERAL INFORMATION

In the context of this study, there are distinct resemblances between Singapore and Hong Kong. Like that of Hong Kong, the population of Singapore is largely concentrated into urban areas and is engaged principally in light manufacturing and commerce. There is a little heavy industry, notably shipbuilding. The commerce of Singapore is directed mainly toward exports and reexports, and, with a restricted land area and few natural resources of its own, it relies heavily for its industrial raw materials and for most of its food supplies on its nearest neighbors, Malaysia and Indonesia, both of them important agricultural producers.

In projections based on the census taken in 1957, the population of Singapore was estimated to be 1.659 million in 1967. Using present rates of growth and assuming that there will be no abnormal movements of population either into or out of the country, it is estimated that it will be 2.840 million by 1977 and 3.406 million by 1982, offering a potential market roughly two-thirds the size of that presented by Hong Kong.

The people of Singapore probably have higher standards of living than any other nation in Southeast Asia. GNP was estimated at $500 per capita in 1960; it rose by 4.25 percent a year between 1960 and 1964 and has been rising at a somewhat higher rate than that since then. It is now believed to be at least $700.

CHARACTERISTICS OF THE ECONOMY

Detailed and up-to-date estimates of national income were not available at the time of this study, but the contributions of specific economic sectors to GDP (in percent) are approximately as follows:*

Agriculture and fisheries	5
Entrepôt trade	14
Manufacturing and construction	13
Retail and wholesale trade	21
United Kingdom Armed Forces	16
All other	31

The fastest annual growth rates appear to be in construction, tourism, and manufacturing. The quarterly index of industrial production indicates that the manufacturing sector grew by 18 percent in 1968 alone.

The contribution to the economy derived from military expenditures by the United Kingdom is an important one, and the planned military withdrawal by the United Kingdom may produce some difficult problems. Singapore's leaders are hopeful, however, that defense contributions by Australia, an increased level of concessionary aid from the United Kingdom, increasing American and Japanese investment, and the development of the shipbuilding industry in converted naval dockyards will ameliorate the effects on the economy.

An unfortunate distortion occurs in the trade statistics as a result of the exclusion, since the 1964 "confrontation" between Indonesia and Malaysia, of all statistics on trade between Singapore and Indonesia. It is believed that this trade has now recovered its pre-1964 level and may account for from 20 to 25 percent of all Singapore's external trade; if so, trade with Indonesia probably amounts to the equivalent of $200 million. Much of it is by barter.

(The external trade statistics, though otherwise comprehensive and apparently accurate, are disappointingly late in publication. The latest available figures are for the first nine months of 1968. This lag is largely due to the need to incorporate Malaysian figures, which are slow in arriving from that widely dispersed country. No differentiation is made in the statistics between exports and reexports.)

Only 7 percent of the population of almost 2 million are engaged in agriculture. Most food requirements are supplied by imports, but Singapore produces almost 90 percent of its meat requirements, 50 percent of its vegetables, and 25 percent of its fruit.

---

*The Singapore Yearbook (1967).

Although much of Singapore's industry is still concerned with the primary processing of raw materials (particularly rubber, tin, timber, rattan, and spices) for reexport, manufacturing is playing an increasingly important part in the economy. Singapore has a complicated customs tariff structure, with built-in Commonwealth preferences and protective tariffs on processed and manufactured goods, though not generally on raw materials. No customs duties are presently imposed by Singapore on the kinds of commodities that may conceivably enter trade between Vietnam and Singapore, except for tobacco and alcoholic beverages. Neither are there any protective or restrictive quotas on the import of raw materials and prime commodities.

In pursuit of new markets in the socialist countries, there is a trend towards state trading, and trade agreements have been negotiated with Hungary, Rumania, North Korea, Bulgaria, Poland, Mainland China, and the U.S.S.R. An important feature of these agreements is an arrangement whereby percentages of the sales proceeds of imports from these countries must be utilized for the purchase by them of products manufactured in Singapore. A state trading organization, INTRACO, was established in November, 1968, for this purpose.

EXTERNAL TRADE

Official trade figures for the last three years are shown in Table 79. Growth rates, in terms of values, are substantial but less impressive than those of Hong Kong, which achieved a 26 percent increase, by value, in exports in 1968. It should be remembered, however, that these statistics exclude the reviving trade with Indonesia and that they reflect (to an unusual extent in the case of Singapore)

TABLE 79

Singapore: External Trade, 1966-68
(In Millions of Dollars)

Year	Exports		Imports		Total Trade	
	$Million	%Increase	$Million	%Increase	$Million	%Increase
1966	1,124.5		1,355.2		2,479.7	
1967	1,183.5	5.2	1,468.8	8.4	2,652.3	6.9
1968	1,230.2	3.9	1,655.4	12.7	2,924.8	10.3

Source: Singapore External Trade Statistics (1967 and 1968).

depressed world prices for rubber and tin in the particular period they cover. These commodities together make up a very large proportion of Singapore's reexports.

West Malaysia continues to be Singapore's leading trading partner, accounting for 21.2 percent of total trade in 1967 and 17.4 percent in 1968. Imports from West Malaysia in 1968 were valued at $270 million. Japan was next in importance to Malaysia in 1968, and Mainland China displaced the United Kingdom as Singapore's third most important trading partner. Other countries having significant commercial relations with Singapore are the United States, Sarawak, Thailand, and Australia. Vietnam also figures prominently (and unexpectedly and rather artificially) among Singapore's trading partners because of its very large imports of petroleum products (3.3 million tons in 1968, worth $130 million).

In 1968, Singapore imported goods and raw materials to the value of $1,655 million, principally from the sources shown in Table 80.

More than a half (55.5 percent) of all imports were derived from Asian countries. In addition to those listed in Table 80, Singapore also made purchases from Brunei, Burma, Cambodia, Taiwan, South Korea, Laos, Pakistan, the Philippines, Sabah, and North Vietnam. Its imports

TABLE 80

Singapore: Imports, by Sources and Value, 1968

Source	Value (In c.i.f. Millions of Dollars)	Percentage of All Imports
Malaysia (West)	$270	15.3
Japan	231	13.6
China (Mainland)	153	9.0
United Kingdom	132	7.8
United States	116	7.0
Kuwait	113	6.7
Australia	72	4.3
Sarawak	69	4.1
Thailand	55	3.4
Hong Kong	48	2.8
India	46	2.6
West Germany	43	2.5

Source: Singapore External Trade Statistics (1968).

TABLE 81

Singapore: Imports, by Class of Commodity, 1966-68

Class of Commodity	1966		1967		1968	
	$U.S. Millions	Percent	$U.S. Millions	Percent	$U.S. Millions	Percent
1. Food and Live Animals	$256.7	18.9	$270.6	18.4	$304.1	18.4
2. Beverages and Tobacco	21.7	1.6	24.5	1.7	30.1	1.8
3. Inedible Crude Materials, except Fuels	251.1	18.5	212.5	14.5	195.2	11.8
4. Minerals, Fuels, Lubricants	206.9	15.3	246.3	16.8	297.7	17.9
5. Animal and Vegetable Oils	19.3	1.4	21.5	1.4	17.0	1.3
6. Chemicals	67.1	4.9	78.9	5.4	83.1	5.0
7. Manufactured Goods, Classified Chiefly by Material	217.6	16.1	265.7	18.0	313.3	18.9
8. Machinery and Transportation Equipment	185.3	13.7	193.0	13.1	246.5	14.9
9. Miscellaneous Manufactures	100.1	7.4	127.6	8.7	132.5	8.0
10. Commodities Not Classified According to Kind	29.3	2.1	28.0	1.9	35.9	2.2
Total	$1,355.1		$1,468.6		$1,655.4	

Source: Derived from Singapore External Trade Statistics (1967 and 1968).

from Pakistan ($26.15 million) and Taiwan ($25.56 million) were quite substantial. Imports from South Vietnam, $540,000, were insignificant.

Purchasing goods from its neighbors in East Asia, to the value of nearly $1,000 million a year (about a half of Hong Kong's imports from the same source), Singapore represents a market of considerable importance. The commodities that have entered into its import trade during 1966-68--and the extent to which they entered it--are shown in Table 81. In the early future, the interests of Vietnam appear to lie principally in the first, second, third, and fifth categories of commodities shown on Table 81.

Singapore's exports are diverse. Reexports of crude materials, particularly rubber, constituted 21.3 percent of all exports in 1967; petroleum products followed with 13 percent. Manufactured goods accounted for 12 percent of the export trade, and food and live animals accounted for a further 11.8 percent. Singapore has a worldwide market for its exports, but its principal customers in 1967, in order of importance, were West Malaysia, Vietnam, the United States, the United Kingdom, and Japan. One reason for the prominence of Vietnam has been explained, though Vietnam has been an importer of more than petroleum from Singapore in the last three years.

TRADE WITH VIETNAM

Figures from the Vietnamese Statistical Yearbook indicate that imports from Singapore totaled $1.543 million in 1966 and jumped to $12.600 million in 1967.* In the first half of 1968, imports were running at about the same levels as in 1967. The most significant item in these years was petroleum products, which amounted to 70 percent of all of Vietnam's imports from Singapore in 1966, 94 percent in 1967, and 90.5 percent in the first six months of 1968. Small quantities of iron and steel were also imported, worth $220,000 in 1966 and $440,000 in the following year. The only other commodities imported to any substantial value were cereals and cereal preparations, $95,000 in 1966 and a little less than $70,000 in 1967. Other imported items listed in official Vietnamese reports were preserved meat, cocoa and cocoa preparations, preserved vegetables, photographic supplies, wood manufactures, tin, and nonelectric machinery and appliances, all in insignificant quantities.

---

*There is an obvious discrepancy between these figures from Vietnamese sources and those from Singapore sources. The former evidently do not include military purchases, and the latter evidently do.

Exports from Vietnam to Singapore were valued at $350,000 in 1966 and merely $190,000 in 1967; in 1968, they appeared to be falling further. The only significant items exported to Singapore in these two years were coffee ($165,600 in 1967), oilseed cake ($118,000 in 1966, but only $5,000 in 1967), and rubber ($146,500 in 1966 and $72,000 in 1967).

Other exports that appear in the trade statistics for these years are the following: live animals; fresh fish; fish bladders; vegetables; tea; cinnamon; flour; peanuts; soybean and other oilseeds; plants used in perfurmery and pharmacy; kapok, peanut, and coconut oil; plaited matting; and iron scrap. None of these was exported in any volume, but the list at least indicated the wide range of potential demand.

The years 1966-68 are not, of course, necessarily typical of the normal trade relations between Vietnam and Singapore over a longer period of time. From 1959-63, there was a substantial balance of trade in favor of Vietnam, as much as VN$177 million in 1960 and VN$265 million in 1963. Thereafter, at least from Vietnam's point of view, the trade deteriorated, though Vietnam's adverse balance did not acquire serious dimensions until 1967, when it was VN$1452.6 million, about $12.3 million at then official rates of exchange.

From time to time, over the years, a fair variety of products have entered into Vietnam's export trade with Singapore. For instance, no less than 44,000 tons of rice went to this market in 1958; the trade in rice fell away in the years 1959-62 (when Indonesia and Hong Kong became Vietnam's principal clients) but rose again in 1963, when Singapore purchased 62,600 tons, almost 20 percent of the record exports of 322,570 tons reached in that year.

Singapore has also provided a small but steady market for Vietnam's rubber, purchasing some every year, though not nearly as much recently, for obvious reasons, as it did in 1959 and 1960 (3,725 and 4,870 tons, respectively). Peanuts were exported to Singapore in considerable quantities in the mid-1960's, over 3,000 tons in each of the years 1964 and 1965; and there was a small trade in vegetable oils from 1962 to 1964, which became quite a substantial one in 1965, when, according to the Vietnamese Statistical Yearbook, this particular export climbed to 18,000 tons.* Cinnamon was sold to Singapore in every year from 1962 to 1968, not usually in large

---

*The figure represents such a large increase over the 150 tons sold to Singapore in the previous year that it can obviously do with scrutiny.

quantities, though 138 tons are said to have been traded in 1963. A little coffee has gone to Singapore in every year on record, 660 tons in 1964, 575 tons in 1967, and 325 tons in 1968. In the early 1960's, preserved duck eggs appeared as an export to this market, over 1 million kilograms being shipped in 1962.

In only one year since 1955 has tea figured to any extent in the trade statistics. In 1965, 222,250 kilograms of tea, worth VN$5.9 million were exported. Rapidly diminishing quantities followed in 1966 and 1967; the difficulties in this case were not concerned with demand but with supply. Oil cake exports reached 7 million kilograms, worth VN$288,000, and, in the same year fresh vegetables reached their highest level, 1.137 million kilograms, worth VN$3.1 million.

Singapore has also provided a steady marked for fish products since 1960, taking an average of about 250 tons a year.

EXPORT OPPORTUNITIES FOR VIETNAM BY COMMODITY

Rice

Singapore imported 250,000 tons of rice in 1967, of various grades and types and from a variety of sources, valued at $46.5 million; it exported 78,000 tons, mostly to West Malaysia. In the first nine months of 1968, it was importing rice at the rate of 308,000 tons per year, worth approximately $61.0 million. The reexport trade in rice from Singapore appears to be on the decline, since Malaysia is aiming to be self-sufficient in this basic foodstuff by 1972 and Indonesia by 1974. However, even without reexports, a large market exists in Singapore itself. It approximated to 170,000 tons in 1967, and, if present rates of per capita consumption* are maintained (they are presently slightly in excess of those in Hong Kong), the Singapore rice market should grow to 250,000 tons by 1975 and to almost 300,000 tons by 1980.

Nearly all of this will have to be supplied by imports. Singapore's acreage of arable land is limited; it is devoted almost exclusively to

---

*There are no official figures of what these are, but knowledgeable importers state that the decline in recent years has been marginal, and they estimate consumption at 160 to 165 catties per head, approximately ninety-four to ninety-nine kilograms.

higher value crops, and domestic rice production is negligible and always will be.

At present, a rice stockpile is maintained, and importers are
required to purchase from it in proportion to their imports. Rice imports are under license, but licenses are issued liberally. There are
a great many sources of supply, but Thailand is by far the most important single one, providing 48 percent of Singapore's rice imports
by value, even in 1967--a year, it should be remembered, when Thai
rice was in short supply and several Asian countries, including Singapore, introduced an import quota system, in order to protect their
supply position. Substantially, the Singapore rice market in 1967 was
shared between Thailand and Mainland China, which provided 31 percent, by value, of all imports; the remaining 21 percent of imports
came from widely dispersed sources--from Cambodia, Burma, Taiwan,
India, Pakistan, North Vietnam, and West Malaysia in Asia; from the
United States, Mexico, Uruguay, and Argentina in America; and, also,
from Australia and the U.A.R. Trade statistics for the first nine
months of 1968 record the purchase of 16,765 tons from Mexico,
10,158 tons from the U.A.R., 4,688 tons from Uruguay, 5,800 tons from
other South American countries, and smaller quantities from North
Vietnam, Taiwan, Italy, and, even, Japan.

In fact, 20 percent of the Singapore market, that is, from 45,000
to 50,000 tons in 1968, was relatively open to all comers. Vietnam
has the advantage of proximity--relative to many of its potential com-
petitors--and it also has the advantage of long-standing family and
business associations between some of its merchants and importers
in Singapore. Once it is again in a position to produce a surplus for
export, it should have little difficulty in recovering its former share
in some of the growth in that market. Depending on the supply position in Vietnam and on Vietnam's ability to provide regular supplies
at competitive prices, it may be able to dispose of 75,000 tons, worth
$13.1 million, by 1975 and up to 100,000 tons worth, $17.5 million, by
1980.

There is some potential, also, for the export to Singapore of
rice bran and broken rice for animal feeds. In 1967, 52,500 tons of
these commodities, valued at $3.2 million, were imported, and, in the
first nine months of 1968, 55,400 tons worth $2.8 million. As live-
stock production in Singapore increases, demand for feedstuffs is
growing (this is described, with its implications for Vietnamese exports, later in this chapter); rice by-products are an important part
of this demand. Burma and Cambodia presently supply 90 percent of
Singapore's requirements.

Timber

In 1967, Singapore's imports of wood in various forms amounted to $23.57 million, 70 percent of this consisting of logs for its wood-processing industries; its exports of timber in the same year amounted to $20.36 million, 99 percent of which consisted of shaped or worked woods. Its wood-processing industries are growing rapidly. In the first nine months of 1968, imports and exports were almost as high as in the whole of the previous year, a growth rate of 20 to 25 percent. Plywood mills had a capacity of 150 million square feet a year at the beginning of 1969, and additional capacity is being installed. One new enterprise alone will increase capacity by 50 million square feet in 1969.

West Malaysia supplies virtually all of Singapore's requirements for hardwood veneer logs (other than teak and ramin), poles, posts, and other wood in the round, and railway sleepers; it supplied 97 percent of its requirements for sawn wood, other than teak. The market for teak was supplied almost entirely by Burma, about 5 percent going to Thailand. Neither Sabah nor Sarawak supplied more than a minute part of any of Singapore's imports of timber.

The prospects of Vietnam's being able to invade this market are uncertain. There are restrictions on the importation of processed timber, such as plywood and veneer, so the potential for the Vietnamese export trade will be limited to hardwood logs, baulks, and rough sawn woods, other, of course, than teak. West Malaysia has overwhelming advantages in this trade--those of proximity to the market and long-established business connections. On the other hand, Malaysia's capacity to supply external markets after meeting the needs of its own construction and wood-processing industries is far from inexhaustible, and Singapore is beginning to explore alternative sources of supply, particularly in Indonesia.

Singapore's wood-based industries are likely to grow, though not as rapidly as they are doing now, perhaps by about 10 percent a year, so its import requirements will increase as West Malaysia's ability to supply them diminishes. By 1975, they may amount to from $50 to $60 million, twice what they are estimated to have been in 1968. It is not yet known whether Indonesian forests are capable of meeting these considerable demands, and it has been suggested previously that Vietnam might capture 30 percent or even more of Singapore's trade in timber by that year. The target may be an over-ambitious one to aim at against certain competition from the flourishing and efficient timber industry of Sabah. The Sabahan east coast ports, however, are not quite as well located as Saigon with respect to Singapore, and a share of between 15 to 30 percent of total imports

to Singapore, with a value of between $7.5 to $18.0 million may well
be feasible.

Rubber

Singapore is the world's principal rubber brokerage center, situated conveniently between the two largest producers of natural rubber,
West Malaysia, whose production in 1968 was 1.04 million tons, and
Indonesia, whose production was 720,000 tons. Between them, these
two countries were responsible for 70 percent of the world's production of 2.50 million tons of natural rubber in that year. In 1967, Singapore imported rubber to the value of $152.7 million and exported it
to the value of $255 million. In the first nine months of 1968, imports
were $92.9 million and exports $203.5 million. The differences between the import and export totals originate partly in Singapore's own
production (12,000 acres are devoted to the crop), to a much greater
extent in imports of Indonesian rubber not included in these figures,
and, also, in the value added that Singapore derives from its milling
and packing operations.

Small quantities of estate brown crepe and flat bark crepe from
Vietnam are still being marketed through Singapore, and merchants
in that market describe it as of good quality, superior to their imports
from Indonesia. A fair proportion of Singapore's rubber imports, from
16 to 17 percent, are in the form of rubber latex, the demand for which
was also noted in Hong Kong.

In 1968, there was a marked increase in consumer interest in
natural rubber, partly owing to revisions in U.S. and United Kingdom
legislation concerning tires; the Singapore price for ribbed smoked
sheet No. 1 rose from between $0.15 to $0.19 a pound to $0.24 a pound
by the end of the year. While uncertainty is still expressed concerning
long-term trends in prices of natural rubber, at the moment, the price
is resting at about that level. A price of $0.25 was quoted in Singapore
on July 20, 1969. On the more efficient Malaysian estates, which have
increased their yields while reducing costs, production costs need
not exceed $0.14 per pound.

World supply and demand for natural rubber are discussed in
Chapter 3 of this book. The demand for both natural and synthetic
rubber has been steadily growing and seems certain to continue to do
so. What the course of prices will be is less easy to predict. The only
valid conclusion at this time is that Vietnam can sell through Singapore, at whatever the world price may be at the time, all the rubber
it can produce. If quality and regularity of supply can be assured, the
prospects are good. Except for large estates, which have their own

marketing outlets, it would be a mistake not to use the expertise and brokerage facilities of Singapore for this commodity.

Tea

In Singapore, tea is almost entirely a reexport commodity, and the trade is small.

In 1967, imports were valued at $1.788 million and exports at $1.813 million. Estimated comparable figures for 1968, on the basis of actual imports and exports for the first nine months, were $1.79 million and $2.2 million, respectively. Total imports of both black and green tea in 1967 were slightly under 4 million pounds (compared with Hong Kong's 1968 imports of 16 million). Three-quarters of these imports were in the form of black leaf of black dust.

Singapore's principal suppliers of black leaf in 1967 were West Malaysia (624,400 pounds) and Mainland China (223,825 pounds), though there were sizable imports also from Ceylon, Argentina, and Taiwan. The principal suppliers of black dust were Ceylon (537,410 pounds), Argentina (313,040 pounds), West Malaysia, Mainland China, and the Netherlands, and small quantities were also imported from Taiwan, Kenya, Mozambique, and other African countries. Almost all of Singapore's green leaf was imported from Mainland China; North Vietnam (with 44,000 pounds) was the principal supplier of the relatively insignificant quantities of green dust it purchased.

Indonesian imports are not reflected in the trade statistics, and it is consequently impossible to establish with any accuracy the extent of retained imports. Indonesia exports 1.75 million pounds of tea to Hong Kong, where it gains ready acceptance, and it is not unlikely that up to 1 million pounds of Indonesian tea finds its way into Singapore. Local consumption is high (85 percent of the population is Chinese) but the preference is for Chinese tea.

Vietnam should be able to acquire some of the small market claimed by North Vietnam, one of the few Communist countries with which, as yet, Singapore has no long-term bilateral trading agreement, and might also intrude on the positions in the market now occupied by Taiwan and some of the African countries, but the trade in tea with Singapore is unlikely to be very large. It might, at the start, amount to about 250,000 pounds of both black and green teas, worth approximately $100,000 at current prices.

Livestock

There is little prospect of much trade in this area. Singapore's domestic production of pork and poultry is substantial, catering sufficiently for its own needs and providing surpluses of pigs, pork, fowls, day-old chicks and ducklings, frozen fowls, and hen eggs for export to other countries. Exports from Singapore were valued in the first eleven months of 1968 at $3.3 million. Most of the egg exports went to Hong Kong and Vietnam.

The only import items of any significance are beef cattle, including buffalo, and fresh, chilled, or frozen beef. In 1967, some 14,500 head, worth $1.5 million, were brought in, and Thailand practically monopolized this trade. Official and well-informed opinion in Singapore was that Vietnam has little opportunity to break into this market. The Singapore authorities are highly conscious of the dangers of livestock disease, and animal health precautions are rigidly enforced, including a period of observation in quarantine. The market for fresh, chilled, or frozen beef is worth more, about $4 million, but this is dominated by Australia and New Zealand.

A much better opportunity for Vietnam is in the market for animal feedstuffs.

Feedstuffs

In 1967, Singapore imported animal feedstuffs in great variety, to a value of $27.3 million. Exports were worth $14.6 million, mainly to Malaysia, so that retained imports exceeded $12 million. In 1968, imports were estimated at $27.7 million and exports at $15.8 million.

Vietnam should have a capacity to export rice bran, corn, sorghum, tapioca refuse, oil cake, fish meal, and broken rice. Its principal competitors for these markets will be Burma, a prominent supplier of rice bran, broken rice, and oil cake, other than copra; Cambodia, which supplies half the market for rice bran and substantial quantities of corn; Thailand, which supplies most of the corn, broken rice, and cassava refuse and, also, some sorghum and oil cake, other than copra; Mainland China, which supplies 88 percent of Singapore's sorghum and one-quarter of its cassava refuse and oil cake; and the Philippines, the largest supplier of copra and coconut cake and meal. The latter commodities are the only ones that Vietnam sends to Singapore in any quantity at the present time. They represent a small market, and, in 1967, Vietnam had only 14 percent of it.

In these various categories, the total market in 1967 was worth $6.9 million. The partial 1968 trade figures suggest that it is a growing one, and, at current prices, it is probable that it will be worth $9.5 million by 1975 and $12.25 million by 1980. One imponderable is the trade in animal feedstuffs with Mainland China, which is probably a feature of Singapore's long-term agreement with that country, otherwise a supplier with whom Vietnam might reasonably hope to compete. Nevertheless, there is still considerable scope for a profitable entry by Vietnam in the feedstuffs market, particularly in fish meal, corn, sorghum, and rice bran. By 1975, it is conceivable that 25 percent of this part of the market could be captured, amounting to some $2.4 million, a share that could increase to $4 million by 1980.

Coffee

Recorded imports during 1968 amounted to 11, 118 tons, valued at $4.8 million, considerably more than in the previous year, when imports were 5,865 tons, valued at $2.8 million. The biggest suppliers were Africa (3,530 tons), Laos (2,080 tons), and North Vietnam (1,336 tons). Exports, however, were about 25 percent lower in 1968 than in 1967. They amounted to 55,562 tons, valued at $32 million, as compared with 72,330 tons, valued at $40.8 million. Main destinations were the United States and European countries.* For Singapore, this is a very profitable reexport trade.

Singapore is not a member of the International Coffee Organization, but is affected by the decisions of that body, because its principal customers are member countries. A decision, for example, by the Organization to withhold export stamps from its exporting members for the period July, 1969, to September, 1969, had inevitable repercussions in the Singapore reexport market, since coffee not accompanied by export stamps was not allowed into the member countries of the Organization.

Vietnam already has a small foothold in this market; in 1967, 566 tons of coffee beans, worth $54,700, were exported to Singapore, and comparable quantities have been exported in 1968. North Vietnam is a substantial supplier, its 1968 exports to Singapore being valued at $1.088 million. There is no visible reason why South Vietnam should

---

*Domestic production of coffee is negligible. The large discrepancy between exports and imports must be due either to unrecorded imports from Indonesia or the run-down of accumulated stocks, or, more probably, to both.

not obtain part of the North Vietnamese and Laotian shares in Singapore's coffee imports, and, subject to competitiveness in quality and price, its present position in this market should be very much stronger than it is now.

There are many imponderables in projections of world coffee markets, but it seems reasonable to suppose that Vietnam could double its present exports to a figure of $600,000 (at present prices) and increase the trade substantially in due course.

Vegetable Oils

Coconut Oil

There is a ready and growing market for coconut oil in Singapore. Between 1967 and 1968, Singapore's exports and reexports of crude oil increased by 149 percent. Most of the crude oil it imports for reexport comes from Sarawak, though there are also imports from West Malaysia. Prices have been falling slightly, from a range of $22.80 to $17.70 a drum in 1968 to $17.00 a drum in July, 1969.

The total value of 1967 imports was about $3.5 million. There should be no difficulty in obtaining a portion of this market; indeed, merchants in Singapore stated unhesitatingly that they would buy at current prices all the coconut oil Vietnam can produce.

Palm Oil

There is no production at the present time in Vietnam, while extensive plantings in Malaysia in recent years are likely to produce large export surpluses. Imports into Singapore were valued at $14 million in 1967, all from West Malaysia. With world supply said to be outstripping demand, prices are depressed, and unless Vietnam can compete in quality and production costs with Malaysia, (which seems improbable in the medium term), little opportunity is presented by this commodity.

Peanut Oil

There is a small demand for this, also. In 1967, 4,000 tons, worth $1.49 million were imported, most of it from Mainland China, although imports are also recorded from Mozambique ($11,000) and North Vietnam ($121,000). South Vietnam could certainly dispose of small quantities of peanut oil in the Singapore market, perhaps as much as $150,000 worth of the trade that now goes to North Vietnam and Mozambique.

Spices

Pepper exports in 1968 were higher than ever before, with officially reported imports of 8,640 tons of white pepper, valued at $5.4 million, and 10,157 tons of black pepper, worth $4.6 million. Sarawak provided 99 percent of these supplies. Prices received by producers fell in 1968 from $42.50 per ton for white and $34.15 for black to $35.80 and $25.80, respectively; but, by July, 1969, prices had recovered to $41.70 and $31. Despite Sarawak's dominance, it does not enjoy any concessionary trade treatment, and there is some chance for Vietnam to share this lucrative trade.

Cinnamon and ginger are imported to values of $370,000 and $200,000, respectively. Most of the cinnamon is recorded as having been imported from Cambodia (787 tons, worth $334,000), and there is at least a strong suspicion that, in fact, much of this may be Vietnamese cinnamon. There is a small but ready market for these commodities.

Fruits and Vegetables

Although strenuous efforts are being made to increase local production, considerable quantities of fresh vegetables and fruit are still being imported annually, $5.4 million worth of fresh fruit, and $9.3 million worth of fresh vegetables being imported in 1967.

Local fruit production consists largely of rambutans, durian bananas, guavas, and soursops. West Malaysia supplies nearly all the market for pineapples, valued at $900,000 in 1967. There is a steady demand for nontropical fruits, such as apples and quinces, mostly met by imports from Australia, but, also, by some from Mainland China. No great opportunities for Vietnam are presented by the fresh fruit trade, although it may be able to dispose in Singapore of small quantities of citrus, mangoes, and avocado pears. As a result of the increase in tourism and hotel accommodation, there is, of course, a growing market for luxury foods, and Vietnam may also find a small market for some of the rarer fruits it grows on the plateaus.

Singapore grows for itself 50 percent of its vegetable requirements and imports only nontropical varieties. An examination of its imports suggests attractive possibilities for some of Vietnam's temperate zone-type crops, including spinach, asparagus, artichoke, cabbage, and lettuce. Tomatoes, garlic, and onions, although capable of being grown locally, are also imported. Imports of tomatoes in 1967 were worth $560,000, coming mainly from Mainland China and Taiwan; India was a principal supplier of onions--$1.3 million worth out of total imports of $1.9 million--the rest coming from Mainland

China, Australia, the Netherlands, Lebanon, and Poland; fresh garlic
came in from Mainland China and Taiwan, to the value of $203,000,
and fresh cabbages, to the value of $1.2 million. The rest of the trade
in fresh vegatables, which amounted to $3.1 million, was shared be-
tween Australia, West Malaysia, Mainland China, and Taiwan. With
the growth in food-processing industries and increasing local demand
as population grows, this is an expanding market, which will offer
scope for a profitable trade. Even as small a share as 10 percent of
the total would yield earnings of the equivalent of $1 million, and the
expectation is that Vietnam could do somewhat better than this.

Marine Products

Only 40 percent of Singapore's fish consumption is produced by
its own fishing fleet, two-thirds of which is presently occupied in
relatively primitive and unproductive inshore and near-water fishing--
but the fleet is in process of modernization, and its capacity to produce
a much higher proportion of local requirements will grow. Imports in
1967 amounted to 45,000 tons, 84 percent of which were supplied by
West Malaysia, where roughly the same conditions apply. Prospects
of a large trade in fish are not, therefore, particularly promising for
Vietnam, certainly as far as fresh sea fish or pond fish are concerned.
However, as in Hong Kong, there is an unsatisfied demand for prepared
fish, particularly salted and dried fish and fish products, which offers
a small but profitable opportunity. In 1967, $193,000 worth of fish
maws were imported, mostly from India and Pakistan. Vietnam was
the third-largest supplier in that year, exporting to Singapore 8.5 tons,
worth $24,000. A larger share of this specialized market could easily
be obtained.

The demand for salted, dried, but otherwise unprepared, sharksfin appears to be insatiable; it was imported to the value of $1.6 million
in 1967 and $2.1 million in 1968, principally from Japan ($870,000)
but, also, from Aden, Pakistan, Trucial Oman, Ceylon, Mainland China,
South Korea, and certain African countries. Vietnam could enter this
trade without difficulty.

Of other types of salted or dried marine fish, over 6,000 tons
were imported in 1967, worth $1.4 million. West Malaysia has the
largest share of this market (70 percent), but the balance comes from
a wide range of Asian countries, with Mainland China and Sabah the
leading secondary suppliers. Crabs, lobsters, shrimps, and oysters
and other molluscs, fresh, salted, or dried, provide another attractive
opportunity. Imports in 1967 amounted to 12,275 tons, valued at $4.15
million, and though West Malaysia dominates this market, supplying
70 percent by value, the rest of the trade is shared between most other
Asian countries and Australia.

The total value of the trade in these special categories--dried, salted marine fish, fish maws and sharksfin, and crustaceans and molluscs--was $6.6 million in 1967 and approximately $7.1 million in 1968. Demand grows in proportion to population and to the development of the food-processing industries. There is an early potential market for Vietnam for up to $1 million worth of these commodities, with ample room for later expansion.

Miscellaneous

Raw Silk

Little demand for silk now exists, nor is any substantial increase in demand foreseen. The only recorded imports to Singapore in 1967 are 2.5 tons from Mainland China, worth $34,000.

Unmanufactured Tobacco

Imports into Singapore in 1967 were 8.5 million pounds, valued c.i.f. at $5.3 million, the United States supplying over a half and India 17 percent. Significant quantities were also imported from Mozambique and the Philippines. Tobacco is not commonly regarded as a crop that Vietnam is likely to produce in surplus after the war, but it is not unreasonable to suppose that, if in the event production is surplus to domestic requirements, small quantities can readily be sold to Singapore.

Duck Feathers

Vietnam is a traditional supplier of this commodity, although the trade with Singapore is small. Total Singapore imports in 1967 were only $100,000, West Malaysia and Australia, between them, supplying 73 percent of the market. Small as it may be, it is a market that Vietnam could conveniently dominate.

Pharmaceutical Plants

Imports in 1967 were worth $4.1 million, excluding ginseng, which accounted for an additional $2.0 million. The United States and Korea dominate the ginseng market, and Mainland China supplies three-quarters of the market for other pharmaceutical plants, the remainder being derived from India, Taiwan, Pakistan, and Spain. Vietnam appears among the suppliers in 1967, with small quantities valued at a little less than $2,000. Considerable investigation is required of the particular requirements of this market, but it is one that should not be ignored and might eventually represent a profitable opportunity.

SUMMARY OF CONCLUSIONS

Singapore provides a profitable and expanding market for many of the commodities that Vietnam should be in a position to export after the war. Vietnam should have no great difficulty in recovering its previous place in Singapore's rice trade and, by 1975, may be able to dispose of 75,000 metric tons, worth approximately $13.1 million. It is possible that the trade in rice may increase to 100,000 tons, worth up to $17.5 million, by the end of the decade.

There may be even more potential in the export of logs, baulks, and rough sawn hardwood timber to supply Singapore's rapidly expanding wood-processing industries, but competition will be strong, and it is difficult to forecast the dimensions of this trade opportunity. By 1975, it may be in the range of $7.5 to 18 million.

Vietnam has been a supplier of raw rubber to Singapore in the past, and there is no reason why it should not become one again. The extent of the market depends partly on the imponderables of world supply and demand, but there is little doubt that, at prevailing world prices, whatever these may be at the time, Singapore, the rubber brokerage center of the world, will accept and dispose of all the rubber that Vietnam elects to offer it. Vietnam has, of course, other outlets for its rubber, and the assumption made at this time is that it will not sell through Singapore more than 10,000 tons of estate brown crepe and 10,000 tons of latex, probably worth together about $7.5 million.

There are prospects for disposing of up to 250,000 pounds of both black and green tea, worth, at current prices, approximately $100,000.

Singapore exports livestock, and no opportunities are presented for Vietnam in this field; however, there is a large and growing demand for animal feedstuffs, and it is believed that Vietnam will have opportunities to export rice bran, corn, sorghum, cassava refuse, oil cake, fish meal, and broken rice. One-quarter of the total market will be worth about $2.4 million by 1975 and about $4 million by 1980.

Vietnam has already a foothold in the small coffee market in Singapore and can probably double its present sales to yield $600,000, with some expansion possible eventually. The prospects for a trade in vegetable oils are restricted to coconut and peanut oils. Of the former, Singapore is likely to purchase whatever Vietnam can supply. Small quantities of peanut oil could also be sold in Singapore, in spite of the present dominance of other countries in this market. A trade

TABLE 82

Export Possibilities, Vietnam to Singapore, 1980

Commodity	Volume	Estimated Value[a] (In Millions of Dollars)
Rice[b]	75,000-100,000	$13.1-$17.5
Timber, Hardwood Logs[b]	160,000-400,000	7.5- 18.0
Rubber[b]	20,000	7.5
Tea[b]	120	0.1
Animal Feeds[b]	32,000-53,000	2.4- 4.0
Coffee[b]	1,200	0.6
Vegetable Oils (Peanut and Coconut)[b]	2,000	0.5
Spices (Pepper and Cinnamon)[b]	200	0.1
Fresh Fruit	_[c]	_[c]
Fresh Vegetables	3,000	1.0
Marine Products (Dried Salted Sharksfin, Fish Maws, Crustaceans, and Molluscs)[b]	600	1.0
Unmanufactured Tobacco	_[c]	_[c]
Duck Feathers	_[c]	0.1
Pharmaceutical Plants	_[c]	_[c]
Total		$33.9 - $50.4

[a]1968 prices.
[b]In tons.
[c]Not estimated; if any, small.

248

in vegetable oils may amount to $500,000 in the short run. Opportunities occur, also, in such spices as pepper, cinnamon, and ginger, particularly pepper, and there are good opportunities for the export to Singapore of specialized fruits and temperate zone vegetables-- even a small share in this market could yield Vietnam as much as $1 million in earnings. There are no prospects for fresh marine fish, but, as in Hong Kong, there is a ready demand for salted, dried fish; sharksfin; fish maws; and crustaceans and molluscs--a trade in which about $1 million can probably be achieved in the fairly early future-- and there are good prospects that it will grow.

One major question concerns the extent to which the long-term bilateral agreements Singapore has entered into with Communist countries will interfere with the operation of normal market forces. In Singapore, unlike Hong Kong, there are obvious opportunities, however, for government-to-government negotiations, which could affect trade between the two countries. Singapore already enjoys a substantially favorable balance of trade with Vietnam and may easily be disposed to some mutually beneficial arrangements under which it will continue to dispose of some of its manufactures in the Vietnamese market. Subject to any effects introduced by such negotiations, the prospects for Vietnam's export trade to Singapore as we now see them are set out in Table 82.

GENERAL INFORMATION

Few of the developing countries of Asia, or, indeed of the entire world, have equaled South Korea's performance in the promotion of exports during the 1960's. The experience of South Korea in developing its own export trade offers valuable guidelines to other countries who want to do the same, and it was partly for this reason that South Korea was included in the countries selected for study in the context of this study.

With a land area of less than 100,000 square kilometers and a population of over 30 million, South Korea has one of the highest population densities in the world. At the time of partition (of what was formerly a single country), most South Korean industry was located in the northern half of the nation. There has been rapid industrial development in the south during recent years, resulting in a large movement of population from rural to urban areas. In 1968, it was estimated that 35 percent of the South Korean people were living in the towns. The population growth rate has been about 2.7 percent, but efforts are being made to reduce this to 2 percent or less.

Although only 23 percent of its land area is cultivated, South Korea aspires to achieve and maintain substantial self-sufficiency in food production. In addition to its agricultural resources, the Republic has some mineral deposits (coal and metals) and a plentiful supply of low-cost labor. By constant attention to increasing productivity, with heavy emphasis on nonagricultural goods for export, GNP has increased from $95 per capita in 1961 to $165 in 1968. The performance of South Korean agriculture, however, has as yet been substantially inferior to that of its industry. Adverse weather conditions in 1967 and 1968 had severe effects on harvests, but even after allowance for this, agriculture has not been holding its own with the industrial sector of the economy.

EXTERNAL TRADE

Promotion of exports has been a first priority in the development program. Exports have increased more than tenfold, from $43 million in 1961 to $622 million in 1969. During the same period, imports have increased even more, from $316 million to $1,656 million, so that the apparent negative balance of trade was actually greater in 1968, in spite of the successful export drive. It should be noted, however, that imports in recent years have included large amounts of capital goods and industrial raw materials; the Korean Economic Planning Board projects (though some consider too ambitiously) exports at $3.6 billion in 1976. Estimates of volumes of particular commodities that will enter into South Korea's external trade in that year are not available, but it is intended that the drive will continue for self-sufficiency in agricultural produce, with some special items produced for export, as well; it is expected that, by 1976, the great bulk of the commodities imported will consist of industrial raw materials.

A shortage of labor may conceivably be experienced in South Korea by that time, though this will obviously depend on a variety of factors, including the degree of mechanization of agriculture and the rate of industrial expansion. If in the event that urban-based industries attract so many people out of the countryside as to affect agricultural production adversely, then the mix of imports can hardly be exactly as South Korea presently expects. In this case, it is not unlikely that the Republic will provide a market for increased amounts of surplus foodstuffs, feed grains, and other agricultural products, which Vietnam may have available for sale after providing for its own requirements.

The progress made by South Korea in developing its export trade suggests a few observations that may be pertinent to its future trade relationships with Vietnam.

As recently as the 1950's, South Korea's exports consisted almost entirely of foodstuffs and mineral ores, the products of its farms and subsoil. Three-quarters of its exports today consist of the products of its processing and manufacturing industries. In the course of this transformation, South Korea has ceased to be comparable to, and competitive with, many countries in Southeast Asia, including Vietnam, whose export trade is still mainly in agricultural, marine, and mineral commodities.

Although South Korean exports of foodstuffs, tobacco, and raw materials now constitute only a minor part of its total exports, some of its exports in these categories are of interest to Vietnam, either because they are potentially competitive with Vietnamese products or because they may suggest new lines of production and new outlets for this country. These particular items (1969 figures) are shown in the following list:*

Commodity	Percent
Clothing	25.8
Plywood	12.7
Wigs, and so forth	9.7
Radios, and so forth	5.9
Raw silk	3.8
Fish products	3.1
Cotton fabrics	3.0
Leaf tobacco	2.2
Synthetic fibers	2.0
Dried laver	2.0
Tungsten ores	2.0

TRADE WITH VIETNAM

In the recent past, South Korea has been an outlet for only token quantities of Vietnam's export products, in spite of the fact that, by and large, the two countries do not produce identical commodities for export and differ considerably in their production pattern.

South Korea's eight most lucrative markets and their relative importance to the economy are shown on the following page:**

---

*Source for data is Bank of Korea.

**Source for data is Bank of Korea.

Market	Percent
United States	50.2
Japan	21.4
Hong Kong	3.9
Canada	2.4
West Germany	2.6
United Kingdom	1.7
China (Taiwan)	2.1
Vietnam	2.1

The prominent positions in this list of Japan, Hong Kong, and Singapore are significant, and so is the appearance of Vietnam, even though it comes at the bottom of it.

In spite of the heavy preponderance of manufactured goods in its export trade, South Korea is still able to trade effectively with countries themselves extensively involved in manufacturing, sometimes in the same commodity field. Price has undoubtedly been a strong incentive to buy South Korean goods. In other cases, of course, South Korea is offering scarce commodities, such as dried seaweed, ginseng, and handmade wigs. It is not expected that, by 1975-80, Vietnamese industry will have developed to a point at which it will be able to compete extensively with South Korea in these existing markets for Korean manufactures; it is only in a few primary items, such as shrimps, fish, and tobacco, that Vietnam and South Korea might then be competing directly for outlets. In general, there appear to be good opportunities for the development of a trade relationship between these two countries, based on a range of complementary products. The economies of South Korea and Vietnam are complementary, rather than competitive.

Official statistics in Saigon indicate that Vietnam's exports to South Korea over the entire period 1958-67 were valued at only $1.2 million (f.o.b. Vietnam) and that, during the same period, Vietnam's imports from South Korea were valued at over $59 million. In 1968 alone, South Korea recorded sales to Vietnam of more than $5.5 million. Vietnam's major purchases in recent years have included cement, sheet iron, and other metals and engines, fertilizers, and oriental medicines (including ginseng). Military purchases, such as clothing and footwear, are not included in these trade returns. In the last two years, almost the only item moving from Vietnam to South

Korea has been scrap iron, shipments of which were valued at about $300,000 in the first eight months of 1969. As in other cases already discussed, the trade between the two countries has been one way and one-sided, partly, but by no means wholly, owing to the circumstances of the Vietnam War.

One factor favoring trade between Vietnam and South Korea is the fact that most of the former's potential clients in Korea have not yet become so large that Vietnamese dealers would be on a totally unequal footing. In South Korea, Vietnam may find a more natural trading relationship than it would in Japan and other developed countries, with their requirements for bulk buying and regular, consistent supplies.

Relating the probable import needs of South Korea with the probable availability of products for export from Vietnam, there is clearly a reasonable opportunity to move toward a better balance in the trade between the two countries. South Korea's total imports in 1967 and 1968, as reported by the Bank of Korea and the South Korean Ministry of Agriculture and Forestry, include a number of commodities that are now produced or may reasonably be expected to be produced in Vietnam. Table 83 lists these items and volumes imported and, in each case, the principal sources of supply during 1967/68.

EXPORT OPPORTUNITIES FOR VIETNAM
BY COMMODITY

The prospects for Vietnamese exports to South Korea up to 1975-80 are described for the items that Vietnam may produce surplus to its own requirements. (See Table 84.) It should be emphasized, at this point, that no official estimates of future South Korean requirements for specific commodities have been prepared.

Rice

In the short term, the outlook is doubtful, but it may become more favorable over time. South Korea has imported varying quantities of rice, depending largely upon weather conditions and their effects on its own harvests. Thus, imports were 139,000 metric tons in 1937 and 247,000 metric tons in 1968, when drought struck the country--from 1964 to 1966, rice imports were insignificant. With better weather and good prices, the output in 1969 was expected to be adequate.

South Korean official policy is to increase agricultural production, and rice is the country's principal crop. Water control is being extended, improved practices are being adopted, and prices are supported by

TABLE 83

South Korea: Selected Imports, 1967/68
(In Metric Tons)

Commodity and Year of Report	Volume	Major Sources of Supply
Rice (1968)	246,803	United States
Corn, Unmilled (1968)	9,655	United States
Cornmeal (1967)	6,606	United States
Soybeans (1968)	4,014	United States
Bovine Skins (1968)	6,977	United States
Natural Rubber (1968)	24,898	Malaysia
Coffee (1968)	47	Indonesia, South America
Wood and Lumber (1968)	1,982,198	Malaysia, Philippines, United States, Indonesia
Wood Pulp (1968)	149,474	United States, Sweden, Canada
Iron and Steel Scrap (1968)	390,927	United States
Bananas (1967)	1,810	China (Taiwan)
Cinnamon (1967)	122	Indonesia
Copra (1967)	2,352	Singapore, Malaysia, Thailand
Shrimps (1967)	1,940	Japan
Unmanufactured Tobacco (1967)	79	Turkey

Source: Bank of Korea.

government intervention. With this emphasis on rice production and with a probable slight decline in per capita consumption, it is improbable that Vietnam can look to South Korea as a sure market for its surplus rice during the period of 1970-75. After that time, it is possible that labor needs in the industrial sector, a modification of South Korean policy on price supports, and population growth may result in South Korea's becoming a regular importer of rice. Should this occur, then Vietnam would be a probable source of supply and might participate in the trade by supplying 40,000 to 50,000 metric tons of polished rice to this market annually. Whether this long-term prospect will be realized obviously depends upon the variables mentioned above, particularly the relaxation of South Korea's present determination to be self-sufficient in rice at any cost. It will also depend, just as obviously, upon Vietnam's ability to meet competition, especially that

TABLE 84

Export Possibilites, Vietnam to South Korea, 1975-80

Commodity	Volume (In Metric Tons)	Estimated Value[a] (In Millions of Dollars)
Rice	40,000-50,000	$7.0-$8.7
Natural Rubber	15,000-20,000	5.6-7.5
Hardwood Logs	800,000-1,000,000	36.0-45.0
Wood Pulp	-[b]	-[b]
Feed Grains	10,000-15,000	0.8-1.2
Oil Cake Vegatable and Oils	1,000-2,000	0.2-0.4
Cinnamon	70-80	0.6-0.7
Soybeans	-[b]	-[b]
Coffee	-[b]	-[b]
Bananas	-[b]	-[b]
Scrap Iron	-[b]	-[b]
Total		$50.2-$63.3

[a]1968 prices.
[b]Not estimated; either small or dependent entirely on production capacity.

Source: Authors' estimates.

of the United States, the principal present source of rice imports into
South Korea.

Corn and Sorghum

The prospects for participation by Vietnam in an expanding
market for feed grains are distinctly favorable. As long as Korea
places primary emphasis on rice production, this policy is likely to
result in the reduction of its capacity to produce other cereals in
sufficient quantity to meet its increasing requirements for both human
and animal feeds. By 1975-80, it may be possible for Vietnam to
supply from 10,000 to 15,000 metric tons of corn and/or sorghum to
South Korea each year. As in the case of rice, the principal competition
is likely to be from the United States.

Soybeans

Unless production in Vietnam becomes more efficient than it
now is, the prospects of Vietnam's disposing of any surplus soybean
crops in South Korea are poor. Soybeans are a major crop in South
Korea, and, in some years, domestic production has been sufficient
to meet demand. Although a need for imports may continue to occur
from time to time, the present competition of the United States and the
possible future competition of Mainland China will be severe, making
it difficult for Vietnam to break into this trade. Possibly, some
special trade agreements might be negotiated, under which South
Korea would take some of Vietnam's soybeans, possibly by barter,
in exchange for South Korean exports to Vietnam. In any event,
quantities would be small, unlikely to exceed 2,500 to 5,000 tons
annually by 1975-80.

Bovine Skins

With continuing emphasis on leather manufactures, South Korea
will probably import larger quantities of hides, but Vietnam is unlikely
to be able to take great advantage of this assured market, since beef
and buffalo production can hardly increase to an extent that will provide
large surpluses of hides for export by 1975-80. The outlook for exports of this commodity cannot be described as better than fair.

Natural Rubber

There is little reason why Vietnam cannot share in the South
Korean market for rubber, providing it can compete with other

producers on price and quality. At present, Malaysia is South Korea's principal source of supply for natural rubber. Imports were 25,000 tons in 1968; consumption will undoubtedly increase as South Korean industry grows, so that that figure should be at least doubled by 1975; if this happens, it is not unrealistic to suggest that, in 1975-80, Vietnam may be able to export from 15,000 to 20,000 tons of natural rubber a year to this market. The outlook for exports of rubber to South Korea appear to be excellent.

Coffee

The prospects for participation in the coffee bean market are only fair. The South Korean market for coffee is a small one, competition for any coffee market is stiff, and a newcomer will find it exceedingly difficult to enter the trade. Vietnam may be able, by 1975-80, to sell 50 or 100 tons of beans a year to South Korea, but this commodity will not be a large earner of foreign exchange in that particular market.

Wood and Wood Products

Logs

South Korea is a major user of wood and lumber and offers an almost certain market for the types of timber it consumes in its important industries of manufacturing plywood and other processed wood products. Timber imports increased threefold by volume between 1963 and 1967 and are quite likely to do so again before 1975. Competition for safe and regular sources of supply of raw materials is keen among the wood-based industries of Korea, Japan, and Taiwan.

Vietnam has some advantage of location over at least some of South Korea's present principal suppliers. Its logging industry, it is true, is still poorly developed, but there is some confidence that the resources exist in sufficient volume to supply both its own wood-based industries and some of its neighbors, and only moderate investments are required to exploit them. The South Korean market is probably capable of absorbing from 800,000 to 1 million metric tons of logs from Vietnam by 1975-80, provided Vietnamese production can be made to achieve such volumes.

Wood Pulp

Here, too, at least from the point of view of demand, the prospects for the export trade are good. Pulp imports into South Korea have

been increasing rapidly in recent years and are expected to continue
to do so. Whether Vietnam can develop a pulp industry that will be
competitive with South Korea's major suppliers--the United States,
Sweden, and Canada--must still be regarded as problematical; if it
does, South Korea will provide an outlet for 25,000 to 30,000 tons of
pulp annually by 1975-80. This would be a totally new industry in
Vietnam. (At the time of this writing, the feasibility of a Vietnamese
wood pulp industry is still being studied.)

Iron and Steel Scrap

South Korea is already importing scrap from Vietnam, and its
demand for this commodity is growing fast. It is expected that an
integrated iron and steel complex will be completed by 1973, and the
demand for scrap will then be much greater than it now is. The extent
of Vietnam's participation in this market, providing prices are in line
with those in other areas, is likely to be mostly a matter of what
supplies will be available. Vietnam has never exported more than
20,000 tons of scrap in any year since 1955; there could, in fact, be
a market for at least 80,000 to 100,000 tons a year in South Korea by
1975-80, but it is questionable whether quantities of anything like this
magnitude will be regularly available for export from Vietnam. By
1975, it will probably be appropriate for Vietnam to consider whether
it should not invest in a steel industry of its own. On the whole, it
seems safer to assume that scrap will not appear to any great extent
in the list of commodities that Vietnam may export to South Korea.

Bananas

South Korean demand for this fruit is not very large at present,
and it is supplied almost entirely from Taiwan, under a semibarter-
type arrangement by which South Korea purchases Taiwanese bananas
and sells apples in exchange. However, as per capita incomes rise in
South Korea, the demand for bananas may very well take the same
course it has done in Japan, and quite a substantial market for the
fruit is expected to develop.

What share Vietnam can capture in this expanding market remains
to be seen. It should be no great problem to produce bananas acceptable
to South Korean tastes and meeting the other requirements of the trade.
There are more difficult problems concerning marketing technology
and transportation in which Taiwan excels, and it has, because of its
relative proximity to the South Korean market, a considerable advantage
over other producers. It would not be realistic to assume that Vietnam
will be able to displace Taiwan in this market to any great extent, and

if it can negotiate entry into the market at all, the quantities it will be able to dispose of are not large, perhaps from 4,000 to 6,000 tons a year by 1980.

Cinnamon

For this commodity, the prospects in South Korea will be as good as anywhere else. Most of South Korea's supplies now come from Indonesia, and there is no reason why Vietnamese cinnamon should not capture a very good proportion of the trade. By 1975-80, it should be possible to ship seventy to eighty metric tons of cinnamon annually to the South Korean market.

Oil Cake and Vegetable Oils

There will be severe competition on these items, both from other suppliers in Asia and from types that Vietnam does not produce, but, as in other Southeast Asian countries, demand in South Korea is continually increasing, and it is thought that Vietnam may be able to export from 1,000 to 2,000 tons of oil cake and vegetable oils annually to South Korea by 1975-80. However, on its past performance, the South Korean market for vegetable oils fluctuates considerably from year to year and probably cannot be depended upon as a steady outlet.

Fish Products

South Korea imported almost 2,000 metric tons of shrimps from Japan in 1967, but this does not represent a normal situation. In the four previous years, shrimp imports never exceeded five tons per year. No need is presently foreseen in South Korea for sizable imports of shrimps or of any other fish products; in fact, South Korea is building up its fishing industry and is already exporting its products in considerable volume, over $25 million in 1968. South Korea should not be thought of as providing more than a sporadic outlet for limited quantities of shrimps and other processed seafoods from Vietnam; it does import some live fish, but transportation of live fish from Vietnam will be difficult and costly.

Manufactured Tobacco

South Korea is a substantial producer and exporter of the types of tobacco currently produced in Vietnam. The only leaf tobacco it imports consists almost entirely of special types used for blending with local tobaccos for cigarette manufacturing. Unless and until Vietnam becomes a producer of these special types of tobacco (and can compete with other producers of them), there will be little or no chance of a trade in tobacco with South Korea.

SUMMARY OF CONCLUSIONS

As can readily be seen, from Table 84, appearing on page 257, the potential export trade with South Korea is likely to consist substantially of three major commodities--rice, rubber, and hardwood logs. Rice exports have been estimated with some hesitation, because of the evident analogy between South Korea's situation and policies and those of Japan; on balance, however, South Korea does seem rather less capable than Japan of fulfilling its policy of achieving self-sufficiency in rice and more likely, in the early future, to abandon it. Easily the most considerable item in the table is hardwood logs, and the estimate given reflects South Korea's capacity to absorb Vietnamese timber rather than Vietnam's capacity to supply timber in these volumes after meeting the needs of its domestic industry and those of other possible markets.

There are also markets in South Korea for feed grains, vegatable oil cake and oils, and cinnamon, and, in these cases, the export volumes and values suggested reflect more accurately Vietnam's capacity to supply South Korea's markets and, indeed, may fall well below it. There are much larger and more certain markets for wood pulp and scrap iron.

For the sake of completeness, soybeans, coffee, and bananas are included in the list, in order to indicate the existence of South Korean demands for these three items, but no suggestions are made concerning export volumes and values. In all these cases, Vietnam will face strong competition from producers who are already firmly established in the South Korean market and who are generally better placed than Vietnam to supply it. Exports of soybeans, coffee, and bananas are unlikely for this reason to become large items in the trade with South Korea, and, if there are earnings from these commodities, they will almost certainly be insignificant. South Korea's disposition to enter into bilateral trade agreements with other countries in order to maintain its exports to them is, of course, a factor that may, in the event, suggest a revision of this forecast.

GENERAL INFORMATION

With an area of 1.2 million square miles (excluding the disputed territories of Jammu and Kashmir), India is the seventh-largest country in the world; with a population, estimated in mid-1969, at 537 million, it has far more people than any other, with the single exception of Mainland China. It is a land of great diversity: rainfall, for example, varies from less than 5 inches per annum in some places to over 480 inches in others; crops range from tropical to temperate in type; over 200 languages or dialects are spoken; and numerous stratified socioeconomic groups exist among the population.

Including landless farm laborers, over 60 million families depend for their livelihoods upon agriculture and allied pursuits. It is said that 82 percent of the population live in the rural areas (there are over 500,000 villages in India) and that 60 percent live in small villages of less than 2,000 inhabitants. The population has been increasing at a rate of 2.5 percent per annum in recent times, in spite of efforts to make family planning programs more effective. Average life expectancy, increasing rather rapidly, from forty-five years to fifty-three years since 1961, has contributed importantly to the population growth rate.

Largely because of the constant pressure of rising population, India has found it difficult to make substantial gains in per capita income. In 1968-69,* it was estimated that the national product per

---

*India's fiscal year is from April 1 to March 31, and practically all its statistical data are constructed accordingly.

263

capita had increased by only 5 percent (at constant prices) since 1960-61; it was then the equivalent of about $72. There are great disparities between urban and rural income and a very uneven distribution of income among the population: as might be expected, there is an extremely large low-income class; a small, but growing, middle class; and a very small group that can be described as wealthy. Agriculture contributes about half the GNP in India, and manufacturing provides 14 percent of it.

In spite of the large numbers of people engaged in agriculture, India has not been able to provide itself with all its food requirements, and large quantities of food grains (wheat, rice, and so forth) have been imported. Only a minority of the population is vegetarian on principle, but, in fact, most Indians eat little meat. An average Indian diet provides about 1,400 calories a day from food grains (rice is the staple foodstuff of three-quarters of the people) and about 650 calories from pulses, sugar, oils, fruits, vegetables, milk, and a little meat, mostly poultry. Even though such commodities as jute, rubber, tea, and coffee are produced in quantity, Indian agriculture is still almost totally dominated by the food crops. Grains are human foodstuffs, and it is rare to find even corn and sorghum used for any other purpose, such as feeding livestock. Only one-third of India's grain production enters into commercial marketing channels, the bulk being used at home or bartered in the villages. Net farm income has increased by 10 percent (at constant prices) since 1960-61, but per capita rural incomes have increased only very slightly.

ECONOMIC DEVELOPMENT AND
TRADING CONDITIONS

Since 1948, India's economy has been gradually changing from being that of a completely agrarian one to one in which industry is becoming important. Since 1951, the government has embarked upon a series of five-year plans, intended to accelerate growth in both the public and private sectors and to double per capita income by 1977/78. The original plan emphasized the development of agriculture, irrigation, power, and transportation, while the next one, starting in 1956, placed priority upon the development of basic and heavy industries. These priorities were continued in the third plan period, but, after 1966, with serious depression and a difficult resources position, India had to revert, in 1967/68 and 1968/69, to annual plans, which were directed principally to agricultural production and allied programs, a reflection of the acute food problem that India faced at that time.

A fourth plan, for the period 1969-74, has been prepared. It gives top priority to industry, transportation, the social services,

and agriculture. Most observers agree that the goals established for
these sectors are extremely ambitious in India's circumstances.
Projected growth of real national income at a rate of 5 percent per
annum is apparently twice what India has hitherto achieved. The fourth
plan stipulates self-sufficiency in food grains by 1973/74, and there
is growing doubt that this can be achieved, particularly as regards
rice, on which progress has been slower than on wheat and other
cereals.

This current economic development plan envisages increased
imports of certain nonfood commodities (principally fertilizer materials, nonferrous metals, and crude oil) and continuing imports of
other nonfood items, including machinery, equipment, and industrial
raw materials, the last of which presumably includes rubber and copra.
Simultaneously, it calls for an average annual growth rate of 7 percent
in exports and for the achievement of a favorable balance of trade by
1978/79. While the trade in India's traditional exports, particularly
tea, jute, and cotton textiles, is expected to grow at a relatively slow
rate, greater progress is hoped for from diversification into metals
and metal manufacturers, iron ore, and chemicals and allied products.
It is assumed that world demand for these items is sure to grow rapidly
and that India can produce them at competitive prices. While tea and
jute will continue to be major exports, they will probably be relatively
less important than they now are. At the same time, some other agricultural and fisheries products are expected to contribute substantially
to India's exports, among them oil cake, shrimps, and even, to some
extent, rice, of the high-quality aromatic varieties that the country
already sells overseas.

In spite of its size, India must presently be reckoned to be only
a minor trading nation, to the extent that its exports make up less
than 1 percent of the world total. Even with the increases projected
for 1980/81, its share of the world's export trade would still be less
than 2 percent. Understandably, India may be preoccupied with its
internal problems, of which the need to grow more food is the most
pressing. Supplies of all types of goods tend to be short, leading to
a sellers' market, a condition distinctly unfavorable to development
of the export trade. As far as imports are concerned, trade is deliberately limited to necessities, and licenses are required. Generally
speaking, only foodstuffs and the goods required for industrial production are permitted to be imported. A large number of commodities
are either banned completely or licensed for importation only by the
actual users. The situation of India's external trade is also strongly
influenced by the operations of state enterprises, the Indian State
Trading Corporation (STC) and the Food Corporation of India (FCI),
and by Indian imports under the PL-480 program. Although the bulk
of the country's trade is still handled by the private sector, the trend

appears to be in the direction of increasing state involvement.

The STC and the FCI are the principal state enterprises involved in foreign trade, the former both exporting and importing and the latter operating primarily as a receiver and distributor of food commodities. Both organizations are government agencies in corporate form, although they have somewhat more freedom of action than regular government offices.

The STC was set up in 1956, under the aegis of what is now the Ministry of Foreign Trade and Supply. Its function is to broaden and enlarge the scope of Indian exports and to arrange for supplies of essential imports on an economical basis. It has several affiliates, the Minerals and Metals Trading Corporation, the STC (Canada), the Handicrafts and Handlooms Export Corporation, and the Indian Motion Pictures Export Corporation.

One major reason for the establishment of this agency lies in the need for a centralized authority to deal with Communist countries, which are themselves similarly organized. Exports through the STC have been dominated by fabrics, textiles, shoes, salt, and dried fish, but have included many other goods, including tobacco, pepper, lemon grass oil, bananas, human hair, and opium. No less than 125 different items were exported during 1967/68. As for imports, in the same year, the STC purchased 73 kinds of commodities, mostly industrial raw materials and equipment, but no rubber, the industrial raw material of greatest interest to Vietnam. Importation of particular commodities is actually reserved to the STC, copra and palm oil being two of them. At the same time, the STC also engages in internal trade and in price support activities for commodities with significant export potential, such as jute. It even engages in production; it has opened a wig factory, and it proposes to manufacture footwear, too.

Practically all the foods imported into our purchased internally in India are routed through the FCI, which dates from 1965. Prospective suppliers will note that the FCI does not itself buy the commodities imported, a function discharged by the government's regular procurement agency, but it does not make some of the decisions on what to buy and it is responsible for distribution. The Ministry of Food is also, of course, involved in policy determinations, but, in effect, only the FCI is granted licenses to import foods. Except for its other dealings in fertilizers (on behalf of other importers, it cleared 283,586 metric tons of imported fertilizer through its port facilities in 1967/68), the FCI's imports have been restricted almost entirely to rice, wheat, and sorghum. Operating through some hundred offices, located throughout the country, the FCI both purchases and distributes foodstuffs. It discharges important functions in price support and in local procurement operations, as well as in arranging for an equitable distribution of available foods among the states. The FCI has also participated in some industrial-type activities, such as flour milling, manufacturing a new food for children (Balahar), and operating paddy dryers and installing improved rice mills. Among the services the FCI offers are port operations, quality control laboratories, and extensive storage facilities.

The PL-480 program requires mention, since it has been responsible for so large a proportion of India's food imports in the last fifteen years. PL-480 foods have been shipped to India in very substantial amounts; India is, in fact, the largest single recipient of U.S. commodities under the special terms provided by the program. The original agreement between the United States and India under the program was signed in 1956.

The terms of these agreements have varied from time to time, but a regular, salient feature is the concessional nature of the sales, payment for which is wholly or partly in nonconvertible rupees, resulting in rupee funds that are then generally used within India for certain specified purposes, such as loans and grants in support of the economic development programs. Obviously, it is difficult if not impossible for other producers of the goods covered by the PL-480 agreements to enter the trade on anything like a normal commercial basis. Wheat, which is of no concern to Vietnam, has dominated this program in India; but over 1.8 million metric tons of rice have also been provided since 1956, though rice shipments have been very small in the last three years. The magnitude of this activity is indicated by the value of the commodities covered by the various agreements, which now stands at over $4.6 billion.

EXTERNAL TRADE

In the two last decades, India has imported substantially more goods than she has exported, with the result that a large trading deficit has been accumulated.

Since 1964, at least, the unfavorable balance has been relatively stable, and, in the last year of record, it has been considerably reduced, reflecting a fall in the volume of imported foodstuffs and, also, some improvement in India's export trade.

Undoubtedly, these continuing trade deficits would have led to serious impairment of the nation's financial position had it not been for concessional sales (particularly under the PL-480 program), which eased India's situation considerably. One result has been a rigid system of controls on imports and another is the adoption by India of a variety of methods to promote its export trade.

Although India imports a wide range of products, there are relatively few items that may reasonably be expected to enter into any future trade with Vietnam. They are listed, together with the values of Indian imports in the last two years of record, in Table 85.

The following information, including information on current sources of supply, is relevant to the discussion of Vietnam's prospects of entering into the trade in these commodities.

In 1968/69, the live animals imported consisted, for the most part, of cattle and sheep, and Australia and Nepal were the principal suppliers. Imports of cereals included 472,109 metric tons of polished rice, valued at $76.6 million, of which Thailand supplied 216,000 tons; Burma, 126,000 tons; the U.A.R., 82,000 tons; Nepal, 22,185 tons; and the Philippines, 19,000 tons; but rice in smaller quantities is purchased from other countries as well, including in 1967/68, for example, Cambodia, Spain, Argentina, and Venezuela. Cereal imports also included a little corn, 845 metric tons to be exact, all from Nepal. In the previous year, corn imports were much larger, 42,828 tons, nearly all of it from the United States.

Imports of nuts were largely cashews, almonds, and pistachios from Africa and certain Middle Eastern countries, although in 1967/68, 135 tons of betel nuts were purchased from Malaysia. The dried fruits imported were almost entirely dates and raisins. Coffee imports were negligible, for India itself is a substantial producer and exporter, and this is obviously true of tea, as well; the imports in this particular commodity group consisted mostly of the spices--485 tons of pepper, from Singapore, Indonesia, and Malaysia; 29 tons of cloves, from Tanzania and Singapore; 55 tons of nutmeg, from Singapore, Malaysia, and Indonesia; 570 tons of ginger and miscellaneous spices, mostly from Nepal; and some aniseed and cassia from Singapore and Malaysia. Imports of cloves were much larger in 1967/68 than in the following year--942 metric tons.

India gets its oilseed cake, 8,934 tons, from Nepal; its tobacco, 334 tons, from the United States and Nepal; and its copra, nearly 15,000 tons, from Ceylon, the Seychelles, Tanzania, and New Guinea. Ceylon was the principal supplier of this commodity, contributing over one-third of the total. India is, of course, a considerable producer of natural rubber, but, in 1968/69, it still bought 4,686 tons from Malaysia, 2,473 tons from Singapore, 1,292 tons from Ceylon, and 1,000 or 2,000 tons from other producers. Its imports of wood in the rough, only 6,000 cubic meters, came almost entirely from Nepal,

TABLE 85

India: Imports of Selected Commodities,
1967/68 and 1968/69
(In Millions of Dollars)

Commodity	1967/68	1968/69
Live Animals	$ 0.2	$ 0.2
Cereals (Including Rice)	690.9	448.8
Fruits, Vegetables, and Nuts	52.3	61.9
Sugar and Honey	0.7	1.8
Coffee, Tea, and Spices	3.1	1.5
Unmanufactured Tobacco	1.9	0.6
Oilseeds, Oil Nuts, and Oil Kernels	7.0	4.7
Raw Rubber	5.9	6.5
Wood	1.4	0.9
Pulp and Waste Paper	13.7	13.9
Jute	2.4	12.4
Scrap Iron	2.2	1.6
Vegetable Oils and Fats	22.1	12.9
Essential Oils, Perfumes, and Flavors	2.4	2.6
Vegetable Fibers, Other than Cotton and Jute	5.6	11.3

Source: Foreign Trade Statistics of India.

but imports of wood pulp were substantial, 68,900 tons, chiefly from the United States and the U.S.S.R.; and a little waste paper was purchased from Nepal.

India bought 44,000 tons of jute last year, nearly all of it through Singapore, though Singapore was obviously not the original producer, and 5,600 tons from Malaysia. It bought even more kenaf, 47,678 tons to be exact, valued at $9.5 million, entirely from Thailand.

Scrap metal, mostly tin plate, was imported to a volume of 11,556 tons from a variety of suppliers, including the United States, the United Kingdom, Japan, Belgium, and Australia. In the group described as gums and resins, the most important items are gum arabic, asafetida, gum copal, and dammar batu. Imports of produce of this type totaled more than 5,000 tons. The vegetable oil imports were predominantly soybean oil from the United States (43,374 tons), but some palm oil came in from Malaysia (760 metric tons, as against 6,448 tons in the previous year) and a little tung oil from Malawi, Malaysia, and Taiwan. Citronella was the most important of the essential oils imported, 70 tons in all, of which 58 tons came from Taiwan and 7.5 tons from Indonesia, but small quantities of such oils as patchouli, nutmeg, clove, and canango also came in; in 1967/68, there was a recorded import of 6 metric tons of cinnamon leaf oil. The extent to which all, or any, of these commodities may offer prospects for the trade between India and Vietnam is discussed in the following section of this book.

As far as exports are concerned, India's performance over the last twenty years has not been particularly outstanding. There has been some growth, but the pace has been rather slow. A gradual shift toward metals, machinery, and equipment, and other products of the engineering industries has been taking place, although the traditional exports--jute, cotton, leather, tea, cashews, and oil cake-- continue to provide the bulk of the country's export trade.

All the same, since 1951/52, the value of exports has ranged between $1,114 million in 1953/54 and $1,715 million in 1964/65, making, of course, a significant contribution to the economy. Table 86 indicates the size and relative importance of the major export items in 1968/69; in addition, it suggests that, in several cases, India is more likely to compete with Vietnam than to do business with it and that the prospects of Vietnam's being able to sell to the large Indian market are distinctly poor.

In recent years, the United States and the United Kingdom have been the principal destinations for India's exports, although Japan and the U.S.S.R. have been moving up rapidly and now occupy the

TABLE 86

India: Selected Exports, by Value, 1968/69

Commodity	Exports (In Millions of Dollars)	Percent of Total Exports
Jute and Jute Manufactures	$294.1	16.2
Tea	208.7	11.5
Cotton, Raw and Manufactured	164.6	9.1
Iron Ore	117.9	6.5
Leather and Allied Products	116.2	6.4
Engineering Goods	113.3	6.2
Iron and Steel	91.7	5.0
Cashews	82.9	4.6
Oil Cake	66.0	3.6
Gems and Jewelry	63.4	3.5
Tobacco	45.0	2.5
Spices	33.5	1.9
Chemicals	31.8	1.8
Fishery Products	29.6	1.6
Coffee	23.9	1.3

Source: Foreign Trade Statistics of India.

third and fourth places, respectively. Nepal, Ceylon, Australia, Iran, the U.A.R., Canada, and West Germany have also provided important individual markets for Indian products.

Among the country's exports, there are several that have particular significance to the export prospects for Vietnam, and both the direction of the export trade and the volumes of the commodities traded in 1968/69 are pertinent to this discussion.

Ceylon, for instance, took most of India's exports of dried fish, which amounted to 5,880 metric tons. The United States and Japan were its principal customers for its chilled and frozen prawns and shrimps, receiving 11,363 tons and 3,207 tons, respectively, with only a few hundered tons being disposed of outside these two major markets. Nearly 1,000 tons of dried prawns and shrimps were also exported, two-thirds of it to Hong Kong, and some to Singapore. About 340 tons of fresh lobsters were sold to the United States.

Although India was a large net importer of rice, it sold 6,766 tons of its high-quality aromatic variety to such Middle Eastern countries as Kuwait, Saudi Arabia, and Muscat; the same countries, together with Bahrein and Qatar, provided markets for 10, 235 tons of Indian bananas. India sold overseas in that year almost 100,000 tons of raw sugar, practically all of it to the United States, with an insignificant quantity going to the United Kingdom; over 28,000 tons of coffee, mostly to the Communist bloc countries; more than 200,000 tons of tea, not only to the United Kingdom, though that is still easily India's best customer for the commodity, but, also, to other Western and Eastern European countries; and 28,000 tons of pepper, to a variety of markets in Europe and the Middle East.

Exports of oil cake, mostly peanut and cottonseed, which were very large--over 800,000 tons--went to the Communist bloc countries, to the United Kingdom, and elsewhere in Europe. The United Kingdom and other European countries took most of India's exports of 52,692 tons of unmanufactured tobacco. Exports of wood products were restricted to a few specialty items, rosewood and teak, for example, which find ready markets in Europe, Hong Kong, and Japan. There was a large export of scrap iron, 402,000 metric tons, almost all of which went to Japan. The United States, the United Kingdom, and certain European countries provided the most important outlets for exports of lac and shellac, amounting to 24,600 tons, but, in fact, such products as these are sold by India just about all over the world. Some 50,000 metric tons of fixed vegetable oils were sold overseas in 1968/69, mostly to the countries of the Communist bloc, but with smaller quantities going to the United Kingdom, Japan, and the United States. Shipments of essential oils were largely of lemon grass

(130 tons, mostly to the U.S.S.R. and the United Kingdom) and sandalwood (123 tons), most of which went to the same two countries but,
also, to other European countries and to the United States.

EXPORT OPPORTUNITIES FOR VIETNAM
BY COMMODITY

For a number of reasons, separately or in combination, we
reach the conclusion that, in spite of the great size of the Indian
market, it is one that offers only very limited prospects for the
Vietnamese export trade.

Because of its great diversity of environmental conditions,
India herself produces in quantity and even exports most of the commodities that Vietnam will hopefully be able to produce in quantities
surplus to its domestic requirements. Moreover, India is endeavoring
to restrict imports to absolute necessities, mostly essential foods
and industrial raw materials, and, in this effort, its import trade
has been subjected to an immense array of restrictions and regulations.
In varying degree, foreign trade is now being conducted through state
enterprises and under bilateral trade agreements; historical trading
patterns in some cases and special concessional arrangements in
others will make it difficult for new suppliers to enter the Indian
market on a purely commercial basis.

In spite of the formidable difficulties created by these circumstances, the fact remains that there is a trade. Between 1958 and
1967, Vietnam imported from India goods valued at $48.3 million,
though exports to India have amounted to only $1.2 million, mostly,
at that, in three particular years. In recent years, most of the sales
to Vietnam by India have been generated by the Commercial Import
Program, financed by the foreign aid program of the United States.
It is reasonable to assume that the future trade between the two
countries will be less one-sided; although the prospects for an export
trade of very large dimensions are not encouraging, there are, at
least, a few commodities that may be both available for shipment
from Vietnam and, also, needed by India. The prospects for the
more probable of these potential exports are discussed below.

Rice

This is the most important food grain in India, representing
40 percent or more of the country's food grain production and occupying
30 percent of the land being cropped. Production has been rising,
but not rapidly, from 1960/61 until 1967/68 by about 10 percent

overall; the new HYV's have not yet gained wide acceptance. In 1968/
69, output reached a record level of almost 40 million tons of polished
rice; in that same year, imports were over 470,000 tons (none of which
came from the United States), and, in 1969/70, it is expected that they
will be as much as 500,000 tons, including 144,000 tons under the PL-
480 program.

The Fourth Five-Year Plan (1969-74) aims at making India self-
sufficient in food grains, including rice, by 1973/74, but there is
some doubt whether this can be done. In recent times, rice production
has certainly been restrained by a consistent policy of supporting other
grains, especially wheat, at higher levels. It has been estimated that,
by 1978/79, India will need 49.5 million tons of rice for human consumption, an increase of 20 percent over 1968/69 production; if performance
should fall short of aspirations by a mere 2 percent, this would imply
a need to import almost 1 million tons. A further factor suggesting
continued imports is that India finds it profitable to export its high-
quality basmati rice and import lower grades, especially brokens.
On the other hand, our measure of the prospects of Vietnam's being
able to sell rice to India should take into account the possibility that
concessional sales, under the PL-480 program, for example, may
continue, even though, in fact, little rice has been shipped from the
United States to India in the last three years.

Subject to rather more in the way of reservation than has been
expressed in some other market areas, it is possible that Vietnam
may find an outlet for as much as 75,000 to 100,000 tons of its rice
in India by 1978/79. It is clear, of course, that it will encounter
strong competition from Thailand, Burma, and the U.A.R., the traditional suppliers, and it may very well encounter strong competition
from the United States as well. In passing, it should be noted that
all India's purchases of this commodity are made by the government
for distribution by the FCI.

Natural Rubber

India is trying to achieve self-sufficiency in this commodity as
well. In addition, it is gradually expanding output of synthetic rubber
and may be expected to continue on this course. India's imports of
natural rubber have not been large: at 10,000 metric tons, they were
unusually low in 1968/69, and they amounted to 16,000 metric tons
during the first seven months of 1969/70. Supplies have come from
Malaysia, Singapore, and Ceylon for the most part, although France,
Germany, the United Kingdom, Belgium, and the United States have
also provided certain processed items.

In an assessment of India's need to import natural rubber, one assumption is that the nation will continue to expand its industrial output, including automotive equipment, and another is that demand may outstrip India's productive capacity, even though production in the rubber-manufacturing industries has doubled since 1960/61. By 1978/79, India's imports of natural rubber could easily be in the range of 25,000 to 35,000 tons a year. It would not be excessively optimistic to suppose that Vietnam might supply from 5,000 to 7,500 metric tons of such a total. India's principal suppliers now are Malaysia, Singapore, and Ceylon, all of whom have close trading relationships with her, though they do not have any special or official preferential position. Rubber is imported by the actual users, consisting at the present time of eight large industrial enterprises.

Copra

India should provide a steady outlet for a moderately large quantity of both edible and nonedible soap stock types of copra. Unlike rubber, the trade in copra is channeled through the STC, which buys and sells the commodity in its own right. India does not expect to become self-sufficient in the group of products to which copra belongs, and imports will probably increase at least as fast as population and purchasing power.

About 15,000 metric tons of copra was imported in 1968/69, and, during the first seven months of 1969/70, another 12,000 tons of imports were recorded. The major sources of supply for the Indian market are Ceylon, the Seychelles, Tanzania, and New Guinea, with most of the buying taking place from July to December. In this case, Indian officials appeared quite receptive to the possibility of additional or alternative sources of supply, providing quality and price of the product were satisfactory.

If, by 1978/79, India is importing 25,000 to 30,000 tons of copra annually, then Vietnam might find an outlet for perhaps 5,000 to 7,500 tons in this market. Undoubtedly, there will be sharp competition from other suppliers, including both traditional ones, as well as such countries as the Philippines and Indonesia, who have not traded copra in any volume before but who will certainly seek to do so. However, copra is quite frequently cited as one of the more hopeful prospects for trade between the two countries.

Vegetable Oils

Besides large quantities of soybean oil (unlikely to be a prominent export from Vietnam by 1980), India has also been importing small quantities of palm oil from Malaysia, Nigeria, and Singapore. Imports were 6,500 tons in 1967/68, but fell to only 760 tons in 1968/69 and to 294 tons during the first seven months of 1969/70.

Commercial plantings of oil palm have yet to take place in Vietnam, but it is supposed that the crop may have at least some of the potential here that has been demonstrated for it in Malaysia. Whether palm oil can make much of an impression on the Indian market for fixed vegetable oils as a whole it is difficult to say--supplies so far have simply been too limited for this to be put to the test. (In the first seven months of 1969/70, India imported 43,000 tons of soybean oil, in contrast to 300 tons of palm oil). The cost of palm oil and soybean oil is roughly comparable in India, about $290 a ton for the former and $320 for the latter, though this is not to imply that the two are completely comparable. It seems entirely possible that, in another ten years, the Indian market might absorb from 2,500 to 5,000 tons of palm oil a year, but this will, of course, be a new and relatively untried product for Vietnam, and it is rather less possible that the industry can be developed in this country quite that rapidly. In present conditions, any palm oil imported into India would be imported by the STC, which has complete and sole authority over the purchase and distribution of this commodity. There are too many uncertainties, both on the supply side and the demand side, to warrant an enthusiastic view of the prospects.

The same is true of tung oil, which India purchases regularly, though not in large amounts--147 tons during the first seven months of 1969/70, for example, and 137 tons in the whole of 1967/68. The principal suppliers are Malawi and Taiwan, and small amounts are also shipped from Malaysia, Argentina, and several East African countries. If Vietnam can supply this product competitively, there might be an outlet for perhaps 40 to 50 tons annually in India by 1978/79.

Carnauba wax (from the wax palm) is another vegetable product imported into India. From April, 1969, to October 1969, imports of the commodity totaled 165 metric tons; Brazil was the major source, with the United States and the United Kingdom providing smaller quantities. There might be a market here for 50 to 100 tons of carnauba a year, but, in present circumstances, when it is not even known whether production of the commodity will be feasible in Vietnam, it may be wiser to make no forecasts. Carnauba is mentioned here simply as a small but interesting possibility that came to light during the study and may repay examination at some future time.

Gums and Resins

This group of commodities contains several items regularly imported by India, the more important ones being gum arabic, asafetida, copal, benjamin ras, benjamin cowrie, and dammar batu. The principal sources of supply are the Sudan, Malaysia, Singapore, Thailand, and Indonesia, but several other European and Asian countries participate in the trade, including the Netherlands, Germany, Afghanistan, Iran, and Japan. Almost 5,400 metric tons of gums and resins (rosin excluded) were imported in 1968/69, and some 3,340 tons were reported for the first seven months of 1969. Like palm oil, most of these items would be new to Vietnam, at least as far as the export trade is concerned, and it cannot presently be said with certainty that they are even adapted to production in this country, though the pine forests of Tuyen Duc may well be capable of producing resins for export. If they can be produced, and at prices comparable to those of the other suppliers, then it should not be difficult to dispose of 500 to 1,000 tons of gums and resins a year in India.

Spices and Flavoring Materials

India is both an importer and an exporter of spices and flavoring materials; in some cases, pepper, for instance, the trade flows both ways. Last year, Singapore, Malaysia, and Indonesia together supplied India with 485 tons of pepper and 55 tons of nutmeg, and Tanzania and Singapore supplied 29 tons of cloves. Imports of cinnamon were also quite small, only 3 tons, though 942 tons of cloves and 13 tons of cinnamon were imported as recently as 1967/68. These two commodities are now subjected to rigid import controls, and trade in them is unlikely to grow in the foreseeable future. Certain other spices, including aniseed, cassia, badian, and cumin are brought into India in moderate quantities, ranging from 25 tons to 100 tons a year.

Apart from the neighboring Asian countries of Singapore, Malaysia, Indonesia, Taiwan, Nepal, and Afghanistan, India's biggest supplier of spices is Tanzania, which provides most of the cloves and the cassia. Without a considerable and, on the whole, improbable relaxation of existing restrictions on imports, the chances that Vietnam will be able to sell cinnamon and cloves to India are poor. The chances of its selling certain other spices--pepper, nutmeg, cassia, aniseed, and badian--may be slightly better, but with strong competition from traditional producers and inadequate experience in this country of the production of these spices, the chances should not be overrated. The largest share of the spice trade with India that Vietnam might hope to obtain in, say, ten years, will probably be within the modest range of twenty-five to fifty tons a year, and even that figure is advanced with considerable reservation.

Citronella oil is by far the most important flavoring material produced in Asia and imported by India. Imports of this product were 172 metric tons in 1967/68, 70 tons in 1968/69, and 102 tons from April, 1969 to October 1969. Taiwan is easily the largest supplier. Small quantities of other essential oils, such as patchouli, nutmeg, clove, and canango, are imported from Indonesia, Malaysia, and Singapore, but most of the imports in this category are received from Europe. Providing Vietnam can develop a capability to produce citronella and, perhaps, other essential oils by 1978/79, there should be possibilities of disposing of some 30 to 40 metric tons per year to India. The essential oils are listed here chiefly for their interest as possible new products, not because they are likely to achieve great significance in the export trade in the early future.

Vegetable Fibers

Jute and jute manufactures have been India's leading export for some time. In recent years, however, production of raw jute and similar fibers has fallen considerably below the requirements of the country's industry, while the political situation has shut India off from its most obvious external source of supply--Pakistan. For these reasons, India has now turned to Thailand for kenaf, relatively large quantities of which have been purchased--24,500 metric tons in 1967/68, 47,700 tons in 1968/69, and 23,300 tons from April, 1969, to October 1969. Quite recently, some difficulty has occurred in the kenaf trade with India, which complains that certain Thai exporters do not observe contract terms as regards quality. These particular difficulties can be overcome, but whether Pakistan will again become a direct source of raw jute for India is problematical.

In the early 1960's, Vietnam made good progress in the development of kenaf as a commercial crop, but, more recently, production has virtually ceased, and Vietnam is now importing these fibers. Nevertheless, it is not improbable that Vietnam will be able to produce kenaf in sufficient quantity to care for its own needs and to provide surpluses for export. Assuming no important change in India's requirements and supply situation, Vietnam may be able to export from 5,000 to 7,500 metric tons of kenaf a year to India by 1978/79. At the moment, India is undoubtedly the best prospective outlet for kenaf exports, but it must be added that this market may not be a stable and enduring one.

Jute, too, is an important import for India. Almost 45,000 tons were received from Singapore and Malaysia in 1968/69, though, in the first seven months of 1969/70, imports of only 5,200 tons were recorded. Some of the jute purchased from Singapore and Malaysia was undoubtedly of Pakistani origin. While jute has been produced in Vietnam, the crop has never been important and has never been given the attention that went into the promotion of kenaf; today, jute cannot be considered anything like as good a prospect for the export trade. India will probably continue to import jute to supplement its own very large production, so a market should be available to those who can produce at competitive prices. In the summary of conclusions presented in Table 87, jute has been omitted and kenaf included, though forecasts of the volume of exports that might be achieved are hazardous, depending both on Vietnam's productive capacity and the extent of the shortage in India's own production.

Other vegetable fibers, notably cotton and sisal, large volumes of which are imported into India, cannot yet be considered serious prospects for the export trade. They are not produced in any volume in Vietnam, nor are there firm plans to extend the plantings of such crops. However, it may be appropriate to give some indication of India's requirements for these commodities: imports of cotton totaled 78,500 metric tons during the period April, 1969-October, 1969, and imports of sisal were almost 6,500 tons.

Corn

Corn is a human food in India, very little being diverted to animal feed. Imports of unmilled corn are not large, compared to wheat and rice. In 1967/68, India received 42,800 metric tons, the bulk of which--39,500 tons--was supplied by the United States under the PL-480 program; in the following year, imports were only 845 tons, all from neighboring Nepal. Between April, 1969, and October, 1969, 10,900 tons of unmilled corn were brought in--2,000 tons from Nepal and the balance from the United States.

Together with other food grains, corn has been given special emphasis in the Fourth Five-Year Plan. Considerable progress has been made in developing HYV's, and improved cultural practices are being introduced. The opinions we heard in India tended heavily to the view that domestic production would substantially meet the country's requirements over the next several years. Since imports have not been large in recent years and since they have consisted mostly of concessional purchases, there must be serious reservations concerning the prospect of Vietnam's being able to sell much unmilled corn to India in the period up to 1978/79. The prospects, if any, are minimal and marginal, and no estimate of potential exports is justified at this time.

TABLE 87

Possible Vietnamese Exports to India,
by Commodity, 1978/79

Commodity	Volume (In Metric Tons)	Estimated Value (In Millions of Dollars)*
Rice	75,000 - 100,000	$12.0 - $16.0
Natural Rubber	5,000 - 7,500	2.0 - 3.0
Copra	5,000 - 7,500	1.0 - 1.5
Palm Oil	-	-
Tung Oil	-	-
Canauba Wax	-	-
Gums and Resins	-	-
Spices	-	-
Essential Oils (Citronella, etc.)	-	-
Kenaf	5,000 - 7,500	0.75 - 1.125
Total		$15.75 - $21.625

*At 1969 prices.

Pulp and Wood

Almost 70,000 metric tons of wood pulp were imported by India in 1968/69, and a similar amount was received in the first seven months of 1969. The United States, Canada, and the U.S.S.R. are India's principal suppliers. There is no doubt that India will continue to import wood pulp in quantity, in spite of efforts to increase its own production--in fact, the expectation is that its requirements of imported pulp will grow substantially. There may be some opportunity for new suppliers to enter this market, but they will do so only if they can meet the competition of the traditional suppliers in price and quality. Since it has not yet been demonstrated (though it is hoped) that Vietnam can produce pulp in quantity at a reasonable price, it would be imprudent to predict exports of this commodity to India, even though the demand exists and the need to import will continue. If the day does come when Vietnam is producing an exportable surplus of pulp, then India may be one of several possible outlets in Asia.

India now imports quite negligible amounts of logs and lumber and is not likely to import very much larger ones in the future. India exports a few wood products, mostly specialty items, such as teak and rosewood; it manufactures some plywood, though production is still inefficient and at high cost, and the industry cannot compete in world markets with Korea, Taiwan, and Japan. Some indications were received of a probable increase in the demand for lumber as incomes improve, but this may not occur for some time, and, in any event, it is unlikely that Vietnam will find a good market for logs or lumber in India against the competition of such favorably situated competitors as Burma and Nepal.

SUMMARY OF CONCLUSIONS

Judged simply by numbers, with its population increasing annually by a number equal to one-half the total population of Vietnam, India appears, at first sight, to be a very large and rapidly expanding market with which a lucrative trade should be possible. But India has low per capita incomes, and it also has severe problems of foreign exchange, arising, in part, from the regular excess of imports over exports. Circumstances almost dictate the restriction of imports to necessities, and, even in necessities, the opportunities to trade are diminished by concessional sales under such programs as PL-480. The trading situation is additionally complicated both by long standing trading-partner arrangements and by the extensive use of bilateral trade agreements, some of which involve payments for imports in nonconvertible currency.

Taking into account what India will need and can probably afford to buy by 1978/79 and, also, the kind of commodities that Vietnam may have available for export by that time, it is apparent that the prospects for Vietnamese exports to India are quite limited. One reason, of course, is the fact that India produces in quantity and, in some cases, even exports most of the commodities that Vietnam itself is likely to produce; frequently, India's needs for import arise from a temporary short-fall in domestic production, a condition in which a stable and continuing trade is not too likely to develop. The possibilities, such as they are, are set out in Table 87. If anything, they may err on the side of optimism; they represent, in fact, what India might buy from Vietnam by 1978/79 in the most favorable circumstance (from Vietnam's point of view), if Vietnam succeeds in producing the commodities listed in quantities and at prices and qualities competitive with those of India's traditional suppliers and if India fails to achieve the production goals it has set itself. In this regard, it will be noted that rice easily dominates the commodities listed in Table 87. Some commodities are included that Vietnam does not now produce in volume, and, in these cases, targets for exports are too speculative to be suggested. Some commodities that Vietnam does produce are more likely to be exported, but in quantities too insignificant to be taken into the total.

Of the commodities listed in Table 87, only rice, rubber, and copra are traditional products of Vietnam, and most of the others (all in fact, except kenaf and some of the spices) represent possible inno-vations in Vietnamese agriculture and industry. It is not yet known with any certainty whether commodities such as these can even be developed in Vietnam, and until it is, exports to India must be consid-ered quite problematical. They are inserted into Table 87 because there is a need for innovations, and they ought to be tried. It will be noted also that the two most important commodities, rice and rubber, are products in which it is India's stated aim to be fully self-supporting before 1978; their place in the table represents a doubt in the minds of India's friends (though not in the mind of many Indians) whether this aim will actually be achieved.

If Vietnam is to develop any sizable trade with India, it is almost inevitable that its government will need to play a direct role in initi-ating and developing the trade. India makes extensive use of bilateral agreements, and Vietnam will probably find it advantageous, and even necessary, to negotiate with India, if for no other reason than to provide the setting conducive to mutually beneficial trade. Vietnam-ese exporters will find trading with India somewhat different from dealing with other Asian markets, in that Indian buying tends to be centered in a few large enterprises: all foods, for example, in the IFC; copra and palm oil in the STC; and rubber in eight private manufacturers. This constitutes a concentration of buying power, which Vietnamese exporters will find it difficult to confront except in concert, suggesting the need for joint action, possibly by means of a trade association or board, to strengthen their position as sellers.

GENERAL INFORMATION

The archipelago of Indonesia, consisting of over 3,000 islands and covering an area of almost 750,000 square miles stretches a distance of 3,200 miles, from Sabang in the western tip of Sumatra to West Irian. Five principal islands make up the greater part of this huge land area: Sumatra, Java, Kalimantan (Borneo), Sulawesi (Celebes), and West Irian, but myriads of other islands, some as large as Ceylon, many only coral reefs, go to make up the whole. They form a highway between the Pacific and the Indian oceans and a bridge between the continents of Asia and Australia. Superimposed on the United States, they would reach from the Atlantic to the Pacific coasts.

Inhabiting these islands is a population that, by 1968 estimates, numbered 118 million, making Indonesia, in terms of population count alone, the fifth-largest country in the world, after Mainland China, India, the U.S.S.R., and the United States. Versatile, diligent, and intelligent, these people form a labor force skilled in traditional agricultural arts but showing indications of a ready adaptability to modern technology, both in agricultural and in industrial progress.

Rich resources in minerals and oil, in untapped forests, and in agricultural capacity are only partially and gradually being exploited; much investment is needed before this potential can be significantly realized. As far as Vietnam is concerned, dwarfed as it is in size, manpower, and resources by this emerging neighbor, a study of the economy and growth of Indonesia is warranted, not primarily to establish the possibility of profitable trade relationships but because of the role Indonesia can, and probably will, play in dictating future patterns and terms of trade within the region, particularly in primary commodities and probably in direct competition with Vietnam.

285

The present economic condition of Indonesia is largely the result of its immediate history. Its development, particularly that of Java, was greatly furthered by the Dutch, whose subjugation of the country commenced in the seventeenth century and which was finally completed in the late nineteenth century. Indeed, much of Indonesia's existing assets in the form of infrastructure--roads, railways, and ports-- and in export-oriented estate production of rubber, tobacco, coffee, palm oil, and so forth owe their existence to Dutch investment--even though the Dutch cultural system, centered mainly on the forced cultivation of cash crops, might be regarded as oppressive.

Following the eviction of the Dutch by the Japanese in early 1942, Indonesian nationalists took the opportunity to organize. On Japan's surrender in 1945, the nationalists were then in a position to issue a declaration of independence from the Netherlands. After a period of resistance and strife, a federal state, formed in union with the Netherlands in 1948, collapsed, and a unitary state was formed in 1950. This ushered in the period of Sukarno's dictatorship, punctuated with events that are still well-remembered widely today: the country's unilateral withdrawal from the UN, the confrontation with Malaysia, the rejection of Western foreign aid, the "Guided Democracy" ideology, the deliberate pursuit of closer ties with local Communists and the socialist countries of the world, and what one Indonesian commentator has described as "the wilful subordination of rational economic principles to prestigious politics."[1] Sukarno's era and the inefficiency of his administration were terminated by the military, which took power in 1966 after an abortive Communist coup.

Today, the government's main task is to overcome the heritage of waste and corruption left by Sukarno, this time assisted by international agencies and by the bilateral aid extended by numerous developed countries. The picture of economic breakdown that faced the new regime can have few parallels in history. The country was in default on a foreign debt officially estimated at $2,400 million. Foreign exchange earnings in 1966 ($430 million) were less than half those required for necessary imports and debt service; tax collection fell far behind uncontrolled government expenditure; and supply shortages had reduced industrial production to below 20 percent of capacity. Estate production was stagnating or declining, and years of neglect and running down of equipment was making road, rail, shipping, and other public services difficult and intermittent.

Inflation reached 635 percent in 1966, but the earnest application of fiscal controls and the determined limitation of expenditure by the new government reduced it to 120 percent in 1967, to 85 percent in 1968, and, it was reported, to a mere 5 percent in 1969.

These improvements, coupled with a rescheduling of debts, increased foreign investment through progressive, flexible investment policies and procedures, and streamlining and enforcement of the previously overelaborate system of controls on the economy (rendered practically inoperative through corruption and inefficiency) have led, in recent years, to some increase in both agricultural and industrial production and to an amelioration of the country's balance of payment problems.

The picture that emerges, therefore, is one of a country of immense potential wealth, struggling to arrest the process of economic deterioration and to overcome the depredations to its economy caused by a decade of misrule and misdirected effort. In this, it is having some success and is poising to take the next necessary steps toward self-sustained growth, based on increases in agricultural production (particularly self-sufficiency in rice), on the rehabilitation and improvement of the infrastructure and of mining, and on some development of the mining, and other, industry.

But there are formidable obstacles to this progress. The concessionary aid and foreign investment now enjoyed by Indonesia must be placed in the perspective of a country fragmented into numerous islands, with great physical transportation difficulties and with a very large and growing population. The magnitude of investment and aid that might well put Vietnam firmly on the road to an economic takeoff after the war would make but little impact on the economy of this potentially great nation. Much has to be expended merely to keep up with population growth. The cost of the necessary infrastructure for development, because of the distances involved and the deterioration of the existing minimal services, is excessively heavy. Although the population is concentrated in Java (almost 70 percent of the population of Indonesia occupy 7 percent of the land area), the resources are widely dispersed. Lack of purchasing power creates almost insuperable problems; per capita income ranges from $80 to $100 a year, and manufacturing capacity is very small. Indonesia, for example, still imports plywood and pulp from such countries as South Korea, made from Indonesian timber exported in the first place. Value added accruing from domestic processing is negligible. The lack of processing capacity is startling: 80 percent of all paddy is hand pounded; most of the wheat flour consumed is imported. Growth in the agricultural, oil, and mining sectors adds very little, at present, to effective demand for consumer products. What consumer demand exists is largely dependent on artificial price levels--subsidized through foreign aid.

The reasonably rapid development of Indonesia, say within the next two decades, depends to a very great extent on the future success of oil and mineral exploration. Either could overcome the country's foreign exchange problems and clear the way to effective implementation of development plans in all sectors. But success is problematical, and progress may be slow. One major limiting factor is corruption and the evasion of controls, which, despite strenuous government efforts, still vitiates much of the endeavor now being made to promote development. In this context, for example, it is an accepted fact that local tire and cigarette production cannot compete in price with the delivered retail cost of such articles manufactured abroad, smuggled into, and sold openly in, the country.

To some extent, the possible future trading relationship between Vietnam and Indonesia can be characterized as being dependent on the relative success each country obtains in furthering its economic objectives. In other words, it could be a race toward self-sufficiency and affluence, the winner enjoying at least temporary trading advantages --for, in the end, it must be realized that both aim at, and are capable of producing, surpluses in many of the same agricultural commodities. It is not oversanguine to hope that, provided Indonesia does not get too great a head-start, Vietnam could well prove to be the more successful one--if only on account of its compactness and, despite the war, the comparative excellence of its infrastructure.

ECONOMIC AND TRADING CONDITIONS

Accurate and up-to-date statistics are hard to acquire in Indonesia. In January, 1970, the latest published trade statistics were dated 1967, although 1968 figures in summary form were available in mimeographed sheets. But these, especially the import statistics, are of dubious value because of the fluctuation of the Indonesia rupiah over the last few years and because of wide variations between years in import patterns.

Trading conditions are still difficult, although the government's policies designed to halt the rapidly deteriorating economic situation and to control inflation have met with some success. Years of excessive inflation have depleted capital resources, both state and private, and, as a result of the government's tight money policy, what credit is made available by the state banks is channeled into the production, distribution, and export sectors. Most imports are financed on a "cash" basis and supplier's credit restricted to limited short-term credit for a very short list of government-specified essential commodities, such as fertilizer, rice, and newsprint. Longer-term credit usually takes the form of bilateral government-to-government aid agreements.

Strict controls on the financing of imports have been accompanied by higher import duties on nonessential imported goods and an attempt to stimulate exports by permitting exporters to keep a larger proportion of their foreign exchange earnings. The success of these measures to channel imports into production goods is indicated below:[2]

	1967	1968	1969*
Consumption goods	43.8	45	28.03
Raw materials	32.5	41	42.15
Capital goods	23.7	13	21.51
Other	-	-	8.31

These foreign trade developments are promising, and exports have reached a level where they can cover the imports of the private sector. In 1969, the balance of trade showed a surplus of $75.5 million, an improvement of 15.3 percent over 1968 exports. The increase in oil export revenues, Indonesia's main source of foreign exchange, totaled 26.8 percent.

It would be fair to say that there is, as a result, a greater feeling of political stability and economic confidence now than the country has known for many years and, at the same time, a realistic sense of the problems, difficulties, and impediments to early achievement of even modest goals.

IMPORT SYSTEM

There is no import licensing, the free market forces being allowed to operate to achieve quantitative control. Government direction of imports is exercised by the level of duty applied to five categories of imports and through the type of foreign exchange used.

Types of foreign exchange for imports fall into three categories:

1. Foreign exchange derived from exports known as bonus export certificates, or "general B.E." It can be used to import all goods on the essential (B.E.) import list.

2. Tied bilateral foreign aid sold through foreign exchange banks as "aid B.E.," which can be used to import essential items.

---

*Provisional.

3. Supplementary foreign exchange, known as "D.P.," which can be retained or freely transferred abroad and used to import luxury goods. Exporters who obtain a price for their goods above a price level set by government (usually slightly below world market prices) are allowed to retain the difference, which becomes D.P. exchange. Importers' commissions are treated in the same way.

General or aid B.E. is cheaper than D.P., and the rate is established three times a week by a call system at the bourse.

Of the five categories of imports that follow, the first three are classified as essential and are contained in what is called the B.E. list, i.e., only these goods can be imported with B.E. foreign exchange.

1. Group A--very essential items, with nil or minimal duty rates, e.g., basic foodstuffs, pharmaceuticals, fertilizers, newsprint, and equipment and machinery for food production and the textile industry.

2. Group B--essential items, with a low duty rate, e.g., a wide range of machinery and spare parts for industry, raw materials, non-luxury vehicles.

3. Group C--less essential items, with a medium to high duty rate.

4. Luxury imports--all goods not on the B.E. list.

5. Prohibited imports--textiles and batik designs and printed matter in the Indonesian language.

IMPORT DUTIES AND OTHER TAXES ON IMPORTS

Customs duty rates vary from 0 to 100 percent over four groups of commodities.

Indonesia is a signatory to the GATT, and the tariffs contain a separate GATT column, but, for all practical purposes, the actual rate of duty charged is the same, irrespective of the country of origin, since parity is achieved by the application to any lower rate of a "special foreign bills retribution." Surcharges can raise the effective rate of duty on certain luxury items as high as 300 percent. There is also a sales tax of from 5 to 50 percent on many imported goods, levied on the c.i.f. price, plus duty and surcharge.

POPULATION

The first national census in Indonesia took place in 1961, revealing a population of 97 million, including an estimated 700,000 inhabitants of West Irian. The only other survey was made by the Dutch in 1930, when the population was estimated at 60.7 million, that is, an increase in the order of 60 percent over thirty years. On the basis of a postenumeration survey of 1962, it was further estimated that, with a crude birth rate of 43.0 per 1,000 persons and a crude mortality rate of 21.4 per 1,000, the rate of growth is approximately 2.2 percent. On this basis, the population was 101 million in 1963, 106 million in 1965, and 118 million in 1970; in 1980, it will be 143 million, in 1990, 176 million; and, by the end of the century, it will have reached 216 million.

There are, however, wide differences among demographers about the rate of growth. Some work on a 2.3 percent growth rate, which doubles the population every thirty years and which implies a present population of 125 million; others have used a 2.4 percent rate of increase.

It should not be forgotten that, at its present stage of development, Indonesia has a high mortality rate. Life expectation, on the average, does not exceed fifty-five years. The main problem in containing growth (and family planning is in its infancy) is that mortality rates may decrease dramatically as standards of living improve and medical facilities begin to be more widespread.

The main pressure of population growth is to be found in Java (67 percent of the population occupying 7 percent of the total land area of the country), and this situation is likely to grow worse. Interisland transmigration has never been successful (the dense forests and sparser agriculture of the outer islands do not attract the Javanese), and even if as many as 10,000 persons a year were to be resettled outside Java, this would account for only 7 percent of Java's expected yearly increase in population. West Irian is the opposite extreme, with 22 percent of the land area and only 0.7 percent of the population. Kalimantan contains 4 percent and occupies 28 percent of the land area.

Much of Indonesia's planned increases in agricultural production will be overtaken by population growth, unless effective measures are implemented to contain it. There is no evidence, at present, that this is happening. The postulated and planned economic growth rate of 5 percent per annum will similarly be eroded.

FIRST FIVE-YEAR DEVELOPMENT PLAN

This recently adopted plan covers the period April 1, 1969, to March 31, 1974. The main feature is the development of agriculture, followed by infrastructure, industry, mining, and oil.

Development in the agricultural sector aims at increasing food production, particularly rice, and at the same increasing and diversifying agricultural exports. The first priority is self-sufficiency by the end of the plan period in rice--a commodity on which Indonesia now spends in excess of $100 million of scarce foreign exchange annually. This involves an increase of some 50 percent from the present level of approximately 10 to 15.4 million metric tons and an investment estimated at over $63 million. Overall investment in agriculture, including irrigation, is estimated to reach almost $1 billion.

Physical targets for agriculture are shown in Table 88.

There is considerable skepticism as to whether these targets can possibly be reached. Many, including rice, have been established on the basis of dietary needs by 1974 in terms of caloric intake. They are nutritional targets, basically. Further consideration is given to this aspect in the sections dealing with specific commodities.

Estate products, rubber, palm oil, tea, coffee, sugar, pepper, tobacco, and copra are given significance. They contribute 70 percent of the country's export earnings, but much rehabilitation, rejuvenation, and modernization will be required.

Forestry, also, is the target of ambitious development. Statistically, there are 48 million hectares of protected forest, 24 million hectares of productive forest, and 18 million hectares due for conversion into agricultural land. There are a further 30 million hectares that fall into none of these categories. At present, only 7 percent of the available forest area has been exploited.

Infrastructural targets are shown in Table 89. The entire infrastructure has suffered from gross neglect, and ten years will be needed to catch up with overdue repair and rehabilitation. The bad state of the roads has led to an overburdening of the railways--the bulk of rolling stock being more than forty years old. Dredging inadequacies have closed navigation channels, and poor port facilities have hindered sea traffic. Telecommunications cover limited areas only. Industrial and mining targets are shown in Table 90.

TABLE 88

Indonesia's Development Targets
for Agriculture, 1973/74

Commodity	Production 1969/70	Production 1973/74	Percent Increase
Rice[a]	10.52	15.42	46.5
Palm Oil[b]	172	275	59.8
Palm Kernels[b]	41	68	65.8
Sugar[b]	677	907	33.9
Copra[b]	1.1	1.5	36.5
Cocoa[c]	8.5	16.25	99.3
Corn[a]	3.37	4.23	25.5
Pulses[a]	0.95	1.40	47.3
Vegetables and fruits[a]	8.30	11.20	34.9
Edible Roots[a]	15.66	18.09	15.5
Fish[b]	1,423	1,969	38.3
Wood[d]	2,900	7,900	172.4
Meat[e]	64.34	107.90	67.7
Eggs[e]	4.69	15.12	222.3

[a]In millions of tons.
[b]In thousands of tons.
[c]In hundreds of tons.
[d]In thousands of cubic meters.
[e]In millions of kilograms.

Source: Repelita (the development plan).

TABLE 89

Indonesia's Targets for the Development
of the Infrastructure, 1973/74

Elements	Production 1969/70	Target 1973/74	Percent Increase
Electric Power[a]	659.0	1,084	64.4
Telephones[b]	177.1	257.5	45.4
Railroads[c] (Rehabilitation)	-	715	-
Diesel Locomotives	285	341	19.6
Roads[c] (Rehabilitation)	-	11,225	-
Roads[c] (Upgrading)	-	6,000	-

[a]In thousands of kilovolt-amperes.
[b]In thousand units.
[c]In kilometers.

Source: Repelita (the development plan).

Overall, productive capacity is to be raised by 90 percent by the end of the five-year period of the Plan. Concentration for the first two years will be on rehabilitation and a more effective use of existing capacity; in the following three years, it is hoped that there will be expansion and development. Few of these projects have reached beyond the preliminary planning stage. Much of the expansion contemplated for oil and mining is dependent on surveys and exploration now under way or yet to be undertaken.

Financial resources for the Plan are estimated at $3.76 billion for the five-year period, of which $2.8 billion is expected to be derived from public savings, the countervalue of program aid and project aid and technical assistance, and $0.96 billion from sources outside the state budget, i.e., direct investment and the increase in medium- and long-term bank credits.

It is admitted that, in the absence of adequate national income and production data and against cost estimates that are not based on

TABLE 90

Indonesia's Development Targets
for Mining and Industry, 1973/74

Commodity	Production 1969/70	Target 1973/74	Percent Increase
Textiles[a]	450.00	900.0	100.0
Fertilizers:[b]			
- P	18.00[c]	168.0	833.0
- N	46.50	403.5	767.0
Cement[b]	600.00	1,650.0	175.0
Newsprint[b]	16.00	166.5	940.6
Crude Oil[d]	293.00	440.0	50.1
Tin[b]	16.16	19.4	19.9
Bauxite[b]	1,000.00	1,200.0	20.0

[a]In millions of meters.
[b]In thousands of tons.
[c]1971 target.
[d]In millions of barrels.

Source: Repelita (the development plan).

any detailed examination of the requirements of most projects, this budget is compounded largely of guesswork and that the estimates of savings and investment are extremely uncertain.

Under the plan, total exports are expected to increase from $672 million in 1969/70 to $924 million in 1974. Imports of foodstuffs are to be reduced from $176 million in 1969/70 to $67 million in 1974. Imports of raw materials and auxiliary goods will rise from $355 million to $680 million and of capital goods from $275 million to $614 million--a total estimated for 1974 of $1,361 million.

Additional to this visible deficit in the projected balance of trade is an obligation to repay (rescheduled) foreign debts, totaling some $2,211 million, which, from 1970/71 to 1974/74, will amount to

more than 20 percent of annual export values. A very substantial
inflow of foreign resources will obviously be necessary even if, as
seems inevitable, repayments are yet again to be rescheduled to
realistic levels in relation to the progress of the economy and to
foreign exchange earnings.

    This brief outline of Indonesia's Five-Year Development Plan
has illustrated some of the formidable obstacles to its full achievement, even though, in most cases and in relation to the country's
needs, the goals are reasonably modest. For Vietnam, there is a
dichotomy of interests. If self-sufficiency in rice and other essential
foodstuffs is reached within the time-frame of the Plan, then the most
certain avenue for an export trade with Indonesia will be closed. On
the other hand, without rising standards of living, greater affluence,
and, therefore, a higher effective demand, the possibility of trade in
a wider range of less essential but higher-valued and, possibly,
semiprocessed foodstuffs may not materialize. At present, for example,
there is a considerable gap between production of fish and consumption
requirements in a protein-starved community--but there is little or
no effective demand for the importation of this commodity.

    As has been pointed out, to a great extent, the viability of the
Plan depends on foreign investment and the success or otherwise of
the exploration, planned and operative, for further oil resources and
mineral deposits. It is just conceivable that Vietnam might have the
best of both worlds from its own point of view. There may be a
continued demand for essential foodstuffs by Indonesia, as a result of
only partial achievement of its agricultural program, and there may
also be a relaxation of foreign exchange restrictions, as a result of
rich oil and mineral exploitation and the value added from increased
processing of domestic raw materials. These factors may inspire
the effective demand necessary if Vietnam is to dispose of a wider
selection of its potential surpluses.

EXTERNAL TRADE

    Care should be taken not to regard any one year's trade statistics
as being fully representative of trading patterns; there are substantial
variations from year to year. Many of the erratic variations in trends
can be attributed to statistical error in coverage. This may particularly be so in cases where an import duty may have been imposed
for the first time or where duty structures may have been altered.
Nevertheless, the 1968 figures can be taken as providing a rough
indication of the flows between countries and of the type and value of
commodities traded.

TABLE 91

Indonesia's Exports, by Value
and Country of Destination, 1968

Geographical Area (Major Recipient: Percentage Share)	Value (In Millions of Dollars)	Percentage of the Whole
Southeast Asia (Singapore: 66)	$175.8	25.5
Near East (Saudi Arabia: 54)	0.1	0.014
Far East (Japan: 94)	182.7	26.5
Africa (Liberia: 83)	1.2	0.2
Australasia (Australia: 93)	73.3	10.6
North America (United States: 100)	112.7	16.3
Latin America	2.2	0.3
Western Europe 36; (Netherlands West Germany 40)	119.9	17.4
East Europe (U.S.S.R. 81)	20.4	3.0
Total	$688.3	

Source: Indonesian Ministry of Trade (unpublished statistics).

1968 export statistics (available only in summary at the time this research was made) offer the figures shown in Table 91.

Of all exports, 52 percent were directed to Southeast Asian and Far Eastern countries, and, of this total, Japan and Singapore acquired 80 percent. Other major purchasers are the United States, Australia, West Germany, and the Netherlands. The picture is one of an export trade clearly oriented towards neighboring countries in the East and in Australasia, with some traditional trading ties with Western Europe, and a relatively recent, but growing, reliance on the American market.

By commodity, 1968 exports (in millions of dollars) were as follows:[3]

Live animals and meat products		$ 7.6
Plantation products		121.7
Small holders' products		194.6
Forest products		16.3
Mineral products:		
1. Petroleum	291.3	
2. Coal	-*	
3. Manganese	-*	
4. Tin	25.8	
5. Others	15.5	332.6
Manufactures and semimanufactures		15.1
Unspecified		0.4
Total		$688.3

These figures exclude what must be a considerable volume of trade restored since the end of confrontation between Malaysia and Indonesia, although much of such trade might take the form of barter or be hidden in reexports from Singapore.

By commodity, the imports shown in Table 92 are as follows:

---

*Negligible.

TABLE 92

Indonesia's Imports, by Value
and Country of Origin, 1968

Source	Value (In Millions of Dollars)	Percentage of the Whole
Far East	$241.7	34.5
Southeast Asia	51.3	7.3
Near East	29.0	4.1
Africa	24.9	3.6
Australasia	19.9	2.8
North America	116.9	16.8
Latin America	0.9	0.2
Western Europe	173.1	24.8
Eastern Europe	41.5	5.9
Total	$699.2	

Source: Indonesian Ministry of Trade.

Commodity	Value
Consumption goods	265.8
Raw materials	244.1
Capital goods	189.3
	$699.2

Imports in that year of selected commodities (1968), with respect to
which Vietnam might conceivably have an export interest are detailed
in Table 93, but further reference to quantities and values made in
the following sections dealing with specific commodities employ the
1967 statistics, in order to provide a more detailed commodity
breakdown.

With three notable exceptions, the sparse list detailed in Table
93 does not hold much interest for Vietnamese exporters. Of all
imports in 1968, 27 percent were in the form of capital goods that

TABLE 93

Selected 1968 Imports, Indonesia
(In Metric Tons)

Commodity	Quantity	Value
Meat and Meat Preparations	1,590	$ 730,000
Dry Salted Fish	1,803	276,000
Other Fish and Fish Products	1,412	310,000
Rice	467,000	92,600,000
Fruit and Seeds	2,944	422,000
Vegetables	2,630	413,000
Gelatine, Soy Sauce, Soy Paste	1,218	465,000
Coffee, Tea	164	76,000
Cloves	15,654	10,806,000
Tobacco Leaf	23,616	8,731,000
Scrap Iron	2,698	186,000

Source: Indonesian Ministry of Trade.

Vietnam does not produce--machinery, railway equipment, vehicles, tools, instruments, and so forth--and 35 percent of all imports were in the form of raw or semiprocessed material--paper, cotton, fertilizer, and so forth. The latter figure excludes the type of primary agricultural products Vietnam produces; apart from rice and some few relatively unimportant food groups, most imported consumables are in the form of processed foodstuffs, textiles, utensils, films, and so forth. Little or no live animals are imported; the country does not import timber other than in processed form; fish, fruit, and vegetable imports are very small. One major food import is wheat flour, which outstrips rice in quantity and value, but this is not a commodity in which Vietnam is interested.

What is of interest is that rice imports (and the figures here do not include PL-480 rice, supplies of which run at around 400,000 tons a year) amount to 35 percent of all consumables imported and a significant 13 percent of all imports of any kind.*

Tobacco imports in 1968 were substantial, even though the country is a producer and large exporter, and so were imports of a related commodity, cloves, for which nearly $11 million of foreign exchange were used in 1968 and a similar amount in 1969. These three major possibilities, rice, tobacco, and cloves, are discussed in following sections.

TRADE WITH VIETNAM

The Vietnam Statistical Yearbook and the USAID Annual Statistical Bullentin indicate that Vietnam has had a fluctuating, and recently dwindling, trade with Indonesia for many years. In the last decade, 1960 emerges as a year when 8 percent of all of Vietnam's exports went to Indonesia, to balance imports from that country, which, by value, amounted to 6.5 percent of the whole. This trade was mainly in rice, flour, and petroleum derivatives. During 1960-66, imports averaged $15.5 million a year and exports $2.55 million. In all years, the visible balance of trade was heavily in Indonesia's favor.

Published Indonesian trade statistics offer more clues as to the types of commodity traded and present a similar picture as far as imports from Vietnam are concerned. The records show that, in 1963, and, again, in 1965, $3.2 million and $1.2 million worth of goods were imported from Vietnam. In both cases, the entire consignment was hulled rice. The only other record of an import from Vietnam is, oddly enough, an amount of $34 of lace embroidery and trimmings in 1964 and, again, in 1967, when the value had grown to $18,000.

EXPORT OPPORTUNITIES
FOR VIETNAM BY COMMODITIES

In the absence of up-to-date trade statistics, this analysis uses 1965 and provisional 1967 figures, in order to provide an indication of the nature, volume, and value of Indonesia's import requirements. Neither year is wholly representative. In 1965, the year before

---

*The discrepancy between these official figures and those quoted on page 293 is due to the use of differing categorizations.

Sukarno's replacement, there was a profligacy in Indonesia's external trade arrangements, stemming from a lack of governmental control, a disregard for the economic consequences of an adverse balance of trade, and comparatively easy access to foreign exchange, as a result of borrowing and tied foreign concessionary aid. In 1967, under a more responsible government tight money policies, manipulation of customs duties, and firm control over most foreign currency disbursements added an opposite distortion to patterns by causing a new emphasis to be placed on capital goods imports to the detriment of consumer goods. The two years were also separated by currency revaluation. The rate of 45 rupiahs to $1 obtaining in 1965 was changed to 10-to-1 in 1966.

In spite of these difficulties, however, it is at least possible to isolate a number of commodities for which there is an effective demand at present and to make some judgments, however rough, on import growth prospects, insofar as local production, population growth, and consumption enter into the equation.

The methodology used is to take seriatim all commodity imports during those two years that Vietnam may conceivably be in a position to supply, establish rough unit prices c.i.f., determine sources of origin, assess prospects for growth in local production and in local consumption, and arrive at a value judgment on the probability of Vietnam displacing current suppliers and/or enjoying a share of the market growth, if any, and to what extent.

For a survey of this nature and given the paucity and incompleteness of basic data, little more can be done, but the isolation of prospects in itself offers opportunity for subsequent in-depth studies of particular markets.

The list is not overlong. Two primarily agricultural, tropical countries, producing similar agricultural commodities and at roughly the same stage of industrial development and economic growth, cannot realistically anticipate a large volume of mutually profitable intertrading activity. And, of course, foreign exchange shortages and lack of domestic purchasing power militate against such trade in semi-luxury specialized goods, such as high-value shrimps, or crustaceans, or temperate zone vegetables, such as asparagus and mushrooms.

Live Animals, Food Products, and Beverages

Of the seventeen groups of commodities into which Indonesia's trade statistics are divided, the main groups of interest to the present study are the imports for the two years 1965 and 1967, valued at $14.6 million and $57.8 million, respectively.

Live Animals

There is, at present, no market for live cattle. In 1965, $452,000 worth of cattle were imported from the Netherlands, but they were breeding stock, and this transaction was exceptional. In 1967, no live cattle were imported. Negligible imports of swine and poultry were recorded for 1965; in 1967, pigs to the value of $1,311 (from Singapore) and poultry, to the value of $360 only were imported. Annual meat production is extremely low--56,000 metric tons only in 1968/69, or less than a half a kilogram per head of population.

There are formidable problems facing plans to increase livestock production: lack of good stock, a high death rate through disease, inadequate grazing, and overconcentration, to the point of reaching maximum capacity of the cattle population in Java. Good possibilities exist for expansion in Kalimantan, the Moluccas, and West Irian but production incentives are low because effective demand for the product is weak. The Five-Year Plan stipulates an increase in meat production to 108,000 metric tons--a 100 percent improvement over five years, and there is no doubt but that if demand and purchasing power improve, Indonesia has the capacity to step up livestock production, possibly to the point of self-sufficiency. But, even then, there is a problem of distribution. With limited transportation facilities and high transport costs, it is, today, cheaper, in many cases, to import essential foodstuffs than to distribute domestic production.

Fresh Meat

In 1965, $265,000 worth of fresh or frozen meat was imported, but this dropped to $130,000 by 1967. Australia was the main supplier. The biggest demand was for beef, followed by poultry. Much of this small intake was for luxury consumption by the tourist trade.

Preserved Meat*

In 1965, canned and preserved meat imports amounted to $262,000; by 1967, imports of this nature had increased to $960,363, 80 percent of which came from Hong Kong and Japan.

These figures of local production, live animal, fresh meat, and canned meat imports underline how limited the amount of meat protein is in the average diet. If local production figures are anywhere near accurate, annual per capita consumption from this source plus imports cannot amount to more than 500 grams a year.

------

*Includes canned meat and meat preparations.

There will, undoubtedly, be a slow but steady improvement in dietary standards over the next decade, but local production will require supplementing from outside sources by increased imports of fresh and canned meat. Australia will probably dominate the market for both commodities, particularly in fresh meat, enjoying, as it does, a comparative advantage, stemming from geographical proximity and the economies of scale; but note should be taken of the present position in the market for canned meat and meat preparations enjoyed by Mainland China, Hong Kong, and Japan. In 1967, these countries exported to Indonesia the following:

China (Mainland)	114,500 kilograms, worth $ 45,300
Hong Kong	230,000 kilograms, worth $150,000
Japan	890,000 kilograms, worth $700,000

C.i.f. prices in 1967 averaged $0.75 a kilogram gross weight, and it would seem that there is every likelihood for growth in demand for low-cost meat extracts and preparations, including canned or powdered soups.

Some relatively minor opportunity might be presented here for an export trade should there be successful promotion and growth in meat-processing industries, based on enhanced livestock production. Processed duck meat especially might find a profitable place in this trade, together with preserved and "twenty-day" duck eggs, for which Indonesians have a predilection.

There would seem to be little or no prospect of finding a market for cattle feed, either of corn or concentrates, since Indonesia has the capacity to produce enough for its own needs, especially as far as cake concentrates are concerned.

Sea Products

Total imports in 1967 were worth $600,000. Provisional figures for 1968 indicated that imports remained steady in value, at around $590,000.

These imports are minute, compared with the volume of fish Indonesia could produce, and very small in relation to actual catches. It is estimated that, in 1967, only 15 percent of the catch potential was realized; even so, 1.09 million metric tons were caught domestically. The growth rate of local production over a ten-year period has been exceptional: a 60 percent increase in sea fish production and a 100 percent increase from inland fisheries. Nevertheless, although considerably more than is the case with meat consumption, per capita consumption of fish remains low, being approximately 11 kilogram a year.

A determined effort to increase production is being made, and $26 million have been allocated to this end in the Five-Year Plan. The 1974 target is 1.969 million tons, an increase of 80 percent over 1967 figures. In particular, an intensive program will be directed to increasing catches of tuna and shrimp for export. But only 1.3 percent of the fishing fleet of 250,000 are motorized, and fishing practices are primitive. Fishing harbors require dredging, and quays, markets, ice supplies, storehouses, and so forth need to be improved or, in many cases, provided. Distribution to consuming areas presents almost insuperable problems without very heavy investment in cold storage, quick-freezing plants, and refrigerated transport. It is probably true that private investment in a relatively small number of modern fishing craft could improve production greatly, but much would be for export, being high-quality pelagic fish and shrimps. Little of this would reach the local consumer. To be realistic, it is doubtful whether, in fact, fish production over the next five to ten years can do much more than keep abreast of population growth, plus, possibly, some minor increase in daily per capita fish protein intake.

There is a fairly small effective demand for imported fish-- mainly dried, smoked, or tinned--which will certainly grow if more foreign exchange becomes available. Hong Kong exported 126 metric tons of preserved molluscs and crustaceans (not canned), worth $177,000 in 1967, which was 85 percent of the total import value of this commodity; South Korea achieved 50 percent of a market worth $146,000 in canned sardines; and Singapore achieved 25 percent.

As is the case with meat, low-priced canned fish is in demand. There is no market for the high-value fish and crustaceans that Vietnam hopes to be able to export in the next five to ten years. Very small quantities of dried or preserved molluscs and crustaceans might be disposed of, but the probability is that consumer demand at home for the cheaper varieties of fish, whether fresh or processed, will militate against an export surplus in such species.

Rice

In 1965, rice imports totaled 818,000 metric tons, valued at $133 million. In 1967, imports dropped to only 56,000 tons, worth $14.2 million. But this was not a representative year. Indonesia has, for many years, been a heavy importer of rice; 1969 estimates indicate that over 700,000 metric tons were imported, 400,000 of which were PL-480 Title I. The probability was that a similar quantity would be required in 1970, at a cost in excess of $100 million in foreign exchange. This situation has been reached because annual average increases in rice production over the last fifteen years have averaged only 1.5 percent, compared with a population increase of over 2 percent.

A fairly typical cross section of suppliers, other than for PL-480, is shown by 1967 figures (in percent by weight) of rice imports by country of origins as follows:[4]

Country	Percent by Weight
Thailand	54.3
Burma	27.1
China (Mainland)	7.8
Cambodia	3.9
Singapore	3.6
U.A.R.	1.4
United States	1.1

But small quantities have also been bought from India, Pakistan, Japan, Taiwan, Australia, and Brazil. When it was available, the red "Java" rice from the Mekong Delta of Vietnam was much in demand.

This biggest single cause for expenditure of foreign exchange constitutes the most serious of the many problems confronting the Indonesian government. Rice cultivation occupies the great majority of the rural population, and rice is the most important food grain consumed. Increased production for import substitution purposes and to acquire stocks for price stabilization is an imperative and central goal of governmental planning.

Current production continues to decline in Java, mainly because the rapid deterioration of irrigation systems through lack of maintenance precludes double-cropping in many areas. The small increases in overall production are owed to greater hectarages being put into production in other islands.

Rice production targets contained in the Five-Year Development Plan (in millions of tons) are as follows:

Year	Production	Percentage Increase
1969/70	10.52	7.34
1970/71	11.43	8.65
1971/72	12.52	9.50
1972/73	13.81	10.30
1973/74	15.43	11.60

It is proposed that this phenomenal increase, in comparison with previous growth rates, should be achieved by the use of HYV's, by rehabilitating the existing irrigation systems (covering 1 million hectares), and by expanding the area under production by 480,000 hectares. If these targets can be met, self-sufficiency in rice by 1974 can be obtained, and calorific intake from rice per head of the population brought to a level deemed necessary by the nutritionists.

This is a most ambitious undertaking. No statistics on per capita consumption of rice exist, but there is no doubt but that levels should and will increase with greater individual purchasing power. The stage where income elasticity of demand for rice is negative is a long way off in Indonesia. It is interesting in this context to note that, although the current year's rice production is estimated to be higher than usual, less local rice is appearing on the market. The presumption is that, at the present abysmally low income levels of average farmers, they prefer to consume more of their own production than to sell some in order to buy more expensive and better foods.

There is much support for the rice expansion program from international and foreign agencies. The World Bank alone is actively stimulating by investment the rehabilitation of irrigation for 800,000 hectares and is sponsoring comprehensive seed production and development programs. Other programs providing complete input packages and extension services for almost 1 million hectares already represent a very considerable injection of fertilizer, of plant protection activities, and of credit, which will undoubtedly help to improve production. At the same time, USAID, as a corollary to these programs, is financing a comprehensive survey of rice handling, transportation, storage, and distribution. Further, World Bank activities extend to a national fertilizer study to determine supply policies and input-crop response relationships, including credit requirements. Additionally, assistance is being provided by the United Nations Development Program and The Asian Development Bank and by projects arranged bilaterally between Indonesia and a number of donor countries.

Many observers, however, remain deeply sceptical about the country's ability to achieve these targets. There are too many limiting and hindering factors, which cannot be improved or removed within so short a time frame. Bureaucratic obstruction and infra-structural inadequacies, the limitations of the institutional factors, and the sheer physical difficulty and heavy investment required to rehabilitate existing land and to exploit new land make formidable barriers to early successful implementation. Many projects are not yet formulated, others not evaluated, many not yet funded, and no direct link has yet been established between project performance and the targets.

Certainly, the next five years should see considerable improve-ment in rice production capacity and activity, but it would be over-optimistic to assume that self-sufficiency can be reached in five years. Production increases should stay ahead of population growth and per-mit higher levels of per capita consumption, but for at least several years to come, Indonesia will need to maintain imports at the 700,000-ton level--that is, some 300,000 tons from commercial sources if PL-480 rice continues to be provided at current levels. Thereafter, and probably for the next decade, Indonesia may require diminishing but still substantial rice imports. It could also be that, because of seasonal fluctuations in local production and limited storage, Indonesia may always be a small importer of rice--certainly of selective better-quality rice.

Here then lies the single largest and, indeed, the only certain opportunity for Vietnam to export to Indonesia. It will involve recap-turing a traditional market, since there will be no growth element in which Vietnam could share with other competitors. It will also be a diminishing trade, from which worthwhile profits can only be expected for, at the most, ten years. It is not possible to be precise about the extent to which this market could be gained. It can only be stated that, if comparative advantages exist as they should in relation to suppliers as far afield as the U.A.R. and the United States and, indeed, over both Thailand and Burma and if price and quality are competitive and traditional trading channels can be reestablished (as no doubt they will be among the traders of Chinese origin, who dominate the trade in both countries), it is not oversanguine to hope that at least 10 percent, and, possibly, 20 percent, of the market could be acquired. Sales of from 30,000 to 60,000 tons of rice a year to Indonesia, dimin-ishing probably to insignificant proportions by the early 1980's, could initially, and for several years, bring in foreign exchange earnings of from $5.25 million to $10.5 million.

Fruits and Vegatables

Total imports of these commodities in 1967, not including pre-served or canned varieties, were worth $654,000. A very considerable growth appears to have been sustained in 1968, although precise figures are not available. In some ways, the 1967 figures are surprising. Indonesia has the range of climate and soils to grow most fruit and vegetables, and, although $650,000 is not a large sum for imports of this nature, it represents foreign exchange that very little effort and planning could save. Again, the probability is that it is cheaper to import than to distribute local production. On the other hand, 53 percent of the value of 1967 imports of fruit were apples (from Australia and Japan), which Indonesia does not grow, 5 percent were grapes (which, like Vietnam, Indonesia could grow), and 30 percent unspecified but coming mainly from Hong Kong and West Germany. Some $54,000 of potatoes were imported from the Netherlands, but this minor market does not warrant the attention of Vietnamese exporters. A further $44,000 of green peas, all from France; $23,500 of edible fungi from Hong Kong, Japan, and Mainland China; $40,000 of onions from a wide range of Asian and European countries and the United States; and a similar value of unspecified vegetables make up the total.

There can be no doubt but that Indonesia could, in due course, supply its needs for most of these commodities and certainly those that Vietnam would be most likely to produce in quantity, but, in the short term, structural market discontinuities and other factors may continue to operate to provide a minor opportunity. The possibility should not be overlooked that, as Indonesia's tourist industry grows, there will be an increasing demand for high-quality specialized fruit and vegetables--avocados, strawberries, asparagus, artichokes, mushrooms, and so forth. It is a significant fact that, today, almost all consumables used in the several large modern tourist hotels in Indonesia are imported, despite management's efforts to establish local sources of supply. New hotels are in the course of erection, and, in Bali, particularly, the future of tourism seems bright, as the country recovers its stability.

Enterprising exporters could find a small but high-valued and possibly profitable outlet here. It is likely to obtain only in the short term, until Indonesian production replaces it, but might be worth altogether $250,000 a year for perhaps five or six years.

Tea and Coffee

Indonesia is a large exporter of these commodities and imports only minute quantities of specialized preparations.

Raw and Semiprocessed Materials

Cloves and Clove Stems

Clove imports for 1967 warrant listing in full. (See Table 94.) In 1965, imports were considerably less, being 4.7 million kilograms, worth $3.76 million, but imports in 1968 and 1969 actually exceeded the 1967 levels. The unusually high demand for this expensive spice is engendered by the national taste for Kretek cigarettes, i.e., cigarettes impregnated with ground cloves and clove stems.

Cloves are the small, unopened flower buds of the tropical tree Eugenia caryophyllata, a member of the myrtle (or Myrtaceae) family. The tree is usually propagated from seeds planted in beds having protective shading. A single tree may yield up to seventy-five pounds of dried buds at one flowering. Flowering begins at about the fifth year of growth, with two harvests a year, and it continues for up to twenty years. Strongly pungent as a result of the aromatic oil, eugenol, contained in the buds, it is used, elsewhere than Indonesia, mainly for the distillation of this oil. The oil is used as an agent for clearing microscopic slides, as an ingredient in germicides and mouthwashes, as a local anesthetic for toothache, in the synthesis of vanillin, and, in perfumes, as a sweetener or intensifier.

TABLE 94

Clove Imports, by Volume, Value, and Country of Origin, 1967
(In kilograms)

Country of Origin	Weight	Value
South Africa	104,800	$ 73,164
Somaliland	105,445	72,882
Tanzania	11,455,428	7,896,075
Morocco	4,352	30,646
Malagasy	1,981,431	1,443,524
Mozambique	103,467	70,097
United States	101,920	75,389
Denmark	50	34
Total	13,856,893	$9,661,811

Source: Indonesian Ministry of Trade.

It is difficult to credit that the legendary spice islands, where, in 1579, Sir Francis Drake bargained with the sultan for seven tons of Moluccas cloves, cannot now meet its own requirements. Until the latter half of the seventeenth century, Indonesia had a world monopoly of clove production, but this was broken when the French succeeded in smuggling seeds to the Indian ocean islands. Now, Tanzania and Malagasy produce most of the world's supply.

The Kretek industry is the single most important light industry in Indonesia and provides very considerable revenue in the form of excise duties. (See Table 95.) Discounting 1965, when political turmoil resulted in some reduction in production, this represents an average annual growth rate of approximately 5 percent. Despite this growth factor, it is understood that factories in East Java are working below full capacity, since cloves are in short supply. The present position of the industry is particularly difficult, since, following poor 1968 harvests in Tanzania and Malagasy, clove prices have increased considerably. At the same time, both Tanzania and Malagasy, with effect from March, 1969, imposed export taxes of 400 percent. In January, 1969, the c.i.f. price of a long ton of cloves in Djakarta was £260 to £270 sterling. Today, the price is around £1,600 a long ton. But the demand stays strong, even in the face of such an extortionate price. It appears that Indonesia will purchase cloves, irrespective of price; although there are indications of a very small shift in demand to the conventional Virginian tobacco, the demand for Kretek cigarettes, bolstered by population growth, seems certain to continue growing.

Although Indonesia still produces cloves in appreciable quantities, their oil content is higher than that of cloves from Tanzania and Malagasy, making them less acceptable by the Kretek cigarette industry. Plans to increase local production are therefore dependent on, and subordinate to, intensive research, which is now being undertaken, to improve the quality of the local species.

Whether or not Vietnam can grow acceptable quality cloves in sufficient quantity to enter this market requires early investigation by agronomists and soil scientists. Cloves are grown in comparatively small quantities in the Mekong Delta and elsewhere,* and, prima facie, there seems no reason why this opportunity should not be taken

---

*Certainly, no exports have been recorded for many years. However, a private estate manager in Saigon tells us that when he first came to Vietnam eighteen years ago, the very first job he was given was purchasing cloves for export. So there is some history of a trade in the commodity, even if it is not very recent.

TABLE 95

Kretek Cigarette Production, Indonesia, 1962-67

Year	Number of Cigarettes (In Millions)	Number of Workers Employed	Number of Factories
1962	4,454.8	19,026	239
1963	5,153.0	19,216	259
1964	6,127.6	21,032	263
1965	5,312.9	16,447	167
1966	7,090.0	19,417	191
1967	8,824.0	22,773	195

Source: Bulletin of Indonesian Economic Studies, Vol. V, No.3 (November, 1969).

by Vietnamese farmers to supply Indonesia with the cloves it requires. The comparative advantage of geographical proximity could help to undercut the c.i.f. price of African cloves.

No other Southeast Asian competitor has so far attempted to capture any of this market. Vietnam could, if early steps were taken, possibly have the field to itself. The difficulty of breaking into an established traditional trade pattern should not, of course, be under-emphasized, but with lower delivery costs, provided Vietnam can maintain a consistent supply and quality, the obstacles should not prove insuperable. There appears, in any case, to be a growth element present that would enable a foothold to be obtained initially. In 1968, imports were recorded as being $10.8 million, an increase of 12 percent over 1967.

The major risks involved in the medium-term capital investment such an enterprise would require arise from the possibility that a clove with a sufficiently low oil content could not be produced (early investigation into climatic factors and soils would be necessary) and that Indonesian researches would lead in the near future to a product more suited to local tastes, leading to enhanced local production and to less dependence on imports.

Subject to these provisos, however, there is a possibility that an early determined effort on the part of Vietnamese producers and exporters could open up trade opportunities, which, conservatively, could be put at several million dollars and which might have the potential to grow to the full extent of the market.

Unmanufactured Tobacco

Local cigarette industries consume most of the country's tobacco production, but, nevertheless, exports, mostly estate-produced tobacco and cigar wrapper leaf, average some $30 to $40 million a year. The popular variety is Virginian tobacco, the demand for which is greater than local supply, and, therefore, some occasional and irregular imports are required.

Earlier in this chapter, it is recorded that 1968 imports of tobacco leaf totaled $8.7 million. The credibility of this figure must be suspect. It is certainly not in keeping with normal trends. In 1963, $1.4 million of tobacco leaf were imported, 96 percent being Virginian tobacco from the United States. There were no imports for 1964, 1965, and 1966 but, in 1967, a further very small consignment of fifty-five kilograms, worth $345, is recorded. The very large 1968 imports, which, as far as can be ascertained, do not appear to have been repeated in 1969, can be rationalized by domestic crop failures or by a desire to stockpile.

Plans to increase tobacco production by 5 percent over the next five years are being implemented; this should keep local supplies in line with the anticiapted annual growth in demand. Small quantities of high-quality Virginian tobacco will, no doubt, continue to be imported from time to time, but it is unlikely that any country other than the United States will enjoy this particular market, unless they can emulate the type and quality of tobacco that enters this trade.

Estate Products: Palm Oil, Corpa, and Rubber

These are crops grown primarily for export, in respect of which Vietnam will be in competition with Indonesia. There are no export possibilities here for Vietnam.

Timber and Timber Products

As would be expected in a country possessing the immense forest resources of Indonesia, virtually no unprocessed wood is imported. In 1967, the only category in this group that was recorded as being imported in more than negligible quantities was "wood sawn lengthwise or square," of which 958 metric tons, worth $78,000, were imported--75 percent from Hong Kong and Japan. In that year, $84,000 of veneers and plywoods were imported, plus a further $1 million worth of plywood packing cases from the Netherlands.

Should the proposals that have been made to erect plywood and veneer factories in Vietnam materialize, there may be opportunities for mutual trading arrangements--logs from Indonesia being exported to Vietnam until such time as local supplies become available and plywood manufactures being exported to Indonesia, it being unlikely that Indonesia will have sufficient capacity to produce all the plywood a growing demand will require for many years. But these are long-range possibilities, which do not represent an opportunity that would warrant inclusion in this particular research.

Indonesia is presently expanding the extent of exploitation of its forests dramatically--mainly through joint ventures with foreign industrial interests. Planned output for export alone is estimated to increase in total value from some $28.5 to $120 million by 1974.

Miscellaneous

Plants for Use in Medicine and Perfumery

Throughout Southeast Asia, there is a consistent and, accumulatively, a considerable demand for plants utilized in Chinese medicine. The market for this commodity in Indonesia is small, but if combined with others--in Singapore, Malaysia, Thailand, Taiwan, and so forth--it makes investigation worthwhile.

Imports during the years from 1962 to 1968 increased in value from $68,000 to $140,000. Hong Kong, Mainland China, and India dominate the market and, in all probability, will continue to do so; nevertheless, it is possible that some of the particular plants in demand that are capable of being produced in Vietnam could be sold to Indonesia and that the extended market in neighboring countries would lead to profitable small-scale trade.

CONCLUSIONS

The prospects for Vietnam finding in Indonesia a substantial market for its exports are not good. This is predictable and understandable. Both are tropical, primarily agricultural countries at similar stages of industrial growth, and both produce or are capable of producing the same agricultural surpluses--foodstuffs and crop-based raw materials. Its possession of considerable mineral wealth alone distinguishes Indonesia and may possibly afford it opportunities for accelerated industrial growth. This advantage may, however, be more than counterbalanced by the considerable infrastructural advantages enjoyed by Vietnam.

Rice is the only probable Vietnamese export crop for which a ready, almost certain, market exists in Indonesia. This market may be large if early advantage can be taken of it but will diminish gradually over the next decade, as Indonesia achieves self-sufficiency in this staple foodstuff.

The clove market presents some valuable opportunities for a new export crop, as does to a much smaller extent that of medicinal herbs and plants, but both require in-depth investigation. Minor opportunities are available in the market for low-priced meat extracts and preparations, assuming Vietnam succeeds in promoting its own livestock production and agroindustry, and for duck eggs. The same situation is found in the demand for processed fish, including dried or preserved molluscs and crustaceans.

There may be a small demand for specialized luxury fruits and vegetables required for the Indonesian tourist industry if determined efforts are made to exploit it. The following list summarizes the possibilities, giving the estimated value range of such commodities in millions of dollars:

Commodity	Estimated Value Range
Rice*	$5.25 - 10.5
Cloves	**
Meat and eggs	0.1
Fish	***
Fruit and vegetables	0.25
Medicinal plants	***
Total	$5.6 - 10.85

*Volume for rice is 30,000 to 60,000 metric tons.

**New crop dependent on research into capability; it could possibly represent an export opportunity worth several million dollars but not within the time-frame of this study.

***Not estimated; probably not more than $10,000.

The importation of rice is a monopoly of a government agency, "Bulog." Cloves are permitted to be imported only by a government sponsored syndicate of importers. Opportunities are thus presented for bilateral government-to-government negotiations. There are not many Indonesian exports for which Vietnam will have a requirement postwar, but oil and petroleum products come readily to mind as offering some possibility of reciprocity.

NOTES

1. Japenpa Pocketbook Series on Indonesia, Serial Number 6901: Development (1968), p. 11.

2. Source for data is from Importers' Association of Indonesia, Year-End Review (1969).

3. Source for data is Indonesian Ministry of Trade.

4. Source of data is Indonesian Ministry of Trade.

17

These three countries are grouped together for a particular reason. Ostensibly, they are less likely than Hong Kong, Japan, Singapore, and South Korea to offer large and reliable markets for the products of Vietnamese agriculture; in fact, their agricultural production is, in many respects, similar to that of Vietnam. In two of these countries, the economies are still essentially agricultural in character, though there has been substantial industrial development in recent years; in the third, Taiwan, though industry is now making a greater contribution than agriculture to GNP, agriculture remains exceedingly important. In all three, domestic production is capable of meeting most of their peoples' needs for foodstuffs and their industries' needs for raw materials.

This is not intended to imply that there is no room whatever for profitable exchanges of any kind between Malaysia, Taiwan, Thailand, and Vietnam. The agricultural commodities these countries produce are not completely indentical in type; thus, Malaysia, an important timber producer, buys teak from Thailand, just as Japan, in spite of its own huge rice surpluses, still buys glutinous rice from other countries--and Indonesia, another considerable rice producer, still buys "Java" rice from Cambodia and Vietnam. Even if production were indentical in all respects, there would still be seasonal variations in harvests, which would, from time to time, induce any one of these countries to supplement its deficits by purchase from its neighbors' surpluses. For many commodities, however, these countries are more likely to be Vietnam's competitors in Southeast Asian and world markets than important and consistent trading partners for it.

A principal interest in including Malaysia, Taiwan, and Thailand in these investigations was to ascertain the methods they have adopted in their own successful efforts to promote their export trade, since

317

these may very well have some application to Vietnam as well. The results of these particular inquiries are discussed in Part III of this study. Another interest was to note the direction of the export trade in these countries, as a useful indicator of the directions that Vietnam's external trade may take, once the war is over and normal commerce is again possible.

MALAYSIA

General Information

The similarities between Malaysia and Vietnam are evident. Malaysia is a comparatively small developing country, with a population of a little more than 9 million,* increasing at an annual rate of 3 percent and thought likely to reach 14 million by 1980 and 18 million by 1990. It is primarily an agricultural country, dependent mainly on rubber and palm oil for its principal exports, but with one major mineral resource, tin. It has important forest resources as well, now being vigorously exploited, with considerable investments in the wood-based industries. Malaysia is still deficient in rice, its staple food, but hopes to correct this in the near future by development of its water resources, the introduction of HYV's, and the use of more fertilizers. It has a rich potential in its fisheries, and its fishing industry is beginning to develop and modernize and become more productive. The development of its industry--mostly the manufacture of light consumer and intermediate goods--is also in an early stage.

As the world's largest producer of rubber and tin, Malaysia is one of the wealthiest countries in Asia, but the performance of the economy in recent years has been disappointing. In 1967, GNP product was estimated at $3,234 million, only 3.9 percent over that of 1966. Export earnings fell by 3.5 percent in 1967, mostly because of low world prices for rubber, palm oil, and tin, but still accounted for 43 percent of the GNP. Private capital investment also fell, and other economic indicators were discouraging or adverse: per capita output rose only 2.8 percent, real per capita income only 1 percent, and unemployment rates in the urban areas increased to about 10 percent of the work force. Domestic savings fell. Defense and internal security imposed a serious drain upon Malaysia's resources.

---

*This excludes the countries of East Malaysia, Sabah and Sarawak, as do all other statistics in this section, unless specifically stated otherwise.

Whether a reasonable rate of economic growth can be achieved in future depends primarily on the extent to which world prices for the major export commodities (some of which have improved since 1967) will be maintained.

External Trade

West Malaysia (but not Sabah and Sarawak) is still heavily dependent on Singapore for much of its external trade. Imports for both Singapore and West Malaysia in the first eleven months of 1968 amounted to $1,921.3 million, of which two-thirds came into Singapore and only one-third directly into Malaysia. Exports were $1,678.2 million, of which 57 percent went through Singapore and 43 percent through Malaysian ports.* In the same period, Singapore imported goods to the value of $1,553.0 million, of which $245.1 million was from Malaysia and $1,307.9 million from other countries; it exported goods to the value of $1,179.8 million, of which $231.2 million went to Malaysia and $948.6 million to the other countries. The Singapore trade is essentially in reexports; West Malaysia uses its port and brokerage expertise to a very great extent, both for its imports and for marketing its exports.

The trade statistics in both countries do not reveal the precise nature of commodity flows in relation to countries of origin. It is certain that a significant proportion of the recorded Singapore exports to West Malaysia are of Indonesian, Japanese, and Hong Kong origin; it is unlikely, however, that more than a minute percentage of Vietnam's exports to Singapore, described earlier in this book, are involved.

As in the case of Singapore, Malaysian tariffs are generally protective in nature, but they are levied not only on processed or manufactured articles but, also, on a wide range of primary products. Some of these may affect future exchanges with Vietnam; there is, for instance, a 20 percent import duty on fish and fish products; a 149.33 percent duty on many fruits; and other duties, varying from 3.3 to 37.33 percent, on many other agricultural commodities that both Malaysia and Vietnam can produce.

In 1968, imports into Malaysia were valued at $2,556 million; food and live animals ($255 million), machinery and transportation equipment ($265 million), manufactured goods ($267 million), and

---

*These figures exclude direct changes between the two countries of goods produced in them.

mineral fuels ($167 million) were the most important classes of commodity brought in, but there were also sizable imports of beverages, tobacco, industrial raw materials, chemicals, and animal and vegetable oils. Over 40 percent of all imports were purchased from East Asian countries, including Japan, Singapore, Mainland China, and Thailand.

Exports were valued at $1,373.4, and 20.6 percent of this went to Singapore, 18.9 percent to Japan, and 15.7 percent to the United States. Australia, West Germany, Italy, and France also provide sizable markets for Malaysia to sell in. Well over a half of all exports were classified as "crude materials, inedible, except fuels," that is, rubber, timber, and tin. But Malaysia also exported $306 million worth of manufactured goods, evidence of the increasing pace of industrialization.

There are only three major classifications in which Vietnamese exports to Malaysia are likely--food and live animals, crude materials, and vegetable oils and fats.

The Statistical Yearbook in Vietnam does not isolate items of trade with Malaysia, but other statistical records show that there has been some trade in the past in peanuts, duck eggs, oil cake, and rice bran. The only substantial item was the last of these: VN$33 million worth of rice bran was exported to Malaysia in 1955 and VN$31 million worth in 1957.

More comprehensive trade statistics are kept in Malaysia, but their accuracy may leave something to be desired. While Vietnamese records show no exports of any kind to Malaysia, in 1967, Malaysian records indicate imports to the value of $883,333 from Vietnam. This is not large, but a rich variety of imports was reported, sometimes in minute quantities. Duck eggs, salted dried molluscs, unmilled corn, cornmeal and flour, melon and pumpkin seeds, potatoes, dried peas, onions, coffee, tea, pepper and chilies, cinnamon, animal feedstuffs of a variety of types, birds' nests, peanuts, copra, soybeans, sesame seed, rattans, kapok, seaweed algae, peanut oil, coconut oil, and citronella oil all appear in the list, and numerous other commodities besides.

As mentioned above, the accuracy of the Malaysian trade records it not above suspicion: Vietnam is shown as having supplied 3,620 tons of coal, for instance, which sounds at least improbable after the Nong Son mine had gone out of production (it is also shown as Malaysia's largest source of supply of citronella oil, though citronella is not yet grown in great quantity in Vietnam, nor is there yet distillation of the oil on a commercial scale). In some cases, there appears to have been misrepresentation by importers, both as to origin and as to the c.i.f. prices of the goods imported. But the list is at least illustrative of the rich variety of produce that enters into international trade in East Asia. This is significant, because, in the early postwar years, quite a large part of Vietnam's export trade may consist of many small shipments of a great variety of items. If the Malaysian records are even approximately correct, in 1967, a year when the entire exports of Vietnam were valued at only $19 million, fifty-seven different commodities were supplied to Malaysia. Some were supplied in quantities valued at $100 or less--but they all added up to almost $1 million.

Export Opportunities for Vietnam by Commodity

Rice

Domestic production in 1967 was 850,000 tons from 756,000 acres, only 105,000 of which were double-cropped, and this was sufficient to meet only 70 percent of Malaysia's requirements. However, by the end of 1970, when the Mudah irrigation project is expected to be completed, Malaysia should have another 130,000 acres of double-cropped rice land, and, with the use of HYV's and other improvements, it hopes by that time to be self-sufficient in this basic foodstuff.

Malaysia actually imported 296,000 tons of rice in 1967 and 203,000 in the first nine months of 1968, mostly from Thailand and Mainland China, so the country may not achieve self-sufficiency quite as rapidly as it expects. But it may very well do so by 1975, by about the time that Vietnam may reasonably expect to have surpluses of rice for export, and the conclusion must be that there will be no exports of Vietnamese rice to this particular market.

Timber

The total value of all imports of timber in log, baulk, or rough sawn form into Malaysia in the first nine months of 1968 was a mere $133,000, and just about a half of this was rough sawn teak from Burma. Vietnam has no prospects for trade with Malaysia in this commodity, but it has some interest in the circumstances and directions of Malaysia's trade.

Malaysia (including Sabah and Sarawak) produced 8.5 million tons of round timber in 1967, an increase of 14.7 percent over production in 1966. A fairly large proportion of production was consumed by the domestic wood-based industries; 34 percent, for instance, was converted into sawn lumber, and there are twelve plywood and veneer mills in West Malaysia, producing, between them, about 120 million square feet a year. In addition, West Malaysia has a chip board mill, a wood-wool slab mill, and a pencil factory, all using domestic wood or wood wastes. But 5.0 million tons of Malaysian timber were exported as logs, to an estimated value of $194.3 million. During the year, the export unit value of timber in the round rose from $28 to $31.6 a ton and that of sawn lumber from $55 to $59 a ton.

Japan is the biggest buyer; it took more than a half of all Malaysian timber exports in 1967. Australia, the United Kingdom, and the countries of the EEC accounted together for more than a quarter, but Malaysian timber went to as many as thirty-five other countries as well. Singapore received 40 percent of that part of Malaysia's production which originated in West Malaysia, and it obviously reexported much of it.

West Malaysia also has two paper mills, which use imported pulp and waste paper. If the production of wood pulp proves to be feasible in Vietnam, then a market for part of the product may be found in this branch of Malaysian industry; this represents the limit of the potential for exports of forest products to Malaysia.

Rubber

As Malaysia is the world's largest producer of rubber, it is surprising that it is a fairly large-scale importer as well. In 1967, 51,500 tons of raw rubber, worth $16 million, were imported, mostly from Thailand, Sumatra, and Cambodia (and a little from Sabah and Sarawak in East Malaysia). This trade does not indicate a possible demand in Malaysia for Vietnamese rubber. It represents, to a large extent, the use of Malaysia by Thailand as an entrepôt for that country's export production and, to a lesser extent, the milling and rebaling for reexport of Indonesian and East Malaysian rubber.

Tea

Tea is still an important crop in Malaysia, though production has begun to fall as land is diverted to more profitable crops. This is reflected in declining exports of the commodity, for local consumption is relatively high, and imports are substantial: 5.53 million pounds in 1967, of which only 379,000 pounds were reexported. Exports of Malaysian-produced tea were 4.3 million pounds.

The normal Malaysian market for domestic and imported teas appears to be about 2.5 million pounds. In 1967, Mainland China was the main source of black leaf (69 percent), with Ceylon, Taiwan, Sumatra, and Hong Kong providing most of the balance. A small quantity was purchased from South Vietnam. However, black dust was the principal type imported, and the market for this was shared between Ceylon (25 percent), Sumatra (32 percent), and African producers (34 percent). Mainland China, Taiwan, Java, and Pakistan supplied small quantities, and so did both North and South Vietnam. Mainland China supplied 60 percent of the green leaf, with small amounts coming from Taiwan, Java, and Sumatra; Sumatra dominated the market for green dust.

There is a small opportunity for Vietnam's tea in Malaysia. Consumption, particularly among the large Chinese community, shows no sign of decreasing, and, as population grows and local production declines, demand for imported teas may very well grow. Vietnam is a traditional supplier to Malaysia and might reasonably aim at selling that country 10 percent of its requirements, about 200,000 pounds, worth about $70,000.

Livestock

In recent years, Malaysia has made itself virtually self-sufficient in pigs, poultry, and eggs, but progress in other types of meat production has been less satisfactory. Imports of live animals in 1967 were valued at $2.58 million. Beef cattle and buffalo made up a good proportion of this total, almost $1 million, and Thailand supplied just about all of them. The market for frozen beef is somewhat larger-- $1.3 million--and is practically monopolized by Australia.

It is difficult to predict whether or when Malaysia will grow enough beef to meet its needs. A good deal of research is in progress into forages and cattle breeding and management, and the probability is that production will increase sufficiently to keep pace with growth of population. It may not keep pace with the additional demands created by rising living standards and a taste for improved diets, and one-half the population of Malaysia will always prefer beef to pork. If Vietnam can produce the quality of cattle now being imported from Thailand--and, in time, there is no visible reason why it should not-- it can obtain at least some share of Thailand's present monopoly of this particular trade.

Feedstuffs

There is a sizable demand for animal feedstuffs, $15.9 million worth being imported in 1967, most of which was retained, since exports and reexports were valued at only $2.5 million. Vietnam already participates, though only to a small extent, in this trade; it provided a small part of Malaysia's corn requirements, the total of which was $3.74 million, Thailand supplying over two-thirds of them.

Corn was the most important item imported, followed by copra and other oil cakes, rolled oats, fishmeal, shrimp dust, and rice bran. Mainland China was the largest supplier of the market for oil cake and shared the market for fishmeal with Thailand, Japan, Pakistan, and Sumatra. Burma, Sumatra, and Thailand shared most of the market for rice bran.

Malaysia's production of feedstuffs is intended to increase with its livestock production, but competition for arable land from higher-valued crops suggests that it will continue to rely to a considerable extent on imports. In a meager selection of opportunities for Vietnam to export to Malaysia, this is probably the best one. Some of Mainland China's present market should certainly be susceptible to penetration. Rice bran, fishmeal, oil cake, and corn are all possible exports from Vietnam to Malaysia, and though this trade may be negligible compared with similar opportunities presented by Japan, it might conceivably amount to $1 million.

Marine Products

In the last three years, the productivity of the Malaysian fishing industry has increased remarkably. The 302,000 tons of fish landed in 1967 represented an increase of 28 percent over the 1966 harvest, and a similar increase in 1968, for which records are not yet available, is confidently predicted. Only 11,000 tons of fresh sea fish, valued at $1.8 million, were imported in 1968--from Thailand, Japan, and Sumatra.

Vietnam is unlikely to benefit from this small and declining trade, but might benefit considerably from study of Malaysia's policies for the development of the fishing industry. In ten years, the number of mechanized fishing vessels has grown to more than 13,000, and there has been a rapid advance in technology, with a wide-spread adoption of trawling and the use of powered equipment and of nylon gear. It seems certain that production will continue to rise and that Malaysia will keep the ability to satisfy its needs.

There are also small imports of dried or salted products, about the same in value as imports of fresh fish. Vietnam appears as the source of very small quantities of salted, dried fish, crustaceans, and molluscs. With its present trade connections with Chinese Malaysian importers, there is no reason why Vietnam should not continue to participate in this market and even enlarge its share of it, but it is unlikely that the market will grow. The probability is that Malaysia will soon be producing for itself all the quantities of such commodities it needs.

Pond Fish

Imports are negligible. There are over 1,400 hectares of highly productive fish ponds in West Malaysia. A well-organized extension service supplies fry to farmers free of charge, and domestic production amply satisfies demand.

Fruits and Vegatables

Generally speaking, Malaysia grows (or can grow) the same types of tropical fruits and vegetables as Vietnam; like Vietnam, it has regions of cooler climates and higher altitudes, where some of the temperate zone fruits and vegetables can be successfully cultivated.

There is, however, an inexplicably large demand for mandarin oranges; 13,500 tons, valued at $3.45 million, were imported in 1967 from no fewer than thirty-three countries, though Mainland China and the United States shared 42 percent of this particular market. Vietnam exported some mandarin oranges to Malaysia in 1966 but has not done so since. Dried fruits, other than citrus, imported in 1967 were valued at $1.5 million, Vietnam contributing 0.4 tons. Other imports of fruit were negligible. There appear, therefore, to be fair opportunities for some trade in mandarin oranges and, possibly, other citrus fruits-- fair rather than good because this is a highly competitive market, though one of sufficient size to warrant Vietnam's interest.

Imports of vegetables, including dried beans, are surprisingly large--over $11 million in 1967. There is little doubt that Malaysia could grow all the vegetables it eats, if its agricultural policy were not so unreservedly concentrated upon rice, rubber, oil palm, and livestock. Imports in 1967 included potatoes from the Netherlands, Mainland China, and Taiwan; dried beans from the United Kingdom, Mainland China, and Burma; dried peas from Thailand, Sumatra, and Mainland China; chick peas from Morocco, India, Thailand, and Turkey; lentils from Burma, India, and Thailand; tomatoes from Mainland China, Taiwan, Sumatra, and Thailand; onions from six different countries, with India contributing nearly 25,000 tons, valued at over $2.3 million; garlic from Mainland China, Hong Kong, and Australia; and cabbage from Mainland China, Taiwan, and Sumatra.

Vietnam has been for many years a source of several of these items--dried beans, potatoes, garlic, and onions--though in small quantities. The demand for potatoes should be of particular interest to Vietnam, which is producing potatoes considerably in excess of local demand, once consumption by allied forces begins to diminish, and it can probably deliver this commodity to Malaysian ports at lower cost than either Mainland China or the Netherlands, which presently share the bulk of a $1.8-million market. The market in onions and garlic is worth about $4 million a year, and is likely to grow; both commodities are in demand for the manufacture of chili sauces and similar condiments. A 30 percent share in the Malaysian market for potatoes and a 10 percent share in the market for onions and garlic are not unrealistic targets and would be worth $1 million to Vietnam; but these commodities by no means exhaust the possibilities.

Coffee

Malaysia produces a little coffee and actually exports about $700,000 worth of beans a year, mainly to Singapore. Imports of coffee beans are much higher, about $1.7 million, coming mostly from Sumatra and Laos, but from twenty other countries as well. In the past, Vietnam has, from time to time, had a share in this trade and should be able to recover it, but the market is small, competition is severe, and the prospects are limited.

Vegetable Oils

Palm oil is Malaysia's fourth-largest export, after rubber, tin, and timber; in 1967, it became the world's largest exporter of this commodity, shipping overseas some $45 million worth. About 35,000 tons of other vegetable oil seeds, nuts, and kernels, valued at $4.3 million, were imported into Malaysia, principally soybeans and peanuts, but, also, some sesame and copra.

This is not an insignificant market, and, in previous years, Vietnam has exported peanuts, copra, soybeans, sesame, and other oil seeds to Malaysia. Mainland China, Sumatra, and Thailand are now the chief suppliers of peanuts, but a good proportion of this market is shared fairly equally by a number of other Asian countries. Sumatra and Java supply most of Malaysia's copra requirements, and Mainland China most of the soybean market. The sesame seed market is dominated by Thailand (63 percent), followed by Kenya and Sumatra.

There is an obvious opportunity for Vietnam in this market; unless Malaysia decides to diversify its crop production more into these specific items, the market may very well grow. The best chances for Vietnam appear to be in soybeans and peanuts.

Tobacco

Malaysia grows a little tobacco and exports some of it (worth $415,000 in 1967) to Singapore and Sabah, but it relies heavily on

imports, which, in 1967, were valued at $7.6 million worth of un-
manufactured leaf and $2.3 million worth of manufactured tobaccos.
The United States supplied two-thirds of the market for tobacco leaf,
and South Korea and India each supplied 7 percent; the rest, valued
at $1.6 million, came from a variety of sources, including Thailand,
Pakistan, Taiwan, and the Philippines.

Vietnam does not yet grow more tobacco than it needs to meet
local requirements, but if, at some future time, surpluses appear,
small quantities may be disposed of in the Malaysian market. The
trade is unlikely to be significant.

Spices

Malaysia imported $3.3 million worth of a variety of spices in
1967. There is a history of trade between Vietnam and Malaysia in
pepper, chilies, cinnamon, nutmeg, mace, cardamon, and anise, and
there is no reason why it should not revive. The most valuable market
is in dried chilies, of which 4,598 tons, valued at $1.4 million, were
imported in 1967; this is now shared almost equally by Mainland China,
Sumatra, and Thailand. The small market for cinnamon ($34,000) is
supplied very largely by Sumatra.

Summary of Conclusions

As seen at present, the opportunities for Vietnam to export to
Malaysia are limited to tea, livestock, animal feedstuffs, dried and
salted marine products, vegetables, coffee, tobacco, and spices.
Some tentative judgements on what the export trade in these items
might amount to by 1980 are offered in Table 96. There are some
obvious reservations; it will take Vietnam, for instance, some time
to develop a beef cattle industry capable of competing with that of
Thailand in quality and price, and the readier market in dried and
salted marine products may be a short-lived one. Some of the
commodities that will enter into the export trade with Malaysia, coffee
and tobacco for instance, are unlikely to do so in significant volume.

TAIWAN

General Information

In a period of less than twenty years, Taiwan (the Republic of
China) has accomplished a transition from being an almost exclusively
agriculturally based economy to one in which industry is the dominant

TABLE 96

Export Possibilities, Vietnam to Malaysia, 1980

Commodity	Volume	Estimated Value (In Millions of Dollars)[a]
Tea[b]	200,000	$0.07
Beef Cattle[c]	1,000	0.1
Animal Feedstuffs[d]	12,000 - 24,000	1.0 - 2.0
Citrus Fruit[d]	-[e]	-[e]
Vegetables (Potatoes, Onions)	3,000	1.0
Salted and Dried Fish	120	0.2
Coffee	-[e]	-[e]
Tobacco	-[e]	-[e]
Spices (Chilies and Cinnamon)	-[e]	-[e]
Vegetable Oils and Oilseeds (Peanut and Soybean)	2,000	0.4
Total		$2.77 -$3.77

[a] 1968 prices.
[b] In pounds.
[c] By head.
[d] In tons.
[e] Not estimated; either small or dependent entirely on production capacity.

activity, though agriculture is still extremely important. External trade was responsible for only 20 percent of the island's GNP in the early 1950's and is responsible for almost a half of it today. Both exports and imports have been increasing steadily, and, recently, an adverse trade balance has also been growing, though not so rapidly as to create serious problems.

With a population of about 14 million on a land area of 36,000 square kilometers, of which only one-quarter is arable, Taiwan has one of the highest population densities in the world. In spite of the pressure of people on resources in land becoming heavier, for population has increased by two-thirds since 1952, there has been a steady improvement in economic well-being, reflected by a doubling of per capita income in this period--from $100 in 1962 to $205 in 1968. In 1952, agriculture accounted for almost 36 percent of GNP and industry for 18 percent; in 1968, industry contributed 29 percent and agriculture was down to 23 percent, a distinct change in the structure of the economy. The agricultural sector has been growing at a rate of 6 percent per annum but industry at a rate of 18.3 percent. In the meantime, the rate of population growth has been slowed from 3.7 percent to 2.4 percent and is expected to fall further.

From 1952 to 1960, Taiwan experienced inflation, prices rising by almost 9 percent a year. Since then, the price and monetary situation has been stabilized, and average annual price increases have been about only 2 percent. It is of some interest to note that many companies that thrived on inflation and speculation went bankrupt soon after stability was achieved.

In 1953, Taiwan initiated a series of four-year plans for economic development. By the end of the fourth plan in 1968, GNP had increased by 275 percent, and industrial output was up 700 percent, while agricultural production had gained 155 percent. Although the influence of the government has been all pervasive in the economic development process, it has been characterized more by steady support and guidance than by widely publicized high-pressure campaigns. While there have been shifts in emphasis from one four-year plan to another, the plans have nevertheless given a high degree of continuity to this very successful development process.

For a number of years after Japan restored Taiwan to the Republic of China, state enterprises dominated the business scene. In part, this was simply because properties established and held by Japanese citizens during the 50-year occupation were transferred directly to the government of the Republic, and, in many cases, Taiwanese private entrepreneurs with the experience and resources to operate these properties were not available. From time to time, the government has served variously as the costodian of private business, the founder of new enterprises, the supplier of raw materials, the buyer of finished goods, and the source of high risk credit. However, the principal purpose of these activities was to prime the pump, and, more recently, the trend has been away from state enterprises and into private ones. In 1952, the public share of industrial production was 57 percent; by 1968, it was only 27 percent.

During the early 1950's, when industrial development was beginning to gain momentum in Taiwan, the main motive for encouraging industry was to displace imports rather than to increase exports. Primary emphasis was on promoting light industries, mostly to satisfy domestic demands for consumer goods and production inputs. As these industries expanded and local requirements were fully met, Taiwan proceeded naturally to export in greater volume. In the course of this evolution, heavier industries have established themselves, and production has been oriented deliberately toward exports, a trend that has been particularly evident in the 1960's.

In evaluating the export potentials of Vietnam, Taiwan has to be viewed not only as a probable market but, also, as an illustration of the way in which Vietnam's own export trade may very well develop. With determined, but not dictatorial, government leadership, Taiwan's export trade has shown strong and solid growth--from $120 million in 1952 to $842 million in 1968. The manner in which this has taken place may possibly provide useful guidelines for Vietnam's own export policies.

External Trade

Taiwan has consistently discouraged the importation of consumer goods; in 1968, such items made up only 16 percent of imports--agricultural and industrial raw materials accounted for 47 percent, while the remaining 37 percent consisted of capital equipment.

All imports have been subject to strict control in the past, and, although, because of the increasing need for capital equipment and industrial raw materials, the degree of control has been moderated in recent years, it is still difficult to bring most types of consumer goods into Taiwan. The control mechanism consists of licenses, limits on foreign exchange, quotas, and tariffs. Vietnamese trade with Taiwan will not be more adversely affected by these controls than that of any other country, but it is clear that the overall market for controlled commodities is necessarily restricted by them. However, most of the products that Vietnam is likely to be able to supply to Taiwan are primary industrial or essential agricultural materials, on which controls and tariff rates are least onerous; in fact, import licenses for such commodities are granted almost automatically.

By deliberate policy, the government of Taiwan has not been receptive to the idea of special government-to-government trading agreements, though it has participated actively in negotiating the terms of trade in certain commodities, for example, bananas exported to Japan and corn purchased from Thailand. In spite of this general reluctance to consider barter or other special trading arrangements, it is possible that Taiwan would react favorably to ministerial level discussions in order to encourage two-way trade with present or potential trading partners, particularly in those cases where there is an extreme imbalance in the trade between the two countries, such as that of Vietnam.

The import business in Taiwan is conducted either by registered traders, by end users, or by government trading agencies. For the most part, importers do not yet operate on so large a scale that Vietnamese exporters would find it difficult to do business with them. Taiwanese commerce has not as yet established very many foreign branches or overseas trading affiliates through which to channel imports and exports, but numerous business relationships have been established as a result of Vietnam's extensive purchases from Taiwan in recent years; these channels should be helpful in starting to reverse the flow. Many of Taiwan's traders are both importers and exporters, and the same is true of Vietnam's.

Although the initial phases of industrial development in Taiwan were quite logically directed toward producing goods for domestic consumption, the objective now is to produce for export, in order to provide employment and reinforce the country's foreign exchange position. The evolution of Taiwan's export trade, from a situation dominated by raw and processed agricultural products to one in which industrial manufactures have taken the lead, has been rapid. In 1952, agriculture provided 95 percent of Taiwan's exports, but, in 1968, only 34 percent, the rest being industrial goods. Exports totaled $842 million in 1968 and provided over 20 percent of the GNP. It is improbable that Vietnam's transformation to an industrial economy will be as rapid, but in time, Vietnam's exports should move toward semi-processed goods at least, and, later, to finished ones.

In several cases, Taiwanese exports include products that Vietnam too may be in a position to export, so the two countries are potential competitors, as well as potential trading partners. The degree of possible competition varies from commodity to commodity: with such items as bananas, plywood, sugar, lumber, tea, and processed fruits and vegetables, it will be difficult for Vietnam to take any of its existing trade away from Taiwan; but with others, including rice and fish, Taiwanese competition will be a less serious obstacle to Vietnam's efforts to expand its export trade.

Among the more important commodities exported (entirely agricultural in origin), several have developed very rapidly in recent years. Bananas, canned asparagus and mushrooms, and wood products are outstanding examples. Taiwan's success in the trade in these products is founded mainly on its ability to supply them at competitive prices and on its quickness to produce for markets before competition for them has developed.

The most profitable outlets for Taiwanese production are obviously in the more developed countries; the United States and Japan alone absorb over a half of all exports. Asian countries, other than Japan, are also important markets for Taiwan, especially Hong Kong, Vietnam, Thailand, and Singapore. There has been an effort by Taiwan to diversify not only the commodities exported but, also, the markets to which they are destined, and this is reflected by the growth of its export trade with North America and Europe. By 1972, Taiwan aims at annual exports of almost $1.2 billion, representing an increase of 12.5 percent a year on the export values it achieved in 1968.

Among Taiwan's exports, processed and manufactured goods are now very much in the majority; even among basically agricultural items, the trend has been toward processing before export, and plywood and canned fruits and vegetables are prominent in its export trade. In 1952, sugar and rice constituted 78 percent of Taiwan's exports, and, in 1968, only 8 percent.

With greater emphasis on industrial production, it has been necessary for Taiwan to import ever increasing volumes of such raw materials as its own agriculture, in spite of the emphasis on self-sufficiency, is unable to supply. Table 97 lists those commodities imported by Taiwan in 1967 and 1968 that represent promising potential exports for Vietnam.

Under Taiwan's latest four-year plan, it is estimated that imports during the period 1969-72 will total $4,585 million, averaging a little more than $1 billion a year. This is approximately the level imports reached in 1968. In 1972 alone, however, imports are projected at more than $1.3 billion. Substantially increased volumes of natural rubber, wood pulp, wood, and beans are expected to be imported. All are potentially important exports from Vietnam, and there are good prospects of disposing of sizable volumes of them in this market.

TABLE 97

Taiwan: Values of Selected Imports, 1967 and 1968
(In Millions of Dollars)

	Value	
Commodity	1967	1968*
Logs (Nonconifer)	23.0	13.0
Soybeans (Dry)	29.8	10.2
Soybeans (Green)	4.5	4.5
Corn	10.3	11.7
Scrap Iron	9.4	7.5
Natural Rubber	4.4	2.0
Pulp	5.0	1.4
Waste Paper	1.2	0.7
Bovine Hides	2.1	1.0
Beans, Peas, Lentils, etc.	7.3	5.9
Tobacco (Unmanufactured)	6.4	0.5
Plants, Seeds, Flowers (for Pharmaceuticals, insecticides, and Fungicides)	4.0	2.0
Oilseeds, Nuts, and Kernels (Including Copra)	2.0	2.2
Jute and Ramie	0.8	0.7
Coffee	0.15	0.09
Cinnamon	0.09	0.01

*First six months.

Source: Derived from official Taiwan trade statistics.

333

Export Opportunities for Vietnam by Commodity

These are summarized in Table 98. Except in the case of scrap iron (a doubtful item for reasons explained in the section on South Korea), wood pulp, and beans, peas, and lentils, it is assumed that these commodities will be available for export from Vietnam in the volumes suggested and that they will be available at competitive prices. On most items, competition from other producers in Southeast Asia is likely to be keen.

A few observations concerning these items, and certain others not included in Table 98, are appropriate.

Among the commodities listed as potentially promising exports, only scrap iron, vegetable oils, and rubber have been of any real significance in Vietnam's present or previous trade with Taiwan. Most recently, very little of anything has been shipped, except scrap. Several of the commodities listed in Table 98 and several others that might have been added to it had the prospects for them been less uncertain have not previously been exported by Vietnam--nor, in some cases, even produced by it--in any volume.

Corn, wood pulp, wastepaper, bovine hides, tabacco, beans, peas, and lentils would certainly have to be included in this category, and logs, coffee, and jute have entered only sporadically into Vietnam's external trade. The lack of substantial experience in shipping these commodities is not too serious an obstacle, however, particularly if there is a good working relationship between buyers and sellers.

Rice is not regarded as a potential export to Taiwan. Except in unusual circumstances, Taiwan has been self-sufficient in rice, and it normally has a small surplus for export. Apart from the long-standing tradition of Taiwanese farmers to place an absolute priority on production of rice for their families, they have a further incentive to grow rice because it is used to pay for fertilizer and for land payments and taxes. In addition, all owners of paddy land in Taiwan are required to sell rice to the government. Assuming a decline in the rate of population growth, a decline, also, in per capita consumption, and a continuing official interest in self-sufficiency, especially in rice, Taiwan is quite unlikely to provide a significant outlet for rice from Vietnam during the period 1975-80. If, however, there should be any shift in emphasis away from rice or if a plateau is reached on production, then it is entirely possible that Taiwan would begin to import this commodity, though, by 1975-80, this would probably not be in large quantities.

TABLE 98

Export Possibilities, Vietnam to Taiwan, 1980

Commodity	Volume (In Metric Tons)	Estimated Value (In Millions of Dollars)[a]
Hardwood Logs	180,000 - 230,000	$8.0 - $10.0
Feed Grains	25,000 - 35,000	2.0 - 3.0
Natural Rubber	5,000 - 7,500	2.0 - 3.0
Waste Paper	_b	0.2 - 0.3
Vegetable Oils and Oil Cake	5,000 - 7,500	1.0 - 1.5
Jute and Kenaf	_b	0.3 - 0.4
Cinnamon	60 - 70	0.05 - 0.07
Beans, Peas, and Lentils	_b	_b
Scrap Iron	_b	_b
Wood Pulp	_b	_b
		$13.55 - $18.27

[a] 1968 prices
[b] Less than $25,000 in value.

335

In evaluating the prospects of exporting commodities from Vietnam to Taiwan, or elsewhere for that matter, consideration has to be given not only to the prospective demand situation within the importing country but, also, to the probable competition from other sources of supply, the trading relationship between Vietnam and the importer, and the expected supply situation in Vietnam itself. In the case of Taiwan, for example imports of beans (soybeans and other types) are expected to increase to $50 million by 1972, and it is tempting to assume that, with the balance of trade now so heavily in Taiwan's favor, there would be a real opportunity for Vietnam to sell beans to Taiwan. Even 5 percent of such a market would be worth $2.5 million a year. However, it is questionable whether, by 1980, Vietnam will have such substantial surpluses as this to dispose of after meeting its own requirements; with strong competition from Taiwan's present suppliers of these commodities--the United States, Thailand, Burma, Mexico, and certain African countries--it has been deemed advisable to avoid an estimate of the size of the share of this market that Vietnam may reasonably hope to capture. The Taiwan market for Vietnamese scrap metal might easily amount by 1980 to between $5 and 7.5 million, but we have borne in mind the possibility that, by that time, Vietnam may very well be importing scrap to supply a steel industry of its own; even if it is not, it can hardly hope to supply Taiwan in the volumes that these values suggest. There is likely to be a market in Taiwan for wood pulp to the value of $1 to $1.5 million, but little probability, even if the feasibility of pulp production is proved, that Vietnam can supply it after meeting its own requirements and those of other client countries (discussed in previous sections of this book).

Other possible trade items ommitted from Table 98 are unmanufactured tobacco, pharmaceutical plants and seeds, and coffee. There are markets for all these commodities in Taiwan, representing a possible total value to Vietnam of from $2 to $3 million; but the amount that Vietnam is likely to be able to be sell to Taiwan of any of these commodities in the face of competition from well-established present suppliers will not have a significant effect on its foreign exchange earnings.

Summary of Conclusions

Among the commodities exported by Taiwan, there are a number that are now among Vietnam's exports or which may reasonably be expected to be available for export in the future. Intense competition may be anticipated on bananas, processed fruits and vegetables, tea, fish products, plywood, fresh pineapples, and, even, poultry feathers. Generally speaking, however, there is no competition between Vietnam and Taiwan on industrial raw materials, such as hardwood logs and rubber, and feedstuffs; these products are imported regularly and in quantity by Taiwan.

Vietnam has been an important outlet for exports from Taiwan; in fact, Taiwan's sales to Vietnam totaled almost $44 million in 1968, when Vietnam was the fifth most important market for Taiwanese goods. Between 1958 and 1967, Vietnam purchased goods valued at $330 million from Taiwan and exported to that country goods worth only $6 million. It is not unreasonable to expect that Vietnam should participate more substantially in the market for those commodities that Taiwan cannot produce for itself and needs to import to serve its fast-growing industries. The size of the share in this market that we suggest Vietnam might obtain is, in fact, rather a modest one-- between $14 and $20 million.

THAILAND

General Inforamtion

Thailand is basically an agricultural country, and the development of industry on any scale is quite recent. Minerals, however, especially tin, contribute importantly to the economy. In 1967, agriculture provided 31 percent of GDP and manufacturing about 13 percent.

The pressure of population on land is not yet severe; the area of Thailand is 514,000 square kilometers, and the population is 35 million, or less than 70 persons to the square kilometer; but population is increasing at the high rate of 3.2 percent a year, fast enough, if unchecked, to suggest that sooner or later Thailand's resources in land will be strained. At present, approximately 40 percent of the land area is cultivated; it is estimated that over three-quarters of all Thais live in rural areas, although Bangkok and its environs have an urban population of 3 million. Per capita, GNP has been rising steadily--from $103 in 1960 to $154 in 1967. Thailand aspires to reach $195 by 1971.

External Trade

Exports have been increasing fairly rapidly during the past ten years, and they reached a peak of over $700 million in 1967. At the same time, imports, mostly of manufactured goods, have been increasing even more rapidly, so that Thailand's balance of trade has become increasingly adverse. This is, of course, a common problem for many developing countries, which, like Thailand, depend heavily on primary products for their export income. Over 80 percent of Thailand's exports in recent years have consisted of agricultural products, almost entirely foodstuffs and industrial raw materials. Rice has been the principal export, and tin and rubber have been important ones; in the 1960's, there has been some diversification in export commodities, with corn, kenaf, cassava, and fish products entering into the country's export trade in volumes of increasing significance. Further diversification is contemplated under Thailand's current Economic Development Plan.

The expansion of the export trade has been accomplished almost entirely by private enterprise. Until recently, the government of Thailand has not taken any active part in promoting exports, and, even now, there is no organized drive or formal program to stimulate external trade. However, 1968 exports, valued at $650 million, represented a sharp fall from the previous year's returns of $730 million, partly as a result of drought and partly because of falling prices in international markets; since imports increased during the year, the deficit in the external trade account rose to $500 million. There is now increasing awareness in official circles of the need to narrow the trade gap, and more attention is being paid to the promotion of exports, leading to greater participation by the government in what has hitherto been considered a purely private activity.

Four commodities--rice, rubber, tin, and corn--accounted for over two-thirds, by value, of all the exports that left Thailand in 1968. (See Table 99.)

Thailand's performance on exports is of special interest to Vietnam because, with few exceptions, the commodities leaving Thailand are either produced or suitable for production in Vietnam and could enter into Vietnam's export trade in the postwar period. It is to be noted that the great bulk of these exports are either foodstuffs or industrial raw materials; no manufactured goods are yet of sufficient importance to be listed separately.

Rice, rubber, and tin have always been the principal constituents of Thailand's export trade, but, in recent years, several new commodities have entered the trade and are now very important countributors to it. Among these, corn, kenaf, cassava, and frozen fish are outstanding. During the last ten years, corn exports rose at a remarkable rate --from 237,000 tons to almost 1.5 million tons; exports of kenaf have increased by 1,000 percent; and exports of cassava and frozen fish products have multiplied sixfold. In 1968, these four commodities together accounted for fully one-quarter of Thailand's export income. Thailand's experience demonstrates the importance of constant

TABLE 99

Thailand: 1968 Exports, by Volume, Value, and Principal Destination

Commodity	Volume (In Metric Tons)	Value (In Millions of Dollars)	Principal Markets
Rice	1,050,000	$199	Hong Kong, Singapore, Malaysia, Japan, India
Rubber	245,000	85	Japan, United Kingdom, Singapore, United States, Italy
Tin	25,000	79	United States, Netherlands, West Germany, Italy
Corn	1,457,845	84	Japan, China (Taiwan), Singapore, Hong Kong, Malaysia
Kenaf and Jute	196,600	27	Japan, India, Belgium, Italy, France
Tapioca Products	720,000	39	Netherlands, West Germany, United States, Japan
Teak*	31,000	9	Denmark, United Kingdom, West Germany, United States, Italy, Japan
Kapok	18,747	5	United States, Japan, Malaysia, Singapore
Castor Seeds	25,786	4	Japan, France, Netherlands, South Korea
Green Beans	44,000	6	China (Taiwan), Malaysia, Hong Kong, Singapore, Philippines
Tobacco	7,500	6	West Germany, United Kingdom, Japan, Laos, Singapore
Shrimps (Frozen)	9,500	15	Japan, United States
Sorghum	53,403	3	Japan, Singapore, Saudi Arabia, Malaysia, Hong Kong
Other		93	
Total		$654	

*In cubic meters.

Source: Official Thailand trade statistics.

alertness to the possibility of market exploitation and development. Among the minor exports from Thailand, there are several that might serve as potential exports from Vietnam, for example, sesame, tamarind, seedlac, and sticklac.

Of the ten leading buyers of Thai products, six are in East Asia, and Japan is easily the most important single market. These six countries absorbed over a half of Thailand's exports in 1967. Exports to the United States and Europe consisted predominantly of industrial raw materials. Except in the cases of Japan and India, shipments to the six Asian markets consisted mostly of foodstuffs and animal feeds.

Manufactured goods, machinery, chemicals, and mineral fuels make up about 90 percent of Thailand's imports. The principal purpose of Thailand's current program of industrialization is to make greater use of domestically produced raw materials and to meet more of the domestic demand for consumer goods; there is, therefore, little immediate opportunity for any other country to sell unprocessed agricultural products or even industrial raw materials to Thailand in any volume. The agricultural commodities imported are generally complementary to local products and consist mostly of certain specialty items (such as apples, potatoes, dried onions, canned and frozen fruits, and vegetables), wheat flour, cotton in its various forms, tobacco, dairy products, coffee, and fish products.

Items imported in 1967 that might reasonably be supplied by Vietnam are shown in Table 100, together with the principal countries from which Thailand presently purchases them.

Export Opportunities for Vietnam by Commodity

During 1958-67, Thailand imported small quantities of a limited range of agricultural products from Vietnam. The total value of such shipments (f.o.b. Saigon) over the period is estimated at only $500,000, and exports of tea were responsible for most of this. It cannot, therefore, be said that Thailand has been of any real importance as an outlet for Vietnam's products, nor is it likely to be one in the future. It may be noted that, during the same period, Vietnam imported from Thailand goods valued at over $22.5 million, rice being the major item.

In reviewing the commodities listed in Table 100, it is obvious that, with the possibility exceptions of tobacco and scrap iron, Vietnam's hopes of winning any significant share of Thailand's limited markets for these items will depend mostly on whether it can meet competition from other producers in Asia. The prospects, such as they are, are set out in Table 101.

TABLE 100

Thailand: Selected Imports, by Volume and Source
of Supply, 1967
(In Metric Tons)

Commodity	Volume	Principal Sources
Tea	1,766	China (Taiwan) and Indonesia
Coffee	4,044	Indonesia
Nonmanufactured Tobacco	9,309	United States
Iron Scrap	25,110	Belgium, Australia, and West Germany
Vegetables (Fresh or Dehydrated)	4,595	China (Taiwan), Netherlands, and Japan
Cinnamon	47	Indonesia
Fish (Fresh, Frozen, or Dried)	2,944	Malaysia, Korea (Republic), and Japan
Silk (Yarn)	135	Japan and Korea (Republic)

Source: Derived from official Thailand trade statistics.

341

TABLE 101

Export Possibilities, Vietnam to Thailand, 1980

Commodity	Volume (In Metric Tons)	Estimated Value (in Millions of Dollars)[a]
Tea	200 - 300	$0.2 - $0.3
Coffee	600 - 800	0.3 - 0.4
Fresh and Dehydrated Vegetables	2,000 - 3,000	0.6 - 0.9
Cinnamon	30 - 40	0.03 - 0.04
Salted, Dried Fish, and Molluscs	800 - 1,000	0.2 - 0.3
Scrap Iron	b	b
		$1.33 - $1.94

[a] 1968 prices;
[b] Less than $25,000 in value.

There appear to be good prospects for fresh and dehydrated vegetables, especially those of temperate zone-type, such as onions, potatoes, dried beans, lentils, peas mushrooms, and shallots, and Thailand might absorb up to 3,000 tons a year of Vietnam's production of these commodities. There are good prospects of shipping a little cinnamon to Thailand, 30 to 40 tons annually, though there will be competition from suppliers in Indonesia. Once again, there should be good prospects of selling iron scrap to Thailand in substantial volume, 10,000 to 15,000 tons a year (for Vietnam has an advantage of location over other suppliers), but the chances that Vietnam will be able or will wish to do this are too uncertain for a positive estimate to be made of potential exports of this item.

There are some prospects, but they are not as good, that Vietnam may be able to sell a little tea, a little coffee, and a few specialized marine products, such as sharksfin, cuttle fish, and other dried fish, as well as fresh molluscs, to Thailand. As far as tea is concerned, there will be strong competition from Taiwan and Indonesia, and there is also an effort by Thailand to promote the use of domestic teas; it will be difficult for Vietnam to sell more than 200 or 300 tons in this market. Against competition from Indonesia and other producers and in view of the likelihood that Thailand will encourage local production, it will not, probably, be able to dispose of more that 600 to 800 tons of its coffee in Thailand. Although Thailand can probably absorb from 800 to 1,000 tons of specialized fish products (but not of ordinary fish), there is a question whether Vietnam will be able to produce in such quantities surplus to its own requirements and to those of other markets.

The prospects for selling tobacco to Thailand are distinctly poor. Thailand produces surpluses of the types now cultivated in Vietnam, and until Vietnam can greatly increase its production of Virginia leaf (which, presumably, Thailand could do for itself also) and contend success- fully with United States competition, these products can be dismissed.

Summary of Conclusions

Thailand and Vietnam are likely to be direct competitors in seeking outlets for production in excess of their domestic demands. With few exceptions, the product mix of the two countries, especially in agriculture, is similar. Some of Thailand's principal exports, including corn, kenaf, and cassava, have not previously been prominent among exports from Vietnam, but they may well be adapted for greatly increased production in this country. In these circumstances, the trade between the two countries is not likely to be substantial. On the other hand, Thailand does offer Vietnam the advantages of proximity and of being already a friendly trading partner, although the trade has been flowing in recent years almost exclusively from Thailand to Vietnam, with very little movement in the other direction.

18

INTRODUCTION: VIETNAMESE ATTITUDES
TOWARD THE EXPORT TRADE

In order to establish more definitely the setting in the private
sector within which substantially all Vietnam's export trade is likely
to be generated, a number of exporters were interviewed to obtain
some firsthand and informed opinions on the prospects. This survey
was conducted in June, 1969, and July, 1969, and covered a score of
traders located in the Saigon-Cholon area, these being selected at
random from a list of firms reported to be in the export business.
The results of this limited study are of some significance, because
they indicate some of the attitudes of the business community upon
which the success of an export promotion program will largely depend.

All were asked to state what commodities they thought most
likely to enter into the export trade after the war, and all expressed
the belief that rice and rubber would continue to be Vietnam's principal exports. Next in order were tea, coffee, and oil cake. Very
few other products were mentioned, even those that have been exported
in some volume previously, for instance, duck feathers, cinnamon,
and fish sauce. The only new export commodity suggested as likely
was corn; and no mention, whatsoever, was made of industrial raw
materials, such as scrap iron and timber. The answers suggest that
existing exporters are strongly influenced by traditional and customary
export patterns and that the private sector will need convincing of the
merits of a broader and bolder program.

Among the problems to be expected during the postwar period,
the most commonly mentioned were those of prices and high production costs. It was clearly recognized that, at present exchange rates
and under existing currency regulations, domestic prices of most

347

products are so much higher than the returns from exports that trade is very difficult, if not impossible, without substantial subsidies. In addition, some, though not all, of these exporters were aware there would be intense competition on most export commodities and that more efficient production will be necessary if Vietnam's products are to be competitive. Other problems rather frequently referred to had to do with the lack of export promotion by the government of Vietnam, the need for quality control, and the need for unfailing fulfilment by traders of their commitments to their clients.

The merchants interviewed were divided in their views on whether Vietnam would find it easy or difficult to regain its previous markets and to expand them. By a narrow margin, the weight of opinion was on the side that doubted or had reservations concerning Vietnam's ability to do this. They argued that Vietnam had been displaced from its markets and had been absent from them in a period of constantly increasing competition. Those who took a more optimistic view maintained that this country's products have always had a good reputation and have traditionally been lower-priced than those of Vietnam's competitors; however, just as many took an opposite view, asserting that quality has not been superior and that prices are too high. There may well have been confusion concerning the application of the question to past or present conditions. A few traders said they believed that the war has given Vietnam publicity that would be helpful to export sales.

Answers to a question on the most promising outlets for exports from Vietnam reflected wide acceptance of the view that France, Japan, Hong Kong, the United States, and Singapore will be the best markets for Vietnamese goods. A few traders also mentioned Germany, the United Kingdom, and a scattering of other countries, but the concentration on the five leaders was obvious. Again, it was apparent that past experience continues to exert strong influence in forming attitudes about future exports.

There was a considerable range in opinions of what the government should do to expand exports; the replies were mostly along the following lines: it should subsidize exports where necessary and/or apply a realistic exchange rate on them; it should permit free competition among exporters and refrain from granting exclusive trading privileges; it should reduce the formalities and red tape that are involved in export procedures at the present time; and it should do more to stimulate production of the commodities that might enter into the export trade. Generally speaking, traders were unanimous in urging that the function of government agencies should be to facilitate and not to hinder the conduct of external trade, with an implication that this is what they actually do.

The answers were rather less certain on what traders themselves could do to promote exports. The responses were varied, but, for the most part, involved three lines of thought: closer cooperation between merchants and producers, so as to improve the marketing structure and practices; the maintenance by merchants of higher standards of integrity, with particular attention to the stipulations of agreements concerning quality, price, and delivery time; and a more aggressive attitude on their part in their sales efforts. One, and only one, trader said that the principal need was for exporters to organize themselves.

Against this background of trade opinions and attitudes, it is apparent that strong leadership will be needed to organize and conduct an effective program for expanding Vietnam's exports. Because this was fairly obvious from the start, this appraisal of the country's export potential was broadened to include a review of the steps taken by other countries to promote their international trade. Experience elsewhere in Asia and some possible procedures for Vietnam are outlined in the sections that follow.

INSTITUTIONS FOR TRADE PROMOTION
IN EAST ASIA

Except under the special conditions prevailing during the war, when domestic production has declined and imports have soared (in part, deliberately, as a measure of price stabilization), it is obvious that Vietnam cannot continue indefinitely to buy from other countries so very much more than it presently sells to them. The huge imbalance in the country's external trade account requires that, as soon as production can be increased, Vietnam should move actively, and at diplomatic levels if necessary, to promote export sales to those markets that are shipping goods to Vietnam in quantity. Once a more normal situation begins to return, Japan, Taiwan, South Korea, and India cannot expect to continue selling to Vietnam without buying more from it in return; this would hold true for the United States when the time comes for its very large programs of assistance to Vietnam to be curtailed or terminated. The suggestion that the principal effort be directed to those who are currently selling goods in great volume to Vietnam does not imply that other prospective outlets should be ignored; all and every potential client will be needed to raise Vietnam's foreign exchange earnings to a reasonable level and to move toward a better balance of trade.

A sustained and well-managed campaign to promote Vietnam's exports in every potential market will be essential if its economy is to prosper. As indicated earlier, exporters themselves advocate the establishment of such a program. Vietnam already possesses the ordinary governmental agencies that handle the procedural routines of external trade. It also possesses an Export Promotion Center, under the aegis of the Directorate of Foreign Trade, which hopes to enter the field of commercial public relations, once conditions permit. It has, in addition, an Industrial Development Center, which is intended to promote enterprises, some of which might contribute to an export program. Nevertheless, the government may well find that it needs something more than these and that the experience of other countries in this field may be relevant to its own requirements. For this reason, it is appropriate to describe the methods used by some of Vietnam's neighbors in Asia in their successful efforts to promote their export trade.

Hong Kong

Trade Development Council

For a favorable image of Vietnam to be created overseas and for the effective prosecution of sales promotion activities, there must be a sense of common purpose and direction, and, for this, a coordinated institutional structure will probably be found necessary. This has certainly been the experience of Hong Kong, which, in 1966, enacted legislation setting up a central agency for export promotion and endowing it with executive powers. In this development, Hong Kong took into account the experience of some fifteen other major exporting countries. In every one of these, there was either a single recognized central agency for export promotion (which might be either inside the government or outside it) or there was one governmental agency and one private one operating in parallel. The need to concentrate the activities of specialized export promotion staff and the value of keeping the numbers of promotional agencies to a minimum are, in fact, widely recognized. In most countries, the promotional function is performed by a central council, which evaluates the overall needs for export promotion, fixes the targets, and either adjusts the programs of other agencies to assemble them into a coherent whole or sets up new programs of its own design. In almost all of these countries, the public funds devoted to trade promotion are utilized by, or channeled through, the central promotion agency. Methods of financing, naturally, may vary; they include outright grants of public funds, a general charge on the community, levies on foreign trade, and contributions from individual firms and associations, and all possible combinations of these. No one country offers an ideal model, but the institutions of several whose situations were comparable to Hong Kong had features in common, which Hong Kong judged to be applicable to its own circumstances:

There was a central policy-making body, fully representative of commerce, industry, banking, and government, established by law, responsible to the government and the legislature for the carrying out of its work, and with full powers to prepare its program and budgets, engage staff, and authorize expenditures.

The objectives and functions of this body were to assist the development of overseas trade and the promotion of exports by organizing and financing, or assisting in the organizing and financing, of any activities that might seem to it beneficial to the achievement of these objectives. These activities included, for instance, the establishment of contacts between overseas buyers and local exporters, the distribution of information concerning domestic products available for export, and advice to governmental information services on the need for explanatory publications on governmental policy in cases where misunderstanding or ignorance might damage the country's image abroad and prevent understanding of its problems. The responsibilities of this central body did not, on the other hand, extend to the maintenance of channels of trade and of international trade relations, functions reserved to the government, though it was expected to familiarize itself with the government's objectives in these matters and to act in accordance with them.

The central export promotion body was commonly given a degree of financial autonomy and was permitted to apply any budgetary and accountancy system it wished, since systems of public accounts were recognized to be inappropriate to the quasicommercial nature of these activities; it was also accorded access to public sources of finance.

Every such body was empowered to employ a full-time chief executive, to whom wide powers were delegated and who was assisted by a permanent staff.

Using these criteria, Hong Kong itself established an export promotion organization, known (for reasons peculiar to Hong Kong) as the Trade Development Council. It consists of a central policy-making council, broadly representative of government and leading trade and industrial associations, with its own executive director and staff. Care was taken to ensure that the Council was properly representative of all the agencies interested in, and concerned in any way with, export promotion. Such representatives are invariably the heads of their own particular organizations.

In deciding the matter of assistance to the Council from public funds, Hong Kong examined the formulas adopted by certain other countries. Denmark and Switzerland rely principally on an assessment of the need for export promotion and its importance relative to other activities financed by the state, while Austria and Norway have adopted formulas related to the values of their foreign trade. Japan, at the start, provided funds for its export promotion agency to the amount of

0.35 percent of its export target for the year in question. Hong Kong's approach was pragmatic: it set a target for the total funds to be made available to the Council at 0.25 percent of domestic exports (which, in 1964/65, amounted to HK$11.5 million), and then considered what formula should be applied to the raising of these resources.

The following criteria were considered appropriate to the levying of new taxes for the support of trade promotion activities: First, any new tax should be equitable in its incidence throughout the commercial and industrial communities. Second, it should be applied at a low rate, so as to reduce to a minimum the financial burden on trade. Third, it should be simple to administer and collect. Fourth, it should have a yield directly related to the value of trade. Because of the complete dependence of Hong Kong's economy on its export trade, the benefits of which are spread throughout the industrial and commercial sectors, the method eventually adopted was a direct levy on the value of all imports, exports, and reexports, collected through a stamp duty related to the value of consignments as shown on the trade declarations filed with the Department of Commerce and Industry for statistical purposes. The ad valorem rate of the stamp duty is HK$0.50 per HK$1,000 or part thereof, with a minimum charge of HK$2.00. This was estimated to produce approximately HK$6.5 million, and it was decided that the balance of HK$5 million, representing the cost of previous government services and commitments to be discharged by the Council, should be met by an annual direct subvention, payable by the government.

It is not suggested that this formula will be appropriate to Vietnam's circumstances. Vietnam's exports will be primarily agricultural commodities, without direct correlation to imports. The device adopted by Hong Kong is recorded simply as a good example of a specific tax structured to meet particular requirements. There is, however, an obvious parallel with the statistics fee levied by Vietnam on exports, which may possibly lend itself to adaptation for trade promotion purposes.

Export Credit Insurance

It was not until 1963 that Hong Kong began to consider the advantages to the promotion of exports of offering some form of public insurance for the credit extended by its exporters to their customers. In 1966, an organization was established to supply this need; in its first two years of operation, it amply demonstrated its value and did so at low rates of premium. Vietnam would be advised to investigate other examples of insurance schemes of this type, but the Hong Kong model has worked well and may prove to be an appropriate one for the circumstances in which Vietnam may find itself after the war. Insurance is an essential aspect of export expansion, and it deserves early and serious consideration.

As international trade becomes more competitive, credit for overseas buyers is an increasingly important factor in determining the suppliers with whom orders will be placed. At this point, it is fitting to mention that Vietnam has previously pursued a policy of cash in advance. However, granting credit to overseas buyers is a risky business. Apart from the normal commercial risks, a variety of events may occur to delay or prevent payment--the insolvency of the importer, or his dishonesty, political developments in the importer's country, a shortage of foreign exchange, a currency devaluation, a sudden embargo on imports, disturbances, wars, nationalization, and many others. An export credit insurance scheme encourages the export trade by selective coverage of such risks and, by covering them, adds the element of security to the selling efforts of exporters and helps them to compete on equal terms with foreign suppliers. Insurance also improves the financial status of exporters, for commercial banks are readier to finance transactions and will often charge lower rates for advances or bills discounted against them when they are insured.

The insurance institution may be a regular agency of the government, and in many countries it is, since the government necessarily has to underwrite these operations. In Hong Kong, it was decided that, on balance, the flexibility essential in day-to-day operations of this kind would best be obtained by a separate statutory organization working within clearly defined policies approved by the government. An Export Insurance Corporation, therefore, was established by ordinance, with a capital of HK$10 million, fully subscribed by the government, which also guaranteed its obligations. Its function is purely and simply to provide credit insurance for Hong Kong's exporters. It does not subsidize exports, nor does it operate on a profit basis, aiming merely at covering its outgoings with its premium income. The Corporation is assisted by an Advisory Board, appointed by the government, composed of members with wide experience in industry, commerce, and finance.

This organization offers the following:

1. A comprehensive shipments policy, designed for export of consumer goods and covering all the policy holder's D/P and D/A business against the following causes of loss arising after exportation: (a) insolvency of the client, (b) the client's refusal to pay within due date for goods delivered and accepted, (c) government action preventing or delaying the transfer of foreign exchange to the policy holder, (d) the imposition of new import licensing restrictions or the cancellation of a valid import licence by government action in the country of the importer, (e) war between the buyer's country and the exporter's country, and (f) war, revolution, or civil disturbance in the buyer's country.

2. A comprehensive contracts policy, which provides coverage immediately after a firm contract is concluded for losses arising from any of the above causes.

3. Coverage for reexports and merchanting transactions.

The corporation pays 85 percent of the amount of loss under all its policies, but, of course, exercises a system of credit control based on the assessed credit-worthiness of individual buyers. This is an invaluable reinforcement to an exporter's own system of credit management. Premium rates depend on the length of credit granted and the particular market with which an exporter may be dealing; the average rate presently in force for all types of policy is slightly under HK$ 0.50 per HK$100, that is, approximately 0.5 percent.

South Korea

The fact that exports from South Korea were expected to reach $700 million in 1969 (they were only $84 million in 1963) is sufficient indication of the success South Korea has had in promoting its external trade. Imports have increased rapidly as well, but this does not detract from the success of the export program. After the Korean War and until 1960, South Korea exported very little at all, but, beginning in 1963, with currency stabilization and increasing emphasis on manufacturing and exports, the country's foreign trade entered into a period of remarkably rapid growth. This development was no accident; rather, it was the result of a well-organized and efficiently executed program, and of the South Korean government's deliberate decision to make expansion of exports their top priority objective. Because this program has been so outstandingly successful and because it has been established and managed by one of the less-developed countries, the South Korean experience is bound to be relevant to other countries anxious to increase their exports. In the following section, the major steps taken by the government and programs it has developed to stimulate exports are briefly described. While all the interests involved in foreign trade have participated actively in these programs, since 1965, the leadership has quite definitely been provided by the government of South Korea, and the results have been extraordinarily successful.

Public Authorities

Impetus was initially given to the export drive by President Park's announcement in January, 1965, that the target for exports was to be the equivalent of $1,000 million annually. At the time, exports were running at a rate of less than $200 million per year; it was expected that the goal of $1 billion would be reached in 1970.

In 1963, a Joint Export Development Committee (known later as the Export Promotion Subcommittee, or EPSC) had been established, but it was largely ineffective until, in 1965, it became the nucleus of this new export promotion program. The Committee was composed of a good cross section of higher government officials and representatives of chambers of commerce and trade associations. There were two cochairmen, the Vice Minister of Commerce and Industry and the Deputy Director of the United States Operations Mission to South Korea. A steering committee directed the work program, and a series of task forces was organized along commodity lines. Although the EPSC was not a regular government agency and could not compel acceptance of its recommendations, it was nevertheless successful in getting most of its suggestions adopted by the various other agencies involved. One reason for this may have been the President's personal interest in the program and his insistence that the cochairmen report to him directly every month. This joint approach was maintained until the end of 1966, when the functions of the EPSC were transferred to committees of the South Korean government and of the private sector, but, in the meantime, two years of close cooperation between the government and the private sector had established basic policies for the export drive and provided a solid foundation for further implementation of the plan.

Within the government, the Ministry of Commerce and Industry and the Economic Planning Board were given primary responsibility for setting goals and designing plans for the export program. The Ministry was asked to design the initial program in a single comprehensive document and the Board was assigned the task of determining the levels of exports that might reasonably be expected to be achieved. For this purpose, the ministries of Agriculture and of Commerce and Industry suggested targets for specific commodities in their respective areas. It is to be noted that the Economic Planning Board is headed by a Deputy Prime Minister and that it controls the Republic's budget; it is in a strong position to influence both the formulation and the implementation of all government programs.

In addition, a South Korean Trade Promotion Corporation (KOTRA) was organized under the aegis of the Ministry of Commerce and Industry, as a wholly owned government agency, supported entirely by the public authorities. This corporation is similar in its organization and functions to Japan's External Trade Organization (JETRO). Its purpose is to undertake programs aimed at expanding exports of South Korean goods; its principal activities include the following:

1. The survey and exploration of overseas markets for specific commodities, the dissemination of information about overseas markets, and the promotion of the export trade.

2. The promotion of export industries and their products to facilitate their entrance into overseas markets

3. The encouragement of export industries and the preparation of merchandising plans for export goods

4. Mediation in export transactions and the inducement of potential customers

5. Operation of trade centers overseas, as well as of the Corporation's National Exhibition Center in South Korea

6. Participation in international trade fairs, exhibitions, and displays

7. Publication of the monthly magazine "Korea Trade" and of other literature and production of films for the promotion of exports.

With fourteen overseas trade centers and representatives in twelve other countries, KOTRA has been a major participant in export promotion programs. It has a staff of about 250 people, of whom 150 are located outside South Korea. Like JETRO, the Corporation is not a sales agency; its sole purpose is to promote sales of South Korean products, individually and collectively. There is, of course, no doubt that organizations of this type are most effective where the products in question are manufactured goods or specialty items; it is not so likely that they could, or even should perhaps, be considered appropriate to countries where staples or raw materials such as rice, rubber, and scrap iron dominate the export trade.

It was recognized by South Korea at any early stage that the financing of business enterprises is an essential ingredient of export promotion. Under the jurisdiction of the Economic Planning Board, an Office of Investment Promotion administers the law relating to the attraction of foreign capital investment. The salient features of this law, under which some 130 businesses have already been established, are as follows:

1. There is no limit on the percentage of equity that a foreign investor is permitted to hold; he can own 100 percent of the stock of an enterprise.

2. There is no limit either on the conversion and transfer of profits and dividends earned on foreign investment.

3. A foreign investor may liquidate the whole or any part of his holdings after two years of business operation, and may then repatriate up to 20 percent of his capital subscription per annum.

4. A foreign investor may reinvest dividends accrued from
stocks or shares either in the same enterprise or in any other in
which there is foreign investment up to an amount equal to his total
initial investment; approval for additional investment is required if
it exceeds the amount of his original investment or if the intended
investment is in an enterprise that has no foreign investment.

5. Foreign-owned enterprises and foreign investors receive
exactly the same treatment under the law as South Korean nationals.

6. Income tax, corporation tax, property tax, and property
acquisition tax on foreign enterprises are waived entirely for the
first five years and are levied at rates reduced by 50 percent for the
following three years. For partly foreign-owned enterprises, these
privileges are granted in proportion to the percentage of stock owned
by foreign investors.

Substantial contributions to the export trade have resulted from
these provisions for the encouragement of foreign investment. Many
of the firms that qualify for these privileges are producing goods for
the export trade. While the Office of Investment Promotion is not
itself a financing agency, it is active in helping to develop a climate
favorable to the granting of credit by banks and other lending agencies.

Another example of government action in the export promotion
program is the Agricultural and Fishery Development Corporation,
sponsored by the Ministry of Agriculture. This is a quasipublic
organization, nominally directed by the Ministry and financed largely
by the South Korean government, but which operates in practice very
much like an independent private enterprise. Its purposes, defined in
the law by which it was set up, are to--

1. Invest in the construction and operation of facilities needed
to store, preserve, process, and market the products of South Korean
agriculture and fisheries.

2. Mobilize domestic and foreign capital resources and to extend
loans for the development of the above facilities.

3. Provide technical and managerial guidance for the development and operation of industries relevant to its purposes and to
secure foreign technological assistance when necessary.

4. Dispose of agricultural and fisheries products in both
domestic and foreign markets and to supply both domestically produced and imported materials necessary to the storage and processing
of these products.

5. Assist in enforcement of quality control.

6. Engage in any other activities appropriate to the growth of industries for storing, preserving, and processing agricultural and fishery products.

As of June 30, 1969, this Corporation had no less than twenty-two subsidiary and affiliated companies engaged in the production, processing, and marketing of crops and fish. It had advanced $3.7 million to these affiliates and had helped to secure for them external loans to the amount of $18.9 million and external capital investment in equity to the amount of $1.2 million. In the first six months of 1969 exports generated by the Corporation and its affiliates were valued at over $4 million.

The essential formalities and records of South Korean external trade are within the province of the export and import sections of the Ministry of Commerce and Industry. In general, these administrative agencies play only a minor role in the making of policy, which is normally the function of either the Economic Planning Board or that of interministerial committees, or both. But the Ministry has made genuine efforts to reduce formalities and red tape involved in the conduct of foreign trade. This was certainly necessary. An inquiry in 1964 revealed that, on a single shipment of cotton textiles, the South Korean exporter was required to take 37 separate procedures, involving the presentation of 94 different forms, to a total of 148 copies. From 84 to 121 man/days of work were necessary for this process. As another example, a South Korean businessman wishing to travel overseas had to complete 32 different forms in a total of 46 copies, estimated to take him or his staff 46 to 67 days of work. Though there has been some simplification of these procedures, the process is still very imperfect and will probably remain so until drastic action is taken to override the natural reluctance of governmental agencies to admit that its procedures are unnecessary. At least, it can be said that South Korea is aware of the problem.

South Korea has developed an elaborate system of export quotas or goals that extend down to individual producers. From time to time, the goals are revised and updated; this is done by joint deliberation and effort of the public and private sectors.

Quality control on export commodities is still fragmented in South Korea, in spite of intermittent efforts to centralize this activity. Some of the larger firms and trade groups have proposed that they be made responsible for quality and inspection; other have suggested that this function be turned over to the South Korean Standards Association or to the South Korean Industrial Development Research Institute,

both semipublic bodies; there is some solid support for the creation
of a government inspection service. Standards have not yet been
prescribed for all commodities, nor are standards always enforced
where they have been established. Governmental responsibility for
quality control is largely divided between the ministries of Commerce
and Agriculture, the Office of Monopoly, and other agencies. However,
some commodities, raw silk for example, are controlled adequately
by the industry itself.

In summary, all South Korean government agencies even remotely
connected with the conduct of foreign trade are given an active role in
the export promotion program. This is a logical consequence of
designating export expansion as the first priority of the government.
Some problems remain, but, for the most part, the governmental
agencies have worked together admirably in the implementation of
this program.

Quasipublic Organizations

Although these are essentially private in composition and control,
there are several so broad in their coverage of the business community
that they have acquired something of a public character. Prominent
among these are the South Korean Chamber of Commerce and Industry,
the Federation of Korean Industries, and the South Korean Traders
Association. The first is a nationwide body, with a membership of
over 350,000 businessmen, and it has thirty-five local affiliates.
Its principal activities include the promotion of international trade,
modernization of industries, stimulation of regional trade, the conduct
of surveys and research, advice on government economic policies,
and the arbitration of trade disputes. The Chamber publishes price
reports, news bulletins, and a business directory.

The Federation of Korean Industries is also national in scope
and has a membership of 130 individual companies and 17 business
associations. Its basic objectives are to promote and strengthen
the role of the private sector in the development of the nation's
economy and to further and diversify international economic cooperation. It also provides counsel on domestic and international economic
policies from the standpoint of South Korea's interests.

The Traders Association is financed entirely from private
sources, but in a sense is more public in character than either of
these other organizations. Government regulations require that every
exporter must belong to the Traders Association and must have a
trading license. Over 700 companies are involved in the export trade,
but less than half this number qualify for the trader's license, the
others selling their goods through a licensed firm. The Association

maintains offices in Tokyo and New York, but most of its activities are centred in South Korea, where it engages in lobbying, assisting potential buyers, and providing information to its members.

Organizations of this type serve a useful and necessary purpose, providing a channel through which the business community can be addressed and by which it can air its views on matters affecting not only business but, also, the community at large.

Private Trade Associations

There are a considerable number of trade associations organized on commodity or interest lines; in fact, there is an organization representing almost every major product that enters the export trade, concerning itself with most of the aspects of producing and marketing the commodity concerned. These associations serve as a forum in which views may be exchanged and agreement reached on the problems of particular industries. Although a trade association has no real power to enforce the will of its members, it can and does exert pressure to accomplish this purpose. Trade associations are active in seeking governmental action considered necessary to their interests. They have also been active in the export promotion program, participating in the establishment of export targets and assisting generally in the achievement of them.

Much of the success of the program to expand South Korea's exports is due to the strong support given to it by all levels of the government. South Korean experience demonstrates that, if sufficient pressure is exerted to achieve a goal, the tendency of government agencies and of the private sector to resist coordination and act independently can be overcome. In South Korea, the President has taken personal responsibility for the smooth operation of the export program, and his requirement of a monthly progress report from his ministers has been instrumental in keeping the program moving.

Another very important factor in South Korea's success in promoting exports has been the adoption and maintenance by it of a realistic rate of exchange. In 1964, the won was devalued from 130 to 255 per dollar, and, since 1965, the exchange rate has been allowed to float. This has been of great benefit to the export trade. Besides adherence to a realistic monetary policy, South Korea has had political stability, which also contributes greatly to the expansion of external trade. In a brief period of ten years, South Korea has emerged as a manufacturing nation, a phenomenon closely related to the rapid growth of exports and to the liberal attitude of the government in making inputs available to South Korean industries.

The government of South Korea is receptive to the principle of special trading arrangements with selected countries. It has such an agreement with Taiwan, under which South Korea buys bananas and sells apples, and a somewhat similar agreement, involving other products, has been made with Indonesia. Through Vietnam's Foreign Trade Directorate, an announcement has recently been made that South Korea is interested in buying chili peppers. Vietnam might find it advantageous to explore further this approach to bilateral trade with South Korea.

In South Korea, there has been a tendency to link imports and exports. It is said to be much easier to obtain permission to import if it can be shown that the company concerned will offset the cost of goods purchased by selling other goods for export. This is not, of course, an unusual policy, and other countries also have employed it in their efforts to balance payments. In general, the regulations and restrictions on imports entering South Korea are rather rigid, as might be expected where there is a large negative balance of trade and a desire to be self-sufficient in consumer goods. Capital goods, raw materials, and essential commodities are admitted freely, however, and once a commodity is placed on the approved list, procedural formalities are reduced to a minimum.

Japan

No Asian country has developed a more extensive and effective program for export promotion than Japan. At all times, there has been a close working relationship between the public and private sectors, reflected not only in the institutional structure underlying export promotion activities but, also, in the manner in which the program is implemented. It might, nevertheless, be a mistake to draw too heavily on Japanese experience in structuring an export program for Vietnam. Japan is, of course, one of the world's most advanced and industrialized countries, and its exports are mostly manufactured goods, many of them highly sophisticated products. In addition, the business community is dominated by a number of giant combines or conglomerates, which exercise great influence in matters of policy. These large companies are generally well able to conduct their own promotional programs.

For the purposes of this study, it may be appropriate to place more emphasis on the manner in which smaller less-developed countries, such as South Korea, Taiwan, and Thailand, have approached export promotion. The account of Japanese institutions concerned with export promotion that follows is, therefore, restricted, both as regards the organizations covered and the extent of coverage.

The Japanese External Trade Organization

This was established in 1951 as a quasipublic, nonprofit agency, and it has become a very large and far-flung organization, whose main purpose is the promotion of trade and understanding between Japan and other nations. It is sponsored jointly by the central and provincial governments and by various business interests. It has its headquarters in Tokyo, and there are twenty-three branch offices in other Japanese cities. It maintains in foreign countries sixteen trade centers, two machinery centers, and forty-eight other offices.

The management of JETRO is vested in a president, a vice-president, six directors, and two auditors. In its head office, there are thirteen divisions set up on functional lines. The services that JETRO provides include the following: (a) the dissemination of information on Japanese products and where to obtain them, (b) assistance in establishing contacts with Japanese manufacturers, (c) displays of the latest Japanese products, (d) market research to help businessmen meet the needs of overseas markets and to assure orderly distribution, (e) the use of literature, films, and other media, to provide information on Japanese trade and industry, and (f) the provision of special services for business visitors from foreign countries.

The organization does not engage in buying and selling but merely facilitates the trade process. Its primary emphasis is on helping medium and small companies, for the larger Japanese concerns are generally well able to take care of themselves. Some of the services it provides are rather unusual: it encourages good design, for example, making awards for this and arranging displays; it discharges the formalities and arranges meetings for visiting businessmen; and it organizes tours of industrial plants. It maintains a very extensive reference library and publishes numerous periodicals and reports. JETRO has been taken as a model by several other countries in setting up export promotion agencies, KOTRA in South Korea being a good example.

Keidanren, the Federation of Economic Organizations

Keidanren is a nationwide organization that represents Japanese business interests. Its membership includes about 100 trade organizations and associations of companies, covering practically all the sectors of economic activity, including 729 leading enterprises in manufacturing (the largest sector represented), mining, commerce, transportation, banking, construction, and insurance. It is a private nonprofit organization, financed entirely by its members' dues.

Keidanren's purposes are to study economic problems, domestic and international, from the viewpoint of Japan; to ascertain the opinions of business circles and convey them to the Diet, the government, and to other interested parties; and to investigate industrial and commercial problems, so as to reach practical solutions and, thereby, contribute to the sound development of the Japanese economy.

In order to achieve these purposes, Keidanren has twenty-nine standing committees, which concern themselves, among other matters, with fiscal and financial policies, taxation, industrial policies, industrial technology, trade and commerce, and economic cooperation. They meet frequently and, when appropriate, submit proposals and recommendations to the authorities concerned. Keidanren's opinions and recommendations are given considerable weight in the formulation of the government's economic policies.

This organization was first established in August, 1946, and it was completely reorganized in September, 1951. In its early days, it concentrated its efforts on the rehabilitation of the Japanese economy, promoting economic development with a view to helping Japan rejoin the international economic community. Later, it turned its attention more toward participation in international development, with emphasis on such programs as those of the International Monetary Fund and the Organization for Economic Cooperation and Development. It is the firm and sincere belief of Keidanren that better economic interchange among the industrial countries and the more rapid economic development of the less-advanced countries will contribute to world prosperity and peace and also to the well-being of Japan. The organization subscribes to the doctrine of freedom of trade and advocates the reduction (within reason) of restrictions on exchange of capital, in the belief that such policies are necessary to Japan's continued economic progress.

Keidanren takes an active interest in providing technical assistance to less-developed areas and in the investment of Japanese capital overseas. It has sent economic missions to several countries, including Vietnam.

Other Organizations and Agencies

There are many other bodies, both private and public, which are actively involved in trade development, including the Japanese Chamber of Commerce and Industry and the Japanese Foreign Trade Council Incorporated. As in many other countries, special interest groups in Japan have their own trade associations, and there are numerous local chambers of commerce as well. The functions of such associations in export promotion is similar to that of their counterparts in Korea and Thailand, and a description of them is unnecessary at this point.

In the government, besides JETRO, the principal agencies involved in external trade matters are the Ministry of International Trade and Industry and the Ministry of Agriculture and Forestry. Both are involved in the establishment of policies, as well as in the procedural formalities concerning exports and imports. The ministries of Finance and Foreign Affairs are also concerned, the former by its control over foreign exchange and the latter by the influence it exerts on trade arrangements overseas. In this context, it may be noted that the yen has been a very stable currency, while Japanese commercial attachés are recognized everywhere as lively and active.

Japan has found it both necessary and desirable to exercise close control over the quality of its export commodities. It does so by means of an export and import trading law, which gives the government wide powers to enforce standards, even to the point of revoking the licenses of offenders and prosecuting them for violations. Other countries, including Thailand, have taken the Japanese approach to quality control as a model. It is strict, but it is effective.

Taiwan

It is sometimes said that Taiwan's export trade has been expedited rather than promoted. As stated earlier, the original purpose of the expansion of manufacturing was to produce goods for domestic consumption. As industrial capacity increased, goods became available for export and, at that point, enterprises were established that produced primarily for export. Traditionally, Taiwan was an exporter of foodstuffs and certain raw materials, but now there is a distinct trend toward the production and export of processed and manufactured goods. In the development of the export trade from $120 million in 1952 to $842 million in 1968, the government has played an active and important role, even to the extent of participating in the establishment and operation of business ventures, but unlike the governments of Japan and South Korea, it has not yet set up a single centralized agency for purposes of export promotion. It is, however, presently considering whether it should do this.

Other than briefly stating the identity and functions of the agencies that regulate the export of goods from Taiwan, this section is concerned with identifying and describing certain associations and organizations that have special roles in developing the export trade. The principal governmental agency concerned with the regulation of external trade is the Foreign Exchange and Trade Commission, which is attached to the Executive Yuan. The functions of the Commission include formulating and implementing foreign exchange and trade policies, examining and promulgating export and import commodity classifications, assisting in the export of products, examining and approving import applications, approving applications for invisible trade, issuing export and import licenses, and studying international markets for export and import commodities. The Commission publishes an annual foreign exchange and trade handbook (in English and Chinese), in which the procedures and regulations involved in imports and exports are listed for easy reference.

Another agency that has both policy-making responsibilities as well as regulatory and record-keeping functions is the Board of Foreign Trade in the Ministry of Economic Affairs, which maintains close liaison with the business community, in general, and with traders and industrial producers, in particular. The Ministry administers inspection and quality control programs, issues certificates of origin, and, also, has some surveillance over the pricing of exports.

Forward planning for economic development, including projections of external trade, is the responsibility of the Council for International Economic Cooperation and Development. This is also attached to the Executive Yuan. The Council's principal function is to prepare and supervise Taiwan's four-year development plans, the fifth of which, for the period 1969-72, is in progress. Agricultural development, however, is planned by the Joint Commission for Rural Reconstruction, whose activities have contributed importantly to increased exports of agricultural products; while the implementation of agricultural production programs is discharged by the Provincial Board of Agriculture and Forestry and the Provincial Food Bureau. They, too, have given important support to the export program by their effective efforts to increase the output of both traditional and newly introduced crops.

The remarkable growth of Taiwan's exports, particularly of industrial goods, is due, in no small part, to the government's encouragement of investment by foreigners and overseas Chinese. Between 1952 and 1968, almost 1,000 applications for investment from abroad were approved, with a total capital involvement of over $300 million. Overseas Chinese, Japanese, and Americans were responsible for 95 percent of these proposals, and most of the enterprises established by them are producing goods for export. There are liberal incentives for investment, including a five-year income tax holiday, reduced rates of income tax after the initial five years, unlimited remittance of earnings, payment of customs duties by installment, help in acquiring plant sites, the acceptance of full foreign ownership, the repatriation of capital, and partial exemption from customs duty for machinery and equipment.

Within the Council for International Economic Cooperation and Development, there is an Industrial Development and Investment Center, which is responsible for the program for attracting foreign capital investment. This is an aggressive organization, with a staff of some forty people. In general, the Center is an expediting agency, seeking to improve the investment climate in Taiwan, to encourage the inflow of overseas capital, to assist the development of the nation's industry, and to provide consultation, communications, advisory assistance, and technical guidance to investors. The Center is located in the same building as (and works in close cooperation with) the Overseas Chinese and Foreign Investment Commission, the governmental agency responsible for administering the laws and regulations concerning investments.

One major factor in the rapid growth of Taiwan's exports has been the program for developing industrial zones. About sixty areas have already been reserved for this purpose. One particular case will illustrate the significance of the effects of this program on the growth of the export trade. This is the Kaohsiung Export Processing Zone, located in Southern Taiwan. The original unit was opened in 1966 on about 70 hectares of reclaimed land in Kaohsiung Harbor, and it has been so successful in attracting factories (there were 95 in operation by May, 1969) that it has become necessary to develop a second unit of 115 hectares, which will accommodate another 200 plants; while a third zone of 230 hectares is planned for development in the early future. The zone has some powerful attractions for investors and factory operators: there is a centralized administration for handling applications and registrations; no import duties are paid on machinery and equipment brought into it; and there are no restrictions or duties on raw materials and semifinished products brought into it for processing. The management provides prompt handling of foreign exchange applications, customs clearance within twenty-four hours for imports and exports, free transportation of goods to and from ships, and loans at low rates of interest for plant construction. There is no obligation to purchase plant sites; there are plentiful supplies of power and water; and there is abundant manpower in the neighborhood.

For administrative purposes, the Kaohsiung zone comes under the Ministry of Economic Affairs, but, in its operations, it enjoys a considerable degree of autonomy.

As industrialization progressed in Taiwan, a need was seen for an organization to advise and assist companies in improving the efficiency of their production. A forerunner of what is now the China Productivity and Trade Center was set up in 1955 for this reason. The Center is a nonprofit semipublic agency, supported by both the private sector and by the government. Since 1959, it has been concerned with the development of domestic and overseas outlets for goods

produced in Taiwan. It continues to provide industry with services in
the areas of producitvity, industrial design, marketing, manpower
training, and collateral appraisal in connection with loan applications,
training being its most important activity at the present time. The
Center publishes an annual "Taiwan Buyers Guide," a very comprehensive business directory, and, also, publishes a weekly trade bulletin
and a monthly productivity and trade magazine. A large reference
library is maintained.

In the same building as the Productivity and Trade Center in
Taipei is the China Display Center, another semi-public organization,
supported by the private sector. Here are assembled displays of most
of Taiwan's manufactured goods. The firms displaying their goods
pay fees to do so, and these charges provide the bulk of the income
required to maintain the facility.

Although the government of Taiwan has not yet set up a specific
export promotion agency, it is presently considering a proposal under
which all government-sponsored trade promotion activities, including
the functions of the Productivity Center, and, perhaps, those of the
Display Center also, would be combined in a new China trade development association. This central trade promotion organization is intended to do for Taiwan what JETRO does for Japan and what KOTRA
does for South Korea. It is recognized that the competition is becoming serious for markets in certain commodities, particularly textiles,
electronics, and light machinery, in which a number of the newer
industrial countries have concentrated their capacity for production
for export. Greater efforts are thought to be necessary to promote
exports and to maintain present growth rates in this sector of the
Taiwanese economy.

Taiwan also has several chambers of commerce and industry
associations, which have taken an active interest in the export trade.
They operate in much the same manner as those in South Korea,
Thailand, and other countries.

Thailand

Generally speaking, the development of Thailand's export trade
has been by private initiative, with little direct intervention or stimulation by the government. However, in recent years, the growing gap
in the balance of trade and some serious industrial problems have
begun to lead to more involvement of governmental agencies in this
important sector of the Thai economy. Imports have been increasing
faster than exports, and there is more and more demand for an
organized approach to market development, which will hopefully result
in increased sales overseas. The pricing problems of corn and

complaints from buyers of poor quality of kenaf are additional reasons for the government to modify its traditional attitude of nonintervention in trade. But in spite of this, official policy is still that there should be the minimum of interference by public agencies in the export trade.

More than 200 individual private shippers are directly involved in Thailand's export trade, and, in addition, there are three kinds of organizations that are associated closely with it.

Private Trade Associations

Authorized under a law of 1966, most of these associations are organized on commodity or special interest lines. There is an association for each of the major export products, the membership being composed of individuals and firms interested in promoting the particular commodity with which the association is concerned. In a sense, these associations act as specialized "chambers of commerce" for the export commodities, serving as forums for discussion of matters related to the purchase, sale, and handling of the particular commodities in question. These trade associations do not themselves engage in business, and they possess no real authority over the actions of their members, but they are useful as a means of gathering, exchanging, and disseminating information.

Quasipublic Organizations

The chambers of commerce and the Board of Trade of Thailand are included in this category. All have been established under the Chamber of Commerce Act of 1966. Eight chambers of commerce are presently functioning, each with a membership based on nationality, Thai, American, or British, for example. The chambers of commerce have only an indirect interest in the export trade; they are probably more heavily concerned with imports and investments in-country.

In the case of the Board of Trade, the concern with exports is direct and substantial. Membership of the Board consists of ordinary members and associate members, but only the ordinary members vote and, in principle, therefore, they control the organization. The ordinary members are the eight chambers of commerce mentioned above, twelve trade associations, six state enterprises, and a cooperative society. There are over 200 associate members, individuals, or organizations engaged in commerce, financing, services, or other forms of business activity.

The predecessor to the Board of Trade was originally set up by the government of Thailand, about fourteen years ago, to represent the business community in discussion with the government of matters of common interest, especially government actions that might affect the business and trade. It is, today, a substantial organization, with a sizable paid staff, financed through the collection of dues and fees. It has important functions in relation to the export trade, and these include the following:

1. Certification of quality for the commodities for which export standards have been established by the government

2. Assistance in negotiating trade agreements (the most recent case being the Thai-Japanese Maize (Corn) Trade Agreement for 1968-69)

3. Arbitration of disputes between buyers and sellers

4. Issue of a weekly commodity price report and periodic reports on exports and imports

5. Publication of special market situation reports and of the "Board of Trade Directory," a general review of the trade situation in Thailand

6. Participation in market promotion, including trade missions and trade fairs.

The Board of Trade of Thailand performs undeniably useful services in export promotion and appears to have achieved some balance in representing not merely its membership but, also, the public interest. It has performed well in the field of quality control, where it has a clear legal base for its activities, but has also been effective in exerting influence on shippers and others to improve the general conduct of foreign trade, a matter in which no real authority has been delegated to it. This semipublic, semiprivate approach to both regulation and development of the export trade deserves serious consideration by other countries, including Vietnam.

Government Agencies

Within the government of Thailand, there are several agencies that directly or indirectly take some part in the regulation or encouragement of exports. As stated previously, the official attitude of the government is to interfere as little as possible in the conduct of this business, but, in spite of this desire to leave trade alone, there is no doubt that, in practice, the public authorities are becoming more and more involved in both regulatory and promotional activities. Briefly, the functions of the various agencies may be outlined as follows:

The Ministry of Economic Affairs bears the principal responsibility for government activities in trade. Its Department of Foreign Trade develops policy on the direction and flow of exports and makes decisions on the extent to which the government should intervene in particular instances. In 1966, for example, the department itself negotiated an agreement with Ceylon for rice purchases by that country, but, in 1968, it assigned responsibility for the negotiation with Japanese corn importers to the Board of Trade. In general, the Ministry's attitude appears to be that government-to-government agreements should be treated only as a last resort. The Department of Commercial Intelligence, another agency of the Ministry, investigates and provides reports on prospective markets for Thai products. It also prepares displays of local products, both in Bangkok and abroad, distributes brochures advertising export items, and assists in the management of trade missions. Also within the Ministry of Economic Affairs is an Office of Commodity Standards, responsible for issuing and enforcing standards on export commodities in accordance with the Export Standards Act of 1960. There are now eleven commodities for which standards have been prescribed by the Ministry: corn, kenaf, and jute, castor seed, salt, tapioca meal and chip, teak conversions, sorghum, silverware, and Thai silk, while rice is treated separately under the commodity standardization program. With a few exceptions, however, the inspection and certification of these commodities has been delegated to the Board of Trade.

The Board of Export Promotion is independent of the Ministry of Economic Affairs, although its functions appear to overlap the Ministry's. The purpose of the agency, as its name implies, is to develop Thailand's export trade, and it is located, curiously, just across the street from the Department of Commercial Intelligence, which engages in similar activities. The Board has only a small staff and a limited budget. It is clear that it finds it difficult to get the support needed to undertake an effective promotional effort. In part, at least, this must be due to interagency competition, for the Ministry of Economic Affairs is generally more influential, and there are suggestions in Thai government circles that the Board should now be brought within the Ministry.

From time to time, the Board prepares brochures and statistics on major export products and issues them in a series entitled "Thai Export Bulletins." The quality of these publications is very good. It also prepares and distributes color posters advertising Thai products. In addition, the Board compiles a "Buyer's Guide," in which export regulations are described and the names of exporters are listed. (The Board of Trade Directory provides similar information.) Recently, the Board of Export Promotion has been participating actively in the arbitration of trade disputes and the adjustment of transportation rates and services. The staff of this Board works closely with the Board of Trade, as well as with the Ministry of Economic Affairs, in attempting to solve trade problems and in organizing trade missions.

Thailand has had great success in attracting outside capital, and much of this is attributable to the favorable climate for investment, largely created by the program of incentives managed by the Thai Board of Investment, by which special concessions are given to certain new business ventures. It is not appropriate to this study to elaborate on the investment program in Thailand, but it is worth indicating that the program has encouraged the establishment of several enterprises that engage in or contribute to the export trade. Export-oriented manufactures are given particularly favorable treatment, and there has been substantial investment, as a result, in increasing production capacity of such commodities as tin, corn, cement, fertilizer, and gunny bags, all of which enter into Thailand's export trade. Incentives are provided as well for activities such as the improvement of rice and rubber processing, which also reflect favorably on the export trade.

The participation of the ministries of Agriculture, Industry, and National Development in promotion of exports is indirect but important. In all three ministries, there are agencies active in programs aimed at increasing production and improving production efficiency. It is by the work of these ministries that the commodities which are potential earners of foreign exchange are produced in the volumes and to the quality standards that allow them to enter into the export trade. There is generally close consultation between these three ministries, concerned primarily with production, and those agencies of the Ministry of Economic Affairs that are concerned primarily with the promotion of sales of Thai products in overseas markets.

Finally, there is a National Economic Development Board; the agency of the Thai government responsible for general economic planning. It is mentioned in this discussion for the sole reason that income derived from exports obviously has a strong bearing on projections of national income and plans for economic development. So far, the National Economic Development Board has done little itself to develop or suggest programs for export promotion, but it has given considerable weight to the estimates prepared by the Ministry of Economic Affairs and the Board of Trade in its preparation of Thailand's five-year development plans. There are indications that the Board will be giving more attention in the future to export potentials.

General Observations

There is obvious similarity in the export situations of Vietnam and Thailand; both are offering for sale the same primary commodities, mostly foods, feeds, and raw materials, and neither, as yet, has a highly organized program for export promotion. Although Thailand's exports far exceed those of Vietnam and some of the Thai institutions concerned with external trade are reasonably advanced, there is still sufficient common ground for Vietnam to benefit from Thailand's experience and vice-versa. The following observations, based upon opinions heard in the course of the present survey, seem to have some clear implications for Vietnam.

Concern over Adverse Balance of Trade. Thailand is deeply concerned over its increasingly adverse balance of trade, which was about $500 million in 1968. There is a fear that, in the short run, certain major exports, including rice and kenaf, for example, may stagnate. There are, therefore, definite moves toward a drive to increase and diversify exports, and the Minister of Economic Affairs is providing vigorous leadership for this effort.

Foreign Ownership. In some fields of business, foreigners have moved in and now participate importantly in the exporting of Thai commodities. A considerable controversy is centered upon those Japanese-owned firms, based in Thailand, which ship Thai products to Japan. This sort of situation can create difficult problems for all the parties concerned.

Regulation of Export Trade. Even when commodities are subject to standard control, some deelers manage to engage in deceptive practices. This is likely to result in more stringent legislation (which will probably be based on Japan's export and import trading law), under which the authorities will be able to prosecute offenders. There have been several flagrant cases of deception recently, involving kenaf shipments, and these have precipitated a demand for stronger regulations.

Market Exploration, Development, and Research. Market exploration and development is receiving considerable attention, and trade missions, brochures, and exhibits are all being used freely to stimulate sales in overseas markets. On the other hand, there is little in the way of research aimed at greater efficiency in marketing or at exploring new market outlets, but there is a growing awareness in some sectors of the export trade of the need for this sort of work.

Policy of Nonintervention. Thailand subscribes to a maximum of freedom in the conduct of its foreign trade, an attitude that is voiced frequently and consistently. The following extract from an article on the trade situation by a prominent Thai official is typical and is worth quoting in this context:

> The export of duck eggs and chicken eggs should serve as
> an object lesson of all the mistakes committed under the
> system called federation of cooperatives, consisting of
> export control and rules and regulations . . . which re-
> sulted in great inconvenience, and high costs of exports,
> and eventual flight of regular overseas buyers of Thai eggs
> to other sources of supply.

However, this policy of nonintervention is currently being modified
where regulation is found to be the only way of controlling those who
would otherwise abuse this freedom and might, in doing so, undermine
the entire trade structure.

Strength of Currency. The strength of Thailand's currency during recent years has contributed importantly to the development of foreign
trade. Prices have been remarkably stable, with the wholesale price
index increasing by only 18 to 20 percent since 1958. Thailand's
political stability has also served to facilitate trade.

Special Credit and Export Insurance Programs. Thailand has no special credit or export insurance programs to encourage exports. Some
thought is now being given to a guaranty plan, somewhat similar to
that used in Hong Kong and elsewhere, under which exporters will be
assured of payment for their shipments.

Export Taxes. The export taxes on rice and rubber and the royalties
on tin are being increasingly criticized as impediments to further
development of Thailand's export trade. The rice premium, because
of its regressive effect and its tendency to discourage the use of improved practices by rice farmers, is a subject of particular controversy. It is held that, as competition becomes more severe among
the exporting countries, it is necessary to minimize or eliminate those
levies that tend to interfere with production or keep prices artificially high.

Singapore

Export Promotion

The problems Singapore faces in the promotion and expansion
of exports are similar in many ways to those that confront Hong Kong,
but Singapore is following quite a different path in pursuit of the same
ends. Its attention has been devoted primarily to industrial promotion by means of the attraction of foreign capital through favorable
investment practices, tax concessions, the provision of industrial
estates, and similar devices. The agency responsible for

administering these policies is the Economic Development Board, which was established by law in 1961.

It was not until 1966 that an Export Promotion Center was established, principally as a means of coordinating, within the administrative framework of the Economic Development Board, the efforts of a diversity of interests in the expansion of exports. The Center was intended to assist local industries in their export drives; to provide information on tariffs, quotas, certificates of origin, and other administrative formalities; and to assist in the organization of Singapore's participation in trade fairs and exhibitions abroad. So far, in its short existence, the Center has, in practice, operated principally as a clearing house for information for export-oriented industries. The need for more active involvement has been recognized, and new policies have been proposed under which the Center would have provided sales teams to organize distribution of Singapore's products in external markets and make direct sales on behalf of its domestic industries. These developments, however, have been superseded to some extent by the creation of a state trading corporation, Intraco, which will be described later.

Singapore's Export Promotion Center in its present form has, therefore, little of the active involvement in, and direction of, export expansion possessed by the Trade Development Center of Hong Kong, nor is it a body integrated into commercial interests and with some degree of financial autonomy. It is financed by a state grant and controlled by the employees of the Economic Development Board, who are quasicivil servants. There is probably not much Vietnam can learn from this particular institution in its present stage of development.

Intraco is an interesting development. It was incorporated in November, 1968, under the Companies Act, as a public limited liability company, 30 percent of the equity being held by government and the rest by banks and commercial interests. The Company has two main purposes: first, to develop export markets for domestic manufactures and products throughout the world and in as many countries as possible; and second, to strengthen the bargaining position of Singapore's merchants in their dealings with socialist countries, where foreign trade is a state monopoly. The Company is intended to operate like a private business, and the active participation of private enterprise is being sought. At the present time, however, its principal officers are all civil servants.

It is hoped that, in due course, the Company will be able to assist manufacturers in the importation of both raw materials and manufactured goods by negotiated bulk purchases. It intends, also, to establish overseas offices in the main commercial centers of North America, Western Europe, Eastern Europe, the Middle East, the Far East and Southeast Asia. So far, Intraco has concentrated its attention upon negotiation of long-term bilateral agreements, in a counter-import program, whereby a proportion of the earnings that other countries get from selling to Singapore is used by them to purchase manufactured goods from Singapore.

It is too early to assess the impact Intraco may have on Singapore's trade. It is undoubtedly going to be useful in obtaining entry to new markets in countries where trade is a State monopoly, but it is essentially a device appropriate to a highly industrialized community, eager to exchange its processed manufactures for raw materials. It seems improbable that Vietnam will find such an institution relevant to the stage of development it will be in in the decade after the war.

Export Credit

In the eyes of its traders, a prime requirement for the expansion of Singapore's exports is the early establishment of a system of export credit guarantees. No such system now exists, but it is said that the Singapore Government has under study a report by a working committee set up to prepare proposals for an institution of this kind. It is believed that the recommendations are for a form of export credit guarantees that closely follow the Hong Kong model and that this is likely to be accepted.

Malaysia

Malaysia is only just beginning to consider a central export promotion organization, and it is also beginning to examine alternative schemes for a system of export credit guarantees. Up to the present, both the government and private enterprise have concentrated their attention in regulating the quality of rubber and timber exports. These highly specialized schemes for Malaysia's major export commodities were outside the scope of this study but would repay examination in detail, particularly those relating to rubber. The Standard Malaysian Rubber Scheme, introduced in 1965, represents a revolutionary departure from the conventional methods of marketing natural rubber according to grades based on technical specifications.

India

In the fifteen-year period since 1955/56, India's exports have increased about 50 percent--from $1,250 million to $1,800 million.

There was modest but consistent growth in the export trade until the end of 1964/65, but then there were two years in which exports actually declined: 1966/67 and 1967/68 were years of depression, the result, principally, of severe drought. In 1968/69, the export trade began to grow again, but at rather a slow rate.

So far, India has not developed or undertaken any special or deliberate program to promote exports. In its national planning, of course, the need to develop the export trade is fully recognized, but recognition has still to be translated into effective action. Today, there is increasing concern in Indian government circles over the country's unfavorable trade balance, and there are those who advocate the establishment of an Indian version of JETRO in Japan or of KOTRA in South Korea. This should not be taken as implying any lack of agencies, organizations, programs, and regulatory measures that, in one way or another, concern exports; on the contrary, India has very many such, but close coordination of effort, strong direction, and adequate financing have not yet been attained, nor has export promotion yet been made a major and overriding objective of government policy. In India's domestic circumstances, this is, perhaps, not to be expected.

Within the government of India, but including representation of private commerce and industry, there is an Advisory Council on Trade and, also, a smaller body, the Board of Trade, which meet periodically to consider trade controls, commodity export problems, commercial services and assistance for export marketing, and the organization and expansion of the export sector generally. The administration of regulations affecting exports and imports is vested in the Ministry of Foreign Trade and Supply, and this agency has also some responsibilities for the development of commercial policy and for the establishment and administration of international trade agreements. It operates a service division, charged with such activities as quality control, transport, publicity, exhibitions, and market surveys. Several state governments in India have appointed liaison officers for the promotion of trade in goods produced in these states.

Outside the government, there are about a score of export promotion councils, which concern themselves with specific commodities. These bodies are made up mostly of growers, producers, and exporters, and their purpose is to provide a channel by which the views of the trade may be conveyed to the government and matters of mutual concern and interest may be discussed with it. From time to time, the councils carry out studies of foreign markets, organize trade delegations, participate in exhibits, disseminate information, assist in quality control, and participate in export promotion schemes. There is, also, a Federation of Indian Export Organizations, performing somewhat the same functions as the export promotion councils, but covering the

entire field of Indian exports, including such matters as the dissemination of commercial intelligence and the provision of facilities for
settling trade disputes.

Commodity boards have been established to assist in the development of certain commodities (tea, coffee, corn, silk, handicrafts, and
handloom products), and these also participate in the efforts to increase
exports. Similarly, the Textile Commissioner, Jute Commissioner,
Indian Jute Mills Association, Indian Sugar Mills Association, Steel
Exporters' Association, and the Cardamom Board are all concerned
in varying degree with promoting exports of the particular commodities they represent; while Indian industry has also given birth to a
number of development councils for purposes similar to those of the
commodity boards.

A government-sponsored but autonomous organization, the
Indian Institute of Foreign Trade, has been established to further
overseas trade by providing training courses, conducting marketing
studies, and investigating trade problems. This organization has
sponsored a series of market surveys covering most of the countries
with which India has traded in the past or hopes to trade in the future;
it investigates such topics as transportation, credit, regional trade,
and the management of export houses; and it issues reports on the
export potentials of many Indian commodities. The USAID has contributed substantially, both in funds and technical assistance to the
Institute's activities, and still maintains an Export Promotion Division
in its Mission to India.

There is a weekly "Indian Trade Journal," as well as an " Exporter's Directory," both published by the Department of Commercial
Intelligence and Statistics. The Journal provides current information
on markets and prices, inquiries from prospective buyers abroad, reports from commercial representatives overseas, and the tenders of
foreign buyers. The Directory is a listing of persons and firms dealing in export commodities. The Department compiles and publishes
detailed statistics on India's exports and imports.

Possibly more significant than any of these is the direct participation of the government of India in the export trade by the corporations
it has established and controls. The largest of these is the State Trading Corporation, which already has thirteen offices outside India and
intends to create another twelve. In addition, there is a Handicrafts
and Handlooms Exports Corporation, an Indian Motion Pictures
Export Corporation, a Minerals and Metals Trading Corporation, and
a Metal Scrap Trade Corporation. These are expected to assist the
private sector, and, in particular, the smaller industries, in developing the export trade, but the main effort is directed to the trading

operations of the corporations themselves. The volume of exports handled directly by these government enterprises is only 5 percent of all exports, but, in some commodities, the proportion is much greater, and the influence exerted is very strong. Some observers believe that India will engage more and more extensively in official trading, and the state trading corporations, already important elements in the country's export trade, will in the future become even more so.

A considerable number of government services and other types of assistance are available to Indian exporters, and the more significant of them are listed below:

1. Fifty-nine priority industries, many of them producing for export, are given preferential treatment in the issue of import licenses. Registered exporters generally have no difficulty in obtaining licenses to import component materials or parts of the products to be exported.

2. Special allocations of raw materials, including iron and steel, are made to manufacturers producing goods for export.

3. Cash assistance by way of export subsidies is provided for selected export products, such as engineering goods, chemicals, and allied products, plastic manufactures, sports goods, prime iron and steel, iron and steel scrap, and processed foods.

4. Customs duties are refunded on products exported, including waiver or rebate of excise taxes and refund of import duties paid on raw materials and components of the exported product.

5. Freight rate concessions are given on certain export commodities moved by rail, and such goods are given priority in transport facilities within India.

6. Through the Export Credit and Guarantee Corporation, exporters can insure against both commercial and political risks capable of affecting payment for goods shipped. Special terms apply where shipments are made to new market areas. Coverage is normally limited to 85 percent of the political risks and 80 percent of the commercial risks. The Corporation also offers a program through which it shares risks with banks lending to exporters, guaranteeing their loans up to a limit of 66.33 percent of the total involved. Premiums for the corporation's policies are not exorbitant in cost and provide excellent support in obtaining loans from commercial banks.

7. Under a Bill Market Scheme, administered by the Reserve Bank of India, exporters can obtain special financing from both the

Reserve Bank and private banks on the basis of export bills. Credit
of this type is even more readily available where shipments are covered
by the Export Credit and Guarantee Corporation insurance policies.
The interest rate is especially low, 4.5 percent, for engineering and
machine products, and normal bank rates apply for other items. Loan
maturity under this particular credit program is normally six months;
for longer terms, the Industrial Development Bank will provide export
credit on specified capital or engineering goods for terms of from six
months to five years at 6 percent interest. In exceptional cases, these
loans may run as long as ten years.

8. Commercial representatives located at Indian embassies
throughout the world relay information on possible trade opportunities
and, to a limited extent, engage more directly in promotional activities.
The quality of this work is uneven, however, and, at the present time,
not all Indian embassies have commercial attachés on their staffs.

9. Quality control and inspection services are readily available
to exporters through the Export Inspection Council and its affiliates.

India's propensity for bilateral trade agreements was mentioned
earlier in this study. Since 1947, it has entered into such arrangements
with no less than forty-seven different partners. This approach to
external trade is now firmly embedded in Indian government policy
and is a factor of which any country that wishes to do business with
India should be aware. At the present time, 47 percent of India's
exports and 35 percent of its imports are moving under the terms
of agreements made with thirty-nine countries. Special rupee payment
arrangements, principally with the countries of the Communist bloc,
apply to 21 percent of all exports and to 12 percent of imports.

Three broad categories of bilateral agreements are being used.
First, there are agreements with twenty-six Afro-Asian and Western
European countries, which express, in rather general terms, an inten-
tion to trade and provide for payment of trade accounts in convertible
currency. It is usually agreed that these treaties have not been very
effective in stimulating trade between India and at least the majority
of the countries concerned. What they were intended to do was simply
create a congenial and friendly climate, in which mutually profitable
trade relationships could develop. To the extent that they do this,
they are considered useful, but such agreements do not, obviously,
create exchanges of goods where the natural conditions for this do
not exist--as, for instance, the Cameroons, North Vietnam, and
Mongolia, with all of whom India's trade continues to be insignificant.
On the other hand, since these twenty-six countries include such
important customers as Japan, Burma, Ceylon, and West Germany, it
must be assumed that quite a lot of the trade would have occurred
whether there had been any agreements or not.

Second, there are four special agreements, with Afghanistan, Burma, Pakistan, and the U.A.R., which originally provided for the settlement of trade accounts, partly in nonconvertible rupees and partly in convertible currencies. These agreements were intended to be effective for twenty years. In fact, trade with Pakistan stopped completely after 1965, and today, the only commodities that India is paying for in nonconvertible rupees are the hides and skins it gets from Afghanistan.

Finally, there are the agreements with eight Eastern European countries, and, also, North Korea and North Vietnam, which provide for settlement entirely in nonconvertible currencies. Trade with the European members of this group (though not, as mentioned above, with the others) has increased remarkably, both in volume and in the number of commodities traded since the agreements came into force. The exchanges with these eight countries amounted to only $10 to $12 million in the early 1950's, and they were $270 to $300 million in 1968. These countries now absorb practically all of India's surpluses of coffee, oilseeds, pepper, ready-made garments, raw jute, waste cotton, raw wool, and raw hides and skins. Imports into India from these countries are mostly capital goods and raw materials.

However, one needs a long spoon when one sups with the devil, and Indian officials and merchants complain that, in a number of cases, shipments intended for Communist countries paying in rupees have been diverted by those countries to others, which, in their turn, pay for them in hard currencies. Rather frequently, the ultimate purchasers are traditional customers of India, and the inference is drawn that these transactions are depriving India of a direct trade in which it would probably get higher prices and be paid hard money. The trade in cashew nuts is a case in point: this is a significant business in India, which imports cashew from Tanzania and pays for it in hard money, only to reexport to the Communist bloc in return for soft. In other cases, these agreements, involving specific deliveries to Eastern European markets, must have aggravated supply constraints, always a source of anxiety to the people interested in promoting India's export trade. Pepper, for example, figures quite prominently in India's commitments to its Communist trading partners, and India has found it difficult, at least partly for this reason, to supply its former market in the United States, which is being eagerly invaded by Indonesia.

Be it said that the U.S.S.R. itself appears to have been an honorable exception to the transactions of which the Indians complain, and that the others have at least promised to mend their ways. There can be no doubt that, on the whole, these agreements have been the primary cause of the growth of India's trade with the countries of Eastern Europe and that this new trade has probably been profitable to India, as well as to them. Indeed, in these particular cases, without the bilateral agreements it is questionable whether the trade would have grown at all.

India's trade with the rest of the world has been growing too, but not, at least as yet, at a rate to secure the goals India has set for itself in its development plans. A suspicion may arise that India has possibly overorganized its external trade, for, at first sight, one cannot fail to be impressed by its array of administrative procedures, governmental agencies, public and private bodies, and service facilities that have been created, very often, to facilitate the flow of external trade but which also serve to control it. As far as export promotion is concerned, some of the inadequacies of the system may be due to the sheer weight of the procedures with which private business has to comply and to the proliferation of expediting mechanisms that have been brought into being; probably, the more serious weaknesses lie in the lack of effective coordination and direction. India has not yet been able to emulate the thrust and purpose that characterize the efforts of Japan and Korea and is now beginning to contemplate major organizational changes that it hopes will permit it to do so.

OBSERVATIONS AND CONCLUSIONS

A complete and detailed program for expanding exports from Vietnam would be beyond the scope and purpose of this book, but on the basis of the investigations made here and in other countries, a number of specific suggestions are possible. The experience of other Asian countries in developing their external trade provides guidelines that may be valuable to both the government and to private business in Vietnam in their efforts to promote exports. The aspects of export promotion mentioned below are considered vital.

Monetary Policy

One factor appears to be common to all the countries that have had outstanding success in increasing their export sales: stable currencies, combined with realistic rates of exchange for their external trade. Naturally, political stability is equally important, and this has been a very significant feature in virtually all the Asian markets described in this report.

Without substantial subsidies, Vietnamese exporters have been finding it almost impossible to be competitive on price. The high level of domestic prices generally makes it unattractive to export for sale in overseas markets. Vietnam presently offers export subsidies on less than ten commodities, including tea and duck feathers, but the program is not sufficiently broad, while the rates of subsidy are too low to offset the unfavorable impact of the exchange rate.

Export Promotion

The trend in most exporting countries is toward establishing some type of central organization or agency that will have primary responsibility for promoting exports. Vietnam itself has such an agency, or at least an incipient one, in the Export Promotion Center. The concept underlying this approach is sound, but its manner of execution needs adaptation to the circumstances of the country involved. It would be unrealistic, for example, to advocate anything on the lines of the JETRO in Japan or of KOTRA in South Korea, with their large home staffs and numerous sales offices overseas, for a country where the commodities being exported are either raw foodstuffs or basic industrial materials, without any particular identification to set them apart from the same commodities produced elsewhere. This also holds true where export volumes are not sufficient to justify the overhead cost of an elaborate structure. Thus, Thailand and Malaysia, and even Singapore and Taiwan, have not yet seen fit to establish a single central promotional agency, though all appear to be moving toward one at their own pace.

For Vietnam, it is strongly recommended that thought be given to the assignment of the export promotion function to one agency, perhaps the Export Promotion Center, and that this organization should then direct its activities specifically to the requirements of developing an export trade that will consist, at least for some time to come, mostly of foodstuffs and raw materials. It should be recognized that this type of agency has been most successful where it does not itself engage in buying and selling, where it does not attempt to be a regulatory body, but where it does seek and obtain active participation in its program by both the public and the private sectors.

As to the type of organization most likely to provide leadership to the export promotion program, there are strong arguments in favor of a semipublic agency, such as the Trade Development Council of Hong Kong. This allows much greater flexibility in operating procedures than is generally to be found in a governmental agency, and it also embodies the partnership of government and business interests, which is essential to a successful export promotion drive. The management of this type of program needs maximum latitude to initiate and conduct whatever activities seem to it to be necessary to stimulate exports. Recruitment and control of personnel, including their salary scales, can be managed best by the organization itself, without the

usually restrictive influence of government civil service regulations.
To emphasize the public/private partnership aspect of export promotion, it may well be desirable to consider funding from both sources,
with a part, possibly the greater part, of the budget being derived from
a small levy on exports or by some other fee, and the balance coming
from the government itself as a grant-in-aid or subsidy.

One further observation is necessary: contrary to what many
people in Vietnam profess to believe, it is not going to be at all easy
to build the country's export trade up to the levels desired. It is
essential that an export promotion program be given high priority and
that it be well organized and aggressively pursued.

Quality Control

This factor involves more than mere regulatory action--it has
strong overtones, also, of business ethics. In Thailand and elsewhere,
there are traders who resort to shady practices, who fail to deliver
goods that measure up to the standards agreed upon. In some countries, on the other hand, Japan being a good example, it is policy not
to permit the sale of inferior goods abroad, even if a buyer wishes
to purchase such products. The purpose of quality control is not only
to ensure that the specifications of contracts are honored, but also to
earn and preserve the good reputation of the entire export business
of the country making the sales.

From the standpoint of quality, the reputation of Vietnamese
goods is reported as mixed; on balance, it would be fair to say that
its products are mostly considered mediocre, with some rating much
higher than others. Not much progress has yet been made in Vietnam
in establishing standards and controlling the quality of exports, and
this is another area deserving of early attention, particularly where
competition for markets is very keen. As the export trade revives
and grows, it is imperative that Vietnam maintain high standards and
establish a reputation for meeting contract specifications on quality.
To accomplish this, it will be necessary to give additional support and
authority to those agencies and organizations that are responsible for
establishing standards and supervising their application.

In most Asian countries, there has been an unfortunate tendency
to fragment the quality control programs; for example, the control of
standards for agricultural products may be vested in a ministry of
agriculture and the same type of program for manufactured goods may
be placed somewhere else. In many, even in most, cases, export standards may very well differ from the grades or terminology used in
domestic markets, and inspection is usually more stringent on export

items. A very good case can be made for centralizing the administration of quality control, insofar as it affects export commodities. There
is need, however, to distinguish between administration of such a
program, the technical activity of drafting standards and grades, and
actually applying these standards. Standards are often prescribed by
an organization different from that which supervises the quality control program as a whole, while actual inspection and certification of
commodities is often performed by private and/or semipublic agencies.

Capital and Credit

It is obvious that capital investment and credit are needed to
produce commodities for export in any country, and Vietnam is no
exception. Without their liberal programs for attracting foreign investment, it would have been impossible for either Taiwan or Korea
to have developed their exports as they have. It is true, to be sure,
that most heavy private investment is needed for the development of
industry leading to the production of manufactured goods, but the exploitation and development of a country's agricultural, forestry, and
fisheries' potential also require substantial capital. Apart from investment in the production plant itself, finance will be needed for
operating purposes if producers are to turn out really large volumes
of export commodities. Producers and traders alike need short-term
credit on reasonable terms. To some extent, the credit needs of Vietnamese exporters have been reduced by the requirement of payment
for exports at time of delivery in Vietnam, but with increasing competition among the exporting countries, some of whom give credit to
foreign buyers, it is highly doubtful whether Vietnam can continue this
practice and simultaneously build up its export trade.

The liberalization of Vietnamese regulations concerning foreign
investment is now being considered, but there appears to be some
reluctance to invite outside capital to come in, in the same hearty
manner as in Taiwan, South Korea, and Thailand. But whether foreign
investors enter Vietnam or not does not in any way obviate the pressing
need to provide the financing required to produce and market the commodities that Vietnam hopes to export. The programs of the Industrial
Development Center and of the Agricultural Development Bank are
not yet financed sufficiently to support the production that would lead
to even a modest increase in the export trade, and commercial banks
have not demonstrated any real interest in extending credit to encourage
production of the country's most likely export commodities--food-
stuffs and raw materials. Even exporters find it difficult to finance
their purchases until they receive payment from overseas buyers.
At least at the start, it appears that the government of Vietnam will
have to take the lead in making greatly expanded credit available to
producers and traders if exports are to grow rapidly.

In order to stimulate sales overseas and, at the same time, encourage commercial banks to finance outshipments, an increasing number of countries are providing guarantees of payment for commodities exported. In some cases, this is done by government agencies, but, in others, quasipublic organizations have been established for this specific purpose. These programs usually appear as insurance plans, operated on a nonprofit basis. As Vietnam changes over to a system in which payment will be due on delivery to the buyer (in contrast to the present system of payment f.o.b. Vietnam), there will be greater need for some form of guaranty of payment. These plans provide for payment of all or a substantial part of the value of the goods in case of default by the buyer, and it is usual to cover a broad range of eventualities.

Another program attracting some support from exporting nations is the provision of credit to buyers of export commodities. This development has not yet gained as broad acceptance as guaranty of payments, but some countries are using it as a further inducement to attract buyers. Export credit is a frequent feature of country-to-country sales involving governments, but, in recent times, it has been extended to regular commercial transactions, either through private arrangements, with or without government support, or through government-sponsored credit arrangements. However, credit of this type is granted more commonly on machinery and other manufactured goods than on foods and raw materials, and it is improbable that Vietnam will find it advisable to introduce any extensive program of export credit in the near future.

Procedures

This is an element in an export program that should be readily amenable to corrective measures, but, in practice, it is usually a most difficult problem. A 1964 study of the procedures involved in exporting textiles from South Korea (mentioned earlier in this book) revealed that twenty-five separate steps were required and that as much as two or three months were needed to complete the process. And it was almost as difficult for a businessman to obtain clearances to travel abroad to promote his export business. At the other extreme, it is possible to get clearance for exports within twenty-four hours from the Kaohsiung Export Processing Zone in Taiwan, and Hong Kong also handles clearances very expeditiously. The Trade Directory, issued by the Export Promotion Center of Vietnam, states that three weeks may be required for clearance of exports where the commodities are regular items (such as rice, rubber, and tea) and that longer will be needed if the goods are other than these familiar commodities. It can be said almost categorically that no agency is going to admit that its procedural requirements are unnecessary and that all agencies will resist efforts to streamline and shorten the process. This was found to be so even in South Korea, where, in spite of the great emphasis placed on export promotion, a very great deal still remains to be done before export procedures are made as simple as they ought to be.

386

In Vietnam, as in most other countries, a critical examination of the procedural requirements concerning exports and the travel required to promote exports is badly needed. This was one of matters all Vietnamese traders, without exception, emphasized when they were interviewed during the 1969 survey. If the decision is left to each agency, it is probable that very little will ever be done to eliminate some of the clearance requirements and to relax some of the others. The very least that should be done is to assemble representatives of all the agencies involved in clearing exports in one location, perhaps the Export Promotion Center, to save a trader the time he now spends in going from one office to another. Another improvement would be a clearance service for exporters, operated on a nonprofit basis by the Chamber of Commerce, the Promotion Center, or by an exporter's trade association. In any event, strong pressure will have to be exerted by the Executive if there is to be any real improvement in these burdensome proceedings.

Trade Negotiations

With the possible exception of rubber and rice exporters, Vietnam's traders have never been particularly strong or well organized, in the sense of presenting a united front in dealings with overseas buyers. With the decline in exports during the 1960's, the position of Vietnamese traders has deteriorated still more, and some have gone out of business completely. It will be difficult enough for them to get back into it, to say nothing of developing the strength needed to bargain effectively with buyers who, in many cases, are both extremely large and very well organized.

In its present very unfavorable trade position, Vietnam may find it both necessary and expedient to engage in government-to-government negotiations, in order to pave the way for increased exports to offset the heavy flow of imports. Although several of Vietnam's largest suppliers are generally opposed to barter or other special trading arrangements for specific commodities, there is some probability that the government of Vietnam can, and no doubt that it should, assist its merchants in finding markets, especially in those countries that have been heavy suppliers of goods to Vietnam in recent years.

Trade delegations and missions sponsored by the government will also be helpful in building the export trade. These missions have been most effective when both public and private sectors have been represented on them and when their programs have been carefully planned in advance of arrival in the countries visited.

Trade Organizations

In any export program, there is clearly a place for the quasi-public or private trade associations, such as chambers of commerce, boards of trade, or exporters associations. These organizations serve useful purposes, providing a forum in which trade policy and problems can be discussed and by which the views of the private sector can be conveyed to governmental agencies. They are also a convenient means of providing certain essential services to traders, for example, price reports, trade news, commodity inspection, and information on procedures.

In Vietnam, the Saigon Chamber of Commerce has taken an active interest in the export trade and is the principal spokesman for the business community on that and other subjects, but trade associations, founded on particular commodities, are generally weak.

Trade organizations are useful as channels for disseminating information, for sounding out opinion, and for exerting a certain amount of pressure to maintain an acceptable level of ethics. There may well be a place in Vietnam for a general traders' association, comparable to the Board of Trade in Thailand and to the Korean Traders Association in South Korea. In the beginning, this might be preferable to numerous individual commodity associations because the number of traders is relatively small and many of them deal in a wide variety of different items. Over time, however, it is expected that traders will also organize on commodity lines, as they have done in most countries.

There is a particular need in Vietnam for exporters to join trade associations. The fact is that Vietnamese traders have been substantially removed from the mainstream of international trade for several years, and, in addition, most of the exporting firms are relatively small in both resources and volume of business. Acting in combination, they will have much better opportunities to familiarize themselves with the current export market situation and to present at least a semblance of unity in dealing with prospective buyers or exploiting potential markets.

Special Services

As trade develops, there will be an increasing need for mediation and arbitration to resolve the disputes that inevitably arise between buyers and sellers. Services of this sort can be provided by a government agency, but, in practice, they are often delegated to a quasipublic organization, such as a chamber of commerce or a board of trade. A good reason for keeping these services at least one stage removed from the government is to avoid direct government involvement in what are basically commercial disputes, for there is a feeling that such differences are better settled in business circles if this is possible. While this is not an immediate and urgent problem in Vietnam, it is one more element of an export program that will need attention at the appropriate time.

In organizing for export promotion, Vietnam may have both a desire and an opportunity to obtain export-oriented technical assistance from external public or private sources. In South Korea, for example, this type of advisory assistance was a most valuable support to the South Korean effort. Assistance is especially helpful in planning the institutional structure through which the export promotion program will be implemented. It can also help in exploring new avenues of external trade, and, in some cases, guidance in techniques of processing and marketing can be provided.

Transportation and shipping services are essential elements of an export program; there is, consequently, a need for an organization of some sort to represent the interests of the public and of traders in matters such as freight rates and frequency and adequacy of service or even to provide services where necessary. The very nature of this factor in external trade implies that some government influence and financial support are often required, although they may be channeled through a quasipublic unit, a transportation center, or a shipping bureau, for instance.

Dissemination of market information contributes importantly to a program for expanding overseas sales. Information is usually designed to keep traders informed on prices, commodity outlook, market requirements, and the general trading situation, and, providing it is a normal function of export promotion agencies, chambers of commerce, boards of trade, and trade associations. Government agencies participate in providing these services but not ordinarily to the same extent as the semipublic organizations. In Vietnam, the Export Promotion Center and the Saigon Chamber of Commerce might provide the initiative in making the service generally available.

Industrial parks and free trade zones are other useful tools in export development where processed or manufacturing goods are involved in the external trade. For some time to come, it seems likely that these techniques will not be a particularly important factor in Vietnam's export trade, because, certainly in the short term, and, perhaps, in the medium term too, most exports will consist of unprocessed foodstuffs, feeds, and industrial raw materials. But, in time, these deivces should be employed to help stimulate sufficient industrial development to provide manufactured items for export. In other places, as described earlier in this book, industrial parks, established originally for industries intended to supply domestic markets, have often found their residents moving rather rapidly into production for export. Hopefully, sooner or later this will happen in Vietnam as well.

FREDERICK T. MOORE, Senior Economist with the World Bank, has had wide experience in development problems of countries in all five continents, for a period of twenty years. He was most recently leader of the Bank's Industrial Missions to Korea and Indonesia.

Mr. Moore was formerly chief economist of a private consulting company and a member of the senior staff of The Rand Corporation. He has also been on the faculties of the University of Illinois and the University of California, as well as visiting lecturer at universities and institutes in other countries.

Mr. Moore did his undergraduate work at the University of Wisconsin and postgraduate work at the University of California.

D. M. I. THOMAS, now in the South Asian Department of the World Bank, has been involved in economic development for more than twenty years. For most of this time he served in the British Colonial Administrative Service. He served first in Ghana, where he was a District Commissioner and also held various posts in the Central Government, including that of Principal Assistant Secretary in the Development Commission; he served later in Hong Kong, where he was involved in the development of the budgetary system, the fishing industry, and the New Territories; toward the end of his service, he was Assistant Financial Secretary to the Colony.

After leaving the Colonial Service, Mr. Thomas worked in Saigon for two years with Development and Resources Corporation of New York on plans for the postwar reconstruction and development of South Vietnam, before joining the World Bank.

Mr. Thomas studied Economics at the University of Wales and Colonial Administration at London University.

CHARLES W. PETERS, now a consultant on agricultural development in Afghanistan, has spent almost ten years on agricultural problems in the Southeast Asian countries. He has worked on farm production and rural credit programs in these countries and has written a series of research reports on his work.

Mr. Peters was formerly senior agricultural economist with a private company in Vietnam and prior to that was in a similar position with the U.S. Government in Thailand. He was head of the Agricultural Economics Department, University of Hawaii, for several years.

Mr. Peters did his undergraduate work in agricultural economics at the University of Oregon and postgraduate work at Oregon State University.

RICHARD N. PIGOSSI is on the staff of the Industrial Projects Department of the International Bank for Reconstruction and Development and is engaged in project identification and appraisal work in Latin America and Asia. He was formerly with Development and Resources Corporation of New York and was an MIT Fellow in Africa, where he served as Economic Advisor to the East African Railways and Harbours in Nairobi, Kenya. He also served for several years as a consultant to The Rand Corporation.

Mr. Pigossi is an engineering graduate of the Pennsylvania State University and received his master's degree in industrial management from Massachusetts Institute of Technology.

DATE DUE

41979